Wine *A Life Uncorked*

Hugh Johnson

Wine *A Life Uncorked*

University of California Press

Contents

To Judy, Lucy, Red and Kitty,
who have tolerated the whole thing.

Preface

THERE IS MUCH to be said, from an author's point of view and certainly from a publisher's, for a subject that has obsolescence built into it. One that renews itself regularly once a year, as the world of wine does with each new vintage, is an especially desirable prize. When I started on my first wine book, forty years ago, I was making no such calculation; I just saw a gap in the market for a simple text relating the glorious variety of the world's wines and the different pleasures they have to offer. It was far from my mind that an atlas, an encyclopaedia and a history would follow from it, and even further that a little crib for the forgetful wine-lover would become an annual as my *Pocket Wine Book*. But I made my bed, as an encyclopaedist, and lying in it has been absorbing, entertaining, rewarding – everything I could have hoped.

It has also left me with notes and memories that mean much more to me than just keeping up (or trying to keep up) the record.

Proust had his madeleine, and I have my claret. And burgundy and champagne and Moselle and Chianti and Coonawarra. Every bottle, every glass of wine connects with bottles and glasses that went before, leads back in memory, forwards in anticipation and sideways in reverie. The wines that really speak to me are those that reverberate on more than just my tongue. Some wines simply have more to say than others. Hearing what they say, following up and linking their stories, is a pursuit with no end in sight – which means, to me, that it is high time to make a start.

Wine is first and foremost a social game; only secondarily an interest like music or collecting. It is about human relations, hospitality, bonding, ritual … all the manoeuvres of social life – and all under the influence, however mild and benign, of alcohol. No wonder its literature grows and grows. So here is a memoir written with a corkscrew; a book of tastes and opinions, a few assertions, a few conclusions – and not a single list. Reader, I picture you as having your own tastes and opinions, as having as much information to hand as you can handle (and the internet beside you for more), and as being eager to understand. We are in the same boat, you and I. I will tell you what I have understood so far. Some of it could be familiar to you; my tastes have not changed radically with age and experience. I have even repeated a few passages you might have read in articles or other books where they suit my purpose. For the illustrations I have ransacked the family albums – a hit and miss affair, it must be said.

Forty – no, nearer fifty – years of sharing wines and opinions about them has left me in debt to countless people; sometimes for the wine, sometimes the opinions, and always the fellowship. To prevent these pages becoming a list of wines, occasions and companions I have mentioned only a few to illustrate my story. These I thank for their participation, conscious or not, but no less the hundreds, indeed thousands, of wine-lovers, wine-growers, wine merchants, wine writers and others who have, as the French say, 'formed' me over the years. No part of my formation has been formal; there has been plenty of room for heterodox ideas and eccentricities to take root. But, in matters of taste, conformity can easily go too far. *Tante teste*, *tante idee*, as the Romans say, or as Rabelais: *Fay ce que vouldras*. It's your opinion that counts, not mine.

Thanks

I have to thank Michael Dover of Weidenfeld & Nicolson for encouraging me to write a non-encyclopaedic book, my first for a long time; Ken Wilson, who worked my pictures into his design to make the most of a mixed bag; all my collaborators at Weidenfeld and many colleagues and friends, especially those who helped by jogging my memory or with pictures of their own. Above all I thank Diane Pengelly, who first became my editor on *The Story of Wine*, and who has been as sensitive and supportive of a writer's weaknesses as any editor could be. It is rare when, finishing a book, one can say it has all been a pleasure.

I   Prospects

A Life Uncorked

EVERYONE HAS a most Frequently Asked Question. I have two. The first is 'How did you get into wine to begin with?' often with a hint of 'Is it too late for me to join in?' The second is 'What is your favourite wine?' I'll come back to the second: the answer is long and equivocal; you may still be wondering at the end of the book.

But the first question has a simple answer, even a road-to-Damascus moment of revelation. It was late at night in my student digs in Cambridge, on one of those rare evenings when I was deep in books and papers. My room-mate was out at what I knew was a dinner with many wines. The door swung open and there he was in his dinner jacket, his face I fancy a trifle flushed. "Taste these," he said, presenting me with two glasses of red wine.

"What are they?" said I.

"Just taste them. Now, what do you think?"

"Very nice," I said, "but this one seems to have more flavour."

"Exactly. And they came from the same place, the same year – just different sides of the road." This was not all he said. Then began a speech about Burgundy, and Vosne-Romanée, and Grands Crus and Premiers Crus, which I thought was a bit over the top for nearly midnight. He eventually went to bed, and I back to my desk. But the seed had been sown, and next time he went out to dinner, I went with him. I paid my first visit to wine country.

It was curiosity that made me first pay attention to wine, and it is curiosity that still makes me impatient to see what lies under every cork. There are disappointments, of course, but you learn to pick likely candidates, at least. Each one adds to the fascination of a subject with an infinity of variables.

Yes, it would be simpler and tidier to live in a world where wine was a commodity like milk. But let me quote the almost forty-year-old first sentence of my first book. "Think, for a moment, of an almost paper-white glass of liquid, just shot with greeny-gold, just tart on your tongue, full of wild-flower scents and spring-water freshness. And think of a burnt-umber fluid, as smooth as syrup in the glass, as fat as butter to smell and sea-deep with strange flavours. Both are wine." And so are glasses of perfumed ruby; of astringent garnet; of carnelian smelling of strawberries; of deep gold, nut-scented or sweet as honey; of purple giving off fumes of brambles and rum.

"Wine is at the same time simpler than people say and more complex than they think." It was French wine philosopher Pierre Boisset who said it. It is one of those remarks that catch you off-balance. Yes, it makes you think; that's the point. But there is another point, and perhaps this is really what he means. Any fool can make a subject complex and any fool can say it is simple. But how much do you have to understand to grasp the essentials?

If I can risk another riddle I would say most people try either too hard at wine or not hard enough. Wine tends to be an all-or-nothing passion. For some it becomes a matter of moment to remember the proportions of Sauvignon to Sémillon in a vineyard in Sauternes, or the career changes of a fashionable wine-maker. They know

BELOW
My first sight of France was with school friends in Brittany in the early 1950s. I am wearing the white cap.

BOTTOM
Precocious, moi? I apparently drew this landscape with vines when I was eight. I have since dug the pond and planted the trees.

the Bordeaux Classification by heart and every vintage declared by every port shipper. For others any suggestion of real appreciation, a short pause to look at a wine, inhale its scent or think it through, as it were, in your mouth, let alone try to describe it, is an incomprehensible affectation. 'I don't know anything about wine but I know what I like,' is the motto of this category. For 'wine' you could substitute art, music, gardens ....

So what does the reasonable, perfectly balanced person need to know? That wine is not one thing, but many. To appreciate it you don't have to swallow an encyclopaedia, but you do have to pay attention. A good memory helps, but a clear focus on what you are drinking is indispensable. If it turns a drink into a recreation, who can complain?

I stand at the top of my cellar steps and the faintest scent greets me: more an atmosphere than a smell. Moist, organic, old – the words are not very attractive, but a congregation of bottles, some of which have lain side by side for decades, is too powerful a presence to send off no signals.

It is a library down there; a library of different takes on the same plot. The plot starts with vines insinuating their roots into the soils of a thousand different fields, feeding on what they encounter in the ground, rock or sand, wet or dry, lean and hungry or fat enough to grow marrows. It ends with the air in a glass rising through your nostrils and your mouth to leave an impression on your mind. The two are intimately, directly, inevitably linked – via a chain of events that can go this way or that in numberless and ceaseless variations. On some nano-scale of infinite variety everything is recorded. Like the wings of a butterfly in the rainforest, a passing shower or a spore of fungus can tip a balance that eventually makes you decide to order another bottle – or not. Much more, of course, can all the decisions of the farmers, engineers, chemists, lawyers, bankers … the army of operatives who intervene on the way.

There are generous decisions and mean ones, intelligent ones and stupid ones, good ones and bad ones. Cumulatively they make not just a bottle or a vintage but an identity, and a reputation. The differences between wines are genetically inherited: the vines and the vineyard are the bloodline. They are also acquired: when the vine is pruned, as the grapes ripen, when they are picked, as they are fermented and matured and bottled and stored again. The wine has its memories: of the stony soil where the vine's roots probed deep, of the stone wall that gave it shelter, of the frost in May that reduced half its shoots and the potential crop to brown rags, of the sun that crept up the rows in the morning and left the grapes glowing as it went down, of the sudden cold showers. When a

depression made its way from the Atlantic in September, drenching the
dark firs on the hills, families setting out for long days in the vineyard
went back indoors and waited. For three days grey flurries of rain made
puddles under the vines. They waited one warm day after the sky cleared,
then took their baskets down and picked from dawn to dusk. The wine
remembers it: the dry days of August in the sweet jam-like concentration
of its flavour, and the downpour before harvest in a flicker of weakness as
you swallow.

At one extreme a wine's identity is as broad as red or white; at the
other it varies between different barrels raised from the same harvest in
the same cellar – and eventually, years later, between different bottles
from the same barrel.

It is a cliché of the wine trade but nonetheless true that there are no
great wines, only great bottles of wine. The eventual unit that is enjoyed
or not, judged better or worse, is a bottle. If there is something wrong
with it, whatever it's called or whatever it cost, it is good for nothing. The
risk is always there because wine is a living substance, and anything that
is alive goes on changing until it dies.

Wine in Ferment

'Wine in ferment' would be the tabloid way of putting it. Rapid and
radical change is not peculiar to the world of wine, but in the conservative world of bottles and barrels an adjustment feels like a swerve, and
recent adjustments feel like revolution. Wine today is speaking in new
idioms, livelier, in many cases, and more persuasive than its old language
(which was full of clichés, to be sure, and near-meaningless repetition).
There is no reason why new generations of drinkers should want to hear
the same old story. The experience of coach building was invaluable for
the first motorcars, but it has little bearing on the cars of the electronic
age, and almost none on aeronautics. Could this be what will happen,
and is already happening, to wine?

Yes, it is still an intoxicating drink. You can make it only by fermenting grapes. These are the constants. The best varieties of grapes were
found long ago and matched to the best-run vineyards. Centuries of
patient assiduity discovered what manoeuvres worked best in what cellars. And the most successful wines were given precise profiles, idealized,
imitated.

But what defined these model wines were constraints, natural or
adopted. Constraints of fertility and maturity, of ignorance, of disease, of
weather; constraints of the market, of legal restrictions, of social norms,
of shortage of cash.

What is progress but overcoming restraints? Why should a new world accept rules and disciplines and shortages not indigenous to itself? Warmer weather (or indeed global warming) will give you riper grapes; irrigation, more of them. The resulting flavours may not be the same – but neither are the people, the circumstances, the way of life or the food. Absurd, then, to hanker after a model made for a purpose that has passed. Admire it, yes, for its elegance, its durability, its ability still to attract attention when fitter, more functional alternatives come along. But did Chippendale say the last word on what makes a perfect chair?

———————————

I am a Chippendale man myself. I live, by choice, in a house built (probably of recycled materials) in Queen Elizabeth's reign and remodelled, though not drastically, in that of William III. The outer walls are brick, its panelling oak, its floors oak or tiles. Its furniture aspires to be of the same age, or at least in the same spirit. Our dining chairs, around a walnut table, are in the reassuring broad-bottomed country baroque style Chippendale would recognize, if not vouch for. Aesthetically, in fact, I inhabit a world fashioned by 17th century English gentry and updated only piecemeal by the Georgians and Victorians, who seem to have been happy enough with the same snug, perhaps a trifle florid, domesticity.

Under the wings of the house flanking the central block are two

The painter Paul Hogarth illustrated my Wine Companion. *He painted this portrait of Saling Hall as a surprise present in 1984. The 'Dutch' gables were added to an Elizabethan house in 1699.*

cellars. Why two? One is a one-room affair approached by brick steps under the main staircase, with brick wine bins of no special age. The other, under the east wing, has three large rooms. They must have been the kitchens and sculleries of Tudor times. Then perhaps cool storage for fresh food and game and very likely cider, which needed storage year-round, unlike the regular brew of beer.

What is clear is the purpose of a fourth, smaller, room, excavated under the hall floor as, it seems, the only item of 18th century modernization. This is definitely a wine-cellar: brick floored, with six brick bins on one side and four on another, insulated from the outside by the big cellars and, I should judge, unchanged since its contents were minutely listed as part of the inventory of the house: "1769, the contents of the cellar at Saling Hall belonging to Mr Raymond: Item, 20 bottles of port. Item, 17 bottles of Lisbon and one pint of Surfet water." Was Surfet water the Perrier of the time?

What am I looking for? A little inner wine-cellar was excavated under the house in the early 1700s.

I shall tell you in due course about the present-day contents of this cellar and the others. First, though, I must justify, if only for myself, the large part that wine has played in my life since I first became aware of it nearly fifty years ago. How come I still pull corks with alacrity, full of curiosity; still get a buzz from each first sip, rolling it round my tongue, sucking it to test its mettle? What sort of test am I putting it to? What do I expect or want it to be? Clearly something more than a mere thirst-quencher. Or a rather long way round to oblivion. Indeed I find myself straight away facing the principal drawback of this great companion. If you drink too much, or even if you drink what feels like enough, your legs become as tangled as your thoughts seem lucid. You may not fall over, but you must certainly not drive home.

Paradox: there is no wine without alcohol. None of its properties is available without the fermentation of the fruit that turns it into a drug. Smell, taste, texture, the kernel of satisfaction in each sip, the complexity of your body's response: none of these belongs to grape juice. How much alcohol wine needs, why some are completely satisfying with very little and others seem lean and limp without a hefty dose, is a subject I will come back to later.

Not a knockout drop, then, and more than a glass of water. What am I asking wine to be? There is some quality the most commonplace wine and the most rarefied both need to pass muster. Call it balance; call it harmony. What it feels like to me is energy, almost as though the wine were a living organism interacting with my tongue and palate. Good wine manages to communicate undeployed reserves of energy, at least to tasters who look beneath the surface to gauge what it will become as it matures. Great wine in its youth (and to the initiated) conveys the feeling of an unexploded bomb.

How does such energy communicate itself to your brain? It seems to consist of contrasting properties in opposition. Sweetness and sharpness for example, in a Riesling from the Moselle – a good wine to examine for clues since it is so transparent, there is no body or breadth of flavour and very little alcoholic warmth to obscure what seems a simple contrast between sweet and sour. When this opposition becomes balance, you're in business. How far from simple it is, though, becomes clear when you compare several similar examples. Analytically they might be almost identical: sugar content so much in grams per litre, acidity ditto; but sense of energy, of something happening to your whole mouth: worlds apart. At one extreme you have something no more interesting than lemonade: perfectly swallowable but equally forgettable. At the other a convulsive, electrifying, high-tension display: charisma in a bottle.

There is a school of thought that says voltage is everything: quite simply the more intense the flavour the better. 'No-one can deny,' says a Californian wine critic, 'that intensity drives the score.' (I'll come to the question of scores later. The word means a numerical rating arrived at by comparative tasting.) Professional wine tasters can easily fall into this trap; intensity is the character that tends to emerge when you are faced with a line-up of fifty or so wines of the same kind. The palate is (or should be) a sensitive organ. Bathe it repeatedly in alcohol, acidity and tannin, and the quieter notes cease to register. Tannin, after all, is the substance that turns skin to leather, acidity forces your sensitivity to retreat in self-defence, and alcohol numbs not only the nerve-endings but the nervous system itself.

Perhaps I should have started by asking what wine is for; there may not be such an obvious consensus. I rarely, for example, drink wine, or more than a couple of glasses of wine, without food – and when I do it is almost always white. Wine for me is essentially what I drink while eating, which is not at all the case with my children's generation. I can only respect their capacity for wine unmixed with solid matter. If they want wine which itself tastes more solid, if that's the word, I can hardly be surprised.

——————————

It depends whether you see wine primarily as a drink or as a recreational substance. In a drink you look for something refreshing and satisfying without too loud a voice, not too intrusive on your food or your thoughts each time you take a sip. How often do you? Some people, I notice, revisit their wine glass at long intervals. They seem to forget about it between an initial taste and a first swallow, and the moment when the plates are cleared away. Others (and I am one) are constantly coming back to it, touching it, looking at its colours and following each mouthful of food with a contemplative sip. Rarely, if ever, a full-throttled swallow. You can call it taster's tic, if you like, or the programmed response of someone who has been to too many wine tastings. When I catch myself swishing the water in my toothmug and sniffing it before I rinse my mouth, I know I need therapy.

At table I am using the wine as sauce or lubricant for my food. A bite, a sip, the food and the wine together in my mouth; it blends their flavours almost as though the wine had gone into the pot. It works when both have the same intensity of flavour, or nearly. If the food is much more tasty, or spicy, or hot or acid, then the wine falls back into the role of a chaser; just a liquid to clear the passage for another mouthful. If the wine is more intense in flavour, fruitier or sweeter than the food, or with tannins that attack your palate, the artistry of the chef goes for nothing. All that is left is texture, and even that can be blotted out by a too-forceful wine.

What does surprise me is anyone's indifference to food after a glass or two of wine. When tasting, concentrating on smells and flavours, trying to analyze them and record my ideas, I can stave off thoughts of food for hours on end – if sometimes with difficulty. But once I start to sip and swallow, my guard is down. The message comes back from my stomach, 'Thanks. That put me right in the mood. Shall we have a look at the menu?'

When your mind starts to turn towards an evening glass of wine, how does the prospect present itself to you? Is your first concern the odds of a heart attack, and the golden opportunity of lengthening them by a micro-fraction if you choose red rather than white? Neither is mine.

What do I consider? My companions first of all. The food in prospect. Wines that I want, or need, to taste. My bank balance. Most powerfully, though least palpably, the crystallizing image of thirst, the anticipation of winey pleasure, forming in my mind as evening approaches. It is, strange to say, quite specific.

I think sweetness, fruity uplift, gripping tannins, scouring acidity or inspiring bubbles. I think grape varieties, regions, countries, vineyards, growers, vintages. There is a list of wine flavours in my subconscious, just as there is an ingrained food menu. You are just the same: lamb, fruit, an egg, salmon, a jam sandwich are all there in your mental menu. For one reason or another (you may even believe it is your body chemistry issuing instructions) one takes priority and becomes what you want.

Of course there are practical factors. Where am I? I would have a different bottle in mind in a restaurant, a summer-house, a mountain cabin or a city apartment. There are chalet wines and boardroom wines and wines for South Sea islands. And in wine country it would be perverse not to drink (or at least try) what is being made before your eyes.

And when is it for? Is this a snap decision for today or a considered one for a special occasion? Is it lunch or dinner or a picnic? Is it summer or winter? Are there crystal glasses or plastic beakers? What sort of occasion, in short, with what sort of expectations? Exceed them, it need be only by a whisker, and everyone will smile.

Question one, though, was with whom? I have dear friends, and close family, who are classed as swine in the wine department; I keep my pearls for other people. I have often poured these brutes a wine I particularly like, and would like them to like. I have tried a nudge, as in 'What do you think of this wine?' It doesn't take long to see a glimmer of interest; a moment longer, perhaps, to see whether it is mere politeness. I am absurdly gratified if one of my swine sniffs the pearl and looks up with a question. A second glass is instantaneous – but then I have to suppress my urge to add footnotes. Voltaire never troubled himself, apparently, with such urges and counter-urges. When he lived in exile near Geneva, he is said to have given his stream of visitors Beaujolais while he drank Corton.

Here is a story about two Australian swagmen who used to meet for a chat under the shade of a well placed tree. By Jacob's Creek, I shouldn't wonder. One day, Barry, the first, turned up with a bottle. He took a long swig, wiped his lips on his sleeve, and passed the bottle to his mate Kevin, who did the same. "Whad'ya think of it?" said Barry.

"Jes right," said Kev.

"Whad'ya mean, 'jes right'?"

"Well. If it'd bin any better you wouldn'a giv'n it to me, an' if it'd bin any wuss, I couldn'a drunk it." The art of wine selection in a nutshell.

———————————

With the right companion, a single wine can be a continuing conversation. It is an experience you share, or would like to share. I'm afraid some of us even speculate about the tastes of wines we have never seen – or even wines that have never yet been made. The conversation is the point.

Way back when there were far fewer bottles of wine in the Johnson household, and a smaller variety of labels to be assessed in the world at large, we used to keep a left-overs bottle in the fridge. Think of it. We actually poured the remaining quarter of a bottle into another with a third left in it, maybe added a third wine we had tasted and liked but not quite finished, gave the brew a gentle shake and kept it for the next day. I don't remember ever actually blending red with white. You have to draw the line somewhere. But nor do I remember any negative side-effects. We were ready, in other words, just to drink, or offer friends, a glass of wine as a commodity that needed no more qualification than a glass of water.

Are you shocked? What a long way we have come. Today I might, if no-one were looking, still dilute Perrier with San Pellegrino. But the idea of casually combining wines seems to belong to another age. Tipping a smidgen of a Cabernet into a Shiraz is what a clever-clogs wine buff might do after a bottle of each to show his mastery of judicious blending. Most of us have come to accept that each bottle has a precious identity that must be preserved. It can be criticized, it can even be poured down the sink, but to sully the uniqueness of its being is sacrilege.

Who is right? Why don't we, why daren't we, make our own *cuvées*? Have we just bought a load of expensive winery PR or are we really spellbound by something Eden Valley has that Clare doesn't, or Russian River offers but Alexander Valley can't? There are plenty of answers to these questions. Enough, indeed, to fill books.

I would not be so reverential. Most budget wine is as much an industrial product as most beers. There is no-one whose pride you would hurt if you did a bit of blending. If there is a taboo, it is in somebody's interest – and that somebody is not you.

Prices and Values

It is easy for someone who drinks for a living to become detached from the realities of a budget. It is one thing to work out for yourself whether the colossal price demanded for a cult wine is justified (the answer is probably No), or to weigh up the relative values of two different châteaux, or two different vintages. Abstract valuation, you could call it. Real priorities are more demanding. The housewife asks 'Is that fair value for the same price as a chicken?' If you are a shopper who hunts down the best and freshest chicken in the market you will have the same feeling about the wine to go with it. You want real satisfaction, not a token. Curnonsky, the first French food journalist (his name was a play on 'Why not?' with a dash of Polish), formulated the basic requirement: food should taste of what it is. It is no different with wine.

Here, let's imagine, are two bottles of red wine. You bought one to go with your free-range bird; it is a well regarded, not exactly ambitious Tuscan wine, a Chianti Classico. It cost, as it happens, the same price as the fowl. The friend you invited to dinner brings a bottle, by chance another Tuscan red, but this one a birthday present. Very special, it must be. You could buy five chickens and a bottle of olive oil for this price. You open both bottles, exclaiming at the shape (very tall), the colour (black) and above all the weight of the expensive one. The bottle empty weighs the same as the other one full. You pour two glasses of each.

The chicken has perfumed the room; a good idea, that sprig of rosemary inside. You sip the Chianti. It blends as perfectly with the bird as its own steaming juices; just seasoning it with fruity acidity, a gentle glow, a brush of roughness as you swallow. You salivate, eat a piece of the thigh, and pick up the second glass. Caramba, the colour! The Chianti was garnet; this is bloody ruby. And Caramba, the nose! A rush of sweet berries and a strong suggestion of coffee. You sip. You forget the chicken. This is Ferrari-powered, Gucci-shod. What is it doing here? What on earth should we be eating with this? Perhaps, at that price, the answer is nothing: you should just sip, and wonder.

There is no stopping a man when money is no object. More, bigger, louder, sooner are not just wishes, they are commands. Once you think you need every chicken truffled, though, you have eliminated ninety-nine per cent of the pleasures of the table. And once you need your wine in overweight bottles, you have laid waste most of the world of wine.

Would I not pay five-chickens-and-a-bottle-of-olive-oil's-worth for a bottle of wine? Indeed I would. A hundred hens, in extreme cases. Such as? Such as an old wine I have heard stories about, whose biography I have read, a wine that triumphantly expresses a specific place and time. I say an old wine because costly wines are not, or are very rarely, made to be drunk young. The costly elements are those that stay submerged under blasts of ripe fruit and wafts of toasted oak. They announce their presence by blocking your tasting apparatus. They may be colossal in the three dimensions of fruit and terroir and the maker's mark of character. But great wine works in four dimensions, and the fourth is time.

Early Days

But back to the Frequently Asked Question. Wine: how did I get into it? My Damascus moment at Cambridge had had its inevitable result. Lectures were no longer my only passion. Cambridge colleges in those days had serious cellars, and no-one discouraged undergraduates from joining in. No doubt there were some bins reserved for the dons, but they did not include the Lynch Bages 1953 or the Lafite 1949. I can still recall how delicious these clarets were. It took no training at all to tell they were very special. My modest bursary did not allow me many trial runs up the Bordeaux Classification. I admit I spent more on champagne – and well remember my father's re-action when I eventually came down from Cambridge with a case for emergencies. It was not that my father didn't enjoy wine himself. He was a barrister, and a member of the Wine Society; their sherries and everyday clarets were on tap at home, and on Sundays Château Les Ormes de Pez. But in Durham, where he came from, champagne sent a message he preferred not to hear.

KING'S COLLEGE, CAMBRIDGE

The University Wine & Food Society was a meeting place for the lighter element at Cambridge, shrewdly viewed by the wine trade in London as a breeding ground for future customers. Under the pretext of our annual tasting match against Oxford, members went onto a punishing training programme, tasting everything on offer – and the offer was spectacular. We had champagne-tastings, sherry-tastings, port, of course, and bordeaux and burgundy without end. Of all the wine merchants who made the trip from London with cases of samples, the most engaging and indulgent was Otto Loeb, a don-like figure himself, founder of OW Loeb & Co in London and in his native Trier on the Moselle. He had London's finest list of German wines, then a major part of our drinking. He also travelled with an open mind, and had recently been to California. (So had I, aged 17, before university.) No-one in Britain knew anything about Californian wine in those days. There was not a great deal to know: the industry was still just picking itself up after Prohibition. When he came to Cambridge with a tasting of Louis Martini, BV, Inglenook, Almaden, Christian Brothers, Italian Swiss Colony – all the major players of the time – we were impressed. This was cutting-edge stuff.

Not only were the college cellars open to us, but the kitchens, too. The butler, Mr Brownstone, and Mr Tabor, the chef, egged us on to give elaborate dinners in our rooms. When a wine merchant came from London, and especially when he brought one of his suppliers, a shipper or the owner of an estate, we pushed the boat out. The food, the silver and crockery were carried by porters across the college shoulder-high on heavy wooden trays covered with green baize.

TOP
*It is hard to believe
I once lived
in the centre of such
an illustrious scene.*

ABOVE
*The University
Wine & Food Society
celebrated its 50th
anniversary at a June
dinner in Wren's Court
at Trinity College
in 2002 – seemingly
without wine.*

Conservative, I should say our menus were. Soup, fish, game whenever possible, and a spectacular crème brûlée which every college kitchen, I gather, claimed to have invented. It came in a great tureen, glazed with an amber layer of burnt sugar so thick that it took several thwacks with a heavy silver spoon to break it. Then yellow cream oozed up through the cracks.

I never played for Cambridge. I suppose there were simply more talented tasters available. My room-mate, my initiator, was the highest scorer and made sure Oxford went home to practise. In 1960 I graduated with what used to be called a 'gentleman's degree' – indicating that it had not been too strenuous. I applied for various jobs where an ability to count would have been useful, but the firms wisely turned me down. Then I wrote to magazines. Condé Nast, publishers of *Vogue* and *House & Garden*, called me for an interview, and I joined the Features department of *Vogue* as that rare thing, a male recruit.

My colleagues were terrifying. The regular recruitment route was via the *Vogue* Talent Contest – open only to women. Four of Britain's brightest, best-educated and most beautiful women are plenty in one office. But in the 1960 December issue I was allowed to write a piece called 'Talking Turkey'. Reading it now I can see that I was under the influence of PG Wodehouse – not a bad place for a writer to be. I knew, of course, very little about turkey or what wine to drink with it. But ignorance is the safest starting point for a journalist. I identified authorities. I rang them up. I wrote down their answers, and my name appeared at the bottom of the article. My star guest, if that's the word, was Mr Nubar

BELOW
My first wine article appeared in the Christmas 1960 issue of Vogue.

BOTTOM
Editorial duties included instructing ladies who lunch (in Chanel suits) on the mysteries of tasting. My boss, Harry Yoxall, is on the left.

Gulbenkian, one of London's most prominent diners-out, a man who had his own taxi, its body conspicuous in wicker-work to make sure head-waiters knew who was coming. "It depends on the weather," was his answer to my question, "and on my guests and on the night before; but it will be either Château Lafite 1949 or Clos de Vougeot 1928." It was nice to recognize one old friend at least. The Lafite, I told my readers, could be had from Dolamore & Co for 39 shillings, a Pommard 1928 (but no more Clos de Vougeot) from Hatch Mansfield for 27/6.

Once a writer has been identified by interested parties, you can imagine what happens. 'This Hugh Johnson, who is he? Never mind, he writes about wine in *Vogue*.' Could I have lunch? Would I like to visit Champagne? It didn't take long. The articles began to spread to other publications. First *House & Garden*, then Condé Nast magazines in New York. I soon discovered that they printed much longer articles, paid much more money, and required a visit from their contributors from time to time. Nor was wine their only interest. José Wilson, the features editor of *House & Garden*, began to send me on travel assignments.

Today almost every magazine and most newspapers have a wine column – most of them sadly devoted to this week's supermarket bargains. Then, there was only a handful of regular wine writers, led by André L Simon, representing the classical tradition, and Raymond Postgate, the consumer advocate, founder of *The Good Food Guide*. Cyril Ray, one-time Moscow correspondent of *The Sunday Times*, wrote a splendidly casual column in *The Observer*. Technical knowledge was evidently not necessary. I somehow learned that *The Sunday Times* might be susceptible and went to see the Features Editor. It was the beginning of an association with that paper that still continues. One snag: Condé Nast did not approve of moonlighting. My name must not appear elsewhere. Nobody at *The Sunday Times* thought my name mattered in the least, so I took the *nom de verre* of John Congreve.

Congreve lasted several seasons and confused everyone, himself included, by switching identities like a hero in one of his namesake's plays. Funnily enough nobody seemed to mind who he was. You never saw him at wine tastings, or the long lunches in the City that shippers gave in those days – lunches that sometimes lasted until after lights out. The chap you did see, increasingly, was me.

This was when I learned that my strings were being pulled by a man I respected but hardly knew, the chairman of Condé Nast and the founder of British *Vogue*, Harry Yoxall. It was probably he who arranged for me to interview André Simon in the Grosvenor Gardens office of the Wine & Food Society he had founded in 1931. Simon was 85, I was 23. Yoxall had evidently decided to help his friend Simon to retire gracefully from

ABOVE
*Was it this lesson in
French geography from
André Simon that made me
dream of a wine atlas?*

BELOW
*Further inspiration came
from Elizabeth David's
greatest book,
published in 1960.*

**French Provincial
Cooking**
ELIZABETH DAVID

his Society by buying its quarterly magazine, *Wine & Food*. It seems I was being groomed to be its new editor (and only the second in its history). I found myself invited back, and introduced around, until that winter I was told to gear up for my first issue, for spring 1963. I have my fumbling efforts here. I daringly introduced the first illustrations in the magazine's history: old woodcuts, which cost nothing to reproduce. But most important for me, I persuaded Elizabeth David to contribute an article, characteristically on an 18th century recipe for ham.

Elizabeth David's greatest book, *French Provincial Cooking*, had been published in 1960. I had plucked up courage to call at her house in Chelsea to solicit an article. I can see her kitchen now: its scrubbed wooden table taking up most of the room, half-covered in books and papers, plates and casseroles and a wine bottle and glasses over by the ordinary white cooker; a great armoire at one end, the walls lined with wooden racks of dishes. And there was a wonderful smell of baking.

Nobody was to have a greater influence on me, either as an editor or a writer, than Elizabeth David. Over the next two years we became friends as well as colleagues. It was challenging: she did not suffer fools gladly, and I must have said and done all sorts of foolish things. I was always on my guard: a laugh could suddenly turn into a frown. But she taught me how to stickle; there was never a more pinpoint stickler for accuracy and honesty. It slowed her writing down to a crawl, all the checking and delving. Her later books became pedantic: no more of the broad poetic brush-strokes that taught England to love the homely dishes of Italy and France and the colours of their markets when her accounts of the single-minded greed of bourgeois French families read like Zola. Her *Spectator* articles were high comedy.

Wine & Food was engrossing; I grew bolder in my search for contributors, persuading Evelyn Waugh to write about champagne and the playwright Christopher Fry to translate three of the poems of Philippe de Rothschild into English verse. Nobody seemed to mind these literary pretensions. At the same time I found my work for André Simon expanding. At the end of 1963 I was given the portentous title of General Secretary of the Wine & Food Society. As such my main job was organizing lunches and dinners for its members.

It seems preposterous now that at the age of 24 I was signing bills at the Connaught and the Mirabelle, London's best restaurants of the day. It is not true, as many assert, that there was nothing worth eating in England in those olden days. The Connaught Hotel was only fifteen minutes' walk from the Society's offices, overlooking the park at 2, Hyde Park Gate. It was well worth the effort, and I made it – as often as possible.

The Saling Hall Cellar

Anyone looking around my cellar would have no doubt where my heart lies: claret, red bordeaux, outnumbers all other wines put together. The slim dark cylinders with their white labels are everywhere, tucked away in racks, stacked in bins, standing on the table or the floor looking expectant – opening time must be near. Even more of a presence are the pale pine boxes as yet unopened, a pile here, a pile there, each with a black brand on the end, some quasi-armorial, some outlines of châteaux, some just resounding names.

It was true for a long time, my preference for claret above all red wines. I am more open-minded now, as the slope-shouldered bottles and the cardboard boxes attest. There is a simple reason, though, why bordeaux will always be in a majority down here. It stays longer. The waiting time can be, and often is, ten years or more; thirty years in some cases. So it accumulates while other equally loved wines pass through.

Burgundy came more recently into my life, and my cellar. There has been a great change in style, in quality and in availability of good burgundy in the past decade or so. And what is true of Burgundy is true of almost every other region and country: it has far more to offer than it did. Does this mean that Bordeaux should change too? It is the debate of our time.

White wines by their nature flow more rapidly. The come-and-go rate is higher, but there are exceptions. Some of the German wines have been in residence as long as thirty years. It's time I drank them; the problem has been – who with? For years my friends groaned when I went into my 'Don't you like Riesling?' routine, but things have got better recently.

In reality there is a two-tiered system in operation: the wines I must taste as soon as possible, regardless of when they will be at their supposed best, and those I am hoarding out of passion to follow their careers all the way. The first you might call my professional cellar – but could you separate what you drink out of curiosity from what you drink out of conviction? If there is a difference, it is in giving a conviction wine the benefit of the doubt. It may have seen better days, but it revives old memories. A wine-lover should be a romantic: romance can plaster over all sorts of cracks. And one sip can be enough to register a new conviction wine.

Clarets like this spend their youth in wooden cases before, at about year seven, I open a bottle to see how they are getting on and put them in a bin.

Which raises the question of objectivity. Critics are obliged to be objective in their assessments. In their public role as judges they should put their preferences and prejudice aside. Which is why 'critic' is a term I have never accepted. 'Commentator', certainly. A diligent dilettante is how I see myself; a dabbler who dabbles deep, but not so deep that the waters of his subject close over his head.

I love what my French publishers call me: *un vulgarisateur*. Think Vulgate, the name of the Bible translated into the common tongue. If a *vulgarisateur* needs a justification, I borrow mine from an old friend and philosopher in Burgundy, Pierre Poupon, who wrote "*qui, ayant ressenti à certains moments la montée incomparable de la joie intérieure, n'a jamais éprouvé le désir de révéler aux autres que le bonheur existe?*" Who has felt his spirits soar with joy and not wanted to show other people that such happiness exists?

There is a story of a young subaltern whose commanding officer wrote: "This officer's men will follow him anywhere, if only out of curiosity." I will open any bottle in the same spirit. It leads to a distressing quantity being poured down the drain – there is, after all, no obligation to drink it. The bottles that always get this summary treatment are the ones they call blockbusters. My block is too precious to me: I taste them, but one glass is plenty.

The bottom left-hand rack in the cellar has become as familiar as wallpaper. The same bottles (or some of them) have been in the same pigeon-holes down there for over thirty years. What am I waiting for? Occasions worthy of opening a 1961.

It was sheer luck that 1961 was the first bordeaux vintage (or vintage of anything) that I bought. I had had my first wine article published in 1960 and had just been introduced to the temptation of a wine list. Avery's of Bristol, I had rapidly learned, was where the cellar-smart went for their wine supplies. The reasons became clear later; Ronald Avery was a wine merchant like no other. My first contact was in 1962 when a list arrived offering an exceptional vintage for laying down. It was the best, it said, since 1959 (not in itself a great achievement) and perhaps even better than that, the crop having been greatly reduced by spring frosts and exceptionally well ripened by a sunny September. The colour of the wine in the barrels, it said, was the darkest that Mr Avery had ever seen, and its nose, though still in a primary state of mere fruitiness, gave every reason to believe that in due course this would become one of the great vintages. The price was exceptionally high, however, due to the reduced quantities available. For this reason Avery's were taking the unusual step of offering a mixed case of three bottles each of the four First Growths at the advantageous price of £50.

Burgundy magnums with their bottoms cut off make good light-holders: a home-made fitting.

I was earning £12 a week; a good wage, everybody said, and shockingly higher than those of my female colleagues. More than a month's pay seemed a lot to spend on wine I would not be drinking for years. It must have been Avery's prose that seduced me. Four of these bottles, one of each of Châteaux Lafite, Latour, Margaux and Haut-Brion, are still with me, so pregnant with expectation that I have no idea what occasion will move me to open them. They have become almost too iconic to touch; though I do, occasionally, easing them from their nests to read the dusty labels, browning at the edges, to admire the colour – still much darker than usual in such an old wine – and to check how much is left. The level in a bottle sinks infinitesimally over the years. How fast depends on the quality of the cork and the temperature and humidity of the cellar. A wine that has never been moved has the best chance of a long life. In that tranquillity my '61s have hardly evaporated at all: the lowest level is at the top of the shoulder where the neck straightens.

Can any wine live up to this sort of expectation? The Latour will, if it has a good cork (and the chance of a bad one is always there). The last time I tasted it my notes became incoherent with rapture. Negresses, in any case, no longer feature in my wine vocabulary. The Haut-Brion was a great wine, too, last time. To be truthful the Lafite and Margaux are worth more in money than in absolute pleasure. Only a mixture of nostalgia and curiosity keeps me from offering them to a broker, who would trade them for a dozen bottles of a younger and more modest wine with far greater pleasure potential.

I fear it is too late now to computerise my cellar. Too late, and counter-productive. Not half the fun, but a good deal of it, is a sort of bookshop browse. You go in looking for a guide to the Caribbean and come out with a spy story. I pop down for a bottle of claret and come back, twenty minutes later, with one of Corbières and one of a South African Sauvignon Blanc that looks prime for an aperitif tonight.

If I were to computerise it, in any event, should I do it the old-fashioned way, under Countries of Origin, or by Grape Varieties, or by Where it Fits into my drinking life? All three, in fact, come into the arrangement somewhere. So do vintages (all my 2000s together), value (there is an inner sanctum), and plain old sentiment.

However good wine is, sentiment makes it better. If it can't make a lame wine walk, at least it can make it worth talking about. Above all, such incidental connections give people who are wary of wine-talk an entry into the conversation. Wine-talk rapidly becomes rudely exclusive. I have a perpetual horror of being button-holed to discuss technicalities by an initiate in the company of people who are not. My answers get shorter and shorter as I manoeuvre to change the subject. (On the other hand I am equally vexed by people who do know one wine from another and who chatter on regardless when I think they should be paying attention to their glasses.)

Half the secret of enjoying wine is to know when to put your critical faculties on hold. Professionals can rarely afford to do this. Pity them. I have little caches of all sorts of wines and vintages that won't show on anyone else's radar but have meaning for me. The obvious one is a vintage memorable for a birth or a wedding. The rewards for remembering and bringing out the bottle at the right moment can make up for any deficiency in the wine. But I am soft enough to hoard a bottle from a grower I liked or an obscure region I visited, or even just from a happy holiday, if I see a prospect of a warm reminiscence at some time to come.

Drinking Dates

I was born in a terrible year. No wine-maker in Europe seems to be proud of his 1939. Except a Bulgarian who dived into his cellar for a bottle of Mavrud, a great heavy burgundy bottle with a wooden label round its neck that he couldn't have scribbled at the last moment. Mavrud is the wine that they claim you can carry in your handkerchief. Age had reduced this one to liquid form, but it was still dark, strong, plummy and highly enjoyable. Château Latour made a 1939 I have drunk several times without grimace. And a Madeira reputedly of my year was presentable. If I thought I could get away with it, I would adopt 1945 as my vintage. I have contemporaries who do.

Every part of home is intertwined with memories of people and events, but a cellar positively provokes reminiscence and commemoration. Its raison d'être is dates. Every bottle is a living memory of a particular time and place. The vintages lying quietly downstairs in the cold and dark are symbolic links to the events of forty years of my life – starting, alas, with a gap. I have nothing from 1965, the year Judy and I were married. The vintage was dismal. We were all too aware of it: we spent a protracted second honeymoon tracking the vintage through Portugal and Spain, France, Italy and Germany, wearing out the windscreen-wipers of our Mini. There must have been some successful wines? Yes, down under: Seppelt's Chalambar Burgundy. I have a note from a dinner a year ago: "Layer upon layer of flavour, velvet. Old cherry brandy; a wonder." Nothing in Europe, though. Like off-vintage children who console themselves with the vintage of their conception, Judy and I are very happy with the year we met. We will eke out our few remaining '64s for a while yet.

1966 was the year of publication of my first book, *Wine*. It was a good year for long-haul claret, good in Burgundy, good on the Rhône and excellent in Champagne. There was nowhere to keep wine in our top-floor flat in Notting Hill Gate. I must have bought the wines I still have when we moved to Islington and acquired the typical 'cellar' of a small London house: the coal-hole under the pavement. Several clarets have followed us from there. Château Gruaud-Larose was the most recent to give us commemorative pleasure.

1967 gave us our first daughter and a new home. I spent far too much of the year away as Travel Editor of *The Sunday Times*: no job for a new father. Lucy's commemorative hoard is largely, lucky girl, Château Yquem. The mellow autumn gave France and Germany some of their best ever nobly rotten sweet wines.

There is nothing left in the cellar from 1968 or 1969. 1968 produced nothing worth buying; '69 was a washout in Bordeaux but a triumph in Burgundy. I had moved on to edit the fashionable glossy *Queen*, a fortnightly with pretensions to controversy as well as fashion. The parties were different from the *Vogue* ones: noisier and longer; but by then the

sixties had swung longer and further. I don't remember having much time in those years to do much wine tasting, or much travelling. The wine in the Italian restaurants where I reasoned with models and photographers was best avoided. I did buy some '69 burgundies, thank goodness, but that would have been in 1970, when I was tempted away from *Queen* by an offer far too good to resist: Would I write an atlas of the wines of the world? The answer took me five clear seconds: if anyone would pay for good enough maps.

James Mitchell had just left my first publisher, Thomas Nelson, to set up a new house with the production director, John Beazley. Like all young go-it-alone publishers they were squatting in borrowed premises, in Covent Garden. They had found a backer in the publisher of maps and atlases, George Phillips. "What else, apart from roads and countries, can we sell maps of?" they asked. "How about the Universe?" was James's typically modest reply. It was done, a huge success; and an *Atlas of the Moon*, too: America had just landed on the moon. "What next? Shall we see if Johnson would do wine?"

So 1970 was the year I spent with clipboards and wax pencils turning survey maps of wine regions into wine maps. A glorious summer, a brimming-over harvest of grapes: much satisfaction all round. That autumn we caught our first sight of Saling Hall. The vines that covered the front of the house were laden, their leaves gold. And it had a cellar?

ABOVE LEFT
My first issue as Editor of Queen. *I had evidently not forgotten the food theme.*

LEFT
James Mitchell (centre) and John Beazley founded their publishing house in 1969 with atlases as their speciality. James was a noisy but irresistible leader.

That did it. We moved in the next Easter.

I have to tell you the story of the second cellar. The estate agent had shown us one, in the west wing: a dream cellar by any standards. Months later, after we had signed the contract, I was going into details with Gooday the gardener. "Where does the rainwater drain to? And what is that door?"

"That's the cellar," said Gooday.

"But that's the other side ..."

"The main cellar," he said. "I'll go and find the key."

This book could be a tour of the space we found down there, a total surprise and an astonishing bonus: the 18th century wine-cellar, a cobwebbed closet reeking of history.

The 1970 clarets were once a large part of our drinking. The oil crisis of 1973 panicked the British brewers who had just invested heavily in wine and wine merchants; suddenly the whole range of bordeaux 1970s reappeared on the market at below half price. When you can buy St-Juliens and Pauillacs at one pound a bottle you need storage space. I was perfectly happy to let friends stack their bargain boxes alongside mine. Red, our son, was born in June 1970; there was never a lack of birthday bottles for him, though they are nearly all gone now.

Almost every vintage of the seventies provided another memorable reason to stock the cellar. 1971 was an excellent burgundy year and one of the best ever in Germany. It was also the year we moved from Islington to Saling and the year my *World Atlas of Wine* was published. I finished it, I used to tell people, in the removal van. It was not far from the truth. There is still a small rack of 1971 Rhine and Moselle Ausleses, some of the most perfect, polished and penetrating sweet wines I have known, now growing pointed with age and smelling more and more, as old *Botrytis* wines can do, of oranges.

1973 had much to commemorate, but few long-haul wines to lay down. Our second daughter, Kitty, was born in January; we started The Sunday Times Wine Club in August; my *International Book of Trees* was published in October. A few bottles of champagne are the sole survivors; no matter if their bubbles are sparse. 1975 was the next vintage to demand cellar room. There had been a dearth of good bordeaux in the early seventies; no really exciting vintage for four years. '75 was destined to be great. Everyone said so. It was a hot summer; the wines were dark, potent and tannic. They are still tannic, some of them like rusty nails. It was certainly a great Sauternes vintage,

Creating a brand. Mitchell Beazley commissioned the artist Adrian George. I can't judge the likeness.

HUGH JOHNSON

THE WORLD'S BESTSELLING WINE WRITER

"Wine - one of the world's great pleasures"

and the last bottles of champagne are still delicious. 1975 was the year I started my monthly gardening column, in a new role as the editorial director of *The Garden*, the journal of the Royal Horticultural Society. I adopted the *nom de plume* of Tradescant. Thirty years on I am still sharing my horticultural thoughts with the Society's members every month.

Drought was the problem in 1976; drought and Dutch elm disease. The immemorial elms had been one of the reasons we fell in love with Saling. With their enormous boles and airy canopies they constituted the entire landscape, the view from every window. They started to die in 1973. We battled for their lives, injecting their trunks with fungicide against the disease. Nothing worked: by 1976 we were felling trees with trunks like hippos – a scene of desolation. Certainly tears from me. The wines to commemorate them? Germany was the success story; the hot summer made sweet wines almost too rich in sugar. Very few remain.

There are memories that always come back in exactly the same format: a frozen moment. I was at the kitchen window when James Mitchell said to me, "You know, Hugh, everything anybody really needs to know about wine could go into a little book like this," – pulling out his diary. He had invented my *Pocket Wine Book* – and scores of other pocket books on everything from antiques to sex. That was in 1977, commemorated in the cellar by an excellent port vintage, now just entering the prime of life.

I need at least one wine from 1979 to mark my favourite book – to date, that is: *The Principles of Gardening*. Not only was it a mind-stretching exercise; it made me give my mind to the garden. It began to look coherent, and our pleasure in it doubled. Champagne is the only '79 we still have. I never bought the clarets of that super-abundant year.

What do I remember when I drink the marvellous clarets of 1982, the best vintage between 1961 and 1990? A year of pleasure, the children at school, the summer warm, the launch of *Cuisine* magazine in New York and my job as its wine editor. (It lasted only two years before *Gourmet* bought it. Out of jealousy, I was told.) A visit to Australia and another to California, but I need to consult my diary to give a year to these: they are not anniversary events to give the '82s another dimension. Nor can I think of any dimension I'd want to add.

There are no '83s left here now. I bought very few, having gone for broke on '82s. If I dwell on what happened in 1983, in any case, I am likely to remember work more than play. I was finishing my *Wine Companion*. The experience made Judy extract a promise from me that I would never write another "bloody great reference book". (Rewriting, of course, doesn't count.)

No wines left from 1984, either; there was none worth buying. I shall never forget the year, notwithstanding. We turned Saling Hall, the cellars and gardens into a film lot to make a silly home movie about wine with a quite starry cast: Virginia McKenna and Bill Travers and their daughter Louise; John Fortune and Neil Stacey. My brother-in-law, Simon Relph (he loves wine too) directed. His other film credits include *Reds* and *Damage*. The delicious clarets, burgundies and champagnes (and Napa Cabernets), of 1985 have to stand in for the missing '84s. At twenty years old the '85 stands as the example of an ideal vintage, good to drink at every stage of its long career.

1986 was the year I became a director of Château Latour, and some believe an even better bordeaux vintage than 1985. It is quite different, more tannic, with a hard edge. Château Latour, unfortunately, is not quite the star wine of the vintage. I don't know what went wrong: I still remember the fresh taste of the new wine. Having an inexperienced director on the board was presumably no help.

1988 is represented in the cellar by long-haul clarets, the best burgundies of the 1980s and lively, vivid champagnes. I was hardly at home at all, travelling all over the wine world making a history of wine for television. We made 13 half-hour programmes, beginning in the misty Caucasus and ending with Beaujolais Nouveau in Tokyo. One of the many lessons I learned doing it was that the film crew wanted to know every detail and taste every wine. In a sense they were the real audience. If I could keep them interested and amused, the show would work for viewers at home. I'm afraid they ended the tour with expensive tastes. The '88s they bought should not let them down. I am still waiting to open the cream of the '89s too. It was a ferociously hot vintage, and the clarets taste of high summer. The Sauternes could hardly be more luscious. Once

Neil Stacey (waiter)
John Fortune and Louise
Travers on the set
at Saling in 1984 for
How to Handle a Wine.
I played a helpful ghost.

more the champagne of the year has been the wine to reflect with while the bordeaux matured. The subject of reflection? The book I wrote to follow the television series: *The Story of Wine*, and the birth of a difficult child, the Royal Tokaji Wine Company.

Our Silver Wedding year, 1990, filled the cellar with good things: claret, burgundy, the Loire, the Rhône, Alsace, champagne, German Rieslings, wines from Piedmont and Tuscany, Napa Cabernets, Penfolds Grange. A grand slam, in fact, and room for only a fraction of the desirables. Since then, I suppose, there have been more splendid vintages than landmarks in life. In 1991 we bought our farm in the Bourbonnais: no wines. 1992 was a great port vintage to toast my collaboration with James Halliday: *The Art & Science of Wine*. 1993 was the first vintage we made in Mézes Mály, once the most famous vineyard in Hungary, but in Communist times almost abandoned. We were lucky: our first wine is sumptuous; we will be drinking it for decades.

There was something of a bordeaux hiatus between 1990 and 1995, but '95 redressed the situation. The clarets will commemorate our buying a wood overlooking the sea in North Wales. It is a vintage that will still be good to drink when most of the dark rows of spruce have been felled and oaks are growing in their place. There are lovely burgundies, too; champagnes, Rioja Reservas and California Cabernets.

1996 was the year we planted our little vineyard in deepest France. No rapid results from that, but bordeaux, especially Pauillacs, to outlast the '95s; red burgundies to hold for years; exceptional white burgundies, Vouvrays, Barolos, reds from northern California and South Australia. With such a choice we will scarcely have enough to celebrate. 1998 was a vintage to buy perfect Pomerols. 1999 was the turn of red burgundies and Tokay. Mézes Mály '99 has qualities to keep it going long past my time.

In 2000 the millennium year provided claret for the next fifty years, and since then every vintage has brought good things to stir memories. 2003 brought our daughter Kitty's first book, *Wine: A Woman's Guide*, and 2005 our first grandchild. My cup is full.

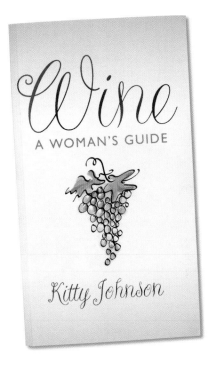

The next generation at work. Kitty, our younger daughter, took me by surprise when she found her own angle on wine – and a lot of new jokes.

Making Lists

I seem to have spent a great part of the past few decades making lists. Lists of wines, or regions, producers, grape varieties, vineyards …. To me lists have a fascination, even a sort of poetry, of their

own. The names of French vineyards can become a persuasive litany –
Cheval Blanc, Les Fourneaux, Les Perrières, Les Charmes (it would be
more humdrum in English translation). And I am not biased towards
France. The lilt in Italian, the swing of Spanish and the earthy vowels of
Australia all get to me. Even, with a little initiation, the tongue-tangling
staccato of Germany.

The World Atlas of Wine is a list that makes itself. I started with the
idea that if there was a vineyard anywhere in the world, I would map it.
Not all at the same scale, of course: scale depends on importance. How to
gauge importance? I chose the evidence of labels: the more specific they
are, as a rule, the more attention is paid to their wine by both the makers
and the consumer. So Burgundy or Germany, their vineyards divided into
tiny plots, each named and legislated for, needed mapping on a scale that
could show their precise topography. These were the most fun to make,
where a path through the vines raised the question of where to cross a
wall or eat a picnic. The intimate details paint the spirit of the place. They
help the wine to come alive. There was no point, on the other hand, in
mapping industrial vineyards on more than a road-map scale, or researching and plotting field-names in regions where they never appear on a
wine label.

There are readers (and wine-growers, of course) who think I must
like, let's say, wine from Paso Robles less than wine from Napa, or Rioja
less than Chianti, because the map is on a smaller scale. It's not that I
value them less, just that the names of vineyards don't appear on their
labels. When they do, they will be on the maps. When the detail helps to
understand the label, it will be there.

My *Pocket Wine Book* is another kind of list. I first saw it as a sort of
aide-mémoire. I wrote down all the wines I could think of, classified by
country. If I used a reference book, it was probably my atlas. I wrote
jaunty little notes on them and devised the hieroglyphics. Where is it?
Red or white? Sweet or dry? The first two editions were almost spacious,
in a taller format than today's, on rather good paper. I had a copy bound
in buckskin for daytime use and one in black leather to carry in my
dinner jacket.

By the third edition we were more business-like. We needed a diary
binder to cope with the quantities on order, so the size shrank to conform
to his machinery. The number of entries, and pages, went up and up.
Soon, rather to my regret, I was putting wines in just because they existed
and someone was bound to look them up. Should I list bad wines, or
would not listing them tell its own story? Need a wine exist to get in? I
decided not, and invented a few to keep readers on their toes. There was a
Coteaux d'Affreux (*affreux* means frightful): "Should perhaps use grapes

*I had a copy of the first
(1977) edition of my
Pocket Wine Book bound
in black leather for dinner
parties. It was taller
(and much slimmer) than
the present format.*

as base." And Domaine Des Gueulasses (*dégueulasse* means disgusting): "Source of much restaurant house wine, most in pubs and theatre bars." There was a Pinocchio, with a variable nose, a von Richthofen .... And there were a few Australians. Beggar's Belief Chardonnay was volunteered by a reader: "Oak and sugar mixture responsible for the majority of recruits to the ABC Club" (ABC stands for Anything But Chardonnay – or indeed Cabernet). St Sheila's was another: "'36 '22 '38 Full-bodied fizzer. Ripper grog, too." Nearly thirty years later, *Pocket Wine* takes an international team to keep it up to date.

But list-making is not what it used to be. Not only are today's lists impossibly long, with names jostling to join them, hundreds a year, but the new names are often detached from reality.

Is there any point in following the inventions of a marketing department that will change its mind next year? I remember a visit to a bookshop in Belfast for a book-signing session. 'Didn't you bring any wine?' was their first question. I went out to find something interesting, perhaps two contrasting wines, to offer and explain to the bookshop's customers. I looked at the shelves in the nearby supermarket in despair. There were so-called Hills and Valleys and Creeks and Ridges from Chile, California, Australia, even from Hungary, all from the same few international grape varieties and none of them, to my knowledge, corresponding to an actual place on the map. I brought a red and a white. At least this provided a real difference (I hoped) through which to demonstrate my art.

I used to think we all agreed on what makes a good wine: certain basic constituents of alcohol and fruit, for sure, but also a sense of origin. I would be as surprised (perhaps pleased, but certainly surprised) to be given a wine in Italy that tasted French as I would to walk down a street in Rome and see a *tabac* or a *urinoir*. The point of travelling was to see different things. The point of importing something was that it had qualities peculiar to where it came from.

How old-fashioned all this sounds. Urban man now lives in interchangeable cities. The country is a theme park. 'Where shall we go on holiday?' 'To the cheapest place with sun, sea and clean bathrooms.' I say this to persuade myself that my subject, wine, is no more homogenized than everything else.

On the face of it, it seems logical to bring the wines of all the world into the ring together and let them slug it out. In roughly comparable groups, for sure, which could mean groups by price, by 'style' (light grape-scented wines, or rich oak-perfumed ones), by origin or, the way it is most often done today, by grape variety or varieties. There is not much to be learned from racing Cabernet against Pinot Noir except which flavour you prefer.

So you arrange a pitting of Cabernets: bottles from Bordeaux, Tuscany, California, Chile, Australia, Argentina … it could be a long list. You don't even look at the labels until after you have tasted. And you write down your opinions. You discover that the wines from warmer climates tend to be darker and more alcoholic. That some have been so flavoured with oak that it doesn't seem to matter much where they came from. That some have fresh flavours with a sense of juice and others are more earthy. Up to this point it is a personal matter: some seem more obvious to you than others; perhaps more interesting, as though there is more to explore.

Then you try to put them in order of quality. Which is better: a dark rich-flavoured one or a fresher, lighter model? Better for what? Which would you choose to take away and drink for lunch and which would you think is the most expensive? Other things being equal, judges tend to think that bigger is better. Wine is no different. If I like the girl with the shy smile and willowy figure it may show I am out of date – but that's my prerogative.

This book is not a list, although it does have an index. In a restaurant you have a choice of everything in the cellar. You can spend hours (even in some cases days) turning the pages of the wine list and deciding what to drink. When you are a guest things are much simpler. Instead of decisions, you have the Table d'Hôte.

Points of View

T HE MAN IN the discreetly striped suit walking up St James's Street (I can see him from the window of the flat where I write) has a pretty settled view of what constitute the good things of life. This gently sloping street, down from Piccadilly to the Tudor red-brick gateway of St James's Palace, is one of them. The inhabitants of the palace and the others adjacent (Clarence House, Buckingham Palace) have his approval. He is deeply attached to the leafy parks that lap round his favourite street: St James's Park with its romantic lake, its duck-thronged bridge, its fountains and flamingos; Green Park with its massive plane trees, its regiments of daffodils, its drifts of fallen leaves. Also to his club where his lunch is cooking: potted shrimps, Colchester oysters, roast partridge; his tailor, his gunsmith and his wine merchants, two of them, facing each other in gentle-manly competition across the road.

Breakfast in St James's. Our view takes in the old shops in London's High Street and Westminster Abbey across St James's Park.

St James's is London's old High Street, its shops clustered at the gate of the palace and bearing, many of them, the royal coats of arms that signify they are or were suppliers to the court. Berry Bros & Rudd was the grocer and still displays its coffee-mill. Now wines and spirits are its business. Lock is the hatter, Lobb the bootmaker, Chubb (recently departed) made locks. What blunt Anglo-

Saxon names they have: Rudd, Chubb, Lobb, Lock. Justerini & Brooks, the other wine merchant, introduces an exotic note, not sustained by Harris the Chemist, Evans the guns, or Fox the cigars. Or indeed the clubs: Brooks's, White's and Boodles. This is the heart of England, where its monarchs have reigned and their ministers wrangled for five centuries. And it is hollow with wine-cellars. With the right keys, it is said, you could walk up, down or across the street underground.

The settled, genteel, some would say stuffy air of St James's lets you forget that this was the Pennsylvania Avenue of the 18th and 19th centuries. World power pivoted here, and the fortunes dispensed and invested from this quarter of London decided fates and tastes over a large part of the globe. Their traces are being expunged from most of it. In the world of wine they are not easy to eradicate. Port, sherry, champagne and claret were all fashioned to please the nabobs of St James's. Cognac, scotch and hock would not have been the same without them. Burgundy indeed is the sole classic wine region where London had only a marginal influence.

The mind-set of our man of tradition is clear. The best white wine comes from Burgundy, the best red from Bordeaux. (Tradition, note, is not fixed in stone: fifty years ago he would have said Germany, not Burgundy.) The funny thing is, I agree with him. Funnier still, so does three-quarters of the wine-drinking globe. Not actually or specifically insisting that their glasses are filled from these precise provinces of France, but positively thumping the table for more of the wine flavours they created.

A cobbler should stick to his last. My career as a purveyor of glass and silver for wine-drinkers in St James's Street lasted for ten years. The memories are more positive than the balance sheet.

_____

How did Burgundy's Chardonnay and Bordeaux's Cabernet come to dominate the modern world of wine? It is easier to say how Cabernet did. The best grape of the most important red wine region was not a difficult choice for the colonists of the vine who planted in California and South

America, South Africa and Australia. It suited California and Chile perfectly; Australia on the whole less well than Syrah from the Rhône. Where Cabernet made good wine there was nothing to touch it. It was deep, durable and recognizable. Full recognition had to wait until the repeal of Prohibition; then it was easy. Equate it with the great wines of Bordeaux and its quality does the rest.

Chardonnay took longer. Even in France there was not a great deal. It was early into California but late everywhere else. There was only a token amount in Australia until the 1970s, and in South Africa it was not even legal. The reason it was not memorable, or particularly recognizable, was that no-one made it very well. Riesling was the recognized white grape, scented and often sweet. White burgundy was a sophisticated minority taste: serious wine-drinkers drank red. It took French oak to make people sit up. It happened in California in the early 1960s. The new element that changed the public perception of good wine was not so much French grape varieties as French oak.

My striped-suited St James's friend is now a harmless old buffer. There is no mystery about where his successors in influence come from. Imperial hegemony lives in Washington and the dictator of taste in Baltimore. His opinions (he is Robert M Parker Jr) go round the world at internet speed. And not only do they travel infinitely further and faster, but they have become, as it were, enforceable. A thumbs up rings round the world as a signal to go and buy, a thumbs down can break a marginal business.

There is another difference, too: one I find more disturbing. Taste in the past was largely a matter of harmless fashion. In American hands it feels more like a moral crusade. Robert Parker deals in absolutes, and castigates those he sees as backsliders.

———————————

New York 1985. Twenty years or so since my first book came out. I am thrilled to share a publisher with my idol, PG Wodehouse – even an editor: Peter Schwed, gruff-voiced, sly and twinkling. Peter thought up the titles of half my favourite books. He even published my book on trees, however much he would have preferred me to stick to wine. His new colleague, Dan Green, is becoming a wine fanatic. "I want you to read this, 'Ugh," he says, giving me a manuscript. I take it away and read vivid, elaborate, highly coloured tasting notes on hundreds of wines. The author is Robert Parker. "Dan," I say next day, "this is great. Extraordinary notes. He seems a great taster, very sure of himself. But what are these numbers – 70s, 80s and 90s – in the margin?"

I had just met the 100-point scoring system that Parker had devised for his newsletter, *The Wine Advocate*. He is a lawyer, Dan told me, who thinks the wine industry needs its Ralph Nader. Nader had recently shredded the automobile industry. Detroit was in retreat. "Wine," wrote Parker, "is no different from any other consumer product." Oh yes it is, I thought. I had mixed feelings about some of my wine-growing acquaintances meeting the same basilisk stare. They do their best, heaven knows. But this was America. There is no need to recount where Parker's scores took him. He had invented a system that supposedly took the mystery, the guesswork out of choosing wine. This guy will not only tell you if it's good, but exactly how good. If it scores more it's worth more. It didn't dawn on me then that so many people would want to buy their critical opinions ready-to-wear.

Robert Parker's method is not that simple. It is spelt out precisely in each of his publications. It is apparently based on the American High School marking

How to promote Robert Parker? Dan Green, my publisher at Simon & Schuster in New York in the 1980s, discusses tactics with Joan Wexler.

system, where you get 50 points just for showing up, so the 60s are dreadful, the 70s pretty poor, the 80s not bad .... The meaning of the scores is clearly explained – and in theory you should be able to cross-reference them to other numerical systems which have been used by the wine trade, especially in England, for years. Some professionals favour points out of seven; a majority go up to 20; others, less eager to be precise, are content with five.

To work, they all need to be qualified. They depend on comparing like with like, for example. But 100 is an eye-catching figure. Everyone is accustomed to percentages. Perhaps I was the only one to be surprised when America seized on the notion as the answer to the conundrum of wine.

Imitators soon showed up, the most prominent the *Wine Spectator*, today a loud voice, at that time a small magazine beginning to ride what was becoming a wine boom. There was a difference, though, between Robert Parker's my-palate approach and a magazine that used a panel of tasters to arrive at its score. An average of scores is a blander result than one man's judgement. A reader following one critic can at least learn his preferences and foibles and, in the long run, aim off for his own.

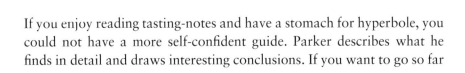

If you enjoy reading tasting-notes and have a stomach for hyperbole, you could not have a more self-confident guide. Parker describes what he finds in detail and draws interesting conclusions. If you want to go so far you can often follow a wine-maker's work through his commentaries. The weakness of any such system is that it is based on tasting, rather than drinking. I can't remember which wine-maker said 'I make my wine to be drunk with food, not with other wines,' but the problem goes to the heart of all test-bench judgements. To everyday wine-lovers (and I am one of them) context is … well, perhaps not everything, but at least half of the pleasure – and hence of my judgement. Who is to say how a wine tasted, as it were, only in combat with other wines, will perform solo at table? The more categorical the judgement, the deeper the trap.

There is no avoiding what you might call 'taster's palate', a seemingly inevitable drift towards the more concentrated wines in any line-up. If intensity of flavours were the sole criterion of quality (there are tasters, and not only American ones, who say that it is that simple) there would be no problem. If balance and nuance are critical (the traditional position, now increasingly seen as European) not only are such judgements debatable, but so is the whole apparatus of tasting by lining up large numbers of wines and pronouncing on them as though each had had a chance to speak.

At least we should be aware of the traditional American taste for sweeter and simpler flavours. Champagne blends used to be adjusted accordingly and labelled either Goût Américain or Goût Anglais. It would save a great deal of misunderstanding, and even occasionally bad blood between critics, if we made the same allowance for cultural differences about other wines.

I have more doubts about expressing judgement in numerical scoring – especially out of the definitive-sounding 100. It is rationalized by giving a maximum of five points for the colour, 15 for the nose, 20 for the palate and a further ten for the overall impression – a feat I myself am quite incapable of. I will admit that I am pretty well innumerate (it took me four goes to pass the most basic maths exam). But to me the link between the colour of a wine and a number is simply missing. If it is the wrong colour altogether I might give it no marks, but does darker (within an acceptable range) mean more marks or fewer? And why? The nose: unpleasant, no marks. Sensational, full marks. There are no absolutes in between. The palate the same. Overall impression: if I were being forced to produce marks this is where I would start. I love it; it must be in the high nineties. Then it is a matter of maths, giving points that add up to the number I thought of in the first place.

The apparent certainty of numbers, remember, is being used to compare and measure the particular pleasure given by one wine with the different particular pleasure given by another. Why is it that wine produces this reaction? There is a convention of star-ratings for restaurants, but who would think of trying to rate Manet and Monet, or Hemingway and Fitzgerald, or Aida and Lohengrin? We have all had dinner-table votes. Was it the Volnay tonight or the Pommard? The Stags' Leap or the Araujo? Consensus comes easily between appreciative friends (and usually follows the most convincing advocate). But would you go out next morning and publish the fact that one was a 90 and the other an 88? Worse, scores have reinvented that old bogeyman, the wine snob, as a more potent force. A wine snob used to be anyone who thought he knew more than you and found a way of rubbing it in. He was also, by extension, a wine bore. Your recourse was not difficult, though: it is all a question of taste. Introduce the illusion of absolutes and your tastes have to shape up. The scene is a wine-shop. Customer: 'I'm afraid I didn't think much of that Cabernet you sold me.' Assistant: 'Parker gave it a 90.' Customer: 'I'll take a dozen, then.'

Another wine-maker's axiom: 'Lafite makes the best Lafite and Latour the best Latour.' If you are looking for the flavour of the one you won't find it in the other. I am a relativist. I admit it. I look for the virtues proper to each wine and enjoy them for what they are. I am a humanist, too: when a grower reveals his personality in his wine it is part of life's rich pattern. I look on fundamentalist judgements as dangerous and misleading.

If I missed the point of what Robert Parker was trying to do with his percentages of perfection, I made a mistake. To me his numbers game was simply irrelevant. He could score away as he liked, and I could enjoy my wine untroubled. It took years for the realization to dawn that his scoring was influencing the way wines were being made. He, of course, would say for the better. We have different tastes. Parker emphasises concentration, strength, density and 'palate feel'. To him 'viscous' – of a red bordeaux – is a term of praise. It makes me shudder. Other things being equal I love transparent wines, clear-cut, fresh in the mouth, with the lowest alcohol content compatible with flavour and satisfaction; wines that merchants are prone to describe as 'elegant'. To me this is the purpose of aging wine; the reason to lay down good claret, or any red, is to purge it of grossness, to give its constituents time to agree and perform whatever chemical choreography is in their destiny. Apart from aesthetic considerations, besides, my experience is that mature wines are kinder to your head. The wines Robert Parker prefers often seem to me to threaten headaches, and not only in their youth.

More important, his scores, backed up with his wide tasting range and comprehensive notes, have the ring of authority. It is easy to assume that his criteria are the only ones. It is convenient for the market to have a single reference point; buying for investment becomes easy if there is a score to put in your computer as well as a price. No knowledge is required; appreciation takes on a mere mathematical meaning. But wine-makers can see which way the wind is blowing, too. It is only too easy to see what the scorer's rules are and what wines he prefers. If by altering your wine-making – perhaps picking the grapes later for maximum alcohol, handling them differently in the winery, soaking the skins for longer to get more colour and density, exposing them to as much new oak as possible, aiming, in short, for density, sweetness and strength (viscosity, even) – you can score 90 points instead of 85, the temptation is hard to resist. If nothing else, self-doubt creeps in. 'Perhaps my wine is rather light,' says the grower, or even the inheritor of some splendid château. 'I was born with the taste in my mouth, so perhaps I'm no real judge. I'd better call in a consultant.' And which consultant? Logically, the one whose clients' wines have a track record of high Robert Parker scores. It is not a theoretical threat. A number of Bordeaux châteaux changed their style of wine in the 1990s, and California's 'cult' Cabernets seem to be on steroids.

My fear has been that the process is irreversible. Once the rule is established that bigger, stronger wines fetch higher prices, who can afford to row against the current? True this is an American phenomenon, but America is an important market for the wines that set the fashion. The growing Asian market is likely to be impressed by numbers (though it may not necessarily prefer stronger wines). Wine is not the only field in which American culture has an imperialistic swagger. In short, would every producer fall in step, and my precious favourites fall by the wayside?

Unmarshalled, though, and with no such heavy weaponry as the 100-point system, the body of those who love wine to drink, not to collect, is framing its answer. My colleague Jancis Robinson threw down the gauntlet when she reacted to a typically fat and florid red bordeaux (you can't call such a wine claret) in the manner of Lady Bracknell. "Really," she wrote, and the stress on the word meant 'You've gone too far.' Here at least was a *casus belli*, a wine to debate publicly. Was it the true expression of its terroir in a hot vintage, or an overcooked monster? It will remain a debate until time has told.

The impish editor of *Merum*, a serious Swiss wine magazine, has another way of expressing his judgement of what is good to drink. He regularly invites eight colleagues to lunch and puts a dozen wines of similar provenance in front of them. The score is measured in centimetres of wine left in each bottle. The empty bottles are the winners.

Totting up scores, of course, is not the only thing you can do with numbers. The most practical notation I have met, and perhaps the most profound, is that used by a Parisian wine-buyer, Pierre Boisset, who for many years travelled round France and further afield buying wine for the firm of Nicolas. He devised a formula to remind himself and tell others how well a wine matched up to its own ideal profile. His method looks at each wine from ten aspects, all of which need to be considered by a professional, but are illuminating for anyone who wants to understand.

The aspects are colour, scent, balance, cleanness, finesse, body, character, acidity, hardness and development. Each gets a mark on the scale of one to nine. Evidently, for some aspects, the higher the score the better. They are the qualitative ones: you can't have too much balance, cleanness, finesse, or (according to Boisset) scent ('bouquet') either. The others pivot around the mid-point of five, taken as ideal. Colours from zero to four are too weak; from six to nine too strong. Body the same: zero to four is on the light side, six to nine the heavy side. The same with character (or 'typicity', defined as the intensity of the tastes that reveal its origin, normally grape variety and terroir together). Over seven points Boisset considers exaggerated for these, under four too vague. Acidity and hardness should also be in the middle of the range. (Remember that this system is as much to describe a wine as to judge it.) And five is the best score for development too: one is the starting point when the wine has just stopped fermenting, nine is *complètement claqué*: clapped out.

The great virtue of Boisset's system is that it gives equal prominence to all the things that might make you prefer one wine to another, including hopes for its future. It is a real buyer's guide. The problem is that a score of 6788966454 is double Dutch to most people. It is shorthand for tasting notes, not a pecking-order judgement.

In the end any ranking of wines is a matter of taste, but before even taste there is a question of philosophy. One school of thought holds that quality is an absolute. It is not a question of whether you like a wine; either it is good or it is not, and a professional judge can tell you exactly how good, with or without numbers. The other school, as though you couldn't guess, is the one I subscribe to. Its laureate is the diarist who once wrote 'I would rather have a worse wine if it had more to say.'

Louder Music

There are numbers, and there are words. It seemed a perfectly harmless question from half-way down the long barrel-vaulted hall. I was lecturing at a literary festival. We had just circulated little plastic cups of four different wines to the three or four hundred in the audience while I chattered on about what made them different. Basic know-your-wine stuff; upbeat, sure: that's my style. Riesling offers one kind of pleasure, fino sherry another, Beaujolais something completely different and so on. It can hardly be too basic. For most people just hearing wine talked about at all is a novelty. Those who have heard it before don't seem to mind a repeat. Put in context, with a guided tour for the taste buds, it makes harmless entertainment, and may even sell some books.

The question? 'You don't like the TV way of describing wine in terms of fruits, do you?' It evidently referred to the BBC's television wine stars of the day, Oz Clarke and Jilly Goolden, who built up a large following playing a free-association game on their evening show. They taste; a performance of swishing and sniffing and sucking and rolling their eyes. Jilly: 'This is fantastic. I get tangerines. I get pear drops. I get lots of lovely ripe melon …' Oz: 'I get lemons. I get just a bit of toothpaste. I get tennis shoes.' Joking? It passed into pub conversation, anyway.

It makes good television, was my answer, but I don't think it really helps anyone to give what sounds like a recipe for fruit salad. Riesling tastes like Riesling more than it tastes like lemons and apples. Surely, once you have tasted Riesling, it becomes a reference. How many apples do you have to eat to recognize an apple?

Next day (and this is the reason I tell this story) I found myself in the news. Wine, the paper said I said, tastes like wine. *The Times* ran a half-page story with a headline about sour grapes and a large picture of my

A scientific approach – or so it appears. A tasting of Australian wines in the Aldwych in central London with the writer Oz Clarke and a Master of Wine, Angela Muir.

nose, followed by a solemn lecture from its wine correspondent. Did I not know that the same aromatic principles were found in wine and common fruits? I was a reactionary, jealous of the younger generation.

If the technology of wine-making has advanced in the past thirty years or so, and we know much more about most aspects of growing grapes, crushing, fermenting, aging and everything that goes on up to the moment of drinking; the business of defining and describing our own reactions has advanced enormously too. Writers used to be alarmingly vague; often intentionally, perhaps. The furthest most could commit themselves was 'Good colour, nice nose, fruity and typical. Good wine.' I scarcely exaggerate. The vocabulary of wine was not only limited, it was stilted by inhibition. If you said what you really thought, it would seem ridiculous, or be unkind to a friend, or would look like advertising.

Rather than try to describe tastes and smells such writers as André Simon, my own mentor, and his friends resorted to similes and metaphors, which often had their own charm. The most popular were anthropomorphic, giving wines human traits, many of them feminine. Wines turned up as pretty little girls, in the full bloom of womanhood, broad-hipped, matronly, benign in maturity or growing frail with age. A wine could have light feet, a paunch or grey hair, virtues, vices, emotions .... Wines called to mind the whole of the human condition. To ridicule these essays is easy, but to call them snobbish is wrong. They tried to express differences, or feelings, for which no technical language existed and, for their contemporaries, in their fashion they could be highly expressive. For me they still can.

Academic discipline arrived in the world of wine in the 1960s. The universities of Bordeaux, Montpellier, Dijon, California (at Davis), Geisenheim on the Rhine and Roseworthy College in South Australia were the most notable. In England the Institute of Masters of Wine began the formal professional training of wine merchants. Giving terms precise scientific meanings both broadens the field of reference and narrows the scope for metaphors. The biggest step came with laboratory instruments that could analyze the chemical constituents of wine and, up to a point, isolate odours and give them names. How much help is it to know that the scent you recognize as lemon can be pinned down to a chemical called isobutoprochlorosniffazine? In description, none at all, but in understanding the behaviour of molecules, how they relate to one another, how they behave and how they may develop, perhaps, to chemists, a great deal.

This sort of analysis was given graphic form at Davis in 1984 by

Professor Anne Noble in an 'Aroma Wheel' that recalled the first practical analysis of colour a century earlier in France. It divided the aromas that might be found in wine into ten groups, ranging from the fruity to the woody and earthy. The greatest French teacher of tasting, Professor Emile Peynaud, also cited ten groups, but divided them slightly differently. Little matter, both give tasters and writers authority to reel off a recipe, as it were, for the wine under their noses. Finding descriptive terms used to mean rummaging around in your memory and your imagination, bringing up sample recollections to match the smell in hand, rejecting them, sniffing again, trying another sample, and often giving up with no exact match. An approved list makes it seem easier. If it is fruity it must be in this long list of fruits, and if there is no precise match I'll play safe with several. This, presumably, is how we arrive at descriptions such as: 'fresh herbs and gooseberry dominate, with a hint of lemon and lime, ripe tropical fruits, melon, guava and pineapple in the finish.' Do you find that tempting? Or confusing?

It is sometimes hard to know whether a new taste has appeared or just a new description become current. 'Fruit-driven' was the vogue a few years ago, applied at first, I think, to Australian wines. Did it mean anything different from 'fruity'? It sounded more dynamic. In many cases I fear it just meant rather sweet. Then came the vogue for 'mineral'. 'Mineral' seems to refer to a sensation rather than a taste. The only mineral I am aware of actually tasting is salt in, especially, certain South Australian reds. The local term 'sweaty saddle' is presumably a reference to the same thing. 'Mineral' unqualified tries to express a certain crisp brightness in the flavour, certainly a positive character. If a writer says 'crystalline' he is, I suspect, building up the same thought (not seeing crystals in his glass). Minerals are linked to soil, of course, so 'mineral' wines reflect terroir. It only takes one writer to pinpoint a character in a memorable word, whether it is 'toast' for oak flavours or 'butter' (my fault this, I think) for certain mature Chardonnays. Once the concept enters the consciousness of tasters, they will cotton on.

Where there are clear and reasonably consistent matches between wines and everyday substances it has one positive effect: it stimulates people who have never consciously thought about the smell of wine to pay attention to what they are drinking. I proposed a simple demonstration for the annual Vintage Festival of The Sunday Times Wine Club in London. We called it the Taste Tunnel. It consists of oversized wine glasses holding some of the reputed constituents of the smell of different wines,

or at least different grape varieties. In the 'Chardonnay' glass we put a slice of melon, a vanilla pod, a few cloves, some tinned peaches and a piece of buttered toast. In the Gamay glass, to match a glass of Beaujolais, fresh and tinned strawberries, red rose petals and white pepper. In the Cabernet Sauvignon glass tinned blackcurrants, fresh mint, slices of green peppers and pencil sharpenings. In the Syrah/Shiraz glass, Liquorice Allsorts, pipe tobacco, stewed plums, raspberries and a little piece of leather. We followed the same idea with Sauvignon Blanc, Sémillon, Muscat and Viognier (an easy one: apricots). There is a glass of wine to sniff and compare with each mixture. It has, I admit, not much basis in science, but it looks extraordinary, our club members love it, talk about it, and drink more different wines as a result. It has been the starting point for people who have progressed to professional tasting – where they learn, of course, that such simplicities may awaken your interest, but reality is more complicated.

Perhaps one day a system of notation will be able to recognize and describe the aromas that make up a wine's total flavour. But music might be a better model for it than colours, or biology, or any of the sciences. Music because different notes act on each other to produce harmony or discord, and more importantly because time is of the essence. A plethora of adjectives is all very well, but verbs are even more telling. It is what wine does, more than what it is, how it starts, develops, lingers and finishes, that gives it character and makes it interesting. Like music, it has more or less volume (intensity of taste) and internal balances between volumes. A brass chord may fill your ears, but a new phrase from the violin, or a whisper from the woodwind, will still catch your attention.

Organic, P. Baines, Chard, Ries ...
SZ yellow straw. V. little nose, fierce st.
caramelly fl. Completely nasty.

Fer Lapo 1990. Chianti Classico

Not aromatic,
Not deep, but red-hearted like a robin. You can smell the rasp on
just warmly Sangiovese — you can smell the rasp as
well as the raspberries. Smooth on entry, then
sandpaper with the fruit. Long and even; good
balance; v. well-made, genial and long.
Scarcely a sensation, but roundly gentilhomme.

How boring this book — & how much better it
would be enlivened with doodles, quotes,
reflections on the brevity of life, the passing
seasons, the flowering of plants & the flowing
successes of children. Very well then ...

ARS LONGER

24.1.02 Kalljob Ries. '99, Hochgewächs, trocken, Zell, Mosel.
11.0°   Clear green Ries. smells appetisingly: finir kennen
        mighty fully fleur. Dry, flesh, fruit, no point.

        Monivar P. Noir, Ries (unfiltered) 1999
        Cheerful light ... Nose caramelly with
4°   burnt oak. Caramel dominant all the way.
        Dull to drink.

Does it persist? Do you hear it again? What message does it carry? So sub-plots of flavour can come and go while a wine is in your mouth, or a theme you just detected at the beginning, say a hint of oak, of late-harvested sweetness or volatile acidity, can grow to dominate and be your final memory of the wine.

To carry the analogy a little further, the quality of an orchestra, a choir or a band, lies in the organization of its energy. Energy is not volume; you can sense it even in the quietest passages. It is reserves of power and skill to be deployed over time. Wine can be the same, its quality can be sensed – to plough on with this metaphorical excursion – like a ripple of muscle under the skin. Judgements of quality that are based on decibels alone are too common among wine critics. We read of 'cartloads of fruit' or 'oodles' of this and that. 'Strawberry-stashed', 'crammed with toasty oak'… volume is constantly being mistaken for quality.

Ernest Dowson was a minor English Victorian poet – not much read today. In the poem that starts "Last night, ah, yesternight, betwixt her lips and mine … " he cried "… for madder music and for stronger wine." The poor man lived and died too soon.

LEFT
*The notebook I keep
in the kitchen to record
every wine I taste at home.
No-one reads it except me.
After many volumes
I decided to spice it up
with doodles.*

The Technical Stuff

"**S**IR," (quotations from Dr Johnson always start like this) "you may scold a carpenter who has made you a bad table, though you cannot make a table. It is not your trade to make tables." It was his defence for having been rude about a play, and the common critic's justification. Although a critic is not how I describe myself, I used the same cover for thirty years, until at last curiosity got the better of me. I really didn't know what I was talking about, I felt, if I didn't make wine with my own hands.

The first hurdle was the ridicule of my friends. 'You'll regret it,' they said with many voices. 'It'll be a millstone round your neck! You'll lose a fortune. Don't expect me to drink it. You'll have to drink it all yourself.' But curiosity is a powerful driver.

We had certainly not chosen the cold upland Bourbonnais as our French bolt-hole for its reputation for fine wine. But it was at least far from the mocking glances of real vignerons. There are good reasons why mine were the only vines on those hills. The same causes destroyed the peasant wine industry of vast swathes of Europe: phylloxera, the louse from America that eats the vines; mildew, the fungus from America; remoteness; competition from the warm south; emigration to America. On balance, America had not been a great help.

Wine-growing survived all these things where there was a population to drink it and where the wine was up to it. In the centre of France there was very little market and no easy transport to one. The wine was not up to much either; it is the land of the oak, not the vine. The most ambitious vineyard in the district had once covered thirty hectares of an estate known for its stag-hunting, not its wine. When I asked about it, the owner showed me his old oak vats, his presses and barrels mouldering in a substantial *chai* beside the splendid stables. "I'd love to see your old label," I said, thinking the vast château would look good on it. "Label?" he said. "Don't imagine it was ever bottled. It all went in barrels to a man in Sancerre."

Sancerre was the obvious model, a hundred and thirty kilometres away to the north. Different climate (the Loire is mild, the Bourbonnais cold and hot by turns); different soil (chalk in Sancerre, granite in the Bourbonnais). Same language – approximately. Peasants, as opposed to hunting aristocrats, planted Gamay in the hope of making red wine. With the local technology it was more often a murky rosé that emerged. I decided on white. Three hundred metres above sea level in a cold climate I had a better chance of ripe grapes, and it is easier and quicker to make. What an admission: but then nothing about being an absentee vigneron is a very good idea.

First the *chef de douane*, the excise chief of the département, had to be brought on board. M Brun came to lunch, Mme Brun in a black leather skirt and high heels that disappeared into the soggy grass. He brought a box of bottles for me to taste, the labours of his other clients. We opened some: I was not so worried by the competition as I was by the problems they had evidently faced. He was a jolly man, not given to making difficulties. Judy had cooked a succulent joint of pork with beans from the garden. He agreed, over a magnum of ten-year-old Grand Cru Chablis that yes, one could argue that a vineyard had been pulled up on the property recently enough for the *droit de plantation* still to be valid. There was no sign of the vines – but the choice of site was not hard. The land behind the farm buildings culminates at a point from which it drops a hundred metres in deep woods, almost sheer, to the river. We call it Tractor Hill: the old tractor lived there – no starter motor. The slope from the top back to the farm faces due south, a gentle saddle with a touch of east and a touch of west, perfectly exposed to sun and wind. Virgil's axiom was that vines love an open hill; this was our best shot. We ploughed the land deep and found the top half was crumbling brown granite. We borrowed a bulldozer that dragged a metal bar a metre deep to open a furrow. We gave it a once-and-for-all manuring with a whole barnful from the sheep that for years had had the run of the place. When the vines had eaten that they would have to forage deeper and deeper for themselves.

What vines was I allowed to plant? In every part of France (it seems even in parts where no-one in his right mind would be planting vines at all) there are three categories: Recommended, Authorized and Don't-You-Dare.

At the time a friend in Bordeaux, Peter Vinding, was replanting an ancient property in the Graves. He had found old vines of a minority variety in these parts called Sauvignon Gris. Grapes called 'gris' have pink or light-purple skins instead of yellow-green (Pinot Gris is the best known). By all accounts it ripened rather early, and it certainly had less of the green herbaceous character than its better-known white cousin. I loved the taste; they were grapes you could enjoy eating. Would I be allowed to plant them?

Nobody said no. A thousand tiny vines of Sauvignon Gris arrived from Bordeaux. I drove to Burgundy to fetch 750 Chardonnay plants so small that they all fitted into my car. This, I judged, on what grounds I'm not sure, would make the perfect Bourbonnais wine: elements of Graves and elements of Chablis. One thousand seven hundred and fifty plants one metre apart each way made 175 ares or 0.175 hectares, well within my planting rights. That is on the classical model of Bordeaux and Burgundy: 10,000 vines per hectare. Modern-style, the same vines could take up two or even three times more room.

Planting Chardonnay vines at Les Boutons, one metre apart in the classic pattern. Here I am taking a turn watering in the tiny plants.

It was May, the perfect time to plant, when roots and shoots are full of vim. Good friends came round to help. I borrowed a tool called a *bicyclette* to dig deep and narrow planting holes. Vines come from the nursery, where they are grafted and grown in sand, with roots like long auburn hair. The hardest part is chopping off three-quarters of the tresses, roots you could never spread out in the hole. It seems such a waste.

The home team consisted of Bertrand and Hermione. Bertrand was 'formed', as the French say, first as a printer, then as a chef, but really loves the open air. If you saw a wiry young man with a cigarette out in the vines or the woods day or night, that was him. Hermione, with a model's figure, a shock of red hair and endless stories, was a neighbouring farmer's wife who made herself indispensable. Milking Jerseys is perfect training, it seems, for cellar work. One day she came in from the vineyard to announce "I've had my eye on your vines. I want to look after them." A comment on my husbandry, I'm afraid. Peter and Susie Vinding came from Bordeaux. Susie is a tiny

dynamo. While Peter and I were discussing techniques and speculating about outcomes, she planted three vines to every one of mine.

They looked desperately vulnerable, my little vines. Especially when the first green shoots appeared. Rabbits! Not much luck with my gun: they keep different hours from mine, the little devils, setting their alarm clocks for sundown and calling it a day just before it is one. A distinguished believer in biodynamism told me the answer. Shoot a rabbit, he said – the difficult part. Skin it. Serve it *à la moutarde* or however you like it best. Burn the skin in a fire. Crumble its ashes into fine powder. Stir three pinches of the powder into six litres of water in a can and sprinkle it around the perimeter of your No-Rabbits-Please zone. Another enthusiast had told me that the cure for Dutch elm disease was a similar decoction of blackberries: pious hope. Nevertheless I followed the instructions. I can only think the rabbits' sense of smell must have been at fault.

Now came the task demanding skill: the wires. It is hard to remember that before the Industrial Revolution there was no such thing. Each vine stood on its own, its branches hanging down. Italians grew them up trees.

Five years on, the vineyard is established and the trim hedges take their place in the Bourbonnais landscape. Hermione strikes a proprietorial pose.

The French practice was to prune them short, making a miniature tree of the trunk and keeping the grapes off the ground by various forms of ingenuity. You could walk through a vineyard in any direction. In most regions today you have to follow the tramlines of trellising: the vines are grown as parallel hedges.

Putting up three-wire fences is no more my thing than making tables. When they have to be strong enough to support vines and their fruit year after year, experience is the key. I called the growers' cooperative of the nearest town that makes wine in earnest, St Pourçain-sur-Sioule, fifty kilometres away. St Pourçain was the wine-supplier of the Bourbons, the dukes who became the royal house of France. Today it makes respectable red, white and rosé for mainly local consumption. It was St Pourçain I was about to put out of business with my wine-making empire. Nobody could have been more helpful. "You're planting vines where? Yes, I think I might find a vigneron who would come and help. I know the very man."

He came, Denis Barbara, tall and shy and a master of the tape, the stake, the hammer, the staple and the vast grey roll of wire. He taught Bertrand and me (when I say I do something on the farm, read Bertrand and I, or just Bertrand) to rig the wires and tighten them until they sang. About to leave, Denis asked me if I remembered receiving, four years before and just before Christmas, a letter from a young lady. She was a school-teacher, about to marry a novice vigneron. The letter asked me if I, as an author, would write a letter to her fiancé telling him how wonderful wine is, and how splendid the race of wine-growers. I did, and four years later here was the very man before me, happily married. Cast thy bread upon the waters ....

———————

The vine is what the Germans would call a guest-worker in France. Its natural home is further south. In France it needs constant supervision and vigilant medical attention. Two varieties of mildew make a beeline for it, and red spider mites are only the most persistent of a dozen bugs that consider its leaves a feast. How to prune it to best effect demands a chapter (which I will spare you). Spraying it against ailments, training it and restraining it is work that seldom stops. Fine to saunter among the green leaves at drinks time; less fine to return the following morning to redo yesterday's treatment, rendered null and void by last night's rain.

In year two the excitement begins. The spring growth is extending to alarming lengths when suddenly, in late May, tiny bunches appear: the clusters of flower-buds. In June they open, minute green leaves with a score of stamens giving off a sweet elusive smell: close to, there is very little; you catch it on the breeze. Folklore says the scent of vine-flowers is a potent aphrodisiac. Besides, a June night is perfect for a walk in the fields. We Pisceans have no quarrel with the theory. There is no vintage, though, in year two, and in year three only a smattering. Year four is when part two of the learning curve starts in earnest. Time to find out who your real friends are: time to pick.

Even the apparently simple task of relieving a vine of its fruit has its wrinkles. 'Why don't you take row three?' Chardonnay. The bunches are perfect, dry, heavy with gold translucent grapes (I am fantasizing) separated by a hair's breadth from each other to let the sunshine in .... The first problem is finding them. You squat down and find the sturdy lower arm of the vine is festooned with half a dozen. You reach with your scissors to find their way blocked with leaves, tendrils, one bunch tangled with another, their stems buried deep in grapes, draped over the wire. You need your other hand to hold a bunch while you cut. This is how fingers are sliced – every day.

Perfect grapes are rare. The reality is usually a spotty crop. Far from the flowering happening in perfect conditions, with every flower being fertilized and becoming a grape, cold and rain interrupt proceedings. Half the flowers get no further than tiny green blobs. A bunch with some developed grapes and some still in embryo is known as a 'hen and chickens', and the chickens contribute nothing to the wine. When on the other hand every flower fructifies, the grapes can be so tightly packed in the bunch that they invite rot. If rain falls when they are nearly ripe they swell and split their skins and in no time the bunch is full of fungus. It is one thing to be aware of the possibilities; another to control them.

A vine can ripen only so many grapes. It is photosynthesis through the leaves that makes the sugar: too many grapes in relation to the leaves and you wait in vain for them to ripen. It is routine in ambitious vineyards to limit the number of bunches allowed to develop on each vine, if necessary by a 'green harvest' in summer before ripening begins. It can be hard to per-suade workers to cut off half the fruit of their labours and leave it lying on the ground. Equally painful, though, to harvest half-ripe, half-rotten bunches and to have to sort them before they are pressed. No-one enjoys stand-ing at the sorting table, sticky to the elbows,

Our grapes were not always as photogenic as the Chardonnay crop of 2003. The plastic boxes are a luxurious touch copied from more prestigious producers.

snipping clean grapes from among mouldy ones. As for the mechanical harvesters that comb almost every modern industrial vineyard, knocking off all the grapes indiscriminately, they make no distinction between good fruit and bad.

Heaven knows how many wine-growers I have seen at work, how many harvests in how many cellars. Watching the process and reading the manuals, though, is not even a preparation for getting your hands dirty. So little is predictable. Bertrand, Hermione and I made five vintages together. You would think it would become routine: far from it.

LEFT *to* RIGHT
Sorting grapes is sticky work. It calls for patience from family and friends. My brother Brian (right) could even be too fastidious.

Bernard, Leo and Thierry operate the grape mangle, the fouloir.

Many hands pretend to make heavy work of the pressoir.

Bertrand forks out the cake of skins left after pressing. I measure the sugar content with the saccharometer.

The first stage of wine-making is to crush the grapes. The old stone barn is our theatre of operations. Even if your plan is to press them straight away (the best idea for white wine) it is far easier if their skins are broken. It takes far more force than we can exert by hand to burst grapes just by squeezing them. It is different with a pneumatic press, but we are only in the handicraft league. Stage one for us is a mangle, in French a *fouloir*. It has a hopper, which takes the contents of one of our plastic baskets. You wind the handle, the rollers seize the grapes and deposit them – a mash of skins, stalks and juice – into a bin below.

From the bin we bucket them into the waiting press. I love this object. It consists of a broad iron saucer on three short legs with a central steel screw standing two metres high. Around the screw fits a slatted wooden cage to hold the grapes. When it is full you cover it with boards and blocks of wood and spin the massive iron press-head down the screw

until it holds the blocks in place. Juice begins to stream out between the slats and run from the lip of the saucer into a plastic trough with the sound of a little cascade. A heavy iron lever fits into the press-head. With each stroke of the lever a ratchet gives a ringing clack, juice streams, the cascade redoubles and the trough fills with the grape juice you are proud to call 'must'.

How sweet is it? The measure of its sugar is the measure of the alcohol in the coming wine. I fill a glass cylinder and lower in a float calibrated to read the potential alcohol, calculated from specific gravity. Ten per cent by volume: we haven't done badly. Should I add sugar to push it up another degree? It takes 17 kilos of sugar to raise the alcohol level in 1,000 litres of wine by one degree. I would if I were doing this commercially. Everybody has since M Chaptal was Napoleon's Minister of Agriculture: his *Traité sur la Vigne* was the vigneron's standard textbook for generations. But his agenda was more complex than just easier wine-making, it was the promotion of sugar-beet as a crop when the British naval blockade cut off France's supply of cane sugar from the Caribbean. 'Chaptalization' of wine was his wheeze to make the wine-growers of the south subsidize the sugar-beet farmers of the north. Once they had learned the habit, wine-growers – presumably drinkers, too – grew addicted.

Why would I want stronger wine? Personally I would rather drink more of weaker, so long as it had flavour. My real goal is to see what nature gives unadorned, to discover the unaltered taste of our grapes and our ground. The only addition, then, is the sulphur wine-growers have used since the Romans: without its anti-oxidant properties the wine

Len Evans, sculptor and wine man, visits from Australia to carve a monumental stone head for us. It surveys the green Val d'Aumance from our wooded heights.

would go as brown as a bitten apple. It comes in a plastic jerry-can in a concentration that demands head-spinning calculations to achieve the recommended dose. No-one is watching: I use a modest splash.

Our fermentation vessels, our vats or *cuves*, are distinctly unglamorous fibreglass affairs. They have two great advantages: transparency (more or less) and virtual weightlessness. I can roll them outside unaided to clean them with a hose. I would be horrified if I went into a serious cellar and saw them, but we have no pretensions, we vignerons of the Bourbonnais.

————————

Bertrand is loading the *fouloir*. Bernard, proprietor of the vast cream cattle you can hear munching ten metres away, and maker of rich sharp cheeses you eat fresh and crumbly, joins the team for the vintage. He is ratcheting the press. Hermione has turned on the little whining electric pump to pump the must from the trough into a vat. Phase one is coming to an end. We have extracted the juice of our grapes. Now nature, with no interference from us, will turn the juice into wine. This is what I still see as a miracle; the origin of wine. It just happens. Where is the yeast? In the air. It comes from the vineyard – perhaps in the bloom on the grapes? By now it probably lives in the stones of the barn where it was born out of fermentation. This is what fermentation is: the furious breeding activity of millions of these little creatures, neither plant nor animal, offered the supply of sugar in the vat of grape juice. Alcohol is half of the resulting waste; the other half is carbon dioxide. You know the yeast has begun to breed when you see the little bubbles start.

It doesn't happen straight away, at least not in this cool autumn weather. It is the last week of September. There is time to let the solids in the liquid settle. Within twenty-four hours most of the scraps of skin and pulp have sunk to the bottom. Time for the first racking – the word for separating juice or wine from its sediment. We pump it from the vat into a clean one alongside, rinse the sludge out of the first vat and pump the must back. On the way it absorbs all the oxygen it wants. Fermentation is only a matter of time now. If you can't bear the suspense you can add yeast from the baker's – or indeed a yeast specially bred and cultured to give specific properties to your wine. Many modern wineries do, and lose originality in the process. A few years ago a handful of Bordeaux châteaux swapped yeasts. Each made a trial vat with another's culture. People who tasted the wines reported a bizarre cross-over of characteristics. Nobody wanted to pursue the experiment. I admit one year I blinked and used baker's yeast. You warm a spoonful in a saucepan with some must and sugar (this is the Johnson method) until it starts to rise like dough. When you add it to the vat, it spreads by contagion.

I have been in Jerez at vintage time when the weather is still so hot that fermentation is almost immediate. 'Tumultuous' is the word they use for the frothing, heaving onset of yeast breeding. Wine-makers rarely let the tumult run its course; they have views on the ideal temperature and means of enforcing them. I and my now-brimming tanks are limited to what the weather dishes out. My technology runs to shutting the barn doors in the morning to keep the sun out and opening them again in the cool of the evening.

In the famously hot summer of 2003, when our harvest started two weeks early and the ambient temperature even at night was torrid, there was very little I could do about it. I remembered many years before seeing a grower in Pomerol heaving blocks of ice from the fishmonger's into his vats – and not in plastic sacks to make them retrievable, either. My inadequate effort was blankets wrapped around the vat and kept wet with the hose. The temperature inside went up to 30° C, briefly, and the fermentation was over in five days instead of ten or so: not what any consulting oenologist would have recommended. How much better the wine would have been if I had been able to cool it I shall never know, but there have been no complaints.

———————————

Fermentation is wonderful to watch – and even better to smell. At first only a few bubbles drift idly to the surface. Then it becomes more general and systematic and the smell of grape juice grows sweeter and headier, joined with the smell of yeast. You can watch it best in a glass jar. I keep a demijohn beside the vat just for the pleasure. On day two the must is clear; day three it is hazy, with a few fine bubbles running up the glass sides to prickle the surface. The fourth day there is total haze, the liquid a pale sandy colour with champagne-like bubbles forming a light froth on top. Days six, seven and eight, racing bubbles are jostling through the whole jar. It is warm to the touch and hissing gently. By day eight in the evening they have slowed down and the jar has a sandy floor, peaky like a wind-blown dune. The yeast cells, their intervention over, are dying and sinking to the bottom. You have made wine.

Not fermentation yet. The must forms a fragrant froth as it fills one of our 700-litre fibre-glass tanks.

Cold weather at this point helps it to clear. My practice has been to wait a few weeks, rack it to and fro once more, add a judicious measure of sulphur (the all-purpose antiseptic of the cellar) and batten down the hatches till spring. More ambitious and painstaking wine-makers often keep working at it, leaving it in contact with its yeasty lees and actually stirring them up periodically with a stick to incorporate some of their flavour in the wine. *Bâtonnage*, they call it: *bâton* is French for a stick. There is another process, though, that your wine may undergo either sooner or later, depending on the weather and the temperature in your cellar: its second, or malolactic, fermentation.

Fermentation, in other words, does not simply mean the ebullient behaviour of yeasts. It originally referred to any unexplained, possibly even magical, boiling appearance. Nobody knew what was going on until the mid-19th century when France's greatest chemist, Louis Pasteur, found the answer. It took another century of head-scratching to understand a further fizzing of the wine when the yeast had taken care of all its sugar. *Le malo* is a bacterial business, nothing to do with yeasts. Lactic acid bacteria apparently seize on malic acid and convert it into more of lactic.

Malic acid is sharp (*malum* is Latin for apple); lactic is creamy (*lactis* is milk). If a creamier, less sharp wine is what you are after, you will know which way to vote. Nobody knew this until the middle of the 20th century. Bubbliness in spring was thought to be just a few yeast cells

The family gets together at Easter to bottle last year's wine. Left to right: Judy, Chris, Lucy, Hermione, Red, Lydia and Kitty. We sealed the bottles with beeswax.

having a final fling (which is not impossible) – and in Champagne is the premise on which the whole thing rests. Now *le malo* is part of wine-makers' repertoire of possible adjustments.

Had I planted red grapes, the routine would be different – but really only in its timing. Harvesting: the same. Crushing in the mangle: the same. But then instead of pressing out the juice we would be loading the whole mash – pulp, skins and even stalks – into the vat to ferment together, preferably at a higher temperature than the white. To extract the maximum colour, and enough tannin, from the solid matter we would try to prevent it from floating, or at least keep pushing it back down when it did. 'Punching down the cap' is the technical term. Another way is pumping the juice from the bottom and spraying it over the top. (These are the sort of manoeuvres wine-makers can talk about for hours.) In some cases a week of this is enough; in others, to give the wine all possible brooding depth and tannic grip, three weeks is not too much. Then comes the pressing, when this process of soaking to extract the goodness – maceration is the word – is done. What comes out of the press is the most tannic of all.

Friend Paul Hogarth painted the label. A white sheep was a rarity in a countryside of dingy brown ones, as was white wine where Gamay is the usual grape.

This is wine-making at its simplest. The refinements can go on forever. Most fundamental is the use of barrels, either (in white wine) for the whole fermentation, or (in red) to finish the fermentation after pressing, or (in either) to mature the wine to a further stage before bottling it. This whole phase of a wine's life is known to the French as its *élevage*, its upbringing or raising, words we use in English about children or cattle, but not about wine. White wines in general need less than red. Wines with no pretensions receive no more than a filtering before they are rushed into bottles. "The only thing we raise around here," say my trusty helpers, "is our glasses."

Elevage

It is a different matter for proper professional wines, wines made with serious commercial intent. Their upbringing is as important as their growing. At Les Boutons we had no cellar; the cellar is the hub, the workshop, the strong-room, the showroom and the nursery of a serious vigneron. He brings up his new wine like a baby. He feeds each barrel daily to keep it full to the bung; he changes its nappies when he racks it.

The way these tasks are done is almost ritualistic. It is always coming up in wine country conversations. Do you, for example, encourage the sediment to fall with a 'fining agent', a coagulant to draw fine specks together and make them sink? The whites of eggs whipped to froth are the most traditional. Unless bull's blood (now archaic, if not illegal) is older. Fish glue is a more modern binder. The choice, and the method, and the timing, are the sort of things that run in families. 'It coagulates them,' as one grower told me.

'It's just been racked,' or 'It needs racking,' is the nervous apology you hear in every cellar when you go to taste – meaning this is not the ideal moment. Gardeners are used to nervous prevarication, too; we do it all the time. Dorothy Parker mocked us: "You should have seen it last week," was her jibe. Was it Parker who had the answer for people who can't abide being shown round gardens? (You pull up a plant, examine it and say 'Planted too deep.') The cellar-tour equivalent doesn't bear thinking about.

To the visitor it is a mystery. How does the vigneron know each barrel? He lives down here with them; any change when he comes into the cellar is as clear as if a stranger had slept in his bed. He knows the smells, he knows the sounds. With new wine he is waiting for *le malo*. In the days when almost all small growers sold their wine to merchants in barrel, they had no idea about this springtime eruption – or if they had seen wine 'fretting' they thought it was the original fermentation starting again because some sugar remained unconsumed. The vigneron can encourage it to happen by warming the cellar, but until all signs of activity are over he does nothing to disturb his wine. You can try reasoning with adolescents, but you soon learn better.

Barrels were France's first gift to civilization. They seem to have been invented by contemporaries of Astérix and Obélix. As the perfect receptacle for preparing wine they still have no peer.

Cave de vieillissement des fûts

And the barrels? To hear a cooper talk (and they are famous for it. Also for swearing) you would think that coopers had invented the wheel. They have a point. The barrel is far from being an obvious construction; certainly a giant leap from the amphora that preceded it. An accidental barrel is hardly likely and, like the wheel, there is no half-way stage. What ingenious mind first imagined planks cut to shapes that could be butted up to each other and hooped together to form a – well, a barrel? The hoops were originally plaited withies; the original shape was a cylinder. Bending the staves to form a belly is not done without effort and equipment: it needs a very strong pull on a running noose of rope or, these days, wire. It is made much easier by steaming the wood or soaking it and standing the half-made barrel over a fire. When the fire started to char the inside it gave another twist to the story: charred oak gives wine a caramel flavour, another resource in the *éleveur*'s armoury.

Oak plays such a large part in the vocabulary of wine these days that we are all pocket experts. The names of French forests drift in and out of the conversation wherever wine is made. One name, Tronçais, is universally saluted: the forest that fetches the highest prices. Its oak has the finest grain, from the most closely packed annual growth-rings. I paid my first visit in the 1980s. I was commissioned by *The New York Times* to write about the world's most distinctive forests. A picture drew me to Tronçais, remote in the unvisited centre of France, the old province of the Bourbonnais, the département of the Allier. It was January, when the leafless trees spread a purple-grey haze over the brown forest floor; more and brighter colours than summer green. I was mesmerized by the endless intimacy of it, the repetition of the rides retreating into the haze, and the scale. There are twenty-five thousand acres of oaks, from seedlings to giants like the Chêne de la Résistance: a thirty-five metre grey pillar four metres round. There are lost lakes, patches of piney moorland, remote woodsmen's cottages with a wistful rosebush by the door. Tronçais was a great natural feature, like mountains or the sea, and its harvest was immense cylinders of scented timber.

My favourite oak in the Forêt de Tronçais is named after a forestry professor from Edinburgh. The Chêne Stebbing is four metres round and 35 high. Oaks for barrels are felled at half this size but can still fetch many thousands of pounds.

One of these cylinders could fetch £12,000, standing. They are auctioned as state property in October each year at the age of a hundred and eighty years, give or take a decade. The forest is ringed with little towns where they are dismembered and the best of the wood split into *merrains*, the pieces that will be sawn to size as the staves of wine barrels.

The best timber is the colour of smoked salmon and smells of wine. So much wine, at least, smells of oak that you might think so. Tronçais and its oak are implanted in my life now. Our farm is on the edge of the forest, where streams leak out of the woods to feed a slow brown river with sudden moods of frothy spate. We had oaks, and planted more: barrels for the future. This is where I planted my vineyard, to make wine without barrels: oak does nothing for a drink-me-quick white wine.

Growers of fine wine with delicate flavours prize oak for its physical properties, not for its smell. A barrel wall is a thumb-thick layer of oak split along the grain, nearly impermeable but not quite. Wine soaks into it to a certain depth, and air passes through it in minuscule amounts that allow gradual reactions in the wine. No other container has these properties – as well as being as manoeuvrable and resilient as a barrel. Oak with closely spaced growth-rings is less permeable as well as being less perfumed. Not only Tronçais has these properties (very slow-growing Baltic oak may apparently be even better) but its name is seen in cellars where price is no object. If the smell of oak is the aim, as it is for instance in Cognac, oak from the easier conditions of Limoges is better. And if only the smell, and none of the beneficial effects, of oak is the aim, I tell you through gritted teeth there are shortcuts that would make you blush. Adding oak shavings, or filtering the wine through oak sawdust, are commonplace practices. Most shameless, it seems to me, is to add oak essence from a bottle. But then upbringing is hardly the word you would use in a cellar that took a cocktail-recipe approach to its produce.

'What percentage of new oak do you use?' is what every journalist asks every wine-maker. A hundred per cent is a huge expense, only for the most de luxe establishments – and counterproductive unless the wine has the concentration and chemical structure to absorb so much flavour. Two hundred years ago new oak every year was the rule, at least for the rich. It was widely believed that even second-year barrels carried bugs. They were crusted inside with tartrate crystals which looked, and were assumed to be, dirty. Besides you sold your wine in its container: what else was there?

Now it is a part of a vigneron's empathy with his wine to sense how much time in oak of what pungency is best. Burgundy is the place to see this sensibility at work. A grower may have a dozen different wines in his cellar. They form a natural hierarchy in his mind: the best (Grand Cru if he is one of the fortunate ones) will have the newest barrels, the Premiers Crus ones that have been used before and the junior wines barrels four or five years old. But not systematically: the barrel can have too much effect or too little. Visiting a cellar like this I sometimes think it is a single organism, of which the proprietor is the brain. Certain conventions are observed: the best wines have the best position, in the centre. Visitors should behave with a certain formality, too: it is a privilege to be invited into this inner sanctum. I have noticed many times that good growers never make up for their wines' shortcomings with a shower of adjectives. Self-respect prevents it. They know their value better than anyone: they live with them.

Precious wines are bottled straight from the barrel. Exactly when is another decision taken by the vintner and his wine, as it were, in consultation. In an era of prosperity, this sort of freedom of manoeuvre is taken for granted. Who remembers now that wine used to go off waiting in the barrel for someone to buy it? The grower had no money to buy bottles. When an argument arises about how long it should ideally be kept before bottling, the folklore can get it all wrong. Barolo is a famous case. Because it had customarily had to wait years in the barrel the practice became enshrined in law, even when the wine was withering away, exhausted.

Experience shows whether wines are at their best soon after bottling, or whether there is another life ahead of them that only a bottle can bring. Much of this book is predicated on this second cellar life. It is extraordinary that what amounts to a single serving can continue on its separate way for year after year, sometimes decade after decade. But our vigneron has only one job: to put the wine in its bottle at its best. You would be surprised what passions are aroused by what this means. In the book we wrote together on wine-making, *The Art & Science of Wine*, James Halliday and I talked of the danger of getting it wrong. If in doubt, we said, prudent vintners are advised to put it through a filter. (White wines are usually filtered; we were talking about red.) There were critics who reacted as though the book said nothing else. The horror of filtering any goodness out of wine! Certainly everything good in the barrel should go straight into the bottle: that is the whole point. If you see a label promising that a wine is unfiltered, that is just what it is telling you.

Of course different regions have different methods and different goals. This is the most straightforward. Wine can be brought up to be sweet, to be sparkling, or to be intentionally oxidized. The cathedral-like bodegas of Jerez, where sherry is kept in Andalucían heat, have a very different purpose and effect from a cold northern cellar. Sometimes blending is part of the process. In most cases, though, bringing up wine is just preparing it for delivery in a stable condition, with all the character, the quality and, to use a portentous word, the integrity it brought out of the vineyard as baskets of grapes.

Appellations and Other Limits

Riesling I had first thought would be the grape to plant in my vineyard, simply because I like the taste. It might ripen well in our spells of late sunshine. Luxembourg can sometimes do it, and that is far colder and further north. At any rate it was only for the family, many kilometres from any recognized region, so why would anyone mind? I had underestimated your French bureaucrat. '*Pas autorisé, Monsieur*' means

'Just you try it, son.' If I'd said Sauvignon Blanc and planted Riesling (and burned the dockets) would they ever have known? The police don't knock when they wander about our land with binoculars looking for poachers. Not worth the risk.

It is commonplace, even fashionable, these days to express impatience with France's system of appellations contrôlées; or any system, Italian, Spanish or German, that regulates and legislates for the identities of wines. The critics', if not the consumers', mood is testy. Why trammel the producer? Why tell him what grape varieties he can grow where? Why can't he add sugar/acidity/oak chips if it makes his wine easier to sell? Whose business is it anyway?

Appellations and their like are indeed imperfect. They were born in the 1930s, in an uncomfortable period when producers needed support and their customers reassurance. Phylloxera had destroyed most of Europe's vineyards. Fraud and trafficking followed on an epic scale. What is government for if not to impose fair dealing? Fair dealing, in wine, means identifying the goods on sale.

In all the areas producing quality wines some groundwork already existed. Bordeaux was relatively new to the game but a rudimentary classification of some of its properties went back two hundred and fifty years, and the very specific Classification of 1855 was a famous success. In Burgundy the first steps towards demarcating the best vineyards were taken in the 12th century, and in the 19th what had been intermittent progress became methodical and profound. By the 1930s what was a Premier Cru and what was a Grand Cru was no mystery. The appellations just confirmed common knowledge. There never was a pan-national way of deciding, defining and finally mapping what was in and what was out, or what was first class and what was second. At Châteauneuf-du-Pape the discussions began in the 1920s when Baron Leroy plotted where certain wild flowers grew: soil propitious for serious wine. In Alsace the whole business only began in earnest fifty years later and is still far from finished.

At what stage, in any case, should government get involved? Should it wait until practice and experience have produced some kind of consensus, and then impose it? This is what Italy did. The problem was the timing. Italy's DOC (Denominazione di Origine Controllata) laws arrived in the twilight of an industry near collapse. In most of Italy, so-called traditions were going nowhere. Many DOCs were founded on a combination of some pretty desperate agricultural practices and half-baked folklore. The best-known instance is the 'traditional' recipe for Chianti, containing so many white grapes that the wine was barely red – and Trebbiano grapes at that, a dismal choice even for white wine. It was imposed by law in 1966. It took a generation, and widespread flouting of the rules, for Chianti to become a respected red wine again.

It is not as though appellations and their equivalents guarantee better wine. They can guarantee its origin, its content, its strength and how it is made. Whether it is worthy of a prestigious name – let alone good value for money – is another matter. The government leaves this to the market. There is a rudimentary check: every year France's appellation authority, the INAO, assembles the local experts to taste every wine submitted for a *label*, the authorization to use the name of an appellation. The experts themselves challenged the INAO. It tried to avoid the issue. 'Our relations with winegrowers are of great concern to us … it is a sensitive matter ….' What percentage, asked the experts (who give their time unpaid), of the wines we taste are passed for a *label*? This is where the serious hedging began. What forced the INAO to produce the answer was a recent French law on the disclosure of information in the public domain. Even Paris was aghast when the figures came out. Ninety-eight per cent of all wine submitted was given the green light. The INAO President resigned. How much else changed?

If this explains the dire quality of so much appellation wine, and the inescapable taste of water in the bargain offers of French supermarkets, it also explained the scepticism of France's competitors. They see the appellation system as cover for lazy thinking, not to mention a gravy-train for bureaucrats. Paris is famous for pettifogging, hassling individuals who show initiative. The story of my own little frustration with Riesling (and many are far worse) gets a great guffaw in Australia. It is incomprehensible anywhere in the New World. If the grape ripens – grow it, is the sentiment, and indeed the law too. The market will soon tell you if you are wasting your time. The indignant Australian (not necessarily Australian, but typically) then asks 'Why no Shiraz in Bordeaux, or Merlot in Burgundy? Chroist, you could make a great Sauvignon in Meursault.' Possibly. Anarchy could be a barrel of laughs.

Don't be fooled by the white coat. This scientific-looking person is not tasting but drinking: there is far too much wine in the glass.

The French justification starts with history. Centuries – if not millennia – of trial and error have brought European wines to where they are. In most cases their grape varieties have been selected on the spot. We know the origins of a few, but most are heirlooms from the mists of time. Many hundreds have local importance in specific climates and on specific soil; their potential elsewhere (and of course the potential of their genes) is a virtually unexplored continent. But the matching of Riesling and the Rhine, Pinot Noir and the Côte d'Or, Chardonnay and Chablis, Merlot and Pomerol, Nebbiolo and Barolo are facts for which we should simply be grateful.

The second justification is more complex. It is not about standards: the INAO story quashes any pretensions along those lines. It is about identities, and why recognizing something for what it is gives us pleasure. Knowing a person's name, remembering the name of a rose, recognizing a voice or a model of car – they all give us satisfaction. Our brains are stimulated by labels – and they guide us through the ideas we attach them to.

What is it about the Côte d'Or of Burgundy that brings it attention and devotion quite out of proportion to its size (its production is one tenth that of Bordeaux)? Yes, its wines can be more than delicious. But equally important there are hundreds of them, from fifteen hundred named vineyards. These vineyards are owned by fifteen hundred different families. So there are more different combinations of vineyard and wine-grower than any one drinker will ever master.

Even if most people shrug (as they do) and turn away to something less demanding, this complexity is its own justification. Côte d'Or wine used to be made (relatively) simple to understand by the négociants who blended and sold it. In the past twenty years individual growers have taken the initiative: they now bottle and sell their own. Whether it is better or not, it is personalized. Are the customers put off by the need to know so many more names? On the contrary, they feel honoured to see deeper into this strange society of privileged peasants, locked into its agricultural routine at the same time as it plays on a world stage.

You might logically argue that when the wine is good enough, something similar might happen elsewhere. In Coonawarra for example, or Hawkes Bay or between Rutherford and Oakville in the Napa Valley. Already plots of dirt ('Eisele', 'Gravelly Meadow') have been designated as outstanding – just what happened in the Clos de Vougeot around 1100 (AD, that is, not am). By 2200 perhaps the fragmentation will have gone as far as it has in Vosne-Romanée – though it will be zillionaires, not peasants, staking out their holdings. But no, appellations follow the complexities of geology, and few slopes are as complex as the Côte d'Or. And bizarre as it sounds it takes more than money. You cannot separate the wine from the social structures of this deeply anthropological place.

An appellation in any case is more than a demarcation. In intention, at least, it is a sort of template. Students, brokers, sommeliers, customers, children growing up in wine-growing families all form their expectations, and shape their lives, around the almost Platonic concept of what the French call the *cru*. Médocness, Nuitsness, Côte Rôtieness (and for that matter Sancerrity) are existential realities. And the same is true, of course, of Rioja, Montalcino, port … nothing limits it to France. More important, it is a bankable action plan. Make the wine recognizable as one of these, the plan goes, and a queue will form, money in hand. Why? Because the public wants to buy enjoyment in a predictable form.

In any case (and this will conclude the argument for the defence) rules make the game. A knock-about with the ball is all very well, but it is when the whistle blows that it becomes interesting. When the referee gives a penalty you grit your teeth – or football would cease to exist. And cricket has never suffered (or not until recently) because the rules are too obscure to follow. Do cricket and the Côte d'Or belong to the same mind-set?

Glasses and Decanting

The question of whether to decant, and if so how long in advance, crops up at every dinner. As far as I am concerned, decanting is routine for almost all red wines and the majority of whites. Decanting white wines raises eyebrows. It was another trick I learned from Ronald Avery, who used to say that old whites needed to be 'really rattled about'. What he meant by this was pouring them from a height into the glasses to produce a noise, the object being to give them a good breath of air before you started 'looking at' them. He did it to everything from Chablis to a precious old German Auslese. How you knew the wine was the better for it I'm not sure, but I have convinced myself that he was right to give them breathing space. If you pour wine straight from a freshly opened bottle and the second glass tastes better than the first, you have proved the point. When I had a shop I even had special white wine decanters made, copying some exceptionally elegant ones I had seen in the dining room of the Madeira Wine Association on that island: almost like clear glass German wine bottles with a lip and a tear-drop stopper.

Decanters are apparently an English invention. The French say *carafe*, with no distinction from a water jug, or *decanter*, borrowing the English word. It was not their practice to decant – and perhaps the English practice only because our principal wine was port, which often had sludge at the bottom of the bottle. The discovery that the wine was not only clearer but also better, more fragrant and perhaps even softer on the tongue a few hours after being so liberally exposed to the air, was no doubt accidental. A last minute racking, you might call it.

No-one has more experience in the matter than Michael Broadbent. He times every wine from the moment it is decanted, taking off his wristwatch and laying it on the table next to his notebook. He records the rise, and sometimes the fall, of the fragrance in a fine wine which to him (and me) is half the pleasure. A bouquet that builds up and slowly opens is the mark of a great wine: one that fades or turns sour is clearly the opposite. That they evolve is not in question, and usually for the better. People who leap to judgement on the first sniff are simply in too much of a hurry. It is only fair to add that there are people of great authority categorically opposed to the whole idea. Professor Peynaud was one. To him the only true sight of a wine was the first glass poured from a just-opened bottle. It is painful to think of the pleasures he missed. I make a habit of leaving decanters which have held very good wines overnight, preferably with a last glassful in the bottom. You would be surprised how often their morning breath is even sweeter.

Trusty friends: the jug (below, left) has held everything from Vin de Pays *to Château Latour; the carafe from a café the same. I designed the everyday wine glass in 1964.*

My favourite decanter lives on the kitchen table, where we eat twice or three times on a working day. (In fine weather we eat in the garden, in warm but doubtful weather, the conservatory.) It is a primitive, one might say naive, piece of glassware. I bought it in a junk shop in the Bourbonnais in central France, and it bears in black stencil the words Rosé du Terroir. If the word 'terroir' evokes ideas of exquisite burgundies, of nuances of ripeness and perfume between *clos* and *clos*, the common reality is more earthy. 'Terroir' in the Bourbonnais simply means 'here'.

Why rosé? Because the workhouse Gamay grape, ripening with difficulty on this granite soil at three hundred metres and often picked too soon in desperation at the September rains, gives wine as pale in colour as it is thin in flavour. There is no false modesty about my decanter: more of an apology for low expectations. Into it I pour whatever red wine we are going to drink. Ironically, of course.

The plain old carafe has had some exciting moments. Does it remember, I wonder, the Opus One or the Grange Hermitage it briefly held? It may be jealous of the crystal I bring into play at dinner parties, but its real rival is a little pot-bellied glass jug, another junk shop find. This one I liked so much that I had it copied by a glassmaker in Suffolk to sell in my shop in London. In my mercantile days I used to offer the world half a dozen models, ranging from a rather beautiful 'claret jug' with a silver handle and a silver lid, to the most classic early 19th century design, a simple bulb with three glass rings round the neck as a grip, to my everyday favourites. Customers at the shop generally came in two varieties: those who insisted on classic decanters and those who saw the friendly portly little Suffolk jug as an ally against snobbery and pretension. A leveller, he is.

You would think that a good wine glass would be a simple thing to design but, strange to relate, not many people have tried. Pretty ones, elegant ones, impressive ones are common enough. I have several two-thousand-year-old examples, made apparently in Syria, a great centre for Roman glass-making. They are little beakers, weighing nothing; like picking up a light bulb. Venetian glass, from the 16th century onwards, is also very light and thin. Lead crystal, introduced in England in the 17th century, was the opposite: thick and heavy, with a lustre that made it glow in the candle-light. As far as the wine was concerned, they were all the same: miserable affairs, making appreciation as we understand it almost impossible. I was once asked to advise on the wine glasses for a hotel in a historic French château. They were to be made in the style of Louis XIV. My answer was that the guests would certainly not want their carefully chosen, beautifully presented and dreadfully expensive wine served in glasses that frustrated all attempts to taste it. Glasses of that period, and for another two hundred years, were too small, frequently too thin, and always the wrong shape for what we now consider the only proper way to drink.

It is only speculation, but I believe wine glasses and wine evolved together. Until the late 17th century there were no fine wines as we understand them. Burgundy, rarely, was the exception. Then claret and champagne were revolutionized. The concept of bottle-aged wine arrived, and with it the possibility of a bouquet worth sniffing and lingering over. All the glasses of earlier periods were mere conveyances of liquid to mouth. So little was the wine regarded that in smart houses there were no glasses on the table; servants brought one, on request, from the sideboard. The etiquette was to drink it down and hand the glass straight back. The essential difference is a simple one of size. You fill an antique drinking glass to, or near to, the brim. If you want to taste the wine before drinking it, taste it in the modern sense of looking at it, that is,

TOP & ABOVE
A short history of glassware. A Syrian carafe and glasses of 200AD on a bar in Pompeii; façon de Venise (left) and English lead crystal of the 1700s.

smelling it and spending time considering it, you need room for the vapour as well as the wine.

The earliest glasses I have seen with a bowl big enough to have been intended for this sort of drinking were made in the early 1800s. They were invariably trumpet-shaped, or at least slightly flaring towards the top. Who first designed a glass with a rim narrower than the bowl, to enclose and concentrate the bouquet? It is not easy to say.

This became a practical problem for me as recently as the 1960s. The Wine & Food Society was often asked to recommend good glasses. As its Secretary I looked for a simple generous glass with an incurving rim at a reasonable price. Then I began sketching egg-like shapes with stems. Then I consulted the ceramics department at the Royal College of Art. David Queensberry, a young professor, had the solution. We would design Everyman's wine glass together.

I still use it. It has won no beauty contests and never appeared at a prestigious wine tasting, but it works. It was made as cheaply as possible, by Ravenhead Glass, out of something akin to beer-mug glass. It gave me a taste for glass design which became serious twenty years later when David Queensberry and I went on to design wine glasses for a Swedish book club.

The problem, as I saw it, was that different wine regions had ideal glasses based on their own tastes or traditions, but that a group of them together on a dining table looked like odds and ends. They had no line, no informing design idea, in common. This was David's job. He drew, and we developed, glasses for champagne (easy: a tall incurving tube), red bordeaux (the model used in senior châteaux, more or less), white wines (similar but smaller), burgundy (with a bowl rather like a balloon for brandy, on a longer stem), sherry (a modified copita), and port or other dessert wines (closer to an egg cup for a duck's egg). Lined up together they glowed and twinkled like a platoon in uniform: different kit for different jobs but recognizably matching.

I had them made by the Reijmyre glassworks in Sweden, far south of Stockholm in the deep forests from which the glass blowers emerge for a break from hunting to puff and twirl their gleaming red hot metal into glasses of astonishing regularity. I fell in love with the place and the process, and went on to create decanters there too. All this led to a partnership with Hennessy's of Cognac in a company bearing my name to sell our glasses in susceptible markets worldwide. At one point we had a dozen boutiques in Japanese department stores, all modelled on my green and gold shop in St James's Street. That was just before the bubble of Japan's frantic new prosperity burst. Our boutiques were short-lived.

By this time wine had become, as it is today, a life-style icon (is that the phrase?) and accessories to its enjoyment were big business. The cork-screw was reinvented several times, and wine glassware ceaselessly. The hyperbole that rapidly attached to the rarer wines, their descriptions and their prices, gave glassmakers a new field of opportunity. Several saw it, one was a genius. Georg Riedel inherited his family's glassworks in Austria; he loved wine, and he pushed the new idea of a glass to maxim-ize its appreciation to unimagined lengths.

Riedel initiated a new science at what you could call the interface between wine and drinker: the contact between wine glass and mouth. A different radius of curve or a different contour of bowl, he claimed, changes the flow of liquid as it comes in contact with your lips, gums, teeth, tongue and palate. He not only claimed but also demonstrated, with most persuasive salesmanship, that you can alter the impact, and hence the flavours, by directing the wine to this part or that of the mouth.

The glasses I designed with David Queensberry for my shop are still the mainstay of our drinking. Top shelf: various glasses for port, Tokay and cordials. Second shelf: for white wine, on the right champagne flutes. Third shelf: for red wine, old champagne flutes. Bottom shelf: for water, and odds and ends.

Wines with high acidity, for example, such as German Rieslings, were best served by a glass this shape; wines with more alcohol and body by that one. What started as generic designs for bordeaux or burgundy were soon refined into the best shape for each grape variety: Cabernet needs

this, Sangiovese that. Burgundy, being the wine with the biggest nose, needs the most capacious glass in which its notes of cherry, plum, mint, beetroot, fur, game, woodland floor, truffle and the rest can mingle and express themselves. And to sniff at the brink of a bowl nearly as thin as cellophane and nearly as big as your head is a memorable experience. The very sound such glasses make as they touch, a musical booming clang, becomes part of the luxurious ritual of totem-tasting. Owning such glasses is a status symbol; owning a cupboard large enough to store them, and the ten different models you need for all your other wines, argues serious real estate.

Michael Broadbent (left), the glassmaker Georg Riedel and his son Maximilian find something to admire.

Are such glasses necessary? The wine trade seems to think so. Georg Riedel's company established a near-monopoly of the world's most high-profile wine-tastings, lending large numbers in exchange for a credit in the programme. Was I imagining it, or did I once see 'Thanks to Riedel for making wine possible'?

Back in the world's working tasting-rooms the trend is to standardize rather than particularize. The Office International de la Vigne et du Vin is the world's data-gathering body; wine's NGO. It agreed the design of a single tasting glass to put all tasters on the same footing, an odd-looking chimney of a thing which funnels all the vapours to your nose – but removes all the fun in doing so. There is still work for designers to do.

II   Bubbly

The Social Drug

CHAMPAGNE is France's greatest palpable contribution to human happiness. Discuss. Gaiety rather than happiness, perhaps, but otherwise no argument. This highly artificial, slightly perverse mixture of wine and gas is the social drug par excellence, the ice-breaker, the mood-maker, the catalyst and the symbol of celebration worldwide.

Or perhaps not worldwide. In 1999, I was asked to launch the new agency for Moët & Chandon in Shanghai. My first visit there had been in 1989, when the godowns were at bottom, the Bund was desolate, the famous Peace Hotel hanging on by its fingernails. Six years later it was a new world: we were lunching on the 88th floor of Asia's tallest hotel, built on what I had last seen as a muddy field. The lifestyle press of Shanghai were assembled for lunch at a vast round table, sipping Brut Imperial and listening politely to my brief account of the champagne story. Dom Pérignon got his mention, and I dwelt rather longer on Napoleon's much-reported friendship with M Moët. The Chinese like powerful men. Next to me sat the editor of Chinese *Vogue* (already), a tiny person in an eye-popping fawn suede suit that made her incredible fawn skin only more sumptuous to behold. "Any questions?" I asked. "Please,"

Having fun in Hong Kong. 'Wine education' is the pretext, provides the raw material and brings the results.

said her tiny voice, like the sound of a skein of silk, "why does this drink have bubbles?"

What would you have said? Because we like it that way? Because alcoholic fermentation produces carbon dioxide which readily dissolves in liquid and accidentally, three centuries ago, did so with memorable effect? I chose a version of the first and was crushed. "Chinese people don't like bubbles." Rather than go on to comparisons with Coca-Cola (not, I gather, a big hit in China) I changed the subject to models and photographers, the charming effect of pétillance against the light and, to be on the safe side, her husband.

I should have spun a fairy-tale about the genius of France, the passionate hedonism of Frenchmen that leads them to cook like angels and dress their women in the world's sexiest clothes. (Was her suit French?) What she wanted was the bottom line. Was Moët & Chandon going to advertise in *Vogue*?

It is difficult to explain, now that we take it for granted, why the wine-producers of one small part of France set about elaborating their product in a different, difficult, and originally even dangerous, way. It was different because the wine had to be bottled before it had finished fermenting; difficult because no relevant technology existed, not even reliable glass for the bottles; and dangerous because no-one knew how much gas would be produced, with what resulting pressure, inside the bottle. The odds were on an explosion. Some years most of the bottles became bombs, some years not so many. But no-one went down into the cellar without an iron mask.

It was not as though champagne was a hard sell as a bubble-free table wine. The area was planted as a commercial rival to Burgundy: better situated for communications on a river flowing straight into Paris, and conveniently close to the rich cities of Flanders.

Souper de Gourmet

Une petite caille, des fruits, du champagne : Monsieur est servi !
(Dessin de R. Préjelan.)
From an old copy of LA VIE PARISIENNE c 1905

ABOVE & LEFT
There is a solemn methodology about a champagne cork, and a very clear motive, to judge by La Vie Parisienne.

The grape vines came from Burgundy: Pinots Noir and Meunier for red and (in a minority) Chardonnay for white, with Pinot Gris and local varieties that are now only memories. The aim was red wine for the upper crust of Paris. It rarely came out very red: Pinot Noir is not a highly coloured grape, and this far north even less so. But it could be delicious as a lightly pressed near-white. 'Gris' is the official name for wine between white and rosé, just stained by red skins; 'Oeil de Perdrix' or 'partridge eye' the fanciful one.

In any case the *gratin* bought it. Several stylish Parisians had properties up on the Marne, the Champagne river. They tipped the sommeliers, and a barrel of Ay or a barrel of Bouzy became the new thing to have in your cellar. The next phase is the controversial one: how did this fashionable, and no doubt delicious, wine evolve into bubbly?

It happened during the time that Dom Pérignon was manager at the Benedictine Abbey of Hautvillers. Much of the abbey is still there: grey cloisters among the vines above the river, with a vivid little museum of life and wine-making in Pérignon's era. He was a famous taster, no doubt of that, and blended and sold wine far better than the neighbours', to the great profit of the abbey. Blending was his secret: he could make better wine assembling the best batches from around the district than from any single vineyard. He was not, on the other hand, keen on the bubbles that arise spontaneously in spring from the cold climate of Champagne. He waited until they had finished popping before he bottled; the bottles, in any case, would have popped their corks otherwise.

Dom Pérignon (or his waxwork image) still sits in his study in Hautvillers Abbey overlooking the River Marne. He was unforthcoming when I interviewed him for a television programme.

Meanwhile, across the Channel, champagne was as much the thing to drink as it was in Paris. A blue-blooded exile, the Marquis de St Evremond, seems to have been a demon salesman, precursor of many a shiny-cheeked, striped-suited habitué of race-meetings and night-clubs. St Evremond's sense of humour had been his undoing in Paris; he chose London over prison, much to London's delight. The English practice, for those who could afford it, was to buy any wine – champagne, burgundy, claret – in barrels and have it bottled straight away, adding an unappetizing array of supposed correctives in the process (sugar being the least surprising). Sugar only encouraged any latent final fermentation.

At this point a document appeared which is supposed to prove that its author, Dr Christopher Merrett, invented sparkling champagne. It reads, in part, "Our Wine-Coopers of later times use vast quantities of Sugar and Molasses to all sorts of Wines, to make them drink brisk and sparkling ...." Dr Merrett compiled *The Mysterie of Vintners* as a paper to be read to, or at least perused by, the newly founded Royal Society as a guide to the treatment of wines in bulk – something close, one imagines, to the learned philosophers' hearts. Perhaps more conclusive evidence of bubbles in the wine of the time comes from the stage: lines such as "See how it puns and quibbles in the glass," (*Love and a Bottle*, George Farquhar, 1698) seem pretty unambiguous.

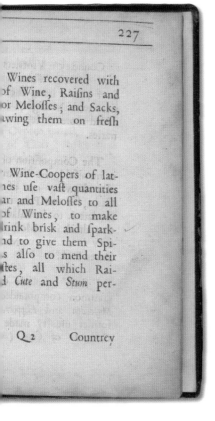

Why didn't the English bottles explode? Because the glass-furnaces of England had switched from wood to coal, burnt hotter and made stronger, darker glass. You had to tie the cork down with string (a special rim was moulded on the bottle to take it). But the result, months or even weeks later when the string was cut and the wine poured, was the first appearance of sparkling champagne.

LEFT
The text that is taken to show that the English Dr Merrett invented sparkling wine.
This is the 1669 edition of The Mysterie of Vintners, *the paper he delivered to the Royal Society in London on November 26th 1662.*

If sparkling champagne merely looked different, it would not be such a big deal. The first experiments, though, showed something far more interesting: it went to your head. Other wines could make you happy, open-hearted, bloody-minded or sick. But champagne made you giggle.

I would love to have been the person who brought the news to Paris, as opposed to Shanghai. Paris would know exactly what to do with giggly wine. But it took a long time for the penny to drop – long enough for the champagne glassworks to adopt the English methods. In the 1690s the law still prevented the movement of champagne in anything but barrels – when it could only have been still. You can't keep bubbles in barrels. Boom-time on the Marne arrived with the 18th century. By this time the fashionable *petits soupers* fuelled with bubbly were developing into luxurious encounters. In Paris the Palais Royal has never entirely lost the reputation it won in those days when, according to the Duc de Richelieu, "the orgies never started until everyone was in that state of joy that champagne brings."

India, when I went on a good-news mission there, again for Moët & Chandon, seemed to be in this kind of receptive mood. The scene was Bombay: a ballroom filled at both ends with jungle, palm fronds and denser leafage, faintly blue-lit from below. In the centre, two long parallel tables were covered with red cloth and gold plates and candles which shone in the darkest, deepest eyes in the world. It was Bollywood in party gear; gossamer saris and heavy gold, the men in dark Nehru coats, the food high-spiced, the chatter intense. Nobody asked why the drink had bubbles. And anything without bubbles, it seemed to me, would have seemed rather sad in this company. There were other parties, too; more confused and intimate affairs. Champagne could scarcely land on more fertile ground.

Not that India was innocent of its own bubbles. One of the least expected, but not least successful, of the many places where champagne technology is now applied to the local wine is in the hills not far from Bombay. An enterprising businessman started, in the 1970s, to produce a light bubbly with all the characteristics of champagne except the flavour. Omar Khayyam is now a staple of good Indian restaurants. And if India can do it, so most certainly can all the more wine-centric countries of the world.

If the giggles are the main selling-point, then, why has Champagne, the cold corner of northern France where conditions are far from ideal for grape-vines, not been superseded by areas with lower costs and higher temperatures?

We come back to the wine. The burgundy-substitute that irrigated the court of Louis XIV (until his physician, as some say, pocketed a big Burgundian bribe and prescribed nothing but Beaune) was no ordinary wine. Even without bubbles it is (and clearly was) something special. Racy, perfumed, delicate, are appropriate adjectives. With bubbles the flavour is (or can be) among the greatest pleasures of the wine-drinking world. But it is not a flavour that can be reproduced elsewhere with much accuracy or nearly so much distinction. Some recent efforts from England are the closest in flavour that I have met – not unreasonably, since the chalk soil of the Sussex Downs is identical to that of Champagne, and the climate only a little more maritime.

Champagne Country

Champagne with a capital C, the province with Reims as its ancient capital, has little of the picturesque about it. In places it rivals the Beauce, the plain southwest of Chartres, as France's dullest landscape. It is land that eats fertilizer but, for big-tractor farmers, renders enormous crops. Vineyards and their relatively busy villages come as a relief after the bare plain. Vegetable matter to nourish the hungry soil used to come from the sole forest on the grandly named Montagne de Reims. For years, until the 1980s, the wine-growers of Champagne were constrained to feed their land with what is known as *gadoux*, the ground-up refuse of Paris. It is better not to think about some of the things that were dumped around the Chardonnay and Pinot.

Photographers manage to make drama, or at least intriguing patterns, out of the giant geometry of vine-rows along the sinuous Marne. Its slopes are gentle, but the seasons bring their moods, autumn especially, when the vines are russet and yellow. In winter the wires sing in the icy wind or gleam with frost, and a haze of smoke hangs in the air as the pruners work their cold way over the fields.

What tourists come to Champagne to see is the urban landscape, and the one underground. The Romans quarried its chalk and left caverns and galleries on a scale that their rediscoverers in the Middle Ages could not believe. What premonition did they have of the industry that would fill them two thousand years later with millions of bottles of wine? Conditions far down in the chalk are ideal: the temperature (10°C) and humidity never change and the space is awe-inspiring. The biggest of the *crayères* open to visitors are those of Pommery & Greno, at the top of the

I photographed my new wife in the vineyards of Champagne (the Forêt de Reims in the background) in the autumn of 1965 when I was writing my first book, Wine.

modest hill overlooking Reims from the southeast. The widow Pommery (widows are oddly prominent in the history of Champagne) turned them into an underground factory in the 19th century. A monumental staircase leads down the thirty metres through the rock to the base of a chalk pit, a vast hollow cone round which you can just make out the traces of the spiral steps used by the labouring slaves. It looks as though a cork would

The widow Pommery's underground factory in Reims used Roman chalk quarries. The caverns are named after the markets for her wine.

be enough to stop the original entrance hole far above. Mme Pommery chose to dig new tunnels at this level, using the spoil to fill the bottoms of pits sixty metres deep. What a spectacle to miss. No-one ever saw the great dark space; no candles would have made any impression.

She made broad drives holding bottles by the ten thousand, and narrow linking tunnels, each labelled with the name of a city where Pommery is drunk: Buenos Aires, Freetown, Kyoto, Manchester …. Huge rusting cogs and pulleys high on the walls, dim in the gloom, are all that is left of a system for moving bottles in baskets which in the 19th century made these cellars the most mechanized in Champagne. From around the corner a long high-pitched rattle, like the sound of a colossal milk-delivery, comes from the new mechanization, the gyropalettes that have revolutionized the production of champagne. They were pioneered here, too. The laborious task (some say art) of riddling, measured in man-hours per bottle, is robotized to go on day and night under precise control with no hands involved. Sentimentalists like me try not to hear the noise, or visit instead the *crayères* across the road which were the cellars of the abbey of St Nicaise until the Revolution scattered its monks and used the great gothic pile as a quarry. St Nicaise is now the house of Taittinger, a warren of chalk-pits more Henry Moore than Industrial Revolution in their strange random forms.

Reims and Epernay are very different places to visit: the capital a grey war-scarred city, Epernay a country town with something of a New-market air. The champagne houses of both sport the sort of preposterous architecture that followed fashion in the Belle Epoque, but Reims adds the gravitas of ancient sanctity in its two grey basilicas, the cathedral and the church of St Rémi. They were prime targets, both of them, for German artillery in the First World War, despite the fact that half the most prominent champagne houses were created by German families. Brewers were particularly drawn to Champagne. Controlling fermentation and handling large numbers of bottles must have been familiar ground.

Troyes is the town that the destruction did not reach, the one to visit to recapture something of medieval Champagne. Its importance then seems improbable now. Reims was the sanctuary, a city of priestly power; Troyes was mammon, the site of Europe's biggest annual trade fair. Champagne has profited as well as suffered from being one of Europe's principal cross-roads. My imagination can never people the rolling plain outside Troyes (there are places where nothing, not even a lonely tree, breaks the horizon) with the cast from Brueghel and beyond that came from Italy and Scandinavia and England and Spain to set up tents here and drive bargains. The majority of long-distance travellers to Champagne today have a restaurant in their sights.

The Rewards of Maturity

How to define the champagne flavour? I start with apple pie. The tart/ sweet flavour of apples is inherent in young champagne. In a good one it is filled out with cherry/plummy flavours of ripe Pinot Noir. In more slap-dash bottlings it can be painfully alone. But a Golden Delicious and a Cox's Orange Pippin are both apples. They are more or less ripe, from a good or less good season, well or badly stored, before ever the cook starts slicing and melting in butter and adding sugar. Let alone making the pastry, short or flaky, done to a creamy paleness or singed caramel brown.

The raw wine is the apples; the pie-making part the second fermentation, when yeast adds baker's shop notes. Mature champagne can evoke the magic moment of walking into a patisserie. Who can say whether it is the tarte aux pommes, the tarte aux mirabelles or abricots, the coffee cake or the absurd Paris-Brest, the wheel of chou paste overflowing with cream and praline, that makes your nostrils flair?

The better the champagne, and the more mature, the more the patisserie. As in all wines, balance is the thing: it should keep you guessing, sniffing again and taking another sip to make sure you are not missing anything. A good vintage champagne runs along these lines for fifteen years at least before entering a new phase. The final reward of great old champagne is not just what the French dismissively call the *goût anglais*, the rich hint of Madeira, but in some cases a delicious hint of creamed mushrooms. You become aware of some delicate *champignon* (to avoid the word 'fungus') making its presence known. 'Wet straw' is another smell often reported with approval.

That a wine celebrated above all for its sprightliness should need aging surprises many people. Not necessarily the ordinary, serviceable but thin wines you meet in everyday blends, but the fine reserve wines that go into vintage-dated bottles. Champagne, indeed, is the last vintage wine of all to be released. You bought 1996 clarets and burgundies in 1998 (or even 1997), but the best 1996 vintage champagnes were not on the market until 2003, seven years after the vintage, and will be gathering flavour, moving from piercing sharp fruit to broader, biscuity tastes, for another ten years or so. The house of Krug did not release its exceptional 1990, one of the grandest champagnes I have ever tasted, until it was 14 years old. A great vintage like this will run, at least in my house, for thirty years or so. It is the acidity, the intense heart of the flavour of any fruit, that preserves it; and the more intense, from vines bearing a limited number of grapes, the longer its lifespan and the more satisfying the finale.

Keeping the finished wine in the cellars on its accumulated yeast cells preserves the wine even longer. It also deepens the cake-shop flavours. 'Yeast autolysis' is the term for the reaction over time between yeast cells and wine. It is routine for champagne houses to keep a reserve of top vintage wines undisgorged for special occasions and honoured guests, giving them their final polish only on the morning of the great day. 'Good Lord,' is the routine reaction, 'it tastes much younger than that.' And Bollinger has made *Récemment Dégorgé* (recently disgorged) its party piece.

Hanging on to champagne longer than my friends do has given me a reputation in some quarters as a necrophiliac. The French, with exceptions, turn away from these warm and golden wines, whose bubbles have diminished to a gentle prickle, and condemn them as 'maderized' – meaning that they taste of Madeira, a wine intentionally exposed to the oxygen in the air until it turns as brown as caramel. But champagne is not exposed to oxygen. The only gas in a bottle of champagne is carbon dioxide, which protects it from the air in a way no other wine is protected. It is the secret not only of its liveliness but also of its longevity.

How long does it live? I should have an answer to the question: I have been buying, keeping and drinking it for long enough. My practice, having the luxury of space at my disposal, is to buy all champagne well before I think I shall need it. There are two upper racks on the far right of the cellar were I range my collection. It is organized by age, then by name. You get to know the colours of the nozzles of favourite *marques*. They wink at you cheerfully as you pass by. Unopened boxes in waiting have a benign presence, too. For the non-vintage wines, which are our regular rations, this means at least a year ahead, and preferably two. I find they all benefit from the wait, shedding any greenness and putting on an appreciable roundness and weight in the mouth. When we needed a substantial amount for our daughter Kitty's wedding, I asked the English shippers of Pol Roger if they could find any stocks that had been stored for a known period to furnish the feast. They found enough that had spent three years in a bonded warehouse. On wedding day I was not the only one who noticed how smoothly it swallowed. On the other hand I would not have bought old stock willy-nilly. Provenance is vital.

I buy far less vintage champagne but from more makers. When I am as enthusiastic about a vintage as I was, for example, about 1990 and 1996, I try to assemble a pretty good set, say six or twelve bottles of each of a dozen wines, to watch their progress over the years. And when the opportunity offers I buy old, even antique, champagne.

The most memorable antique I ever had was the Perrier-Jouët 1911 – a whole dozen bottles of it, so it was no single lucky survivor. Somebody was foolish enough to sell the case at Christie's in its prime, at a mere 75 years old, and I was lucky enough to buy it at the price of the current non-vintage. My old patron, André Simon, had once described 1911 gnomically as "the last of the great vintages". Did that mean the best before the Great War, when the Champagne vineyards became the battle-field of the Marne?

It was a famously hot year, and famous also for the riots that trauma-tised the region. In an early attempt to set legal limits on where champagne grapes could come from, an anticipation of the appellations contrôlées of the 1930s, the authorities admitted growers in the département of the Aube, many kilometres south of the Marne, Reims, Epernay and the heart of Champagne.

Gastronomically it is perfectly justified: the Aube, though half-way to Chablis, grows excellent Pinot Noir. Geographically and politically, though, it looked outrageous – especially to the citizens of such villages as Ay, who set fire to the warehouses of shippers they did not trust. Wine riots have been a common feature of life in the Midi, almost the second sport after Rugby, but they were new in the north and became so violent that forty thousand troops were called in. The law was repealed, the rioters (less three dead) went home – and the vintage was glorious.

We opened the first bottle of the case in July 1993, under an apple tree in the garden before a dinner of the Bordeaux Club – six friends who meet three times a year. My note, written next day, goes "Still straw pale with masses of tiniest bubbles, even faint froth on pouring. An astound-ing bottle – supremely lively and champagney, with depths of very best Madeira. Sublime." I wish I could have found words to do it justice.

Its condition was even more astonishing given the state of the cork: as hard as a bullet. It came out with the ease of a stopper. What had held the pressure in? When you have a first bottle like that, with 11 to go, the prospects are bright. Only two of the 12 let me down. Why was a whole case, in its original thick cardboard and tissue paper, still around? It turns out that house of Perrier-Jouët was founded in 1861; 1911 was its 50th anniversary. For its centenary in 1961 the firm had relaunched what was left of their greatest vintage ever.

I have had other brands of 1911: Moët was excellent and so was Clicquot. I had the sweet Clicquot as well as the Brut: the Brut had aged better. And that is not the oldest champagne to reach superlative status in my notebook. That place goes to a Sillery 1864, also sold at Christie's – and Sillery, once the most famous village in the region, the fief of one aristocratic producer, was not even a high-pressure sparkling wine, seemingly not even made of the classic grapes. It was still, or just 'creaming', and pressed largely from 'Fromenteau', or Pinot Gris.

A 1921 Pol Roger was a famous wine I have had in the cellar, and 1928 Krug. Total recall, alas, is not possible, but such wines leave deep impressions. Other survivors do for reasons not connected directly with taste and smell. I once told the late president of Bollinger, Christian Bizot, that I had had a lovely bottle of Bollinger 1945. "You were lucky," he said. "I remember when I was a boy and they were bottling the '45. They had to borrow a tractor with a belt-drive to work the bottling machine. It was bottled whenever the tractor wasn't ploughing." The image of Champagne today is hang-the-expense. It was not always so.

And the Bubbles?

Carbon dioxide is the gas we breathe out and plants breathe in. It causes global warming and suffocates unlucky cellar-workers. It is the principal by-product of alcoholic fermentation. The fact that it is highly soluble in wine (or water: just look at Perrier) was of no account until the invention of bottles. The only evidence of its peculiar physiological effect was when harvest-hands helped themselves to the still-sweet juice in a vat that was half-way through fermenting, a drink so delicious that in Burgundy they call it *paradis*. It is, of course, totally unstable; a passing phase. Perhaps the widely held belief that an excess of it gives you the colly-wobbles was a rumour started by proprietors to save their stock from depredations and keep their workers sober. I have never drunk enough of it to find out.

Why it takes effect on the drinker's morale so instantaneously was once explained to me by a physician. Apparently carbon dioxide is not welcome in your bloodstream. When it is present, as it is when you take exercise, your heart circulates your blood more quickly to diffuse it through your veins to the skin, where it evaporates. A mouthful of champagne takes a considerable quantity of CO_2 straight into your stomach. The porous stomach wall instantly absorbs it into your bloodstream, taking the alcohol with it. Your heart then quickly circulates it, and your brain feels the effect. Your lips part in a smile.

So much gas is dissolved that persuading it all out is difficult. Just how persistent it is was brought home to me by a friend who habitually decants his champagne. Conservative is a moderate word for this country-dweller, a man who has never had to buy his own furniture, and who serves old wine after the manner of his ancestors. I once saw a champagne-decanter in a museum as an example of eccentric 18th century glassware. This friend just uses a glass jug, pouring each bottle of champagne gently down the inclined lip to lie golden and tranquil beneath a thin froth. Is the champagne flattened? Not at all. It seems to have more flavour than ever. It looks prodigiously generous. And it is much quicker for the host to distribute and the guests to consume: no waiting for the froth in each glass to die down.

The most unbuttoned champagne I ever drank, and the bottle that gave me a whole new way of seeing it, was brought out to us in the shade of a fig tree on a hot day in Tuscany, the prelude to an epic lunch. It was in a crystal bowl full of splintered ice, lying naked, decanted into a crystal flask where it lay, a colour between silver and gold, a few bubbles creaming on top, with the perspiration of the flask adding mist and sparkle at the same time. I can taste the first sip of that wine now: so fresh and pure and clean as it touched my tongue that its silver cool spread round my whole body. (I should, of course, have drunk a glass of water.)

———————

Champagne is above all portable: it survives knock-about journeys in a way you would not ask of a red or white wine of equal value. You expect to be able to open it anywhere at any time. You don't need a corkscrew. At moments of triumph and moments of despair it is always there, on tap.

There is sometimes discussion about champagne on planes up at ten thousand metres. Can it be unaffected by the lower cabin pressure – half that at ground level? Learned voices say it changes character. My evidence says that it can taste its most delicious with the prospect of a long flight ahead. But then while I was a British Airways consultant I was not cooped up at the back of the plane. First Class passengers, of course, had to be given labels they recognized as very expensive, and travellers on Concorde used to make specific demands ('I'm terribly sorry, sir, but I'll make sure it's on board this evening'). Conversely, producers of very expensive champagne want to be seen by First Class passengers. British Airways' orders for Krug and Dom Pérignon were alarming, and the hospitality of aspiring *marques* (not to me, I hasten to say) correspond-ingly warm. Passengers behave in peculiar ways in the air, and champagne is no discouragement. The Steward's Tale, I often think, would make a rip-roaring addendum to *The Canterbury Tales*.

The harmless theatre of champagne is part of the fun, too. In Epernay they like to pretend that the traditional, and the fastest, way into a bottle is by cutting off its top with a sabre. I was taught the trick for my tele-vision series on the history of wine, practised assiduously, and brought it off rather well, I thought, on film. The trick is to hold the bottle (a magnum is best) well out in front of you and run the blade of the sword smartly and firmly up the shoulder. You hit the collar where the wire cage holds the cork in and pop, the bottle breaks cleanly, the cork flying off into the scenery.

I was required to repeat the performance, though, at a launch of the video in a theatre in Chicago. The props they provided were a bottle of New York sparkling wine and a choice of a carving knife or a US Navy cutlass. I chose the cutlass and marched on stage. I swung my weapon hard and the world disappeared in a mountain of foam. The bottle had exploded in my hand. Luckily, no-one was hurt.

Champagne is 'elaborated': a word that means more than just 'worked on'. The implication is complicated – and indeed the 'méthode champen-oise', as it used to be called ('méthode classique' is the new term), in-volves a longer series of manoeuvres than you need to make any other wine.

No region is more adept at showmanship than Champagne. You are invited to go and see the whole performance – though the last time I took a tourist tour round the cellars I was amazed at the rubbish the guide was talking. (And at some of the visitors' questions: 'Is it all made of grapes?')

Pressing (gently) and fermenting (cool) are the first steps. You get raw wines of many different characters from different sites and the three grape varieties of the region: Pinot Noir, Pinot Meunier and Chardonnay. You select and blend according to taste. Some producers make most of their wines from their own vineyards, most buy either grapes or wine or both. Then you bottle, in the spring after the vintage, adding a calculated dose of sugar. The fermentation of this sugar produces the gas – but also, and this is where the elaborate manoeuvres come in, a lot of dead yeast cells that make the wine cloudy.

Champagne became an industry when the widow Clicquot (she gets the credit, anyway) developed a way of eliminating the yeast without decanting each bottle. I won't spoil the story: it is worth going to see how patient, philosophical, cold cellar-workers spend their lives labouring in caves giving us brilliantly clear champagne. In modern cellars you will see, too, how the whole laborious business of 'riddling' is now done by ingenious mechanical monsters.

What makes one champagne better than another, or distinctly different in flavour, are the multiple choices along the way. Which vineyards? Which grapes? How hard are they are squeezed? Are they are fermented in steel tanks or in barrels? There are an infinity of possibilities at a blending session where there might be a hundred wines as candidates for inclusion. Total confusion is the result when I am invited to try my hand. I like one wine, I like another; I put them together and hate the result. Add a third and it's worse. Add a fourth and it gets interesting. Would a fifth make things better or ruin it? I emerge at lunchtime with grovel-ling respect for the professional and a powerful thirst for the finished article.

Nor is the finished article the easiest wine to taste. Each spring in London the PR arm of the Comité Interprofessionnel du Vin de Champagne puts on a mass tasting of a hundred or so champagnes in the stately Banqueting House in Whitehall. A ceiling painted by Rubens is not a requirement for judging champagne; indeed nobody looks at it. The window through which King Charles I walked to the scaffold is full of bottles waiting to be opened. The *bon viveurs* are there, planning lunches; the conscientious, scribbling notes. I start off with a will, taking little sips of wines I have not met before and queuing at the communal spittoon. After a dozen I am at sea. The problem, as James Halliday, Australia's most experienced wine judge, puts it, is that your mouth feels like the inside of a washing machine, full of churning foam. Some are clearly richer, some sharper, some aromatic, some dull or with funny flavours, but a cool appraisal of so many is beyond me.

A champagne press is the biggest model of all, taking four tons of grapes at a time. It applies extremely slow and gentle pressure.

On Your Marques

Favourites? Of course. Wines that stand out for their boldness, freshness, sweetness of savour. Ideally a balance of all these. I certainly have habitual favourites: champagnes I drink regularly, order by the case or in restaurants. I am pleased when I recognize them in the ruck at a blind tasting, but not surprised if I don't. The longest-established is Pol Roger, the first champagne house I ever visited, as a guest of the anglophile Odette Pol Roger. Her salon, in the Avenue de Champagne in Epernay, made a profound impression on me in my early twenties as the epitome of French country taste. I was to learn later that such deep armchairs were

I must have fancied myself as a still-life photographer when I took this picture in Madame Pol Roger's salon. Another relic of a visit to Champagne forty years ago.

considered entirely English in France, but her bold chintzes and flowers in phalanxes became my model of decoration, just as Pol Roger's White Foil (they have since changed the name of their non-vintage) summed up my perfect refreshment. Years later I found my taste was shared by one of Bordeaux's most blue-blooded proprietors. I called one afternoon in the panting dog-days of August to find him in his dark green salon sipping from a tall tumbler. He offered me the same drink: White Foil and water. He had cracked one of life's most serious problems: champagne alone cannot quench a thirst.

Forty years on, Pol Roger is still the family champagne of weddings and feasts. But the champagne rack in the cellar is eclectic, with a steady turnover of names I learn as I go along; either independent growers, smaller *marques* or *cuvées*. Of the regulars, Bollinger, Clicquot and Roederer represent what I think of as the heavy brigade: champagnes with a robust feel of wine about them. Alfred Gratien is in the same category: for long storage. I buy Charles Heidsieck's 'mis en cave', an idea other houses will surely follow: the bottling date of each *cuvée* tells you its effective age and gives a clue to its character. Jacquesson has more recently started similar numbered *cuvées*: 728 was code for a wonderful 1998 blend. Deutz is another *marque* I order regularly, and Ruinart has a vital freshness I love. Recently Billecart-Salmon has become a favourite; I like Bruno Paillard's rather austere taste and the strong definition of Clos des Goisses, a single-vineyard wine from Philipponnat. Among the de luxe *cuvées* I buy Pol Roger's Sir Winston Churchill, Taittinger's Comtes de Champagne and Pommery's Cuvée Louise, Dom Pérignon as the silkiest and most spoiling, and Krug to share with other enthusiasts.

No champagne is a thirst-quencher, but with Krug the idea is wholly absurd: each sip is so packed with flavour that a full-mouth swallow would leave you gasping. Krug's Grande Cuvée has consistency on its side; Krug's vintages are so various that each is like the same melody in a different key, or on a different instrument. Rémi Krug once set me to taste each vintage back to 1964. (He likes to talk about his wine. The story goes that after an intense session he once said "That's enough about

Krug. Let's talk about you. What do you think of Krug?") My notes read like the fanciful paradoxes of a medieval philosopher. "Sour chocolate and green straw." "Crystallized fruit." "Soya." "Seaweed." "Fulfils by extremes." "Like Don Giovanni" (Rémi's contribution). "Marmite and caramel." "Baked apples." "Mille-feuilles." By the 1982 the "greengages" were being joined by "nuts" and "coffee". By 1981 it was "almonds and sous-bois." The glass of 1976 glowed like a golden tulip and smelt like burnt toffee, creamy mushrooms and ginger; "A cello chord," I wrote. The 1973 was mint and lemons, beeswax and unspecified flowers; the 1964 only gently bubbling, toffee and cream; "Perfect now for Gruyère," said my host.

Years ago, when we were house-hunting, we went to look at an old rectory near Bath. The house was much too big for us, but I had heard it had a cellar. What a cellar. It was built in fine creamy masonry like the house itself. It was approached down theatrically broad stone steps. And it was lined with deep rectangular stone bins for wine. Over each bin was a slate label inscribed in chalk. Running round the room it read Bollinger, Moët, Pommery, Roederer, Mumm, Perrier-Jouët, Heidsieck .... It was not difficult to picture the parson at his desk upstairs, scratching away at his sermon. Sunday morning. The text for today is from Timothy. Austerity and self-sacrifice. Pommery perhaps, before lunch; and a bottle of the Bollinger '09 with the lamb. Yes, austere is the word for it – but it finishes well.

Polishing the image of a *marque* is an art the French have perfected. Other nations may have their Tiffanys and Rolls-Royces, their Armanis and Porsches and Patek Philippes. Only the French can take a standard product, a bottle of wine or perfume, and rub it until a genie appears. Louis Vuitton was just a trunk-maker, Hermès a saddler. Pétrus is just a bottle of red wine; Krug or Dom Pérignon a bottle of bubbly – until it becomes a code for sophisticated hang-the-cost living. It is not done quickly, but in the hands of a French team – discreet, quiet-spoken, ruthless; their names hinting at *l'Ancien Régime*, their offices in the 16ème – the image of the *marque* takes shape.

The price is crucial. For these Prestige Cuvées it must be 'aspirational' – out of reach, in other words, to all but the rich. And even they, chic and sleek as they are, have to purr very prettily to be allowed their share. For other brands the question is definition: how to stand out from a hundred of similar quality. Those who can afford it pick a niche for themselves in the market and defend it like an animal its territory. Moët & Chandon like to be seen as the champagne of the fashion world, Veuve Clicquot as the champagne of the social season, Pol Roger as everything that is most English, Mercier (is it Mercier now?) as the fizz that Formula One drivers shower each other with. The *super-cuvées* have their social flavour too: Krug claims the seriously rich, Taittinger Comtes de Champagne a certain stratum of chic, Roederer Cristal everything suggested by the word 'bling'.

I travelled once with a famous Japanese photographer whose assignment was to convey the essence of a luxury champagne in his trade-mark black-and-white pictures. His cameras, large and small, were never put away. A hand touching the bottle, the hem of a skirt, the back of a man's neck, the wire cage holding the cork, a reflection in a car window, a vapour trail, the smoke from the mouth of a bottle just opened .... He shot whatever he noticed, and his photographs were printed with all the solemnity that heavy eggshell paper can convey. Pretentious? Who am I to say?

Grande marque is a title self-bestowed by the dozen big houses that have made the running in Champagne throughout its history. They are most people's entry-point; their familiar names give the comfort of reassurance when you are spending more money than usual on a bottle of wine. This was the case, at least, until recently. The buying-power of supermarkets challenges all brands: *grandes marques* are not excepted. As the region and the industry inexorably fall under the control of fewer and bigger companies (two out of every five bottles exported now come from firms belonging to Louis Vuitton Moët Hennessy) the merry-go-round of historic names seems less and less important. If the banality of a High Street name on your bottle makes no difference to your enjoyment, there is money to be saved. You can now pay less for champagne as good as the standard wines of most of the famous names, and better than some. It almost certainly comes from one of the big growers' cooperatives of the region. To detect which one, from the coded fine print on the label, is a popular game among bargain-hunters.

Champagne in any case has progressively become cheaper in relation to the price of other luxury wines. In the 1940s, for example, the best vintage champagne in one of the best restaurants of the day cost twice the price of the best bordeaux. I have a wine list here, memorable for recording the conditions of London in the Blitz of 1940. The restaurant was Pruniers in St James's, the sister-house to the smartest place to eat fish in Paris and just downstairs from where I am writing. Wartime regulations restricted the price of restaurant meals and rationed the number of courses you could order. What was billed as the Air Raid Lunch was 8/6 and the Black Out Dinner 10/6, the equivalent, let's say, of £11 and £14 today. Black Out Dinner consisted of four courses, including oysters.

The best – or at least oldest and most expensive – bordeaux on the wine list was Château Haut-Brion 1904 at 28 shillings (around £37 today), the best champagne Bollinger 1928 at 37/6 (around £50). Comparable wines today would be listed at perhaps £1,000 for the bordeaux, £200 for the champagne. "Owing to the recent bombardment," reads a note at the foot of the list, "it is preferable for the red wines to be decanted." Mme Prunier showed a true Londoner's *sang froid*, but I'm not sure that decanting would really help an old claret that had just had a near-miss by a bomb.

––––––––––––

It is not the least astute of Champagne's marketing manoeuvres to operate a system of 'declared' vintages not very different from that of port. The term 'declared' is never used, but there is the same sort of unanimity-with-variance about which years are good enough to produce a 'vintage' wine. In the last decade of the 20th century 1990, '92, '93, '95, '96, '97 and '98 were all bottled as vintages by at least a few *marques*. In the seventies it was 1970, '71, '73, '75, '76, '79. In the 1960s: '61, '62, '64, '66, '69. The frequency is increasing. You can credit either growing demand or global warming. Whatever the cause, the intention is to make a vintage year something of an event, and its wine almost a brand within a brand. The producer keeps the initiative. His non-vintage wines level the peaks and troughs. How many of the problems of Bordeaux would be solved if its châteaux could adopt a similar system?

At the other extreme from the *grandes marques* are the purely fictitious names picked from a salesman's catalogue of labels in the certain hope that few people will know the difference. This is where the restaurant proposal of a single glass is an ally. Admittedly you often pay almost the retail price of half a bottle. It is a reasonable pact, though. Ordering a glass of champagne as you sit down buys you time to consider your options on the menu and the wine list. It establishes you as a customer with at least a little style. It mellows you for what is to come – and it tells you whether the management cares about champagne. If they scrimp on it, you can draw your conclusions.

I avoid half-bottles, however tempting it may be to pick one from the wine list. In my experience they rarely taste either as fresh or as full-flavoured as bottles. Maturity of the wrong sort seems to set in early. I do buy a few, and keep them in a reassuring little stack beside the rack that holds senior champagne bottles waiting for their moment. We often open one on a quiet Sunday evening. Otherwise they are for emergencies and moments of crisis. But even in crises I notice that they lose the full champagne thrill sooner than they should. Until 2002 some houses decanted their halves from full bottles at disgorging, which would certainly account for a lack of zip. The practice is no longer allowed, but the zip still goes disappointingly soon.

Magnums are another matter. I wish we had more occasions to justify them. Logically any party that calls for two bottles is better served with a magnum. Morale soars when a magnum appears. Champagne keeps and matures almost twice as well in them (but of course the rare calamity of a bad cork is twice as vexatious).

A silly riddle went the rounds a few years ago: How do you tell a poor champagne-grower from a rich champagne-grower? The poor one polishes his own Mercedes. Champagne vineyards rarely come on the market. Families stick to them like glue: fifteen thousand families in all, most of them with other professions. How do you sell champagne grapes? is the next joke. You pick up the phone.

For a grower there are two possibilities: sell your grapes or make the wine yourself. The trend today is for ambitious growers to go it alone. If there is news from Champagne this is it. The wine and the region are mercifully free of the fashions that come and go elsewhere. Nobody is so foolish as to play with gimmicks. Champagne has already been perfected, and fiddling with the formula would be absurd.

What has changed is that the *grandes marques* are no longer alone at the top: individual growers have successfully challenged the established view that champagne was, is, and should be a wine blended from different grapes from different sites. The regulations are not helpful. The whole of Champagne has only one appellation contrôlée – the biggest by far for a fine wine in France. It has always suited the *grandes marques* to keep it that way. The only distinctions, in their view, should be between their brands. But why not, the argument goes, offer alternatives: wines that express a single vineyard, the appeal of burgundy added to the appeal of champagne? It started with the notion of the Blanc de Blanc: champagne made from Chardonnay only, leaving out the Pinots Noir and Meunier of the classic recipe. Lighter, purer, fresher, more refined … you can see the selling points stack up. Blancs de Blanc have not overtaken mainstream champagne, and never will. Chardonnay is too scarce: only 28 per cent of the vineyards. They reach high points of their own, and the comparison is another pleasure to add to the list. (Personally, I always miss the Pinot Noir.) Rosé is another. It used to be considered a naughty little sub-culture, frivolous, for the ladies. You made it by adding a soupçon of red wine to the white – something that would land you in jail in any other part of France. It is still not mainstream, but it is certainly pretty, and can be delicious, so why not?

The *grandes marques* themselves started the idea of single-vineyard champagnes. Krug, in the later 1970s, issued an exclusive bottling of a Blanc de Blanc from their walled Clos du Mesnil in one of the highest-ranking Chardonnay-growing villages. Bollinger, about the same time, launched their Vieilles Vignes Françaises from a singular plot of Pinot Noir vines at Ay that were never killed by phylloxera. The vines are still grown *en foule* in the chaotic fashion – a trunk here, a trunk there, with branches pinned down to root in between – that you saw everywhere in France before phylloxera made grafting necessary and wires appeared to make tidy rows the norm. Neither of these wines has the classic champagne character; certainly not the seamless balance of their conventional cousins. Are they less expensive? Silly question.

When I paid my respects to Bollinger's peculiar plot in 1979 I asked if I could take some cuttings. The continuity of these straggling vines is a powerful notion. In effect the same plant, renewing itself every year, has been producing champagne for centuries. With a cutting I could have part of the same plant at home.

It is enormous now. It grows over an iron pergola in the centre of our walled garden. In good years it produces twenty-five kilos of its small black grapes and, in very good ones, when autumn is late, gives me an October crop as ripe as it would be in Champagne. I have no press, there is not enough of it to tread, so I crush the grapes with, I confess, a potato-masher, leave them to collect colour from the skins for two days, then ferment the juice in a gallon jar. I make no great claims for my partridge

BELOW LEFT & BELOW
My Pinot Noir grows on a pergola in the walled garden at Saling. A fine late autumn can give us a healthy crop just ripe enough to make wine.

eye. You would shudder at its acidity. But the smell is the quintessence of Pinot Noir; the very soul of Champagne.

Champagne with Everything

Individual growers do, on the whole, charge less. They have lower running costs and no glossy PR machine. They have always been suppliers to the locals and some have mail-order customers all over France. The French still drink sixty per cent of all champagne, and they are less impressed by the *grandes marques* than we ignorant foreigners. The idea of the small supplier is deeply appealing to the French psyche. What is new is the appeal of the *petit fournisseur* to sommeliers in smart restaurants who want to put their individual stamp on the wine list. They need to propose wines of different styles for different dishes, something most champagne-drinkers never think of.

Already there are names to conjure with. Perhaps Salon was the first; the creation of an eccentric millionaire who simply wanted his own brand. Salon is all Chardonnay from the village of Le Mesnil. It is issued only in top vintages; a powerful but I have found rather jagged, clumsy wine. Of the new generation Jacques Selosse of Avize is leader. He throws overboard the long-nurtured concept of consistency in champagne to make each of his wines as 'expressive' as it can be. He ferments it in barrels of different ages from different coopers and forests, discourages the malolactic fermentation that would soften it, omits the final *dosage* of sugar that would bring it into a pre-conceived line. The result is almost shockingly intense flavour and sometimes scouring acidity. Every region has its extremists; their wine is meant to be a challenge, to stimulate, to provoke, to see what happens if …. Compared with them the luxury brands, the Roederers and Dom Pérignons with their consistent flavours, are up-market comfort-wines, operating in known territory. Everybody learns from people like Selosse – if only, just occasionally, what to avoid.

Originality can take many forms. The Aubry brothers of Jouy-lès-Reims, where most of the vines are Pinot Noir, have revived historic grape varieties that had fallen into disuse, taking cuttings from gnarled old stumps they found in neglected vineyards. They make a wine they call Campanae Veteris Vites which, to be unkind, helps to explain why three of the varieties are no longer mainstream. It is interesting to taste these flavours from the past, sharp and somehow evocatively wild, but modern champagne is something else. The Aubrys also make one of my favourite rosés, palest salmon in colour, at only half the standard champagne gas pressure, hence gently frothy. The bottle is polished satin-smooth, quite beautiful with its green label. They call it Sablé.

The more stylistically varied champagne becomes, the better its chances at table. A hundred years ago its regular place was a sorbet-like inter-mission mid-meal – an arrangement we would consider barbaric today. Then it took on different roles in different markets. Its most consistent drinkers, the French, relegated it at least in common use to the end of the meal, as the partner to dessert. Anglo-Saxon blood runs cold at the idea of dry champagne with creamy puddings – or anything sweet, for that matter.

The English have maintained, and steadily increase, their enthusiastic consumption before – indeed without – food. Champagne often invades the menu by default, as it were; the last glass of the aperitif bottle drunk with the first course. Choosing a brand, or a vintage, on the basis of affinity with a dish is relatively uncharted territory. Choosing a succes-

Visitors to Hong Kong used to have a chance of firing the noonday gun. The target was the O in a Sony advertising hoarding.

sion of different champagnes to accompany a whole menu is posi-tively avant-garde. I have detected fanaticism among chefs and sommel-iers when the QED is that champagne can complement any flavour. Expen-sive oriental delicacies? Why not? I suffered an entire menu of abalone in the cause in Hong Kong: abalone marinated, boiled, stuffed, in fritters, with fungi, with tamarind ... on it went. The different vintages of Dom Pérignon were a great relief.

In Osaka the trophy dish is fugu, the Russian Roulette fish. Connoisseurs of this dangerous delicacy gather like conspirators in a functional café under the railway where the thundering of trains overhead drowns their sighs of rapture. They eat nothing else: the whole meal is fugu. First course fugu sashimi, cut as fine as cellophane. A gristly chew; no flavour to speak of. Second course fried fugu. The best part of the fish makes a fair tempura. Pièce de résistance: fugu stew. All the other parts boiled up: fins, tail, eyebrows, the lot. All the parts but one, that is: the liver, a mere whiff of which will kill (or so I'm told) a Sumo wrestler. Experts report near-death experiences from the flesh adjacent. It starts to paralyse first your lips, then your face, as you eat. The wine for the occasion? Why, champagne. (I drank saké.)

In champagne country, however, it is a serious matter. Does the whole idea sound rather indigestible? I fear it would be with acidic young non-vintage wines, but those are not usually the ones in question when senior gastronomes get going. I shall arouse your envy, I fear, if I recount the experiments in which I have played a willing part. With Richard Geoffroy, for example, the blender of Dom Pérignon.

The Royal Champagne is a hotel out in the vineyards on the long south slope to the River Marne from the Montagne de Reims. In front the sun catches the river with a glint; in the distance you can make out the Côte des Blancs on the far bank. Behind is a strange forest; no-one knows why its beech trees are contorted into writhing serpentine forms, or how old this seeming curse may be.

The Royal Champagne that evening had laid on what seemed a fairly difficult menu. Scallops with their corals in a sauce of orange sea urchins was the opening move. Scallops are perfect champagne fodder, rich and caressing. Sea urchins (they sound better in French as *oursins*) have a strong tang of the foreshore about them; they taste like iodine cream. Geoffroy played his powerful young champagne, the new vintage (it was 1985) of Dom Pérignon with this, on the grounds that *oursin*-power needs a bold response.

Saumon à l'unilatéral came next; a neat name, I thought, for a simple salmon fillet in wine lees, cooked on the skin side only: a dish with a fat, even greasy, flavour. Out came Dom Pérignon Rosé of the same vintage. There is a presumption these days that Pinot Noir is the ideal match for salmon; there was enough Pinot Noir about the rosé, red fruit and a trace of tannin, to pursue that argument. The third course was ravioli of foie gras with a creamy dish of green Le Puy lentils. Geoffroy played the ripest and most opulent wine in his hand, Dom Pérignon 1976. It was sufficiently different from the rosé to shift the meal into top gear. Another glass tasted sweeter with powerful cheese, the local Maroilles, and another brighter and more refreshing with two remarkable desserts, a roast pear with acacia honey and liquorice cream, and a tart of fresh figs and almonds. Champagne with sweets was perfectly justified. Champagne with everything, in fact. But what champagne.

New World Bubbles

CHAMPAGNE is inherently a vulgar – at least in the sense of popular – taste. Everyone understands its attractions. It is less intimidating as a result than its equivalents in value and prestige. The owner of a bottle of Château Lafite can easily be self-conscious about it. He thinks long and hard about which of his friends should share it. Ostentation, flattery, many various motives might, he thinks, cross their minds; because it is expensive, yes, but also because it is seen as a sophisticated taste, almost inaccessible to those not in the know. And the vintage: is it a good one? One of the best? A bin-end? Of course a good host can give his great bottle a modest introduction, just enough explanation to make it seem appropriate, inevitable almost. Champagne produces no such qualms. To joke about the label is easy – whether it is Roederer Cristal (the automatic choice, apparently, of footballers) or the local supermarket brand. People who analyze and memorise the tastes of different champagnes like me are very much the exception.

For the same reason champagne is considered fair game by imitators, and its imitations are serious currency worldwide. Which of the New World countries was the first to do it I'm not sure. Australia and California were both in the running. What happened in California before Prohibition is now largely forgotten, but neither country was shy about using the name Champagne, or indeed Chablis or Burgundy, despite the protests of the French that Champagne is a place, not a synonym for fizzy wine. The difference was that Champagne's objections were heard because it had the money.

In California, Korbell was the first brand I encountered that appealed to me. I went to see their vineyards in the 1960s, out toward the coast in Sonoma. An extraordinary sight, I remember, because they ran through what had in the not-too-distant past been redwood forest. The butts of giant trees stood out among the vines, the size of small cottages, black (perhaps they had tried to burn them) among the sparkling fresh green of vine-rows coming into leaf. The cellars, like most in California in those days, had a log-cabin feel. The vats were smooth towers of warm brown redwood. A number of the wines, all I think sparkling, were rather sweet and had various off-putting strong flavours. But the white-labelled Natural had enough acidity and not too much sugar: Wild West Champagne was a fair name for it. There was another German-founded house with the confusingly similar name of Kornell that used Riesling to make what I always thought were unrefreshing wines.

The German heritage was not as strong as the Italian among those pioneer wineries, but one German name had been exalted to the level of myth, despite having died as a fact with Prohibition. Robert Louis Stevenson, who crossed the continent by train and fell in love with the Napa Valley, made the acquaintance of Jacob Schram, climbed the hill through the redwoods and red-barked madrones to his white-boarded, verandahed, turreted house in a clearing to drink his wine, and called it "bottled poetry."

Schramsberg was reborn in the 1960s and taken in hand by a young professional couple who were discovering wine and northern California

Distant summers remembered: a picnic with Jack and Jamie Davies in the Schramsberg vineyard.

at the same time: Jack and Jamie Davies. Schram had made Cabernet, and no doubt some white wines, but the Davies' dream was champagne. My first visit there was particularly memorable. I had borrowed a little dark green MG two-seater from friends in San Anselmo. I swept up the steep curves of the drive through the woods in fine style. I was ravished, as Stevenson had been, with the white house in the clearing and deeply impressed with the rock-cut cellar tunnels behind, which Schram's coolie labourers had hacked and blasted in the 1860s.

In 1998 these cellars were the scene of a surprise birthday party when I was lured there on another pretext. They are, in the manner of all caves, dark until someone switches on a light. When they did, deep in the ground, I was confronted with a garden. Grass, box hedges, lemon trees, a rose arbour – and in the garden what was apparently my own writing desk. Molly Chappellet is a long-time friend, an epic gardener and the designer of San Francisco's most stylish parties. She had plotted with my wife Judy, who had abstracted papers, books and family photographs from my study and smuggled them over. She had cultivated grass in trays for the lawn, rushed the roses in at the last minute before their flowers had had time to fade. As I stood, astonished, my family and old friends started appearing from dark places in the rock and guitarists burst into twang. And that was only the aperitif. In another cave, a long table was waiting with soaring branches of white magnolias, reflected in a surface of black glass. And goldfishes swimming among orange tulips in the candlelight. And a dinner to make your head swim. Only in the Napa Valley ....

It was out of this cave-mouth years before that Jack Davies had brought the bubbly we tasted, cool and gleaming, that hot day on the verandah; not champagne, but the closest America had come to it. Jack made nothing else; he raised the bar for all other bubbly-makers in California. Better even than the wine, though, I remember my descent. The MG needed a push to start it, but that was fine with a mile of steep downhill to get it going. It spluttered, but no fire, and still hadn't started when I arrived at Highway 420 and coasted to a silent stop in a congregation of Hell's Angels.

They were impressive. The California chapter took themselves seriously. Their vast lean-back, legs-out bikes had long holsters from handlebars to front wheel: one bike, one rifle. And one black-leather girl. Without protective cover I had to come clean. "Good afternoon, gentlemen. Do any of you know how to start a car?" As a first move it was all right. Three heavily chained angels started peering under the bonnet. But suppose, I thought, they don't know, and have to admit it to their cohorts. Will the rifles come out to show who rules the road around here? They didn't. They didn't say much, either. Or smile at all. But one by one they remounted, chains jangling, roared up and swung their bikes back onto the highway. I flagged down a passing car.

Schramsberg remains among the best bubblies of California. Jack Davies is dead; Jamie and the boys carry on. The model is Krug: rich and winey rather than bright and tickly, especially the Cuvée J Schram. I hear they are now listening to the old man's ghost and making some Cabernet again. From their vines high on Spring Mountain, just west of St Helena, it should be good.

In bubbly terms, of course, Schramsberg is now a minnow beside the massive Californian operations of Moët & Chandon, Louis Roederer, Taittinger and Mumm, the great names from Champagne that fill America with fizz. When Domaine Chandon arrived in Napa in 1970, part of their rationale was to prove that sparkling wine could be sold in America without borrowing the name of Champagne. 'From the house that brought you Moët & Chandon' has proved just as effective, to everybody's satisfaction.

The debut of wine-makers from cold Champagne in the very warm Napa Valley was not easy. They had never picked their grapes in August before. Chandon rented space in the nearby Trefethen winery, in Napa's most splendid remaining wooden barn: I remember some pretty sharp smells from the first vats. There was a lot to learn about temperature control, and even more about where to grow Pinot Noir and Chardonnay to achieve anything like the Champagne balance of ripeness with acidity.

The answer was grapes from cooler areas. Carneros at the south end of the Napa Valley gets the breezes from San Francisco Bay; Taittinger built a replica of their château near Epernay there. Anderson Valley, far north and close to the Pacific in Mendocino, seduced Louis Roederer and Pommery, whose wines are called Pacific Echo. Roederer's Quartet is intended to reproduce the rich dry style of their non-vintage champagne: it is considered California's best shot. Iron Horse, a long-term favourite of mine, makes snappy fresh fizz in Green Valley in Sonoma. The challenge is always to pick the grapes before they are fully California-ripe. The result, in most cases, is a smooth, not-too-dry, who-would-argue style of sparkler.

In terms of climate and soil there is not a great deal to choose between northern California and Southern Australia. Neither is remotely like Champagne. Which of course does nothing to prevent Australian wine-makers from making bubbles, and doing it very well. Victoria is the most bubbly-minded state – and has been ever since the gold rush of the 1850s.

There were limited options for miners celebrating a strike; the most obvious one was a round of the most expensive drink on offer. They liked the pop of a well-shaken champagne bottle opening – and no doubt squirted their friends as racing drivers do. Some drank it from a bucket, others bathed their girlfriends in it. Few, I suspect, paid much attention to the taste, but those who did were heard to say that perhaps Messrs Moët, Mumm, Roederer and the rest had not reserved their best *cuvées* for Australia. Surely the local vineyards (and plenty were being planted round the goldfields) could do better, at half the price.

It was not that simple. Even when you found a Frenchman who knew how, the local wines were the polar opposite of the acidic stuff they used in Champagne. You needed reinforced bottles. You needed a cool cellar. And you needed workers for the tedious part who would not rather be out digging gold, or even herding sheep.

The company best known as bubbly specialists from the start was Great Western. Goldminers whose luck had run out were persuaded to dig tunnels for cellars instead. By the time it was bought by its present owners, Seppelt from Barossa, in 1918 it was a flourishing company, and not only for sparkling wine.

Moët & Chandon settled on the Yarra Valley as their choice for a predictably consistent fizz in the 1980s, when the efforts of such pioneers as James Halliday at Coldstream Hills had proved how well they could grow Chardonnay and Pinot Noir. When James and I sweltered out to Coldstream from Melbourne in March 1987, the reputed secret of its delicate wines, its cool climate, was not especially evident. But later that night, when we gathered on the balcony of his house for a barbie, I heard the cry I have heard after supper in great vineyards round the world: "Darling, fetch me my shawl." Cold nights, growers tell us, lock the fruit flavours in the ripening grape.

Moët comes to Australia: Len Evans (sitting), James Halliday and I taste some of the early results with Tony Jordan (right) in charge of operations.

The most memorable wine of that chilly evening for me, though, was the sparkling Shiraz, Australia's very own contribution to the bubbly world. I had tasted a sparkling red burgundy many years before, and in my first book had likened it to a fat old man dressed up as a fairy. Maybe that one was. But Seppelt Sparkling Shiraz in 1987 (it may have been the 1982 vintage) was a revelation. There was something Italian about the tingle of gas and the tang of tannin together against a background of considerable body, and I guess a certain amount of sugar. I loved it. Lombardy's Lambrusco should be like this. I must ask for it the next time I am faced with the rich food of Bologna.

Of sparkling wines other than champagne, my cellar holds very few. They come and they go; not often, I have to admit, leaving any very distinct impression. Away from home it is a different matter. Travelling, I routinely drink whatever bubbly the locals recommend. If it is the closest shot at champagne that conditions allow (and almost without exception the sparkling wines of the New World are just that) it is hard not to judge it in that spirit. How close is it?

In Europe there are very distinct variants. England goes straight for the Champagne model, and does it with such effect that I have known Champagne's own citizens flummoxed. Ridgeview is the brand we drink most often; Nyetimber is a bit tastier, but less deceiving. Germany with its Sekt stresses the fruity flavours of German grapes; yeasty flavours blend badly with them. When the grape is Riesling, two good things are combined: Riesling and bubbles. I am not sure that one and one, in this case, ever add up to more than two. Nor, I confess, have I ever seen any specific attraction in the Cava that flows in an unending stream from what they say are the world's biggest bubble-cellars in Penedès near Barcelona. Like champagne, it ranges in quality from the sharp, thin and dreary to hand-made wines as fine as art can make them. Some wines just don't speak my language.

Italian bubbles are different. When they speak the champagne dialect the accent is charming and the vocabulary perfect. Especially, I have found, from Ca'del Bosco near Brescia, east of Milan, though this house is by no means alone. More entertaining altogether are the specialities of Asti and the Veneto, Moscato Spumante and Prosecco.

I suspect sales of Prosecco have multiplied in recent times. Certainly you used to meet it in Venice – and were not allowed to forget that it is the basis for the fizz and peach juice Bellini invented (was it by Hemingway, or for him?) at Harry's Bar overlooking the Grand Canal. Now it is everywhere; the faintly grapey, fairly dry, very cold and fizzy answer to a long day's thirst. I once started collecting the words used in different cities in Italy for a glass of something cold. Venice says 'Ombra'. Apparently they all mean the same thing: 'Just a small one, Luigi; and don't put the bottle away.'

My brother has had the good sense to live in the Maremma, the south Tuscan coast, for many years. His garden is my favourite place to sip Prosecco, flinty-cool in a big thick wine glass, nibbling from a bowl of

anchovies in oil from Porto Santo Stefano. Just visible under a fringe of
olives and oaks, beyond the rising and falling of green intervening hills,
the coast curves out from the Bay of Talamone to form the purple
peninsula of Argentario. The dark shape on the silver horizon is Giglio.
In winter the snows of Corsica peep like a topsail into view. (I don't credit
the Prosecco with the scenery.) If the same aperitif is going down in every
foreign household in Tuscany, and Umbria, and around all the coasts of
Italy, the farmers of the Veneto had better keep planting their little white
Prosecco grapes. Bisol is the brand I know best, but on the one pilgrimage
I made to the Prosecco capital, Valdobbiadene, fifty kilometres north of
Venice, I realized that even in the making of this simple refreshment there
are many variables and much to learn. That bubbles are born not only the
laborious champagne way, for example: Prosecco is made in tanks by a
method known as *charmat*. They dissipate quicker, the flavour remains
simple (with no yeast in the bottle for a second fermentation the bakery
flavours never arrive), but the smile is the same.

Each time I drink Asti Spumante I wonder why we don't drink it more
often – and then I remember. The first sip, the first glass, of this sweet
featherweight is simple ravishment: hot-house grapes on ice with bubbles.
The bubbles, and a little juicy sharpness, usher the sweetness along while
it goes cleanly down your throat. Another sip, another glass, and I find
myself swallowing it in gulps, trying to chase away the thirst which grows
with each sip. It sounds the perfect recipe – and it is lucky the alcohol content is half a wine's-worth. Sadly, though, it palls. A bottle goes a long way.

*The view from Fonte
Pitacchio. My brother Brian
paints and gardens and gives
his friends Prosecco
high above the coast of
the Maremma.*

The sparkling wines of the New World (primarily for the moment Australia, New Zealand and California) can have the edge over champagne at afternoon weddings, and parties where the conversation takes precedence and the food takes time. To put a finger on the difference is hard. A little more alcohol and a little less acidity? A less vivid, less penetrating style? New Zealand versions, in my experience, have more flesh, to the extent of plumpness.

Then there is the whole class of Crémants from France, from the Loire, Burgundy and Alsace. The term used to mean sparkling at lower pressure, 'creaming' rather than frothing. Champagne agreed to give up this traditional second string to its bow if its French imitators (they could never be admitted as rivals) abandoned any reference to the champagne method. Whatever the terminology, the central Loire has a long tradition of bubblifying its less-than-ideally-ripe Chenin Blanc, with Saumur as the reference point. This is full-pressure fizz, clean as a whistle if not usually very interesting. The Burgundy version has more flavour, as the Chardonnay is a fuller-flavoured grape than the Chenin, and comes closer in style to champagne. I have often ordered a glass of Crémant de Bourgogne in Burgundy after a hard day's tasting – though in summer I am more likely to ask for beer. The Alsace version is made primarily of the mild-mannered Pinot Blanc.

The business of bubbles is not limited to these major poles of French wine-growing. The little enclave of Limoux, in the hills of the Corbières near Carcassonne, claims to have discovered the trick independently centuries ago. It certainly does it well, with the local Mauzac as the main grape but increasing proportions of Chardonnay and Pinot Noir. If I were looking for a champagne-substitute, Blanquette de Limoux would be high on my list. In a completely different vein, mountain-fresh rather than cake-shop rich, so would the sparkling Seyssel made by Varichon & Clerc in sight, or nearly, of the Alps. Finally Luxembourg is worth a mention. This unexpected vineyard on the Moselle has mastered its own style of rather austere but extremely pleasant bubbly.

Bubbles give a drink an extra dimension. If they can't redeem a bad wine, they can give point to a dull one. Exhilaration is what they add, but the fun will be over the moment the froth dies down if the wine is not tempting in itself. Champagne has canonized Dom Pérignon on the evidence that he found the flavours of luxury in unpromising materials. He coined a rival to burgundy, interpreting the Pinot Noir as the grape of delicacy and style. If the evidence is true, he invented the whole art of deliberate blending: he was the first perfectionist. The bubbles? Just a happy accident.

III   White

Sports Day at Loggerheads

SPORTS DAY. An English school tradition kept alive by Australia's High Priest and Headmaster of wine, Len Evans. Loggerheads ("Trish and I are always at Loggerheads") has the best view of the Hunter Valley, over vineyards and ponds and Len's tame piece of bush where kangaroos graze and pose and bounce about. The Hunter is a hundred and sixty kilometres north of Sydney, in an area apparently too hot and wet for grapes, which still makes some of Australia's most stylish wine.

Riesling in unlabelled magnums, seafood by the bucket.

A hundred of Len's friends have gathered to celebrate his 70th birthday, a three-day event starting with a Great Wine Dinner, Australian style, and ending with an Imperial Ball at which everyone dresses as an Emperor or Empress. Len is Napoleon with his Josephine. Judy and I are instructed to be Oberon and Titania. All the wine is in Impériales, rare Australians, First Growth clarets, Château Yquem; each one eight bottles' worth under one mighty cork ….

Saturday is Sports Day; dress code: sporting whites. We all turn up in cricket flannels but, to make sure, Len gives us matching baggy white T-shirts. The most energetic sport is a Treasure Hunt. The prize a Jeroboam of Bollinger – without the cork.

Loggerheads is a tin-roofed bungalow, colonial-style, with wide verandahs around a courtyard garden. The centre is filled with a long white tent shading a long white table. Outside it two enormous cauldrons are bubbling, drawing crowds to breathe in their fragrant steam. Sydney Harbour has been emptied of its prawns, its crabs, its Bay bugs, its oysters and mussels and everything crustacean for the feast. When we sit down it is at an empty table – just an immense white plastic cloth.

Then the seafood arrives, in buckets, to be poured out in a pink, grey, red and pearly river right down the centre. This is bare-knuckle stuff: every man for himself.

Now the *coup de théâtre*. Between each pair of guests, flanking the red river in enfilade down the table, appears a tall green magnum. No label, just dewy condensation from the cold Riesling inside. Did we drink it in paper cups? It would not have mattered. It was Petaluma's new wine, from the Clare Valley in South Australia, made by Len's most famous disciple, Brian Croser; sharp, rich, dry, whistle-whetting, grape-fragrant as only Riesling can be. It was like a dynastic

Nobody was surprised by Len's appearance as Napoleon, with Trish as Josephine.

marriage, the sweet fresh flesh of the sea and the cutting fruit of Australian vines. It celebrated the bond that goes round the world, the perfect partnership of food and wine.

A table in view of the sea, fresh fish and cold wine is a formula that never fails. My notebooks are full of ecstatic scrawlings from the world's coasts. Sometimes I think I must be a merman, and a half-cannibal one at that, to enjoy browsing on the seabed as much as I do. I remember a particular plat de fruits de mer at Honfleur in Normandy which was quite simply that: a predators' banquet on all the stony, scaly or limpid beasts that lie, crawl, or proceed in illogical little flicks among the wrack and the wrecks, stirring up the sand or disguised as pebbles. There were shrimps and oysters, whelks and mussels, winkles and cockles and clams. The napkins were sea-green with crustaceous designs. The plate was virtually a bivalve in pottery. The wine, palest green from a dark green bottle, was as cold and as tangy, almost, as the sea itself.

A toss of a lobster-pot from the harbour wall, where pyramids of tarry rigging were black against the moon, the café-restaurant Aux Deux Ponts was like an extension of the seabed, the only difference being that the water boiled. I returned there with unabated appetite for grilled sole, steamed turbot, moules marinières, night after night.

The sea itself is an important actor, with all its nautical props.

The sight of a tubby little fishing boat, and the smell, stale and fresh at the same time, on the jetty, starts an urgent craving for fish, fish, fish, fish (as Fats Waller put it), fish.

I won't say that all the beckoning quay-side cafés come up to expectation. Bergen was a bad let-down. My fault, no doubt for letting the guidebook persuade me for a moment that boiled cod could be worth trying. The place was as tarry as can be. Upstairs, one felt, there could only be a sail-loft. But the jug of melted butter which we were relying on to gild a most unhappy monochrome of cod and potatoes, both boiled, turned out to be margarine. As for the wine, Bergen was barren.

Then there was the restaurant at Juneau, in Alaska, where an enormous and wholly delicious slice of king salmon (the beast in question had weighed almost forty-five kilos and the slice was in proportion) was presented with spaghetti bolognese on the side. And on the other side, as it were, a roaring hot mama belting out 'The Lady is a Tramp' to a growling cornet.

The search for fish has taken me to some curious places. The struggle to photograph them – I have what I am told is an unusual urge to photograph fish before I dispatch them – has led me into even odder ones. How should I have explained to the lady beside whom on the park bench the struggling lobster landed, out of a clear sky, feet upwards, that I had only poured a jug of water over it on its dish on the balcony above because the sun had dried its shell to an unphotogenic brown – in Portuguese?

For several years our favourite haunt was a little hotel on the harbour wall at Le Crotoy, at the very mouth of the River Somme in Picardy. Chez Mado was just across from the jetty where Mado's boats brought Mado's fish to land. Madame Mado Poncelet, when not slipping out to Mass in her red two-seater and her Pucci shirt, presided in a house where they might have stopped The Creation at Day Two.

From the delicate pink mounds of shrimps that appeared beside your aperitif to the moment when you felt you were jolly lucky not to get lobster coffee, you were subjected to the fruits of the Channel – and more particularly the bay of the Somme – without respite. When breakfast came up to your room and the shutters were thrown back, you were just in time to see the night's catch chugging by to the jetty. Before you turned in you watched the boxes of flapping silver from another expedition being swung ashore.

The nearest fishing-boats to home are on the beach at West Mersea.

The world's most sumptuous oysters were reputedly first implanted here by the Romans to supply their British capital, Colchester. For those who can't wait to get their oysters home, a hut on the beach, The Company Shed, provides a table and puts the day's catch (not just oysters – whatever the boats bring in) on a plate for you. The rest is self-help: you bring your bread and butter, mayonnaise (they ban salads as messy things) and your own wine.

The taste of fresh fish is as elusive as it is strong. Descriptive words are hard to find. Salt and sweet certainly apply, but sharp, nutty, fruity – or any evocation of another foodstuff – scarcely ever. Lake and river fish are often earthy, or muddy, but the difference between a sole and a salmon, a brill and a tuna, is easier to describe in terms of texture and richness or oiliness than taste. The taste is largely determined by how it is cooked, whether poached, grilled or fried or sauced or indeed not cooked at all.

"Fish is far too watery a creature to blend happily with wine." Another point of view is always salutary – especially when it is the voice of your old tutor. This was André Simon in the 1940s in an uncharacteristically testy mood. I remember him leaning blissfully over a plate of sole gougères, slim fillets fried crisply in breadcrumbs. The Meursault-Charmes, mature enough to be just touched with gold, had found its perfect match. What did he mean, too watery?

There are fishes that are too oily to be good partners to wine. I challenge anyone to find a match for mackerel. Herring, even simply fried, let alone smoked or soused in vinegar, is at best awkward. In Amsterdam in summer, when they lower little raw 'green' herrings by their tails unadorned down their throats, they chase them with smooth cold gin.

But it is true that the food/wine relationship works differently with fish. It is harder to give wine priority. Gourmands are given to saying

Le Crotoy on the Bay of the Somme is just one of hundreds of quiet harbours living on seafood. Our resort summer after summer for greedy weekends.

things like 'What Pauillac really needs is lamb,' or even, I'm afraid, 'The thing for the '90 La Chapelle would really be a salmi of wild boar.' Red wines, to their followers, suggest specific kinds of meat. Different cuts of meat and game in turn suggest specific red wines. Well-hung grouse, vivid young red burgundy; roast pheasant, well-aged claret. With fish it tends to be the more expensive fishes with the more expensive wines. Status rules.

You cannot go wrong with Chablis. Why? Because it has more character than personality. It stands firm; it doesn't show off. It has no specific flavour, nothing aromatic about it; rather it has a specific shape in your mouth, a little sharp, a little fat, nothing to do with fruit. Premiers Crus are more positive – especially after three or four years. Grand Cru Chablis grows rich and assertive with age; then it is time for cream sauces. Young, Chablis supports the fish and satisfies the drinker without drawing attention to itself. Happily there are many other wines around the world that can play the same role.

The different sea coasts of Australia naturally link up with perfect sources of suitable wines. Loggerheads is in New South Wales. The problem with Sydney is choice. Try to believe that thirty years ago there was hardly a restaurant worth the name in town. The eccentrics who were interested congregated round Bulletin Place, where the same Len Evans ran a club-like establishment that became Australia's first forum for wine and food, separately and together. Guests who bored him, I am told, found themselves paying for the very best wines for guests who did not. "You're not drinking?" I once heard him ask. "You don't have enough personality to not drink."

Seafood traditional at Doyle's on Sydney Harbour.

Doyle's represents the early days; a shack on the beach (it is much more than that now) where the oysters are fresh and the cooking basic. You take a ferry to Watson's Bay from Circular Quay. One day we were sitting on Peter Doyle's beach discussing a bottle of the gentle, insinuating Semillon unique to the Hunter Valley when we noticed sand in our oysters. The wind was whirling it along the beach. We looked towards Sydney to see black clouds, and white sails in disarray. A regatta was scattered, the yachts going over like skittles. "Come with me," said Doyle, and we found ourselves fishing increasingly blue yachtsmen out of the water into the Doyle launch.

The Bather's Pavilion represents what has changed. It stands across the harbour at Rose Bay, looking out at the Heads and the Pacific beyond, a stylish relic of bathing days when men swam in long drawers. Seafood here is like jewellery. Fabergé dreamt up this white bowl of prawns with poached quail and salsify, a clear red tomato jelly and a green watercress pool.

Bay bugs came next, those strange undersea beetles full of sweet meat, in a bowl with sweet pork, broccoli, green perch and delicate mushrooms. Then tuna sashimi in a miniature Dagwood sandwich with herbs and thin slices of cuttlefish, more herbs, and sweet peppers. Then a scallop perched on an oxtail ravioli on a cabbage leaf with gingery soy sauce. Then a gnocchi parcel ('cappelletto', they called it) of goats' cheese and sweet onion with anchovies and olives and chives. Then a meltingly perfect slice of Arctic char (salmon to me) on a crab and potato cake with yellow caviar and aïoli. Confused? Stay with me for the roast Barramundi on leek and cauliflower purée with prawns. And fruit.

It could have been confusion. If we had tried permutations with different wines I would have been lost. On the principle that fish is fish, we drank a bottle of Crawford River Riesling (all the way from Victoria, I'm sorry to say). Its clear faintly grapey flavour, sharp enough to be heard, unified the meal. We were happy: the view of the harbour was sublime. (Bankers, we learned, surf on Thursdays. So that's who it was splashing about out there.)

Why drink inter-state? Why not the excellent wine of New South Wales? There are two classic New South Welsh white wines, the Hunter Valley Semillon we drank at Doyle's (which its pioneers labelled Hunter Riesling) and the famously rich-textured Chardonnays from the same region and one or two others. The Semillon of such producers as McWilliam's (Lovedale and Elizabeth) and Tyrrell's, Rothbury Estate (before 1995), and Tower are curiously timid wines when young, of no great alcoholic strength, gentle and lemony. After ten years or more they take on flavours described as 'lanolin' and 'toast', but zesty still, an intriguing and seductive style you find nowhere else. I love them, but feared the assault of so many powerful fishy and other flavours would bury such subtlety. My reservation about a Hunter Chardonnay was just the opposite. The warm climate of the Hunter gives Chardonnay a golden glow. Add oak and it turns to cream. Most growers do, remembering

How tastes change. Each course at The Bathers' Pavilion, across the harbour, is a composition. These are Bay Bugs, a reason to visit Sydney in themselves.

how one of them, Rosemount, made Australia's first Chardonnay champion – not very long ago. Who would believe today that Australia had no Chardonnay vines at all until the 1960s? Oaky cream or creamy oak is the last thing fish needs. The first is a sharp squeeze of lemon: hence the Riesling.

An autumn day in Kyoto. The Sunday crowds are out to stroll and meditate and giggle and photograph each other among the maple trees. Where Hokusai drew the long arc of a bridge across the Kyoto river you can hire a skiff to row up the broad water between hills of brilliant colour. It is already November; you need a coat. Families lean on their oars and drift down towards the bridge in ecstasy at the tapestry of orange and scarlet and gold. And then the fish boat moves in. He rows just upwind of you, enfolding you in the vapours from his little stove. Resistance is impossible.

We are all innocents beside the Japanese when it comes to fish. My education started in a lecture theatre of the Ecole Technique Hotelière Tsuji in Osaka. I opened the door to be faced with a hundred students in black examining the shining blades of their foot-long knives. First you cut the medula oblongata. 'We call this Iki Jime: live kill. This way the fish is freshest.' You learn a thousand other cuts before you are let loose in a serious sushi bar. My education continued, in the hands of Shizuo Tsuji, proprietor of the school, with a visit to Osaka's ancient public baths to learn how to bathe (sit on a stool and scrub, then boiling water immersion along with everyone else) and how to enjoy having little masseuses running up and down your spine.

This was preparation for a visit to Fuki Sushi, Osaka's (Japan's?) most revered sushi bar. There are six seats at the bar; ten chefs behind it. When Professor Tsuji comes in the ten yell '*Hai*' in well-drilled unison, trailing off in volleys of apologies: '*Simasen, Simasen, Simasen.*' There is no menu, no discussion. The whole menagerie of the sea is sliced into a succession of exquisite mouthfuls, liturgically ordained: a prawn still alive, just stripped of its shell, then the carapace blackened in a flame. A slice of fat tuna belly, marbled pink and white, then a sliver of cuttlefish spiked with wasabi. Each is laid gently on the pale board before you, timed precisely to your swallow. The industrious slicing goes on, punctuated by loud claps

My tutor in the Japanese arts of the table, Shizuo Tsuji, took me out on the Kyoto River. The boat behind (and upwind) is frying fragrant fish.

(moulding rice is a noisy business) until every fish has been anatomized. Then the envoi, five centimetres of hot caramelized eel. And all the while with sweet apologetic nods the kimono at your elbow is filling your cup with warm sweet saké.

———————

I am here to teach Japan about wine. 'What wine, Hugh *sensei*, [this is seriously honorific: *sensei* means teacher] should we be drinking with sushi? One wine with all, or different wines with different fish?' That would be difficult; at this rate the corkscrew would grow red hot.

I think it's called a Morton's Fork, when either answer to a question condemns you. If I name a succession of different wines, we have the hot-corkscrew problem. If I breezily say one wine will do, they will think I know nothing of the subtleties of sushi. I name alternatives. Are you looking for a simple solution? Champagne. More finely tuned? A single glass of non-vintage champagne, then Chablis of the youngest vintage, then a Premier Cru Chablis three or four years old. This formula of brisk and bubbly, followed by simple, pure and fresh, followed by flavouring with more substance, seems to echo the progression of a classic sushi meal. It certainly conveys the idea of crescendo. The Riesling alternative works for some. A little humour helps it along (but I'm giving away my professional secrets).

Humour, I discover, is something the Japanese understand. The day before flying home I was discussing airline food with a Japanese friend. Late that evening he appeared in my hotel with a beautifully wrapped parcel. "Bento box," he said, "for flying tomorrow." Excitement: this was the bento ultimate. The label said Fuki sushi. Next day I smugly spurned the airline meal. "I've brought my own," I said, unwrapping my box. My sushi was beautiful: a whole box of the plastic models they put in the window.

As for tempura, Tsuji-*sensei* told me, the best is the simplest, most urgently required by hungry men in a hurry. A quick fry-up, in fact. Which is why his black Jaguar slid us down to Kobe docks one evening to a waterfront café where seamen in dungarees were scurrying in and out. I'd like to say I instantly grasped why these crisp, pale, featherweight packages of battered white-fish, battered onion-rings, battered prawns, battered shiso leaves were superior to anything in grand hotel tempura restaurants. (We drank beer for the ten minutes our meal took.) But my *sensei* had instilled the principle into me: tempura equals hurry. Think tempo. Forget wine.

I rarely do forget wine, in fact, and have filled notebooks over the years with meals and the wines I have drunk with them – often in Japan. Travelling alone often means eating solo at unusual times – for which the sushi or tempura bar (in hotels it is often both) is ideal. You have the chef for company, and soon pick up at least the names of your favourite fish. One notebook records supper at the Okura, Tokyo's grandest and most staid hotel, accompanied only by a bottle of Trefethen Riesling from the Napa Valley.

Oishi; that's the Japanese for scrumptious. Don't forget. *Megochi* is a tiny flat white fish with a long tail, definitely *oishi*. Then three green ginkgo nuts on a toothpick, good for virility. Good. Lotus root looks like Gruyère. Trust the French (the table in the middle) to chain-smoke through sushi. ¥17,000 each: that's £500 for their supper, plus wine. Look at that: half a bottle of Chablis, ¥10,000. Ebi, you can't beat shrimp. The Riesling loves it. That's the difference between saké and wine; wine keeps reminding you it's there. My head is starting to swim. *Mouth and Mind*, that's what I'll call my next book. What did she call me? *Genki* – that's another lovely word; bouncy, or something like that.

A tutorial. Brutus Magazine had me teach a TV star, Honami Suzuki, how to taste wine. In return, I was taught to paint scrolls (between us, an early effort).

In an English Garden

IN WINE COUNTRY there are a dozen settings for perfect enjoyment, given congenial company. Fire- and candlelight comes high on the list. The deep napery and clanging crystal of a three-star restaurant evokes a totally different kind of pleasure. Why is it, though, that for me first place is always reserved for drinking out of doors?

I fancy the answer has much to do with the English climate. Why are the English the first nation in gardening? Why do almost all the common sports and games have English (or Scottish, you golfers) origins? Because in a climate without extremes it is almost always possible, if not pleasant, to spend time in the fresh air, and when the sky is clear it becomes very pleasant indeed.

If the seaside comes first among my perfect places for tables it is for the fish and shellfish straight from the water, the salty air and what the French call *le grand large* itself: the endless sea and sky. Second place, and very close, goes to a table in the garden. My favourite table is on the lawn under an apple tree. Apples make deep dappled shade; there are few summer days when their air-conditioning fails.

I go barefoot on the cool grass, reading, talking, listening to the birds, watching the vapour trails in the summer sky, trying to pin down the memories triggered by my wine. It is Riesling from the Moselle: a slender green bottle. This is wine of a different persuasion entirely from the savoury, structured offerings of France – and of any other country. It is as though the grapes were not transmuted by fermentation into another

substance, wine, but as if in some Buddhist sense their souls migrated.

The karma of golden grapes from this summer-green country is always lively, apple-crisp, juicy, however sweet it may be. You are never aware of the alcoholic wineyness, the warmth in the throat that is common to all other wines. Without this support it relies entirely on its internal vitality, the wound-spring effect of acidity and sweetness locked together. Half-cock attempts are rightly dismissed as 'sugar-water'. Not this bottle.

There is an international freemasonry of Riesling-drinkers. We know each other by signs non-initiates might miss, among which a slim green bottle (sometimes brown) is the most frequent. We claim unique properties, magic powers almost, for this singular white grape. Not that there is so much competition. Only Chardonnay comes close in quality – and without the crutch of oak, would Chardonnay be so interesting? Riesling alone makes pure wine, innocent of oak, that precisely reflects its origin in a spectrum from flowery and feather-light through tense, dry, and mineral-laden, to unctuous and creamy or to a piercing liquor like celestial marmalade. Only Riesling can make wine of inconsiderable strength, a mere 7·5 alcoholic degrees, that drinks joyfully from birth and can put on flesh and flavours for twenty years. This is its Moselle manifestation. Only Riesling can ripen on dry Australian hills and emerge lime-fresh with pin-sharp focus. Only Riesling can grow to massive power and density on a rock ledge above the Danube or on the sunniest slopes of the Vosges, on a gamut of soils from sandstone to marl, and keep its essential form and character, the nervous energy of its fruity acidity.

Nerve, tension, the character of freshness in the mouth are vital for any good white wine – just as a measure of tannic grip is for any red. It is the very essence of Riesling: fruity acidity that can hold the sweetness of honey, as it were, at arm's length, the two elements balancing each other so that your mouth is aware only of a supremely salivating moment. The ability of this grape to keep its cool in the utterly different conditions of Germany and Australia is one of its fascinations. Historically, though, and spiritually, its home is in the hills that pitch down to the Rhine and the Moselle.

This garden bottle bears the steel-engraved portrait of another country house: Scharzhof, the quietly comfortable domain below the Scharzhofberg of the Egon Müller family for four generations. The hall is the place where you taste at Scharzhof: a gloomy room, dark stairs rising opposite the heavy front door, the antlers of old victims on the walls and, over to the left, lit by a green-curtained window, a small round table with a ring of golden glasses catching the light.

There is a routine to tasting a new vintage in Germany. I tasted each one for many years with the father of the young Egon Müller. He said little as he sipped. You start with the Kabinett wine, a thing of little substance, fragrant and sharp. The smell is fresh grapes, promisingly sweet. The taste is hardly sweet at all. You judge it (if that is what you are doing) on its place in a scale from weakly sharp to an electric shock of silvery acidity that runs straight down your throat. You mount the ladder of ripeness. A Spätlese is next, from measurably riper grapes: potentially two or three degrees of alcohol stronger. It should have the same voltage but more substance and more sugar, making a tighter knot of flavour, with a sense at this stage that a door is shut: you are being excluded from witnessing something interesting. *Gedeckt* is the word; it means 'covered'.

The speciality of the estate is its Ausleses, late-harvested wines of golden sweetness picked far into the yellowing of the leaves. In good vintages there are several, the last made in tiny quantities, designated by an all-gold capsule in place of the regular gold and white. Colour-coded capsules are a German institution. At times, especially in the Rheingau where proud estates proliferate, the various tints and stripes were like signal-flags at sea; you needed a midshipman to look them up for you.

At Scharzhof you taste at a round table in the hall. The late Egon Müller steered me through many vintages of his sublime Moselle.

You don't need a code-book at Scharzhof, or even a code. The progression is palpable. Just when you think the wine has reached the limit of expression, that no further flavour could possibly be packed into a sip, the next glass screws the knot tighter. They have become seriously expensive, these jewels eked out of the waning sun. It takes decades for their gridlock of flavours to resolve into a flow. It is worth the wait.

The late Egon Müller loved his library. From the hall you moved into this entirely book-lined room, the colour of old bindings, with deep armchairs. This is where you learnt the rewards of patience in bottles reaching back to the Second World War. Egon Senior was an officer on the Russian front in 1945 when his father died. Through the fog of war the order reached him that he should come home. He arrived in time for the most catastrophic vintage. The spring had brought a devastating frost. There were only old men and women and children, and very few of them, to work in the fields. Weeds were as high as the vines and the vines were almost bare of fruit.

I heard his story at a dinner at the British Embassy in Paris in 1995 to commemorate the end of the war and the extraordinary vintage that accompanied it. Egon Müller was the only German present. He had brought his last two bottles of the '45. Among all the wines at that dinner his was the most memorable: still pale green, with a fresh, gentle, smoky fragrance and a flavour beyond words, sunny and strong, intense and tender with an echo of honey that sounded long after you had swallowed. An Auslese? There was no selection, Egon said. There were not enough grapes. The vineyard had spoken with a single voice.

The British Embassy in Paris was the scene of a dinner to celebrate the 50th anniversary of the greatest vintage of the 20th century. The mansion was bought by the Duke of Wellington from Napoleon's sister Pauline Borghese.

Learning German

My education in German wine started with Otto Loeb, the most indulgent and intelligent of the wine merchants who cast their pearls before the swine we were as students at Cambridge. In the 1960s in London each new German vintage was a matter of moment. OW Loeb & Co invited their customers to a tasting at the Charing Cross Hotel of the latest and the penultimate vintages from thirty or so of Germany's best estates. The level of knowledge and comment in the crowd was remarkable; these were collectors, and astute ones. The wines of the Moselle were Loeb's first interest. He was a native of its capital city, Trier. But the great estates of the Rheingau, Rheinhessen, the Palatinate and the Nahe were well represented. And they were making glorious wines.

My tutor, interpreter and travel agent when I began to visit Germany in the 1960s was Peter Hasslacher, whose German cousins owned the famous firm Deinhard, of Koblenz and London. There is another advantage to the lightness, the transparency and relatively low alcohol content of most German wines: you can taste formidable numbers without tiring and losing track. I found a hundred was just possible, at least if you skipped the samples whose smell you didn't like. I could not get close to that in Bordeaux in Burgundy, let alone California or Australia.

The Palatinate, or Pfalz, I soon learned, makes the most sumptuous wines. In those days they were never dry (or if they were, we never saw them) but nor did they cloy. It was not, or not obviously, acidity that kept the balance going, but seemingly mineral elements drawn from the soil. Forster Kirchenstück, Freundstück and Jesuitengarten are names you rarely hear today, but we would taste and talk sagely about the geology of the Mittelhaardt with a passion that now only Burgundy seems to provoke. The Mittelhaardt, the core of the Palatinate, lies next door to Alsace. It feels almost subtropical after the Moselle. Trees grow enormous there; you even see stunted palms. The town houses of Deidesheim, Wachenheim and Bad Dürkheim have a feeling of bourgeois prosperity remote from the little Moselle Valley settlements. The Nazis, I learned, did their best to beggar the Palatinate by removing the Jews

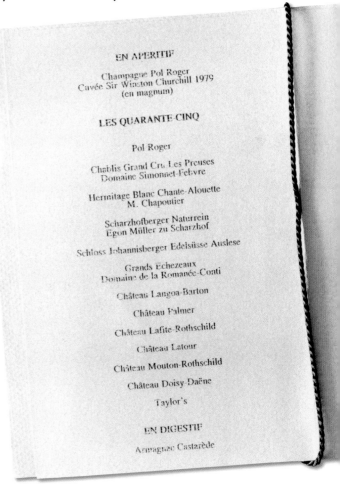

EN APERITIF

Champagne Pol Roger
Cuvée Sir Winston Churchill 1979
(en magnum)

LES QUARANTE-CINQ

Pol Roger

Chablis Grand Cru Les Preuses
Domaine Simonnet-Febvre

Hermitage Blanc Chante-Alouette
M. Chapoutier

Scharzhofberger Naturrein
Egon Müller zu Scharzhof

Schloss Johannisberger Edelsüsse Auslese

Grands Echezeaux
Domaine de la Romanée-Conti

Château Langoa-Barton

Château Palmer

Château Lafite-Rothschild

Château Latour

Château Mouton-Rothschild

Château Doisy-Daëne

Taylor's

EN DIGESTIF

Armagnac Castarède

The wine list of the Embassy dinner. The greatest surprise was the single German wine: an extraordinary Scharzhofberger made under dire conditions.

who, as in many other places, were the motor of the wine business. To keep wine flowing they obliged cities around Germany to adopt wine villages willy-nilly and buy all their wines.

Only a few deeply entrenched and aristocratic producers were seemingly prosperous in the sixties and seventies, notably the 'three Bs', Burklin-Wolf, Basserman-Jordan and von Buhl. The rest of the business was largely done by Germany's most effective wine cooperatives. There were new ideas in their cellars, and bargains to be had from villages unknown outside the region.

The Rheingau, fronting the Rhine in one of its most theatrical stretches as it flows west from the congestion of Frankfurt, Mainz and Wiesbaden, had and still has a totally different *Zeitgeist*. Its great institutions were abbeys, and their successors aristocrats. Several of them had been trading on their coats of arms for too long. Its wine, in any case, is a tougher proposition than the bracing freshness of the Moselle and the plump cushion of the Pfalz. It is Germany's Médoc, where a certain austerity is part of the package and a touch of hauteur in Schloss or château has not on the whole been bad for trade. I was especially attracted by the wines of Hochheim, the original of the English term Hock. Hochheim lies on the Rheingau riverbank just upstream and nearer to Mainz. To my thinking it is the Graves of the Rhine. A perceptive taster once said Médoc and Graves were like glossy and matt prints of the same photograph. It makes sense to me.

Wine tasting in Germany was always an intimate affair. This office breathes the atmosphere of the Rhineland I grew to love.

If Riesling has a true spiritual home it is in the most massive and marvellous of all Germany's cellars, the Cistercian abbey Kloster Eberbach in the Rheingau hills. The founders of Eberbach came from Burgundy, fresh from the foundation of their new abbey of Cîteaux in the plain between Beaune and Dijon, and from planting their prize vineyard, the Clos de Vougeot. Cistercians liked lonely places. They loved the fringes of civilization: in Yorkshire, where the Dales begin at Fountains and Rievaulx; in Germany, where the skirts of the Taunus forest flow down to the Rhine below Mainz. I have been to Eberbach in summer and winter, when it has been a furnace and when it has been a fridge. Its Gothic spaces, its vaults and cloisters and echoing stairs, its dormitory a hundred metres long and its vast echoing church offer no respite. The monks' respite lay in the

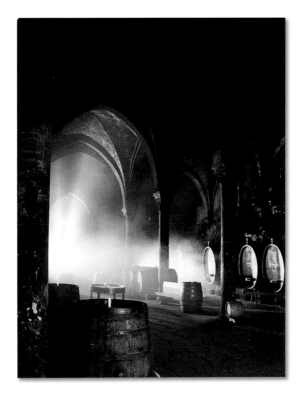

gated, vaulted, barrel-lined cellars barely discernible in wayward candle-light. And so did their fortune.

One would imagine they started with red wine. If they brought their vines with them from Burgundy, they would have been an early form of Pinot Noir. Pinot Noir, 'Spätburgunder', still grows in parts of the Rheingau. But it is too cold at Eberbach. Their German Clos de Vougeot, surrounded like the Clos by a massive drystone wall, was a workshop for white wine – and, at some point lost in the Middle Ages, the propagation of a revolutionary white grape, the Riesling.

The name Steinberg has exactly the right hard ring to it: stone mountain. It doesn't exactly conjure up fruity little wines, or indeed glasses of gold succulence. The great wines of the Steinberg were and are hard-etched, mineral as much as vegetable.

In Bordeaux or Burgundy there was never a question of what the wines should ideally be like. The template was in place: you just did your best to match it. Germany is different. Certainly in the Rheingau there are two traditions. The older is for dry wines, formerly aged for years in big casks to grow soft and, by modern standards, brown. The grapes were picked earlier and more acid; the wine needed years to mellow. The younger, for sweet wines, came in as something exceptional, at first only when the weather showed the vintner the way, then, and more artfully, as a matter of routine. Today dry wines are back in fashion, at least among German drinkers, but for years they were out of countenance, discouraged even by Germany's unfortunate wine laws.

I became one of the first to learn these laws, not through any passion for jurisprudence but because I was writing an atlas while they were being framed. They were due to appear in 1971. My atlas, too; so my correspondence with the ministry in Mainz became hectic. I could hardly believe what they were telling me. The great majority of Germany's ancient vineyard names were being abolished. New names for new divisions and subdivisions of the vineyards were being invented, often bearing a suspicious resemblance to the historic names that were being swept away.

The traditional measures of quality and style were being bulldozed into a mere reading on a saccharometer. It was government gone mad, with no regard for the confused consumer, let alone the perfectionist producer. It was just populist vote-catching, levelling down to the thousands of small wine-growers who in many cases could have been better off planting potatoes. And it ruined the German wine industry.

When at one point I objected that all land was not equally apt for growing grapes, and that a thousand years of experience indicated the better bits clearly enough, I was howled down for being élitist. Land-owners who could have raised their voices seemed to me remarkably acquiescent. Even under the Revolution the French government never pretended that Château Lafite and Château La Pompe were of equal standing, that all that mattered was the sugar content of their grapes. In Germany it has taken thirty years for the principal quality producers, banded together as the Verband Deutsches Prädikatsweingüter, the VDP, the association of quality wine-producers, to win back the ground they lost in the 1970s. Some of the most dedicated, meanwhile, invented their own ways of doing things.

Bernhard Breuer of Rüdesheim was one of these. The purity of Rheingau wine was his passion: he longed to know how best to express the terroir (only the French have the term) of his family's vineyards. One winter evening he and his brother gave me a rather eccentric tasting of all the poor vintages from the family cellars, going back to the 1920s; orphan bottles that nobody wanted. It was a revelation to see how certain flavours, or at least a certain character, emerged time and again from behind unfortunate degrees of acidity, and even traces of rot.

There was, and is, a great lesson in this openness, this lack of pride. You could call it the grower's humility towards his land. It is the polar opposite of the race for high scores and gold medals that consumes the wine world today. Does it earn the farmer a living? Self-esteem, satisfaction and fascination, yes, but not necessarily a new Mercedes every year.

And yet Germany's wine country is hospitable and unproud. It is a valuable and charming tradition to keep open house. Surprising numbers of vintners hang out welcoming signs. *Weinstube* is the word. They need passing trade, so they offer a modest meal in their garden or by the fire-side. With it comes a list of the wines in the cellar. My spirits rise when I see eight or nine offered 'open', by the glass; and rise higher still if the lady of the house produces a turntable, a roundabout for the middle of the board with holes in it for eight or nine glasses.

You need a few friends to play. There is no better way to get gently fuddled and learn (or think you are learning) the lie of the land and the variety of its produce. The vintner, in his list, often supplies useful terms to start you off. This wine is *herbig*, meaning crisp and green; this one *fruchtig*, and the next *lieblig*, or charming. Except that they come in intriguing permutations and sprinkled with many more adjectives. In the Moselle and the Rheingau they are mostly Riesling. Nobody bothers, or should bother, with any other grape on this privileged soil. In the Palatinate and Rheinhessen, the broad stretch of farm land fronting the Rhine between the Palatinate and Rheingau, you will meet wines from Scheurebe (highly perfumed), Sylvaner (light, vegetal), Müller-Thurgau (a mongrel, soft and elder-scented), Grauburgunder (Pinot Gris: heady, even thick), various modern varieties with such names as Bacchus, and steadily more reds.

─────────────

Bernhard Breuer led the Rheingau towards dry wines. He had a kindred spirit in a man whose lineage embodied the long history of the region: Erwein the 29th Count Matushka, whose ancestors, the Greiffenclaus, had lived in the lofty keep of Schloss Vollrads for six hundred years. In the seventies Count Matushka took it upon himself to teach the world that Rheingau Riesling could make wines for every occasion and every dish. He invited great chefs to his castle to regale journalists. His menus were as ingenious as they were sumptuous. He made wines everywhere along the scale from very dry to extremely sweet. The result, sadly, was confusion. His peers in the other castles that line the Rhine were not so adventurous, or so conscientious. Matushka had to mortgage the ancient estate and eventually, when the bank turned on him, took his own life.

You can argue that in Germany, as anywhere else, a grower who really wants to know his land will not intervene, and doing nothing leads to dry wine. All, or most, of the grape sugar will ferment into alcohol. In any case there used to be no way of stopping it – even if the process could take a very long time. There is a chemical means of control: adding sulphur.

It has been known since Roman times, but scarcely used until impatient Dutch merchants invented the sulphurous 'Dutch match' to make wine stable for transport earlier in its life (take one match, light, and place in barrel). Before time became money, a big barrel of wine in a cold cellar sauntered its way to a stable state, burping occasionally as gas gathered in its depths; pickled, as it were, in its own acidity. When Thomas Jefferson stayed at the best inn in Frankfurt they were serving the wines of Hochheim, Rüdesheim, Johannisberg and Marcobrunn, the great vineyards of the Rheingau, of vintages stretching back sixty years – and still in their barrels. You could say Rhine wine was treated in rather the same way as sherry: a shocking concept to modern minds.

Indeed the ability to choose how sweet your wine is, to stop the fermentation at a chosen moment and keep it stopped with fermentable sugar still on board, is a 20th century development. Wine-makers used to be reluctant to talk about how it was done. Often the nose-prickling, cough-inducing smell of brimstone gave the game away.

What made it simple, clean and reliable was the invention of very fine filters by the firm of Seitz at Bad Kreuznach, a few kilometres south of the Rheingau on the River Nahe. Once you could filter yeast cells out of your wine there was no risk of fermentation bubbling on. Bottle it in a sterile bottle (not quite so straightforward) and it would remain exactly as you intended. At this point temptation crossed the wine-maker's path. Why not adjust the sweetness upwards? Why not keep some of the must in sterile conditions, as grape juice, and add it to the wine before you bottled it, thus combining the flavours of wine and fresh grapes? 'Süss-reserve' became the prop of vintners who found the old patient ways too trying for their nerves.

Worse, by then there was plenty of technology available to make vines produce twice, five times, ten times as much wine as before. A vine can produce a huge amount of liquid, but only a finite quantity of the elements that give it flavour (imagine making lemonade with one lemon and as much water as you want). German producers were more sorely tempted than most: they could so easily adjust the flavour. In the 19th century the best German vineyards produced something in the order of ten hectolitres per hectare. In the 20th some made a hundred, or even two.

Breuer, to come back to him, was not one of those, and nor were any of the members of the VDP. The restraints on production and discipline of definition (What is a Spätlese? How rich should an Auslese be?) that the wine laws liberalized to the point of absurdity were adopted voluntarily by VDP members and rigidly policed. The old distinction between better and worse vineyards was the one thing that was banned.

In the first three editions of my Wine Atlas all the German vineyards were tinted a uniform pink as though they were all equally good: a travesty of the truth. It took 23 years and countless discussions with the VDP and others to reach a near-consensus on a provisional (and of course unofficial) classification. In 1994 I was bold enough to distinguish, in tints of pink and purple, between ordinary vineyards, First Class vineyards and Great First Class vineyards, very much after the fashion of Burgundy with its Grands Crus and Premiers Crus. I don't claim the result was perfect or complete: I could not even start on areas where there was no track record of distinctive wines, however good their produce has subsequently become. The Pfalz in particular is full of them. The VDP has since battled on towards a full classification (they published a first shot in 2003) but meanwhile new government initiatives, categorizing certain wines as 'Classic' or 'Selected', have only made a jigsaw into a cat's cradle.

The Rheingau, largely animated by Breuer, took a different direction from other regions (not that any are identical) to reinstate the primacy of its dry wines. By 2001, after years of debate and adjustments, they had arrived at a concept of a First Growth, or Erste Gewächs, which must be dry, must satisfy all sorts of criteria, but has not much to do with a First Growth in anyone else's language. Bernhard Breuer died as his campaign came to a bruising conclusion. If none of this exactly helps you to enjoy, let alone understand, what Germany's incomparable vineyards offer today, I declare myself blameless.

As with all fine wines, the great pleasures come to those with patience. I look at the German wine-rack in my cellar: there are a few dusty bottles from the 1950s, made by families still recovering from the war, with no modern technology. 1953 and 1959 were two great sweet-wine vintages. Their top wines are fading but fascinating, like photographs of the time. One or two bottles of 1964 from the Moselle and Palatinate, kept only for sentiment now. A last bottle of a wonderful 1967 Rheingau Auslese: it was a year when edelfaule, the benign fungus, took over the last of the crop and turned it to cream. But the first vintage I bought in earnest, and kept with joy, was 1971.

What an irony that the greatest German vintage of our times (mine, anyway) coincided with the new laws that almost ruined German wine. It was a big, healthy, stress-free harvest with opportunities for the conscientious to make great wine at every level from Kabinett (until the new laws came in you could label any wine free of the artificial boost of sugar as 'Natur') to the rarest Trockenbeerenauslese – for which see the sticky pages of the Sweet section.

For thirty years the '71s kept pace with the rather similar Bordeaux vintage of 1970, also a huge success, which gave millions pleasure over many years. Today the idea that Rieslings and Cabernets have the same lifespan sounds bizarre. We have been sold the notion that German wines should be bottled and drunk almost as soon as possible – which is true of the mass-produced sugar-water most German cellars produced during the 1970s and 1980s (and 1990s too, I fear).

The bridge of Bernkastel from the steep slate slope of the Doktor vineyard. Only south slopes will ripen Riesling here, but no white wine is more delicately sumptuous.

You would expect a 1970 claret from a top château to be faded in colour thirty years on, its grape aromas replaced with more ethereally sweet ones derived from the earth and the cellar. (From the bottle, in reality, but I think of these elaborations on the original theme as deriving from the cellar where it has lain, feeding on itself, while governments come and go.) With German Rieslings, whether grown on the slate of the Moselle, the schist of the Rheingau, the sandstone of Nierstein in that small part of Rheinhessen that fronts the Rhine, or the volcanic soil of the Mittelhaardt, there is a comparable evolution. The colour darkens to gold and even orange (at least in sweeter wines), the crushed-grape character of Riesling disappears and scents from the soil emerge, mingled with honey and a unique smell that makes me think of filling-station forecourts. Australians, not beating about the bush, just call it 'petrol'. But Australian Rieslings are almost born with it; it takes over (at least in budget models) from year two or three. In Germany, in fine wines of fine years, a hint of forecourt begins to tease you at ten years or so and should never become full-frontal. I imagine the main difference is in summertime temperatures. California's Rieslings (the few that are left: California made good Riesling but couldn't sell it) have a suggestion, or more than that, of gasoline.

———

What did those German settlers think they were doing, planting Riesling from chilly Germany in Napa and the close-on-tropical Barossa Valley? Poor mutts, you might think; they weren't to know. They do now: the hills east and north of Barossa, Eden Valley and Clare Valley have fine-tuned their Rieslings to take on the Fatherland. You look at the brown hills, the sheep, the massive white-barked gum trees, the summer landscape when the only thing that stays green is a grape-vine, and you think

'What a plant.' What an instrument the Riesling is to sing in such different keys with the same lyrical voice.

I remember my first walk up to a vineyard called Steingarten, and my first taste of its wine. This was in 1972, on my first visit to the Barossa Valley. As we sweated up the stony hill we were totally exposed to South Australia sun. Colin Gramp, who took us, had cunningly concealed a cold bottle at the top. The wine was pale green, dry, its taste flickering between leaf and mineral. I probably said 'Not bad, Colin'; Australians appreciate a laconic limey. I didn't forget the hiding-the-bottle trick, either; it turns a promenade into a party every time.

Riesling is still a journey of discovery. For me the Clare Valley came next. Jeffrey Grosset's Polish Hill wines mature just as Moselles do, from spiky youth, where acidity is the main feature, to complexities of limes and honey and petrol and even Turkish Delight. His wife Stephanie runs a rival establishment in the same building with rival Rieslings (she calls them Mount Horrocks) which make a compelling comparison. Hers are (looking at my notes) gentler, more peachy. I was probably suffering from the sympathetic fallacy, or being sexist, or anthropomorphizing when I wrote that. One must be careful.

Stephanie Toole makes some of Australia's most persuasive Rieslings in cellars she shares with her husband Jeffrey Grosset in the Clare Valley, South Australia.

This soil-honey-oil equation can become extraordinarily teasing. Are you one of those who stops by a rose-bush and can't tear themselves away? Pick one, let the cool petals brush your lips as you breathe in the mixture of lemon and tea and talcum powder and xxxx that defies description. It always stays just out of reach.

I must not harp too much on the need to age these wines. They are, after all, so delectable when they have just been bottled. Subtle shadings are not clear in the blast of honeyed grape that greets you, but the pleasure prin-

ciple is. Then comes a period of clamming up, when for two, three or sometimes more years (the better the wine, unfortunately, the longer the interval) there is not a great deal to sniff. You can appreciate the electricity in the flavour, the pent-up energy, the balance of powers, but fulfilment is frustrated. This is when you drink the older vintages you have prudently put by.

I'm afraid you may not believe my answer to the question 'What is the oldest wine you have drunk?' 1540. Yes, fifteen: it was 424 years old when I gave the last glass its quietus. It was, naturally, a bottle with a history, bought at auction from the cellar of King Ludwig II of Bavaria

ABOVE
*There is one bottle left
of the 1540 Steinwein –
at a secret location
in Germany.*

ABOVE RIGHT
*The cask it lived in for
two hundred years is still
in the Residenz cellars
at Würzburg.*

who had inherited it from his forebears' cellars under their Residenz in Würzburg – the one with a Tiepolo ceiling over the stairs. Its history is exactly recorded. There are not many vintages like the one 24 years before Shakespeare was born. The next that looks at all statistically comparable is 2003.

Super-vintages in those days were celebrated with super-barrels. The one in which the 1540 lodged, at least for its second century of life, is still in the Residenz cellar. No doubt the King would have liked to have bottled it earlier had he had bottles, and if someone had invented the cork. It was eventually bottled in the early 1700s; was it perhaps considered too special to drink? It reached London in the hands of Rudy Nassauer, an importer of many good things, and appeared one morning in 1962 in his Mayfair shop for a dozen or so fortunates, of whom I was one. What was it like? Ancient Madeira, but less acid. The point was not so much its varietal character as its dogged grasp on life. It was most definitely alive, and that life had ticked over quietly for longer than the life of any creature (or do tortoises keep going this long?). After that there is a 255-year gap in my grasp of old vintages.

Does this make you eager to try the latest batch? Bavaria has only one wine region, where the River Main wanders through the far north, a long way from Munich. This is Franconia; its capital is the baroque city of Würzburg, and Frankenwein can still be something else. The outward sign is its bottle: squat, pot-bellied and unblushingly known as a goat's scrotum, *Bocksbeutel*. The wine-growing soil here is chalky clay, the same formation, or nearly, as in Chablis and Sancerre five hundred kilometres to the west. The grape that likes it best is the Sylvaner, looked down on elsewhere as a commoner. Riesling ripens reluctantly in clay, and in a continental climate. But in Franconia Sylvaner can make wine as clean, strong and appetizing as Chablis of a high order. At home I have kept bottles long enough for them to become the white wine equivalent of gamey: fifteen years or more. The capacious Weinstuben of Würzburg (the biggest are ancient charitable institutions) rarely offer, with their various sausages, anything more than two years old.

———————

Does the German wine tradition travel? The Riesling is a great traveller, but the German style is unique. It is so specific to the valley of the Rhine that its disciplines and distinctions stay at home. No other country or region plays so singularly on the sugar in its grapes. You can argue that none has to grapple with such a cool climate. Alsace is the oldest and biggest non-German proponent of the style, and Alsace has been in and out of Germany time and again in its history. On a clear day its vineyards can see the Rhine.

But Alsace is the sunniest region of France – or so the statistics say. The height of the mountains, the Vosges, on its western flank tucks its east-facing vineyards into a rain-shadow. This is golden-autumn country where the grapes reach levels of ripeness Germany's vintners rarely see. Riesling is their best grape; it hangs on to exciting levels of acidity even when it is sweet enough to make monstrously strong wine. Alsace vint-ners, though, are not content with one grape. Their insurance policy, and often their pride and joy, is the treacle-textured Pinot Gris and the least reticent of all white grapes, the Gewurztraminer. Also (less easy to understand) the Pinot Noir.

Enrolment in the Confrérie St-Etienne, the wine brotherhood of Alsace, involves drinking from a gargantuan tastevin.

Wine merchants are given to saying, and have been saying in my hearing for forty years, that Alsace is underestimated, is excellent value for money, is on the verge of a break-through to become as popular as burgundy. Not yet. Germany buys huge quantities of it. In France it is on every restaurant's wine list (and frequently in the bins of super-markets) as a recognisable purse-stretcher. In the Anglo-Saxon world it remains a speciality for initiates. The reason? My conjecture is that while there is a large amount of fair-to-middling quality there is only, as else-where, a small amount of the good stuff, and that identifying it is not easy. The majority is made by cooperatives (which in Alsace is no insult).

A dozen or so top producers are internationally known, there are a handful of stars, but few wine-lovers know their way around the villages, the tall bottle associates it with Germany, and it is far from clear from the label whether it will be dry or significantly sweet.

The wines have changed. The Alsace tradition is for dry wines with a fair, but not immoderate, charge of alcohol. Then in the 1960s and 1970s, led by the highly regarded house of Hugel (their yellow label is seen everywhere) ambitious vintners started to make sweet late-harvest wines. They were described as either 'Vendanges Tardives', literally Late Harvest (when the grapes were super-ripe) or, pushing to the limit, as 'sélection de grains nobles'. 'Noble berries' are shrivelled ones, the pick of the end of the crop, whether shrivelled into raisins by desiccation or shrivelled by *Botrytis*, the 'noble rot' – of which much more later. Vendanges Tardives are rich sweet wines suitable, in Alsace parlance, for foie gras. 'SGNs' have aspirations to be Château d'Yquem. Literally, on one occasion when Johnny Hugel, head of the firm, a gruff and beaming character saluted in every French restaurant on earth, invited journalists to lunch at the best-known restaurant in Alsace, L'Auberge de l'Ill. My memory of that bright spring day starts with the fact that one of the brother proprietors was half-way up a weeping willow when we arrived, arranging its branches. An eye for detail, I noted.

Johnny Hugel is on the right of the producer Marc Beyer, the vintner who is speaking, at a lunch at the Auberge de l'Ill in Alsace to discuss the rival merits of Alsace, Burgundy and Bordeaux.

I will skip over a menu that included indecent amounts of all that is richest in the notorious cuisine of Alsace, and wines from Burgundy to indicate that this was no parochial affair. The finale was a blood match: Hugel's finest SGN against a great vintage of Château d'Yquem. Whichever won on points (and I forget) this story really belongs in the Sweet section – and that is the point. The finest Alsatian wine was no longer a

table wine. Dry wines were relegated in favour of sweet. Not in every cellar, it must be said. Many would say that the regular star performer of Alsace is the house of Trimbach, known for steely dry Rieslings. There is a clear trend, though. When I asked the worthy Monsieur Muré (I have drunk his Clos Vorbourg for many years) why his Riesling seemed sweeter than before, he replied that it depends on the vintage.

That wouldn't wash in Burgundy. Chablis or Meursault with that sugar level would be sent back. In Alsace the important thing, says my correspondent, is to pick the grapes at the maximum ripeness and leave it to nature. Natural yeasts may not have the capacity to ferment all the sugar. If global warming is giving them riper grapes than their yeasts can cope with, would we have them interfere with nature? He makes it sound like a moral issue. Olivier Zind-Humbrecht of Turckheim is most vehement of all. His wine-making is as hands-off as his biodynamic cultivation is hands-on. He encourages every wine to become whatever is latent in its composition. Enthusiasts follow such makers wherever they lead.

Alsace wines are not for the flavour-shy. There still exists a café wine of no pronounced character under the name of Edelzwicker (Zwicker before ennoblement came its way). The faintly cabbagey Sylvaner (I love it) and the plain faint Pinot Blanc persist as minor themes. But all the emphasis is on the loud-voiced varieties. And certainly they do the trick, if you want to draw attention to your hospitality. Never underestimate the power of a tarte à l'oignon and a glass of Gewurztraminer. I am surprised, when I look back at my notebooks, how rarely I have deployed such a conclusive weapon. Except that in too many notes I have written 'too much alcohol'. In my book, if I am aware of the alcohol in the flavour, there is too much.

That there is no need for excess is shown by this note on a Gewurztraminer Réserve from the Clos des Capucins of Théo Faller, one of my favourite Alsace vintners. "Pale gold, smelling so strongly of roses (and grapefruit) that the pinky-mauve frou-frou of 'Columbia Climber' in a vase beside it was in direct competition. A lovely lightish interpretation, dry in character, delicate but tenacious, excellent with smoked eel."

As you have deduced, such wines as these – German Rieslings especially – take up a great deal of space in the Saling cellar. The rack on the left just inside the door is for the orphans, single bottles of interest, or wines that don't fit into one of my loose categories of regions and varieties. They stand on the table and on the floor in cardboard boxes, too. (Don't let anyone tell you that wine dies next day if the bottle is not lying down. In a cool and dampish cellar a good cork is in no danger of drying out in days, weeks, or a few months. Even in a warm kitchen, a week or so presents no risk.)

Psychologically it is important (to me, not them) that some wines are kept standing. Once a bottle is lying down on its side it looks installed, part of the décor, as though that was its fate, rather than to be opened and enjoyed. There is a population that has to be kept moving, not allowing me to go for the familiar. Old favourites are for entertaining: I like to be quite sure what I am giving our guests. The daily routine is living dangerously – or at least inquisitively.

A look at my kitchen tasting book jogs my memory. "A pretty poor substitute for lemonade," was my recent note on a Spanish white wine. "Everything I dislike: fat and heady with a bitter aftertaste," was one from Argentina. "Oak, limes; just modern wine. Could be from either hemisphere, or the moon." (Spain again.) "What happened to this famous [Chablis] house? Old and watery at five years!" "No wonder they oak the stuff. A hole rimmed with alcohol." (An Australian 'unwooded' Chardonnay.) A commentator's life is not all roses.

On the other hand "Really snappy, full of flavour, like a cross between Chablis and a Frankenwein. Fine texture and reasonable strength. V.g." That was a Grüner Veltliner from Langenlois, a stray from Austria reminding me that Grüner Veltliner is becoming a darling of the critics these days. I love a fresh peppery Veltliner, and sometimes a richer, more mature one; but I wish I got on better with Austrian wines in general. They have all the fashionable attributes of minerality, 'focus', crystalline purity and 'pure varietal fruit' – and another appeal, too: new oak rarely comes near them. Analytically I can see they are highly impressive. Need they be so hard-hitting, though? They taste like the expressive word they use in the Wachau for a super-ripe wine: *Smaragd*. To me the concentration that comes with small crops and very ripe grapes can be a mixed blessing – best mixed, I sometimes think, with a drop of water. It depends on whether you are a sipper or, like me, a swallower. I have the same problem with Austrian Rieslings: perfectionist selection can make them, however steely and polished, just too explosive for my taste. Blockbusters? Heading that way.

It sounds absurd, but I do sometimes find wine-makers can try too hard. My frivolous nature demands that wines be easy to drink, and above all tempt you on to the next glass. Austria has transformed itself in twenty years from the country with the least, rather than lowest, reputation in Europe to a model held up for the others – including the Germans. We are asked to forget the generally pretty slapdash wines we drank in euphoric carelessness under the arbours of the Viennese suburbs.

Wine has to be bottled these days even to be trusted not to harm you. The vigneron's self-respect demands that it be entered in competitions. 'It was all an illusion,' the critics tell us, 'that stuff you used to drink from the barrel in the corner was rotgut.' The consequence? We pay five times as much for wine made with infinite precautions – and somehow miss the joy. You needed no precautions back then; you just asked for a glass of what the others were drinking. Vienna, but also Prague, of all unlikely places, brings me memories of vivid wines, a little cloudy and gassy, juicy with unfermented sugar and unadjusted acidity. Exciting.

Wines like this remind me of a wine-hunt for the Sunday Times Wine Club during the Cold War. Tim Bleach, the Club's wine-buyer, had had such success in Bulgaria that we couldn't find enough lorries to bring the Cabernet over. Drivers were not keen on the paper-work at five frontiers between Bulgaria and England. Eventually we got in touch with drivers coming home from taking bathrooms out to Arabia and persuaded them to divert to Sofia. Tim and I were asked by the Bulgarian government to help with its primitive system of appellations. The first Controliran tasting, I remember, was chaos.

Tim Bleach was buyer for the Wine Club when he and I tasted our way round Eastern Europe. This was a line-up of Austrian wines.

On one of these trips we had a rendezvous, Tim and I, in Bratislava; he from Sofia and I from Budapest. We stayed at a hotel full of grey suits and waited for our official escort. No-one went anywhere without a minder. Midday next day and no sign of him. We set out in my Austrian car with no clear idea of where we would find wine and no word of the language. Vineyards, we told ourselves, are usually a pretty clear indicator.

We discovered a new, broad and entirely deserted road heading west into Moravia. For Soviet armoured divisions, we speculated, on their way to Germany. When we saw vines we turned off, and eventually stopped at a village called Znojmo; pleasant, tidy and with not so much as a café or a shop. We stopped the only person we saw and tried our German. No comprehension, but an idea, gestures and smiles. We passed the afternoon in her sunny sitting room listening to Schubert and eating cake, waiting for … the village schoolmaster, it turned out, whose French was better than our German. His mother was secretary of the local wine cooperative. Of course we could visit it – and the Sauvignon Blanc was dry, scented and worth the trip. Vladimir still updates me on what has become a successful little region.

Little did I think that within a few years one of Germany's greatest vintners would be working in Slovakia, on the estate restored to his wife's family after the Communist years, to make a Riesling to partner if not challenge his great Moselle. Egon Müller takes Château Belá almost as seriously as his Scharzhofberg. We shall see.

————————

German-style wines of course are not the only ones to drink in the garden. Nor are all German wines, or Rieslings, good garden wines. I have admitted my gardening obsession: the apple tree is not the only tippling corner. There is the table by the swimming pool (under another apple tree), the shady summer-house overlooking the water garden or the Temple of Pisces. Experience has taught me that, to do their stuff alfresco, wines need to fit into the outdoor mind-set. They should not be too subtle, or too strong. Nor should they be too serious. Somehow the garden is never the place to serve your best lovingly decanted bottle of claret, or to sip old vintage port. But then more frivolous wines can blossom into something beyond your expectations as you sit quietly at the end of the day, among your flowers, under your favourite tree.

Chablis

IT HARDLY SOUNDS a resounding encomium to be the default wine, the no-brainer that fits in with almost any situation, friend, dish, time of day and day of year. But Chablis is that. Chablis is also my favourite white wine, the wine I buy and drink most of for pleasure and out of interest. The Chablis rack in my cellar (far end on the left) has more traffic than almost any. Can I say why? Because it is the natural partner for the fish and shellfish I love, and because it works supremely well as a drink. To say it has the essential qualities of water sounds a pretty back-handed compliment, too, but just as the cool volume of water when you swallow leaves nothing to be desired, so the stony freshness, the flinty, faintly sour fluidity of good Chablis has an elemental completeness. Sweeter? Absurd. Stronger, oak-seasoned, drier, more aromatic? All absurd. Chablis, I sometimes think, was sent down to earth as a model for all wine-makers to imitate.

Which of course they did. For generations, any dry white wine looking for recognition was simply labelled Chablis – in California or Australia, Spain or Bulgaria. They never came close, of course: wrong country, wrong grapes, wrong vineyards. In due course they planted the right grape, the Chardonnay, but followed a different model. The Chablis flavour still eluded them. Meursault was an easier target. Recipe: Chardonnay, nice and ripe; ferment, or age in, or at least flavour with, oak. *Et voilà*. There is an area of Australia, California and South America as big as Burgundy earning a nice living by it.

Not that all Chablis does honour to the name, by any means. Its enormous, seemingly effortless, popularity puts plenty of temptations in its producers' paths. The area of northern Burgundy blessed with the appellation has expanded in thirty years from 730 hectares to over 4,300. It has not been indiscriminate: the expansion has been on land geologically related to the original, if not identical: all on the calcareous clay of ancient seabeds, molluscs often still visible. And before it was destroyed by phylloxera, the region's vineyard was bigger by far. Now it is compromised, like almost all Europe's greatest vineyards, as much by lack of labour as by lack of the right soil. Most Chablis today is harvested by mechanical monsters that bring in every grape, good or bad, ripe or unripe, healthy or rotten. But so is most champagne, and we are happy. I am not sure whether the base level of quality suffers or not. The monsters' owners argue that the ability to start picking at a moment's notice, or to stop for rain to clear, is as important as selecting the bunches – and that sorting can be done back at the cellar before the grapes are crushed. The others, of course, argue that nothing beats hand-picking. It is certainly the way the best wines are made.

The euphony of a name is important. Would Chablis be asked for everywhere if it were called Pernand-Vergelesses? The two pretty syllables do have another meaning, I was surprised to learn, in the aftermath of the tempest that destroyed trees in most of France in 1990. *Un chablis* is the forester's term for the utter confusion in a wood after a storm: trees uprooted, trees broken in half, trunks lying at all angles. Shambles, perhaps, in English; certainly not a cool glass of wine.

Not only euphonious, but simple: all Chablis is called Chablis; the superior vineyards are labelled Premier Cru and the best Grand Cru.

Harvesting machines are now the norm in most of the world's vineyards. In such regions as Chablis they are controversial: hand-picked is more expensive. How much do customers care?

The three are tastably different, age in different ways and have different destinies. Crucial, of course, is the producer's name, a universal problem, but in Chablis perhaps less so than in most regions, and nothing like so fraught as in the Côte d'Or. Chablis has a highly competent cooperative cellar that sorts the wheat from the chaff among the less professional growers. Its name, La Chablisienne, is seen on bottles at all levels, including the top. It all sounds, and is, a stress-free proposition compared with the bunkers and water hazards on most of the world's wine-courses. Without great rubbish-strewn depths, then, is it also free of inspiring heights? That tends to be the world's assumption. The most expensive Chablis is less than half the price of a Montrachet of any kidney. Is this a fair valuation?

Not in my book. I have memories of, or notes on, hundreds of bottles that at the time called for a memorial, or at least an attempted description. The oldest was 44 years old when I drank it, a 1926 bottled by Avery's of Bristol in half-bottles of heavy glass the colour they call *feuilles mortes*, dead leaves; green with a hint of brown. Half-bottles of Chablis that old would have been disposed of by most wine merchants, but Ronald Avery knew the value, opened one for me and then sold me a case. It was, I am ashamed to say, too good to share. We lived in a little London house then. The two memories come back together with total clarity: the singular sumptuous taste of this Chablis-sherry, with all its flinty fruit intact but sherried to a taste of toast and a creamy texture, and the summer nights, the open window to the garden, my green-striped chair and my crossed legs, the book on my lap, my white shirt, and my feeling of guilt, drinking it alone.

No-one refills old wine bottles any more, let alone washes them by hand as they did in Chablis in the 1960s.

Here is a more recent note, for Chablis Premier Cru Les Beauroys 2000 from Pascal Bouchard. "The colour of straw with a hint of green. Nose faint and mild at first, the first sip round and easy, then delicately sour as it fills the palate with flavours of green and gold plums. There are minerals in its sugar-free flow. It opened up as it warmed in the glass; at its best after dinner." This is typical Chablis behaviour, especially for a Premier Cru. It is slow-release wine. Served restaurant-style from an ice bucket, it never gets past the faint and mild stage. No wonder so many prefer the hard-to-miss Sauvignon Blanc.

This word 'sour': I have to get it out of my system – or into yours. It could hardly have a worse press. The Moët-Hachette International Wine Dictionary defines it as "smelling of vinegar, volatile," and so do others. How do you describe, then, the flavour of sour cream, which is both less than acid, and more? The sourness in Chablis reminds me of the turning, curdling taste of cream or cheese, a very different thing from vinegar, and in the context as vital as lemon on oysters.

And here is another Premier Cru of 2000, Montée de Tonnerre from Louis Michel. "Just about a gold standard in fine very light green high-intensity Chablis. Even better uncool and opened up at the end of dinner than crisp and pebbly at the beginning." Of the same wine from the 1990 vintage, at the same time, I wrote: "Still palest lemon. Fresh, really spring-like at first sniff, then sour minerals (flints give the right idea) and apples. Also lemons, or maybe limes. Very dry and somehow profoundly light (or vice versa) and exceptionally long." That one was just on the wane. Somewhere in between three years and thirteen, then, the Montée de Tonnerre was giving everything it had. But here comes a Grand Cru, Les Grenouilles, again from Louis Michel but 25 years old, the 1976 vintage in 2001. "Uncannily pale, rich on top but with bare rock below, like a river running over stones. Long-simmered greengages and honey, almost like a phantom Sauternes. How can it be so supremely in balance? And so *long*?"

Why am I suddenly quoting so many laborious descriptions? Because good Chablis is the perfect example of my favourite axiom: great wines don't make statements, they pose questions. To end with an exclamation mark is easy; with a question mark, perhaps not more difficult, but far more interesting. To me, it is elusive flavour that most needs pinning down with words. It is important to add, though, that any account of a mature wine comes with a health warning. Everything depends on where the bottle has been kept, and how transported. And this seems to apply with double force in the USA.

I was once on a book-tour in New York with a publicist so persuasive that the New York Daily News (baseball was more its line of country) sent a reporter to interview me in my hotel, the stately St Regis on Fifth Avenue and East 55th Street (publishers' budgets seem to have shrunk since then). "Tell me all about wine," said this reporter. I called room service for something that would make a clear impression: a bottle of Gallo Chablis Blanc from California and another of the best authentic Chablis on the list, a two-year-old Grand Cru Les Clos. I showed the reporter how to open the bottles, pour, and smell the wine before tasting it. The first sniff told me I was in trouble. The Gallo wine was in perfect condition. It was nothing remotely like Chablis, but you could drink it.

The Grand Cru, at seven times the price, was brown-tinged, smelly, flat – completely oxidized. But how many customers, I wondered, would know that this ditchwater was a travesty and how many would decide not to bother with French Chablis again?

Chablis the region is low-key wine country. It has no famous sights, no magnificent cellars, no châteaux worth the name, one good restaurant; not a great deal to remember compared with Beaune and the Côte d'Or. Scenically it is a continuation of the Aube, which is a continuation of Champagne. Its soil is the same: pale clay. Its buildings are grey limestone. Grey plays a large part in the picture, the sky quite often included. When I drive on south to what most people think of as Burgundy proper, through green valleys inhabited only by cows, it is like putting on warmer-tinted glasses. Down there the landscape glows. The same distance southwest, on the other hand, Sancerre is painted in the same greys. You are still on the same prehistoric seabed.

There is not much that is glamorous about Chablis: just plain bourgeois enjoyment.

On the open plateaux that surround Chablis, blocks of vines suddenly cut into cornland. Is this where the Portlandian, or the Kimmeridgian limestone starts? Portland in Dorset on the English south coast gave its name to this geological formation – and the grey dignity of its stone to St Paul's cathedral. Kimmeridge is the coastal village with the most obviously oyster-derived stone. You can count their little shells. Happily millennia of breeding have enlarged them to a size worth eating. The context is outrageously apt: wine for oysters growing on oyster ancestors.

In the little Chablis villages of Fontenay and Fleys and Béru and Préhy there is little but tractor traffic. Chablis town is adopting airs, but all my early memories there are of a hotel that could have represented northern France in any *concours* of discomfort. How well I remember those creaky bedsprings, that patch of linoleum in the corner of the room where the bidet was barely screened, those dress-fabric curtains, that memory-laden mixture of Gauloises and Eau de Javel, cigarettes and bleach, in the unheated hall.

Past the glass door in the dining room, though, the priorities were made clear. It was as warm and perfumed as a fresh baguette. There was the butter-and-parsley smell of cooking snails, a deeper note of butter browning in another pan, a whiff that made you look under the pink napkin at the stone-coloured cheeses. *Luxe, calme et volupté.* I shall deploy this delicious phrase here, though I could have kept it for a more obvious object. Here it means comfort, calm and a sense of the sensuous; a feeling that nothing will be allowed to get in the way of carnal enjoyment. In the dining room, that is.

Now you can stay at a luxury hotel, les Clos, where the bathrooms are warm, where a log fire greets you in the hall, where the wine list weighs a kilo and the chef-proprietor speaks English. I am absurd to have the slightest regret, I suppose.

If there is a showplace in town it is l'Obédiencerie, (it sounds like a monastic house of correction; perhaps it was) just behind the church. Michel Laroche, a principal producer who is also, as they say, *très businessman*, has converted this survivor of Chablis' gothic past into cellars, offices and a museum of the way Chablis once made wine. Why should I suppress the memory of the grilled oysters he served on my first visit? Only a little butter, and a good shaving of shallot, I remember. The wine (in a magnum, as Chablis should be: I'll come to that) was Les Blanchots, a Grand Cru in which Laroche has some ancient vines; and the vintage 1973. At ten years old it was prime; crying out for oysters.

Can it take all this to squeeze a grape? Medieval technology in Chablis.

Laroche offered to work his medieval press for me to film for television. Burgundy still has many such engines, but few proprietors who are game to set them going. It is astonishing to see to what lengths their ancestors would go to get the last drop out of a grape. I am sure you have seen the model, it varies little in historical pictures of the vintage from anywhere. The biggest available tree trunk, roughly squared, is the weight and the lever. In this case its free end (the other is tethered) is pierced with a massive wooden screw turned by a capstan. The grapes, in complete bunches, uncrushed, are piled high on the floor below the screw and covered with boards. Then away go the capstaneers, leaning on their bars like sailors. The screw, unlubricated, lets out fearsome groans and explosive cracks as it brings the tree trunk down. Juice trickles, then flows (it never really pours) from the grapes into a channel in the floor. Then they unwind the screw, restack the grapes and start again. It seems impossibly laborious – and, you ask, what did people do who had no wine-press, no tree trunks and no money?

The stainless steel equivalent is much less fun. The press is a horizontal drum the size of a good-sized engine of the days when trains had boilers. The grapes, pre-crushed, pour in through a lid. Earlier models work by pushing two pistons together, one from each end, while the whole affair slowly revolves. Intermittently the pistons draw back and a system of steel chains breaks up the caked pulp, releasing more juice through slatted sides into the gulley beneath. Gentler as well as more efficient, though, is the pneumatic or air-bag press, another revolving cylinder, but with a long black bladder inside. The bladder is empty when the grapes go in. As it inflates it squeezes them against the pierced sides of the drum. There is nothing abrasive to crush the pips and stalks.

The vast majority of Chablis ferments in *inox*, as the French call stainless steel; tall tanks with water-jackets to warm them up or cool them down. Most of it stays in steel until it is bottled, in the summer after the vintage or the summer after that. The old guard use old oak, both for fermentation and for the vital period of *élevage*; either barrels (the classic Chablis *feuillette* is the smallest used in France, holding a mere 135 litres; the *pièce* of the Côte d'Or holds 228) or tubby old *foudres* holding up to four barrels-worth. A few challenge convention by using new oak.

Why would you use new oak, with its unmistakable smell, for Chablis, whose character is all about flint and green fruit and hayfields and a whiff of lemon? Oak is what the Montrachets and Meursaults smell of: it is the trade mark of the Côte d'Or. Nobody would, is the answer, for the lightweight wines of run-of-the-mill vineyards, Chablis Villages. But concentrated, tightly wound wines, Grands Crus if not Premiers Crus, can not only absorb and dominate the flavour of oak (its users argue) but can also profitably add it to their structure and character.

Oak is the ideal physical container: it allows a slow exchange of wine and oxygen, even through planks as thick as your thumb. The argument is about what flavours it might add, and using old seasoned barrels with no flavour left is the solution. There are small cellars still lined with old *foudres*, glossy and black with time. Cleaning them perfectly is not easy, there are obvious arguments about their obsolescence. Is it their microflora, their porosity or their neutrality as inert containers that seems to condition their contents at least as well as steel? Or is it perhaps that growers who take such trouble to defend tradition have their hearts in the right place?

I remember one cellar visit years ago in a heat-wave, when the tasting-glasses in the cellar were beaded with condensation. The tradition here is to use small round *ballons*, as it is in the Côte d'Or. I used a photograph of one sitting on the bung of a black barrel in my first Wine Atlas. The light from the cellar door caught its green depths through the dewy beads and made readers, they told me, react as I had done. The cold, plummy, pebbly hay-meadow taste was absorbed by your eyes and appeared miraculously in your mouth. More often, though, I have come on cold winter days when you group round the barrels stamping your feet. In these crystalline conditions every nuance of the cold wine is hard-etched without flattery.

So enthralled was I at one such session (it was with Michel Laroche in 1988) that I ordered a whole barrel – for myself. Not many *feuillettes* leave Chablis full these days, I fancy, when almost all wine is bottled where it is made. The rationale is presumably authenticity, since bottling wine is not a skill it takes too long to learn. I still have the chubby little cask of pale oak empty in the cellar as a souvenir, not only of a most pleasant wine (not a great vintage, '87, and I paid a modest price) but of a hilarious evening. We dressed the cellar with vine-branches, set up a table with oysters and bread and ham and cheese, and let our friends take turns at the spigot. We bottled half of it in magnums, a better measure than bottles, to my mind, for such a versatile and sociable wine. If there are four people at table and one wine is to last the whole meal, you would need at least two bottles. A magnum is not only more handsome; its wine keeps in good condition for longer and eventually, in my experience, reaches greater perfection.

BELOW &
BELOW RIGHT
*The little Chablis barrel,
the* feuillette, *is ideal
for home bottling.*

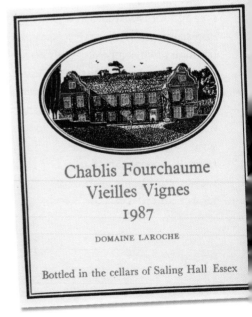

Chablis Fourchaume
Vieilles Vignes
1987

DOMAINE LAROCHE

Bottled in the cellars of Saling Hall Essex

Tasting convention in Chablis is the same as in the rest of Burgundy. You get your eye in with the new wine either at 'Villages' level (or with the junior appellation, Petit Chablis), then taste wine of the same rank one year older. Then you move on to Chablis Premiers Crus (most good growers have several different plots) to finish with a Grand Cru, if any – and if you are lucky, an older bottle to drink over the parting reminiscences. You soon discover what is on your host's mind. In spring, frost is never far from it. It can be devastating here. In the 1950s it almost put paid to the whole notion of Chablis. Now every vineyard is littered with little black stoves; on a clear night their flames flicker all around and their smoke hangs like fog between the wires. The high-tech solution is water, sprayed on from pressure nozzles as the temperature falls to zero to form a freezing protective film around the vulnerable new shoots. They can withstand zero, but no lower.

If it is not frost, it is some controversy: new plantings on the wrong soil, machine-harvesting, using new barrels and, of course, price. What should Chablis cost? Its name makes it a frequent supermarket loss-leader, which creates expectations that it should be cheap. If it is, it will also be pretty thin in flavour. Yet even thin Chablis is often a good and typical drink. Which makes the wild-beast roar of a Premier or Grand Cru wine from a really uncompromising perfectionist almost alarming. I once sent back a Premier Cru from one of these, Jean-Marie Raveneau, or at least asked the sommelier if it smelled strange to him, too. It was cheese I thought I smelled, a dairy character with a herbal note as preface to a mouthful of almost painful intensity. "But isn't it wonderful?" he said. It became wonderful when we sipped it with scallops and endives in a creamy cheese sauce, and better still when it had lost its chill and the cheese board had arrived. Cheese is an unexpected aroma in Chablis (though always an excellent partner).

The affinity of Chablis for shellfish is one of the truisms of the table. There is no point in originality when something works so well. The iodine element in oysters finds its echo, and the sweetness of prawns its antiphon. But at the end of the meal cheese can sometimes pair off with Chablis equally well. There is still work for poets to do. That wine from Raveneau: in the end I pinned it down to orange blossom, spring weeds and bonfire smoke, with a hint of almonds and nail-varnish. Does it sound undrinkable? That's the problem with words.

The Golden Drop

HE TWO FACES of Europe will never become one: the northern and the southern, the cool and the warm, the strict and the easy-going. It is only a morning's drive from Chablis to Meursault, but the two are the corresponding Janus faces of Chardonnay. Somebody brought up on the stony purity of Chablis sniffs something like corruption in the golden flavours of the Côte d'Or.

My brother purrs with delight when I give him a mature Meursault. Once he quoted Rupert Brooke's poem about Grantchester, its old vicarage and everything sensuous: "To smell the thrilling-sweet and rotten /Unforgettable, unforgotten /River-smell ...." No, if Meursault smells like a river something is seriously wrong, but thrilling sweet and rotten comes close to the decadent appeal of great white burgundy as it grows old – and indeed great red burgundy, too.

To be provocative one could argue that red and white burgundy are two sides of the same coin. That they have more in common than, say, red burgundy and red bordeaux. Burgundy, in this argument, falls just short of being a full-on red wine, lacking the deep structural tannins of a Cabernet. Pinot Noir makes white wine in Champagne, whose essence is the two burgundy grapes blended together. In Meursault they grow both grapes, calling some of their red wines Volnay. Suppose they blended them. If two and two make five in Champagne, why would they make only three in the Côte d'Or?

If red burgundy could be called an androgynous red wine, white burgundy is something more than any other white. It fills a space in the wine list that no other wine precisely fits – except other Chardonnays in the same mould. Happily it is a mould that produces passable likenesses with relative ease, and spitting ones excitingly often – galling to the owners of the great original, perhaps, but a glorious boon to the rest of us. The discovery is so recent that I still have proto-types in my cellar from California in the 1970s. Few people, it is true, keep a white wine for thirty years, but these are moments of history.

How do I define this mould? Chardonnay is not one of the aromatic grapes with a give-away smell. The distinctive smell of Chablis seems to be more a product of the place than the grape. Young, the grape may make you think of apples, but more for lack of any other peg than because of a real resemblance. A blank, then? More of a hand-some, fine-grained, just-creamy canvas promis-ingly stretched on a stout frame. When good quality Chardonnay is young, you feel it as much as you taste it. Texture means substance. Like any vine it can be overcropped to produce watery wine, but bearing a limited crop it puts more 'extract' in its juice than most. Extract is, along with alcohol, sugar and acidity, what gives you the feeling you have wine in your mouth.

If anything is surprising about Chardonnay it is that, until recently, so few people grew it. Far from being difficult, it is the lazy wine-grower's friend: healthy, reliable and generous. Yet only Burgundy and Champagne had consider-able plantations, and in the Côte d'Or it is very much the junior partner to Pinot Noir, with less than twenty per cent of the vineyards. Why the restraint? Because it is only in our times that local loyalties have been cast aside and grape varieties been seen as brands in their own right.

Home-grown Chardonnay. Ripe, the grapes become translucent. Few varieties are easier to grow.

The model for Chardonnay to emulate could hardly be more obvious. The wine country you see when you close your eyes and dream is Burgundy's Golden Slope, or something close. Do you see neat parcels of close-spaced vines like little hedges? Do they face, at different tilts, down a long incline topped with woods? Are there random stretches of dry walls in honey-grey stone? Are there villages on the lower ground, more honey-grey stone clustered round a church with a grey slate steeple? You have been there, at least in dreams – and so has everyone who has travelled up or down France's main north–south artery.

One of these stone-walled fields is Le Montrachet. Montrachet, by common accord over several centuries, makes the world's greatest white wine. Which is it? Even when you find the two villages that bear its name, Puligny and Chassagne, you are left looking for the gates and guardians that signal celebrity. Even for a signpost. Then you see two tourists mooching by a little stone archway halfway up the slope. They have found it: France's most celebrated vineyard, indistinguishable from a whole hillside of similar patches, whose walls could do with mending and roadside grass with cutting. The golden grapes from here (Chardonnay does turn gold, gold with a gleam of green, when it ripens) make wine with an almost shocking resonance, a sappy strength of savour that the other fields can only envy. Why? The answer is a long one, full of caveats and provisos, geology and hydrography and hours of sunshine. More to the point is the demonstration, Burgundy's party piece for the privileged, when one of the growers with a stake in these fabulous fields sets out their wares.

Not much to show for such a place of pilgrimage: the arch that marks Le Montrachet.

You, a stranger, cannot buy Burgundy. If you wait long enough, a Bordeaux château, even a First Growth, might come on the market. Land in Burgundy stays in the family. Dynasties roll on, marriages between them complicate and blur the picture, occasionally a neighbour negotiates a lease or quietly buys a parcel. Once in a blue moon a local (always a local) tycoon takes over an estate. But you and I are on the outside, looking in, at families who are proud to be *paysans* of their unique *pays*.

When I first stood in a cellar in Burgundy, glass in hand, while the grower went from barrel to barrel with his pipette bringing me samples of nine different white wines, I was convinced that he had deliberately put them in order of quality and, naturally, price. There was a clear enough crescendo from a simple light wine through gathering themes of sun, fruit and warmth, stone and steel, earth and oak to see the performance as a deliberate climb up a ladder of ripeness and concentration. Clever fellow, I thought. There's quality control for you.

It was not him, though; it was the soil that was doing it. And this is where the relation of man and terroir becomes almost mystical. Different plots make different wines. The plots exist only because they have been marked out, distinguished and named by their cultivators. But how did their proprietors know where to draw the lines? Was it really a process of trial and error and endless attentive tasting, vintage after vintage, down the generations? Of conclusive discussion with neighbours and rivals, too? Did their experiments allow quite different distinctions: say all the grapes from higher or lower, or further north or south along the hill? Did a parcel get picked out because it ripened earlier or later, or the ground was drier or stonier, or had a browner or a whiter cast? All these things, maybe; but how many combinations is that? Perhaps all we need to know

No vineyards are more precisely delineated than those of the Côte d'Or. Every parcel has a name, a character and a value.

is that – with the strong proviso that the grower is up to it – the distinctions hold good. The wines are consistently different. Then, if you like, you can start awarding medals. Wouldn't it be marvellous to discover that you liked the least popular? What an economy that would be. Curiously, though, as every tasting in a good cellar shows, the crescendo effect is provided by nature. There is some message, some transmission of energy (that's what I believe it is) in the wines from the best plots (the nearer to Montrachet the better) that plays on the same string in us all.

You would think that such fine-tuning would make a proprietor almost nervous of his soil. Anything that changes it would surely put out the whole elaborate calculation. Many, to their shame, are downright cavalier, dosing it with fertilizer and herbicide and fungicide as though it were what horticulturists call 'a neutral substrate'. Now the mood, though, is swinging the other way; *lutte raisonnée* (a 'rational battle') is what most growers say they wage against pests and diseases. More and more declare themselves and their practices 'organic'.

A few admit to mystical urges and practise 'biodynamism'. Anne-Claude Leflaive is one of these, and the inheritor of a domaine among the finest in the Montrachets. The Leflaive cellar should be the place to taste the parcels of Puligny at their purest. She herself has the aura of an abbess, keen-featured and prematurely white-haired, and her cellar the earnest austerity of a dairy. If the land is allowed to speak in its most natural, unforced voice; does it say what you expect?

There is land even in the best Burgundy villages that is geologically beyond the pale: usually the lowest land where the slope peters out into the plain. Bourgogne Blanc is the only appellation it can claim. At an early tasting of the 2002 vintage Leflaive's Bourgogne Blanc was pale, green-smoky, limpid and lemon-sharp, pungent without richness. Charcuterie, I thought, was what it needed.

The move onto the village terroir, where the limestone begins, gives the appellation Puligny-Montrachet. Immediately the wine has a sense of coming from somewhere; no more greenness, something more like a yellow plum with a faint trace of nut. The next glass to taste is a Premier Cru from the heart of the slope going towards Meursault: Clavoillons. The new elements are honey and a denser texture. I think the reminder of honeysuckle in the smell comes from the barrel, but this is not remotely oaky. Evidently it wasn't in a new barrel, or not for long.

A move sideways next, to Leflaive's new Meursault vineyard, under the donkey's back. At least that is its name: Sous le Dos d'Ane, a Premier Cru at Blagny, high on the southern Meursault hill. There is not as much difference from Puligny as I expect. It is broader and more grainy, as it were open-pored, but still tight (there's a contradiction) and lively. Now to the parcels of Puligny Premiers Crus that are the special pride of this house: Les Folatières, Les Combettes and Les Pucelles.

The first I find smothered in oak; intense, dry, unsilky. "More finesse," says Anne-Claude, where I might have said "Less flavour." The second is ravishing: all silk, delicately smoky with oak, so finely balanced that I am mesmerized by the retreating flavours. The third has more horse-power but less charm; high-impact, intense, complex, lemony and long. To keep even longer but, I fancy, an even finer wine.

There are three Montrachet cousins, as it were: Bienvenues-, Bâtard- and Chevalier-, each hyphenated to Montrachet. The appellations of Burgundy are a work of art in their own right: never were so many shades of rank and meaning packed into so few words. At two, or even four, years old these are still works in progress; ten is the age to start drinking them. Bienvenues smells honeyed and bosomy, then bites. Bâtard flashes a green-gold light. Why do fine white wines contain chlorophyll? No answer, but it is always a good sign. "Silky, sulky, sour," is what I wrote in my notes, inebriated with words I fear. What are "cross-currents of energy"? A switchboard? Energy, though, is the point: the quality that all good wines possess, and a few to an electrical degree. When you meet them, greatness is only a matter of time, but for now their future flavours are stifled in a silk cocoon.

There is no doubt about the differences that motivate these metaphors – only about whether the metaphors convey them. There is no doubt about the fields: all visible from the village, all within a fifteen-minute walk. But my head still hurts when I try to understand the relationships – let alone their ramifications – when a bottle of Chevalier is worth three times more than a bottle of Clavoillons. I can't blame anyone who finds the whole business too nerve-racking. Are Burgundians all neurotics? They are certainly the only farmers in the world who have turned the most intimate details of their agriculture into a judico-cultural monument. Is it their fault if it is discussed with as much passion as a production at Bayreuth? The cynic can't help asking – especially in a restaurant after an expensive disappointment – who benefits?

Someone has to do it: Bill Baker, glass, and spittoon are daily companions, discriminating for England among the world's finest wines.

There is no getting away from terroir in Burgundy. It explains the landscape, the culture, the economy, the social structure – even the folklore. In Puligny it seems mysterious; on the hill of Corton, on the other hand, it stares you in the face. I once walked up this prominent pudding-shaped hill with the Professor of Geology at Dijon University, the genial Noël Leneuf. From the south the hill looks round, with the village of Corton to the right, then the plain, and to the left a cleft in the Côte and the village of Pernand-Vergelesses. The top is a beret of thick scrubby woods. Leneuf produced his geology kit: a penknife and a plastic bottle. Half-way up he picked up a stone and gave it a squirt from the bottle: hydrochloric acid. The liquid fizzed in reaction. "Hard limestone," he said. "And this," (scraping with his knife in the ground) "is the limestone clay that Chardonnay loves."

This clay and this abrupt hill, facing southwest, out of alignment with the Côte, give Corton-Charlemagne a character of its own. Rather than fine and penetrating with fruity acidity like a Puligny, or mild and mealy like Meursault, the hill produces something austere and flinty, almost burly in youth, certainly tongue-tied. Some call it the Chablis of the Côte d'Or: Grand Cru Chablis, that is. Like a great Chablis it can enter a charm-free period and stay there for six, seven, maybe ten years. Even when it emerges, 'charm' is hardly the word for such a dense, dry, less fruity than mineral puzzle of a wine.

There are two principal producers of Corton-Charlemagne: the négociant Louis Latour and the domaine Bonneau du Martray. Are there any more ancient estates in Europe? The Bonneau land, its boundaries unchanged, was given to the church by Charlemagne in the year 775. Jean-Charles Le Bault de la Morinière was an architect when in 1994 he inherited it from his parents. It had been in the family for so long that generations (and this is not unknown among owners of even the greatest properties) had taken it for granted. But twenty-five acres makes a lot of bottles. Corton-Charlemagne is one of the biggest Grands Crus and the Martray estate is the biggest holding of a single Grand Cru in Burgundy. In Jean-Charles' father's time (not any more, I hasten to add) selling so much wine was a problem. I thought perhaps I could help.

At that time I was often in Japan working as a consultant to Jardine, one of the great far eastern trading houses. Nightclubs are an unavoidable part of a visitor's life. You squeeze into a lift to take you to a dark and noisy room where you are squeezed between Russian girls in fishnet stockings baying for champagne. Regular clients have bottles of Cognac and Scotch with their names on them. Bubbles, I found, were not what everyone wanted. What about one of France's greatest white wines, I wondered. If prestige is what you are after, beat Corton-Charlemagne. A crash course was what was needed. The 'mama-sans' that reign over these prestigious resorts know nothing of burgundy, or even wine. My colleagues at Jardine had the answer: a tasting party. The Daimyo Oda Nobunaga had a famous wine-tasting party, so history records, in 1572 – just the sort of precedent traditionalist Japan approves. We invited the mama-sans to the Imperial Hotel one afternoon for a tasting-lesson and lavish feast. I was tutor.

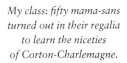

My class: fifty mama-sans turned out in their regalia to learn the niceties of Corton-Charlemagne.

Where would you start with a classroom of fifty geishas in full fig and three vintages of Corton-Charlemagne? In honour of the Imperial, the ladies I had met in severe couture at work were in kimono and war paint, mincing heels and towering wigs. I toyed with geology and decided on

haikus. I briefed them on the Emperor Charlemagne, introduced them to wine tasting, and set up a haiku contest: My Feelings on Tasting the Emperor's Great Wine of France. I'd like to say the poetry in the Japanese soul came pouring out. Half my class headed for the buffet. Five or six, though, were still at their desks, chewing their pencils, when the last lobster was gone. And the wine? Dom Pérignon, I fear, remained the people's choice.

With twenty-five acres of a single Grand Cru, Jean-Charles has a problem more familiar in Bordeaux than in Burgundy: to make a single homogeneous wine from as many as two hundred barrels from 16 different parcels. Following Burgundian logic you might expect subdivisions to emerge: Charlemagne l'Empereur, Charlemagne Barbe Blanche ... but who would tinker with such a *patrimoine*? Instead, his philosophy is generous simplicity; this is a man who matures his wine for decades and serves it in magnums.

I started this chapter with Meursault: in my mind the archetype of white burgundy; the place where Chardonnay expresses itself so differently from its Chablis persona that it could almost be a different grape. Meursault should be buttery, mealy, nutty, grainy (tick the one you recognize) less inclined to fruit and flowers than Puligny or to flint and spice than Corton-Charlemagne. The broader flavour of Meursault is the one that merges with the taste of oak to make the touchstone Chardonnay the whole world has in mind.

One of my favourite roles for it is as Act Two of a three-act dinner at the seaside. Act One is shellfish and Chablis. Act Two is a rich fish, turbot with its creamy strata of flesh in hollandaise, and a Meursault Genevrières or Charmes, a serious Premier Cru. Act Three is whatever you like. Probably just coffee and chocolates and brandy; the craving for a full-bodied wine has been satisfied. To drink a series of white burgundies, or Chardonnays, as you might several clarets at a sitting, with the object of comparing them, is unusual. I'm not sure I've ever done it, in fact. I wonder why. Most people are in too much of a hurry to reach the reds, perhaps.

Memories of the British Airways tasting panel confirm, though, that the demand for both Chablis and Meursault is insatiable. We assembled at least once a year to trawl through fifty or sixty samples of them to find a wine we felt happy with, with the proviso that there was enough of it. The best wines are rarely made in two-thousand-case lots, which is what the airline needed. Sometimes at the end of an hour of sniffing and spitting we would look at each other ruefully. "There's really nothing here," Michael Broadbent would say, and Jancis Robinson would nod agreement. Ever optimistic, I would drag them back down the long white formica table to number 37. Another sip. "Specious," Michael would say.

The British Airways tasting team circa 1995. Michael Broadbent (standing, centre), Jancis Robinson, Colin Anderson and your humble servant.

"I don't think it's quite clean," from Jancis.

"How about 45, then?" from me.

"Come on, Hugh. You're a trier, but people have got to drink this all the way to New York." It must be some sort of tribute to our consistency, if nothing else, that time after time we chose a Meursault from the same négociants. Once Peter Nixson, who runs the BA wine cellars, told us that a First Class passenger had complained because he was offered only Chablis or Meursault. He wanted Chardonnay.

Jancis recalls in her rather premature memoirs (she was only 47) the first time we met. It was at a tasting of pioneer Canadian wines at Ontario House in London. She noted, she says, that her elders (all of us) exchanged comments on the wines that were often completely contradictory, and yet we seemed in perfect accord. One would say 'that's a fruity one' and the other 'yes, isn't it lean?' She concluded quite reasonably that it doesn't seem to really matter what you say – although it might matter what you write. There may have been, I remember, another reason that day: the wines were far from special. Perhaps we were trying to avoid saying so in front of our hosts. At some point a year or so after this meeting Jancis asked me a version of my Most Frequently Asked Question: "Can I have your job?" or words to that effect.

"Yes," I answered, and indeed she has: first, for many years, as wine correspondent of *The Sunday Times*, and more recently relieving me at the tiller of *The World Atlas of Wine*. This, of course, in addition to all her own books including *The Oxford Companion to Wine*, and her website of news, debate and countless tasting-notes that ensures her laptop is never off her lap.

The sages of Burgundy have never quite been moved enough by Meursault, never found that coruscating quality that defies denial, to name any of its vineyards a Grand Cru. It is true, you would have to lower the bar a notch from the Puligny level. A Meursault Perrières is worth a Puligny

Combettes, let's say, but rarely a Chevalier. There are Meursaults, though, as memorable as most Corton-Charlemagnes. (How this argument must have grumbled on down the years.)

It is a big open crossroads of a village. You can sense money, at least by Côte d'Or standards, in its bourgeois houses and long concealing walls. There are merchants as well as vineyard-toilers here; the litany of double-barrelled names tells the story of dynastic marriages – though not in a form that helps you to follow it. And Meursault, just Meursault, no vineyard name attached, from one house is often more exciting than Meursault Premier Cru La Goutte d'Or from another. Did I mention the human factor? I have booked my next lifetime for cross-referencing terroirs and their all-too-human guardians.

This of course is the reason it is always worth going off-piste, or at least outside the obvious main arena, to the villages higher on the hill and tucked into combes whose farmers can be just as conscientious but whose land comes under less intense public scrutiny. The tiny stage-set hamlet of Blagny has been absorbed into Meursault, but beyond it Auxey-Duresses and Monthélie, and higher still St Aubin and St Romain, all grow lovely Chardonnay. The best Auxey is very serious wine indeed. Wines from Montagny and the Côte Chalonnaise to the south can be delicious. The question is whether they can ever offer the richness of Chardonnay grown in easier conditions. In California, for example.

California

I can tell you exactly when it was that the effulgent sun of Chardonnay first shed its golden light on the New World. There was a Eureka moment, and it was down to barrels brought to California from Burgundy. There had already been Chardonnay vines in California for a century. I believe it was the labels of the Almaden winery at Los Gatos that first mentioned the connection. They were composed by Frank Schoonmaker, who had lived in Europe and fallen in love with wine as a youth during Prohibition. When it ended in 1933 his articles in *The New Yorker* were America's first reminder of what it had been missing. "His whole life has been spent as a human bridge over the Atlantic ...." I quote my own words, since in 1967 I was the editor of the first British edition of his *Encyclopedia of Wine*. Few people, indeed, had more influence in my wine education. Schoonmaker was both an importer (he lived half the year in the south of France) and a consultant to the wrecked California wine industry.

Of Chardonnay he wrote: "In California, due to its extremely small yield per acre, it is not widely planted; its wine, almost always sold as Pinot Chardonnay, is perhaps the best white table wine made in the

United States." Small yield, that is, compared with the notorious Thompson Seedless which produced the great majority of California's white wine at the time.

Schoonmaker's 'best white' was not about to be confused with white burgundy until someone gave it the French kiss of oak. I sometimes wonder whether even the makers of burgundy were aware of how much of its character was contributed by its barrels before they had the shock of tasting something from a far country that seemed remarkably familiar. For the record it happened in 1957, at Hanzell Vineyard in Sonoma. By the early 1960s the secret was out: buy French barrels. Those bottles have all gone, but I have only just finished the 1973 Pinot Chardonnays of two of the pioneers, Joseph Heitz and Beaulieu Vineyards. The BV was fine, without brio. The Heitz wine smelled of freesias and ginger and cream, so persistently that I couldn't bear to wash the glasses till the next day.

The excitement of such sumptuous new wines was extraordinary. Everyone knew the Napa Valley could make wonderful Cabernets. By 1966 the word was out about Chardonnay. 1966 is the 1066 of California wine; the year Robert Mondavi opened the first new winery in the Napa Valley since Prohibition. And it was not Mâcon Blanc they set out to make – they had Montrachet in their sights. Montrachet was the name of a yeast cultivated expressly for the job. The barrels were to come from Burgundy's best cooperages. The grapes and where they were grown seemed less important than getting the technology right; there was, after all, no track record of where Chardonnay performed best – let alone gave the wine best suited for fermenting and aging in barrels.

I was the wine correspondent of *Gourmet* magazine at the time. It was clear that the news from California was not reaching its East Coast establishment readers. I was coming to the end of a long series of articles on the wines of every part of the Old World. Portugal, Austria … they were pretty names, and possibly holiday destinations, but it was hard to imagine any American drinking their wines. "How about California?" I said to the editor. "Our readers don't drink domestic wines," was her answer (I got an even cooler reception when I asked "How about Australia?"). I prevailed, and set out for the coast. The news I brought back should have drawn plenty of corks, but it was not going to encourage gourmet tourism. The only place to eat in the whole Napa Valley was the Grapevine Inn, which, I wrote, could burn a hamburger with the best.

The appellations of new wines are not the names of places but of people. If you knew where Bill Bonetti or Brad Webb was making Chardonnay (respectively at the Freemark Abbey and Charles Krug wineries) you had the key. Joe Heitz was in his Napa cellar, and Fred

McCrea up at Stony Hill. The numbers grew rapidly. By the early 1970s Chardonnay was the height of fashion and every California winery made one, with the Napa Valley still leading the way but next-door Sonoma in hot pursuit.

The gold rush mentality suits California; it is not so good for Chardonnay. A few wineries kept their heads and looked for grapes ripened as slowly as they would be in Burgundy (not easy in Napa) to give a good balance of acidity with strength. A few refined their game with real passion. Chardonnay Corner in my cellar has (relatively) recent memories, even one or two bottles, of wines from the 1970s. Still, it's not a bad list: Chateau St Jean, Stony Hill, Zaca Mesa, Freemark Abbey, Iron Horse, Chappellet, Chalone, Firestone (these two far to the south) and many from Trefethen.

I always thought John and Janet Trefethen had the right philosophy: moderation and patience. Only they (as far as I know) deliberately kept back Chardonnays (also Cabernets) as 'Library' wines to release again at ten years or so. When they started building a new home on the western hills, Janet started a tradition of harvest picnics around the oak-shaded spring on their property. When I started introducing California wines to Japan the Trefethens were in the first wave. (It broke at a Tokyo banquet with the Crown Prince, the veteran US ambassador Mike McCarthy and Dianne Feinstein, mayor of San Francisco.)

The note I made on a Trefethen Reserve Chardonnay of 1979 gives the idea: "Bright light gold; the leafy Napa scent blending with melon and green tea, rich but firm. Racy acidity has kept it in perfect condition. Balance outdoes flavour; one of the best Napa Chards ever; elegant, keen and long." What did I mean by the leafy Napa scent? It was a tell-tale character of Napa Chardonnay that something apparently got left behind in the ripening process. At least that was my impression. Golden-ripe, sweet and strong they might be, but a trace of what some call 'asparagus' and I call 'leaf' almost always remained. Too much and it was coarse and off-putting. Faint, it is the terroir speaking.

TOP
Bill Bonetti made great Chardonnay from the 1960s on using French oak – but not too much.

ABOVE
Janet Trefethen gave great picnics: note the hard hats, soup in paint pots and prawns in dumper trucks.

By the 1980s Chardonnay-spotting had become a national pastime. You couldn't go into a restaurant without the sommelier, suppressing a smirk, intoning 'You haven't tasted the new Hyman Kaplan release?' It spoilt good meals for me all over the States: that January day in Chicago; a good appetite, fragrant promise from the kitchen as we sat down at a sunlit table, and the sickening smell of raw oak and syrup from the proffered glass. And the kick; these wines are full of alcohol. One sip was enough. Indeed one sniff. Going for $75. Never again.

Oak got seriously out of hand. The smell of a carpenter's shop is fine when you are buying a table, but not in your glass. For customers who had never tasted good wine it was simply the smell of 'premium', or 'super-premium', or whatever they designate designer-label wine. I felt a killjoy pointing out that no French wine would ever be sold reeking of its container. If a producer did use an expensive new barrel – few did – it was because his wine had the inbuilt character and concentration to absorb the extraneous oak flavour. By the time it was sold (or at least by the time it was drunk) oak would be a just-perceptible nuance, or at most one note in a chord. 'If I want to taste oak I'll go lick a plank,' as an older wine-maker put it.

Australia

Australia's Eureka moment came ten years after California's, but to a country with a more mature wine culture. No Prohibition had interrupted life. The Tyrrell family had been making wine in Australia's oldest region, the Hunter Valley, for a hundred years. Murray Tyrrell's uncle, Dan, had seventy vintages to his credit. It was claret, burgundy, and Chablis (and Riesling) they made, blending their grapes, and if necessary their regions too. It argues a practised, if not a refined, taste if you are prepared to truck your grapes hundreds of kilometres to achieve a flavour you can't quite manage on your own. It means understanding terroir – if only to contradict it.

The small group of Hunter wine folk included Len Evans, whose penchant for opening the world's best wines for his friends is part of Australian folklore. Was it after a bottle of Montrachet that Murray Tyrrell decided to have a go? 'What varietal did you say this one is, Len?' The Hunter was already famous, and with reason, for its unique style of delicate, slow-aging white made of Semillon and called Hunter Riesling – or any other name that would sell it. Even when Tyrrell made his early Chardonnay he apparently blended in Semillon – out of habit? In 1973 he labelled this blend, aged in French oak, Vat 47. I first tasted it in Bristol: Avery's of Bristol were ahead of the game in California as they were in France. Indeed their habit of modifying burgundy to their customers' taste had just been outlawed by Britain's entry in 1972 into the Common Market. In 1972 I had made my first visit to Australia. Up to then I had thought California had it all.

My notes on that visit are sadly sketchy, but they record my first meeting with Len. "A little Welsh bull," I wrote, "bosses and boasts in a loud voice; 42, pretty blonde wife Trish. Old Lindemans Chablis tastes of caramel, Len says a 'honey Hunter'. 1952 Mount Pleasant Pinot Hermitage ..." blah, blah, blah (as Len would say).

There was so little Chardonnay planted in Australia that it remained an open secret while they worked on it. Brown Brothers of Milawa was an old family firm like the Tyrrells'. Max Lake was a Sydney surgeon with a weekend place in the Hunter. Petaluma was a new enterprise in the Adelaide Hills (Len was behind that, too) and Leeuwin Estate was an eccentric plantation in the remote Margaret River south of Perth (inspired by Robert Mondavi). There were many others; these were the ones I visited. The one that really rang the bell, though, was a newer Hunter outfit, Rosemount Estate. Rosemount coined an unmissable new style of Chardonnay; just the wine that anyone not knowing the Australian taste for understatement might have expected. To me it looked and tasted like alcoholic Golden Syrup (oak-aged, of course). The Show judges were impressed, the market loved it, and sweet 'buttery' Chardonnay looked set to become the Australian norm. It was certainly an unstoppable bestseller. Something passably like it, what's more, could be produced from irrigated vineyards at many tons per acre at far less cost. And oak-flavoured by using sawdust. Chardonnay was on a roll.

The strange thing to me was that people liked it as a social drink. 'The thinking man's Martini,' was how someone described it at the height of the boom. Sometimes it tasted almost as strong. There are many white grapes that make the perfect wine for sipping, for refreshment, for finishing a bottle before you sit down for a meal. The first is Riesling; its innate freshness has all the aperitif qualities. Sauvignon Blanc can be a good bright swallow. Chenin Blanc, Pinot Blanc, Pinot Gris ... there are plenty of wines I would cast in the role of refreshment, but Chardonnay with a dose of oak always seems to me to call for accompaniment: a glass of water at least.

Australia had more work to do than California, and a wider range of possibilities. California's climate is famously subject to one great influence: the Pacific. Where you are in relation to the Pacific, its cold currents and its afternoon fogs, matters more than anything else. You can roast up north in Sonoma or shiver down south in Monterey if the configuration of the hills between you and the ocean dictates it. Carneros, the southern

ABOVE RIGHT
*Yeringberg at Lilydale
is a complete Victorian
winery, a survivor
of Gold Rush days.*

BELOW
*Len Evans and James
Halliday have always
supported each other.
Sydney in the 1980s.*

tip of both the Napa and Sonoma valleys, is blessed by cool draughts
crossing San Francisco Bay. Chardonnay and Pinot Noir are happy there.
Higher up both valleys, the ripening regime is quite different.

Australia is still being explored. The Hunter Valley was a strange
place to grow grapes in the first place; it works only because cloud cover
prevents them from cooking. But around the south coast there are infinite
possibilities: in the inland hills of Victoria, in South Australia where
ocean rains from the Great Australian Bight water the Adelaide Hills and
Clare Valley, around the distant south of Western Australia and along the
surfers' coast of Margaret River. Some have even been
tried and discarded in an age that looked for different
things in its wine, and have made a comeback because
taste has changed in their direction. The Yarra Valley,
just north of Melbourne, is one of these.

It had given up on wine when I first went there to see
the perfectly preserved Victorian (in both senses) winery
at Yeringberg. I was brought back ten years later by
James Halliday, one of Len Evans's great friends and
disciples, a formidable lawyer and wine show judge
who had decided to prove his mettle by making his
own. I became marginally involved in his venture,
Coldstream Hills at Lilydale in the rolling country
upstream on Melbourne's river. James let me taste
Chardonnay and Pinot Noir from grapes grown in

some of Australia's most beautiful vineyards, on red soil where 'mountain ash', the vernacular for *Eucalyptus regnans*, one of Australia's noblest trees, pushes up from hidden creeks and thickets of deep green wattle to improbable heights. Show me a good tree and I'm your man.

Everything I look for in Chardonnay was there. Well, not perhaps the flint of Chablis or the nuclear power of Montrachet, nor exactly the mealy/buttery/nutty/grainy breadth of a model Meursault. But richness, freshness, definition, succulent fruit and the bone structure of just the right acidity. James's first vintage was 1985. He fermented it in oak: it was by no means overpowered. My last bottle, drunk in 2003, was as good as ever.

The highpoints of Australian Chardonnay don't seem to me to form a pattern. The Hunter Valley makes soft golden wines; but there are exceptions. What the best have in common, whether they come from the Yarra, the Mornington Peninsula or Geelong on the coast south of Melbourne, the Adelaide Hills or the Margaret River, is succulence in restraint, fruit that is sweet but not sugary, acidity that starts your saliva, and a touch of smoke to make you sniff again.

The American writer Alexis Bespaloff photographs Tim Hamilton Russell, a South African pioneer of Chardonnay, against the backdrop of Table Mountain.

The wonderful thing about Chardonnay is that it is do-able. Italians have done it: Angelo Gaja first. In South Africa Hamilton Russell did it first. In Spain, Jean Leon. New Zealand has only to avoid *too* much fruit flavour. Sicily, Israel, even Malta are cracking it. It starts with the determination of individuals who understand the goal. As they figure out the best plots, the Bâtards and Chevaliers of the future, I shall need to extend my Chardonnay Corner.

The Loire: a Light Touch

"HERE IT IS," said Uncle Ronald. "Let's have a swim." We had been looking forward to the Loire all the sweltering day, rocking along in his silver Citroën, the model that looked like an overgrown dodgem car. It rocked even more than most because the boot was ballasted with wine. It was part of Ronald Avery's unusual system to keep his Citroën parked at Cherbourg aerodrome, a modest field with occasional flights from Bristol. And to keep several cases of wine in the car. We had arrived on the Bristol flight laden with burgundy bottled in Bristol. The aim, as far as I understood, was to demonstrate to his suppliers in Beaune that he could do the job of bottling better than they could. Presumably storage in a car was part of the durability test.

Uncle Ronald takes his ease. At lunch, Pouilly-sur-Loire, 1966.

There was the Loire: my first-ever sighting of France's most famous river. I had imagined it running through parkland, between files of enormous planes, with glimpses of pale stone châteaux among the trees and here and there a castle on a crag above a bustling market town. Here at Pouilly its beach was as wide as if the tide were out: a waste of shingle and sand and carcasses of willows with more of a promise than a sight of water beyond the dunes. Uncle Ronald rocked down as near as he could, jumped out of the car and stripped off. Judy and I followed, wearing very little, into the slow-flowing water. It was too warm to be refreshing: more of a baptism than a bathe. Then we got back into the car and headed for lunch. I forget the name of the restaurant, but we ate *sandre*, to my mind the Dover sole of inland waters, and drank Sancerre. My photo shows Uncle Ronald in his element: lunch over, another bottle ordered, only three hundred kilometres to drive to Beaune.

The Loire of royal châteaux is further downstream. It is still placid, immense, wandering through sand banks and willowy shallows, when it cuts in Touraine through a low range of limestone hills. The soft rock builds beautiful castles; it also forms convenient caves – half the inhabitants of such villages as Montlouis and Hureau are troglodytes. The possession of such perfect cellars can shape the destiny of a region. Long, slow fermentation and ideal long-term storage for wine are a given.

It is cold in these caves. In May you still need a sweater and a coat. The mouth of Philippe Vatan's cave near Saumur is big enough to swallow a truck; then the floor slopes down, the walls form naves and vaults and aisles around a gleaming farm of steel tanks on one hand, and on the other a dark alley of bull-size barrels. There is a whole new language of wine to learn here, smells to discern and tastes to untangle. The Chenin Blanc is not an obvious grape: its smell seems to relate more to mineral than vegetable – or rather the amalgam of the two you find in moss on a damp rock; in this cave, for example. I have no precise word for the flavour but it can turn from steely to buttery without ever tasting of fruit. The notes I write with a cold hand sticky from a cold glass may not be much help either.

In any case "certainties are boring," as my host muses, extracting his nose after a long session deep in his glass. He seems a reserved man, his lined face serious (or perhaps he is just chilled to the marrow). He has a few stock phrases: *'fruits à chair blanc'*, *'fleurs blanches'*, *'texture inouïe'*. I'll go a shade further than white-fleshed fruit and wonderful texture: honey, melon, mirabelles, minerals, lanolin. Then he is off, the way growers go: about his limestone, his pruning, his stinginess with manure and his clairvoyance about the precise moment to pick. You can't describe the wine, but you can tell whether you like it and which barrel has more to say even if you can't speak its language.

Why this inarticulate grape? Why here, and nowhere else in France?

In a cold cave at Montlouis in Touraine. Jacky Blot is another grower who lets his Chenin Blanc express whatever is on its mind.

Why would a drinker, who can choose these days from round the world, home in on a puzzle wrapped in an enigma? The history question is not too hard to answer. The Chenin Blanc goes back to the Middle Ages, when Anjou and Touraine were centres of monastic wine-making. The mercantile Dutch promoted it as a good grape for the sweet wine they liked, in vineyards they could easily reach by sea. It was not their style, though, to buy it where it was already grown and prized and the market was established. I fancy it is not a coincidence that about the same distance up another river they penetrated in their 17th century heyday you meet wines with a similar tendency. Bergerac is to the Dordogne what Anjou is to the Loire, and the whites of Bergerac and Montravel are traditionally on the sweet side for the same reason.

The Dutch developed their own sources around the River Layon, the other side of the Loire from Anjou. The results were unpredictable: sometimes sweet, sometimes dry, but sometimes sensational. Never mind if you couldn't describe it. Its taste was part of the scenery of Touraine and Anjou, the local cuisine (rillettes, salmon …) was adapted to it, it formed a natural duo with the local light reds of Saumur and Chinon, and the chic restaurants of Paris added it to the roster of excellent provincial specialities. A glass of something smooth and silky, faintly honeyed, made a good aperitif. They coined a new definition for its character between dry and sweet: *sec tendre*. 'Tender' pretty well describes its insinuating softness. In years when *Botrytis* took over, the fungus dissipated the water and concentrated the sugar, the wine turned gold and lined up perfectly with foie gras. How much the world owes to the diligent gourmets who pursued such experiments. You may mock, but they stand the test of time.

Jo Pithon (with corkscrew) makes Coteaux du Layon in every nuance from dry to sec tendre *to sweet to* moelleux. *Vineyard and season decide.*

The epitome of the dry school is the Coulée de Serrant. The vineyard is yet another monastic creation, on a steep southeast slope overlooking the Loire. Its owner is Nicolas Joly, France's most famous biodynamist. Biodynamists follow the phases of the moon in their operations – and not just the moon, but the whole zodiac. They have a homeopath's belief in minute doses – in this case, of compost energized by a decoction of plants, stirred in a prescribed rhythm and buried in the vineyard in a cow's horn. It is easy to be sceptical about what sounds like witchcraft, but harder to argue with the results. If you forgo all the rapid remedies offered by science and technology, if you are prepared to spend twice as long in your vineyard doing by hand what others do by machine, at the very least you will know what is going on in the finest detail and care passionately about the results. 'The farmer's boot makes the best muck,' or however the saying goes. Some of the world's best wines come from biodynamic estates; more and more, indeed; the tendency is catching on more rapidly than I expected. Among others the domaines Leflaive and Lafon in Burgundy, Zind-Humbrecht in Alsace and Chapoutier on the Rhône are all sworn to biodynamism. It is fair to say, of course, that many more equally excellent estates take a more measured view of scientific progress.

To articulate the quality is as hard as to believe in the principle – especially with such a tongue-tied grape as Chenin Blanc. Soil and season play an even larger part in its flavours than they do in more aromatic varieties. I brought a bottle of Coulée de Serrant 1999 up from my cellar to see what words I could find. (Loire wines have a corner to themselves; no large quantities: not many stay for long.) The label advises decanting well before drinking and serving without chilling. It works.

Could this be the oldest vine in France? Henry Marionnet of Soings in Touraine has a vineyard of Romorantin, a local white grape, planted long before phylloxera. It makes four-dimensional wine.

The note I wrote at lunchtime runs: "Firm, minerally, dense and silky, rich but totally dry, like the sensation, rather than the flavour, of white plum flesh. Will something more specific happen as it opens up? An inarticulate star: you just have to sip and think." Six hours later: "Strong but sumptuous. Where does this smell like Yquem come from? Extraordinary proportions: generous in flesh, firm in structure – and with this haunting suggestion of Sauternes."

Serrant is exceptional, but it is not alone. More and more growers in Anjou and Touraine (where the great name is Vouvray) are aiming for something on these lines: uncompromising dry wines, often made in oak, with no preconceived model and their ears tuned to the whispers of a quiet voice. They could become a fixation with me, too: I try one as often as I can.

For a bottle of Coulée de Serrant you could buy six of Muscadet: any Muscadet. There is no such thing as a Muscadet Grand Cru, or any ranking or even social pretension in this democratic, low-key, drink-me-quick neighbour. Muscadet lives at the mouth of the Loire, a bare hour's drive west from the Chenin vineyards of Anjou, in a different geographical realm of granite and river-washed deposits. The Médoc is the pebbly outwash of the Garonne and the Dordogne, the Muscadet vineyards the mixed bag of sand and clay dragged from the heart of France by the immense perpetual tide of the Loire. There are soils here that will grow almost anything, the reverse of the classic vineyard recipe: soil too poor for proper farming. Any sense of place in Muscadet country is provided by the smell of sea air and that luminosity that says the Atlantic is just over the horizon.

Each individual French region poses the same question: Who thought of that? What creative genius realized that the ocean and its products would need a vineyard of their own, that it would be a poor outlook for the north of France if Normandy's cider were the only chaser for the oysters and crabs and prawns of its endlessly fertile coast?

The answer, once more, is Dutch merchants looking for cheap white wine. But fertile soil at the cloudy mouth of the Loire holds no hope of the golden October syndrome. Providence decreed that the wine of Brittany would be appropriately watery. This is not an insult: water is a wonderful drink. Can we please have something that combines the neutral limpidity of water with enough tangy cut, a few cells of lemon and a suggestion of seaweed, to put on the table with a plateau de fruits de mer? Muscadet is it. What makes a good one? A very faint prickle of gas is good for freshness, and a sense of yeast in the background fills out what can be a rather bleak dryness. Hence the tradition of keeping Muscadet on its lees (*sur lie*), its deposit of dead yeast cells, until its springtime bottling.

I admit I am one of that captive audience who rarely looks further. I am too busy popping little brown shrimps in my mouth, buttering my bread and adjusting my napkin round my neck for the onslaught on the bivalves. I glance at the label when the waiter brings the bottle to see that it is a young one. By the summer it should normally be of the previous year. There are so many Muscadet-makers (almost all their names seem to end in 'ière': Boutonnière, Bretonnière, Fruitière, Mercredière ...) that trying to follow a favourite is not easy – and by the second glass it is not top of the agenda. Would that there were more wines one could treat so casually with satisfactory results.

Greed sated, though, I do consult the wine list again for a second bottle with more impact. The first would taste thin with the brown-buttery sole that is on its way. A few estates, and one or two merchants, designate *super-cuvées* for two or three years' aging. The 'M' of Louis

Métaireau is one example, Cardinal Richard of Chereau Carré another. I have even had Muscadet fermented in new oak by some enthusiast clearly tired of the essential simplicity of his wine. Where there is concentration, age can add a nutty note and deepen the maritime tang. "Good Muscadet," I once wrote, "should smell like the bilges of a trawler." Very slightly. In a sense Muscadet is a dead end. It is not on the way anywhere either topographically or technically. I can't see new wine regions planting its grapes or imitating its laid-back style. More's the pity; there's always room in my life for something so uncomplicated, reliable and cheap.

Nor are there many aspirants to make the sort of wine the Chenin Blanc makes along the Loire, if only because it is a marketing nightmare. Each vintage can produce wine anywhere on a scale from sharp and thin to unctuous, and the wines of the best years need many years to show their real form. The solution here is to make it fizz: Saumur in Anjou is the centre of the Crémant de la Loire industry, but it is no champagne. True, there is far more Chenin Blanc in South Africa than France. Presumably we can thank the Dutch for this, too. There its virtues are good acidity under a hot sun and a sense of fruit without an aromatic identity, which makes it a starting point for anything from sparkling wine to 'sherry' or brandy. When South Africa turned its attention to more fashionable varieties in the 1990s it tended to sniff, and so did we, at the fresh, dry and rather sweet wines it sells as Steen. I have always thought them one of the world's reliable bargains but, as Muscadet shows, bargains have a low profile in the world of wine.

It has only to refresh me. I don't remember what vintage this was, or where: just the sharp touch on my tongue as it went down.

My favourite Chenin from the New World comes from California, a wine with fragrant associations from one of the most beautiful vineyards of the Napa Valley, a lofty amphitheatre on Pritchard Hill. Far below sparkle the waters of Lake Hennessy. Far beyond lies Mount St Helena and a succession of grey-blue hills. This is Napa's first new-age winery in a strictly contemporary building, a three-sided pyramid of rust-red steel, built by Donn Chappellet in 1969 just after Robert Mondavi set out to relaunch the valley. Donn has unfaltering taste. He modelled his Cabernet on Château Latour, his Riesling (now sadly defunct) on the dry wines of the Rheingau, and his Chenin Blanc on – a Californian model. It is Chardonnay without the apples or the oak, wine with a heft but no sweetness; crisp, fresh and dry. I last met it with a rich dish of clams by the Napa River. Strange how one remembers these things.

So long is the Loire that the vineyards we think of as being at its upper end, Sancerre and Pouilly of the Fumé kind, are actually precisely at its mid-point. There are 496 kilometres of valley upstream of the Pouilly bridge, and 496 down. It is strange to think of the Loire flowing past Beaujolais, but there it is: a river capable of carrying barrels northwards to market hundreds of miles before it has any of its own to offer.

By its mid-point it is unmistakably the Loire, the lazy river in an outsize bed we met with Uncle Ronald. It wanders towards, then away from, then back to, the only hill worth the name in hundreds of miles of easy progress, the hill of Sancerre. Here on the left bank, and across the bridge on gentler contours at Pouilly, the soil of Chablis (or a close relation) comes to the surface and the white wine picks up its flinty energy.

Such is the French demand for red wine that Sancerre was apparently once planted almost entirely with Pinot Noir – a forlorn hope, I would have thought. Pinot Noir is still the apple of many growers' eyes, pallid though its wine is, and remote, in most years, from serious redness. Sauvignon Blanc is its bugle call. There is no fumbling for similes with Sauvignon. We all recognize the herbal smell known to its admirers as gooseberry (leaves as much as fruit) and to its critics as cat's pee (in bad cases, tom). It is an aroma that passes (is this an unfortunate metaphor?) straight from fruit to wine and stays there, scarcely altered, as it ages. At its best, from Chablis-like soil in Sancerre or Pouilly, it rides a smoky-silky vehicle, piquant and vital, lip-smacking and lingering. Its culture is well understood in scattered communes west of Sancerre, even on less ideal soil. When we lived just to the south in the Bourbonnais we would call in at Ménétou-Salon, *chez* Pellé or *chez* Clément, for a dozen of their marginally toned-down and marginally cheaper versions. They became almost an integral part of our lunchtime salads.

This is how Sauvignon Blanc made its name: as a grape you couldn't miss, with a summery style, from conveniently close to Paris. The role of Paris in promoting (above all in consuming) these provincial products should have all possible credit. They might have disappeared without it. The fact that Sauvignon is a bigger player in Bordeaux was less obvious; Bordeaux found it too raw and pungent to drink straight. A better plan, they found, was to blend it with the more grown-up Sémillon. In dry white Graves the same. Young, the blend went well with the icy oysters they love to eat in tandem with hot little spicy sausages. Nothing prepares you better for foie gras and Sauternes. Well aged? It is one of my regrets that white Graves in stately maturity is almost unknown today.

It used to be modelled, more or less, on fine white burgundy; even matured in old barrels. The Dutch tradition was probably responsible for a dose of sulphur that kept it quiet for years. If you were exceptionally lucky your twenty-year-old bottle was a dream. It was one of the many enterprises of the tireless Len Evans to revitalize dry white Graves. World domination, his friends joked, was his ultimate aim. With a financier partner he bought Château Rahoul at Portets and brought his protégé Brian Croser from Australia to make the wine. It began to be remarkable, and so did their little Sauternes château, Padouen, which had another friend, Peter Vinding, as resident manager. Len's financier, alas, died and the company (they invested in the Napa Valley, too) closed down. Peter, however, had the bit between his teeth and persuaded other friends to help him buy the Château de Landiras, vestigial ruins of a castle and a vestigial vineyard on the southern fringe of the Graves appellation, where the pine forests of the Landes begin to dominate the landscape. Like Château Loudenne in the Médoc, where Peter had worked previously, Landiras became a staging post for aspirant wine-makers and their mainly British friends. Susie Vinding's table, laid with the austere elegance of a classical Danish interior – white china and white napkins the size of towels – saw famous bottles from many countries come and go. Peter's trials with Sémillon, Sauvignon Blanc and Sauvignon Gris, with different barrels, yeasts and temperatures, taught us a good deal about Graves, white and red. 'A white Pomerol,' he said his aim was. It takes a little imagination.

Peter Vinding's tenure of the Château de Landiras was all too brief, but produced some memorable wines. This was the 1990.

Peter's creative probing produced some notable results. 1993 was a difficult year for white bordeaux. Ten years later the Landiras white Graves was still light gold, crisp and succulent. Crisp and succulent is exactly why you blend Sauvignon and Sémillon. But many less sophisticated bottles have indicated what old white Graves could be. There is a brasserie on the broad avenue of the Allées de Tourny in Bordeaux, opposite the Grand Théâtre with its 12-columned portico, where for

forty years I have stopped for my oysters and sausages. For years they had a stock of Château Respide, a venerable white Graves (I forget the vintage) which I suspect had survived an overdose of sulphur (it was suspiciously pale) to come through not far from perfection: dry, buttery, with just a glint of steel. My lunchtime formula: the oysters, then a big dish of braised endives, brown and bubbling with butter, sugary and bitter. Which called, of course, for a glass or two of a good red Graves.

———————

If I want to tease a friend (perish the thought) who knows all France's best white wines I have one trick up my sleeve that has yet to fail: an old white Rioja. Admittedly I know of only one cellar that can pull off this trick, but it is the exceptions that drag the world of wine along and if one can do it, I argue, so could others.

The cellar is López de Heredia, a living monument to tradition dug deep in the river bank of the Ebro at Haro, the wine-capital of this rugged region of northern Spain. I recorded my first acquaintance with Haro forty years ago, evoking the foul-smelling fires of rubbish and the ragged gypsies squatting by them. Fascist Spain was a melancholy country. The wine I still hoard comes from precisely that time; its inspiration is indeed bordeaux. It is the 1964 Viña Tondonia Blanco, aged fifteen years in barrels black with age in cellars dripping with damp, to a state of lemon-scented wax-textured equilibrium. A further twenty-five years in bottle only refines its perfect poise. What useful lesson is there in this? That a well balanced wine, made by the simplest methods with minimum intervention and naturally stabilized in a cold barrel, has nothing to fear. Rhine wines were once perfected in the same way. But can we be surprised that haste and hurry, in making and marketing, shorten wines' lives?

Rioja apart, Spain was no place to look for fresh white wines in the seventies. (Fino sherry has freshness of a different kind.) The rest of the country was a blank; so much so that, researching for my Wine Atlas, I thought I must be missing something. I went to Madrid to meet the man described to me as Spain's gastronomic authority, the Conde de los Andes (is there a grander title anywhere?). He invited me to lunch at Madrid's most aristo club. There were, I recall, two white-gloved flunkies for every guest. "I shall show you the best we have," he said, as the golden wine splashed from the crystal jug. It was Rioja. "That," he said, "is all there is." The only part of Iberia offering refreshment of the sharply fruity variety was northern Portugal and, very tentatively, Galicia, Spain's northwest coast.

Portugal's vinho verde was better-known in, and an essential – even fashionable – resource of, the 1970s. Its vogue seems to have passed with what was then the isolation and potent identity of its country, the Minho. Remembering the Portugal and Spain of their Fascist years is like remembering an entirely different place. On my first Portuguese visit at vintage time the dusty roads were crowded with ox-carts. The screech of wooden axles joined the fiddlers and pipes as the sound of harvest. It was a land of nothing but natural materials. Buildings were granite, grey timber and white plaster. Transport was oxen and donkeys. Vines grew up trees or on tall pergolas of hewn granite posts surrounding plots rather than fields, where everything grew hugger-mugger under low grey skies.

One evening we stayed at Monçao, at a hotel on the River Minho famous for its lampreys. Settlers from the Portuguese colonies of Angola and Mozambique came back in the lamprey season to eat these exquisite eels with hot chillies and sharp red wine. That night in the dining room a large party was listening to speeches that made our blood run cold. At the airport we were given tins of sardines and pamphlets illustrating Angolan atrocities. Portugal changed forever in 1974. Its expatriates flooded back (tens of thousands from Paris, I was told) and rebuilt the Minho in concrete. Its half-fizzy white wine, made of half-ripe grapes, was made more comfortable and less shrill. When I last tasted vinho verde recently, in Oporto, it was more like prickly Muscadet.

Spain north of the Minho, meanwhile, brought its white wine to market. Galicia has found a way to make its Albariño a model of low-strength, gently scented, bracingly sharp refreshment. The green hills and grey eucalyptus forests along the coast south of Santiago de Compostela look like no other Spanish wine country, and their not-quite-dry but citrus-sharp wines have more of the Loire than the Douro about them.

Sauvignon Blanc, the grape, has overtaken its native vineyards in fame and importance. It is the obligatory alternative to Chardonnay in any aspirant region of the New or Old Worlds. I often read, incidentally, that there is something offensive, simplistic, I'm not sure what, about this cleavage in two of the wine world. I take the blame for it: I believe I coined it in my first book. Europe was the old world, the one vineyard with ancient roots; its one-time colonies the new. By any reckoning today, however, there are New World regions in the Old World. Wine's New World starts where a vigneron has a temperature-controlled steel tank.

Temperature control was the key to fresh white wines in warm countries. Spain and parts of Italy needed it just as much as California and Australia. Chardonnay got away first, then married oak and conquered the world. Sauvignon Blanc was seen as a lighter and fresher alternative – and of lower value because no-one had ever tasted a great one. Nor did it gain with age.

I taste Sauvignon from around the world, but sadly I am rarely seduced. Yes, its nettly freshness is a boon in a summer wine. Who can argue about its part in Sauternes and Graves? But each move to empha-sise its qualities only reminds me of its limits. Two moves have made waves, if not history. First in the 1970s was Robert Mondavi's brainwave:

to marry it with oak like Chardonnay and call it Fumé Blanc. A huge hit that everybody imitated. I struggle to like the smell of Sauvignon and oak together; pungent sometimes to the point of nausea. (Taste, I repeat, is a personal matter.) The second wave was the New Zealand revolution.

The top floor of the 17-storey New Zealand House in London, near Trafalgar Square and commanding one of the best panoramas in town, qualified definitively as wine country in June 1984. Twenty or so wine journalists assembled, their expectations not, I suspect, as high as the venue, to taste the new vintage of New Zealand wines. A buzz soon started. Five or six of the wines were Sauvignon Blancs. This was Sauvignon with the volume turned up. I remember the surge of scent, the snap on the tongue, the hundred-amp shock through the system. Like Sauvignon or hate it, here it was in primary colours. Some tastes, I thought, are simply better at low volume.

Now we know that this is New Zealand's potential, perhaps for any grape variety. Her latitude corresponds to the places in the northern hemisphere where fine wines were born. Her volcanic soils can be embarrassingly fertile. In many places warm days are followed by cold nights; the recipe for concentrated fruit flavours. Whether the wine was calculated to demonstrate all this with the most pungent grape variety I somehow doubt, but there was no doubt about the impact. A new wine idiom had arrived. It could recruit drinkers who had scarcely noticed wine before, and it has.

Marlborough in the 1980s. John Simes showed me round Montana's Brancott Estate, five miles from the sea on Cloudy Bay. Windy Bay would be as good a name.

Touched by the Sun

THE TABLE IS SPREAD in cloistered shade. It needs to be: your eyes crease and smart when you look beyond the awning and the trees at the bleached tan of the landscape. The slow ceiling fan only shifts the hot air around. Pick at a salad? No: hot countries seem to insist on hot food – and in serious quantities. I remember the weight of an Argentine steak overlapping the edges of my plate while the sausages and chicken still sizzled on the grill, waiting to be eaten. After the antipasto and the pasta, a haunch of wild boar and a bellyful of beans is sure to be demolished. After the jamón Serrano there is a pan of paella a metre across. And that is not even considering curries. And to drink? None of your thirst-quenching spritzers, your pallid northern Rieslings or Sauvignons, your compromise rosés. We'll start with a young red, purple and potent, and go on to drink an older vintage or two, brick-red and leathery, to feed our nostalgic fantasies.

It works. I've never understood why. Do we sweat out the alcohol? Other things being equal, hotter countries make stronger wines. It is counter-intuitive that they turn out to be what you want: the food and wine is of a piece. I wonder if it is a matter of psychology. Does warm weather not make you more outgoing? Are there extrovert and introvert wines? Are my love of precision and finesse and nuances of terroir just a psychological reflex; a way of saying I am scared of drink? It would almost be a relief to abandon analysis, dump ratiocination, forget the fine print of appellation, producers, varieties, vintages .... It won't happen, though, in our latitudes.

In regions where wine comes as naturally as leaves to a tree, whether it is red or white is of secondary importance – or was, before it began to be valued as a tradable part of the folklore. White, if anything, was more valuable. We stayed with friends near Alicante once in great comfort. We cooked; a maid cleared up. There were carafes of red wine, white wine and water on the table. The white wine and water she put in the fridge; the red she threw away. In those days brown was a popular colour, too. Brown wine is the antithesis of modern oenological correctness.

An old formula that still works: fresh fish, tomatoes, onions, bread and a soft, sunburnt white. Anywhere in Spain.

Freshness is all. Protection from the corrupting air is vital. Nobody makes brown wine these days – except by mistake. Or do they?

It was the same in all southern countries. Not the least of the attractions of little harbour restaurants on the Mediterranean coast was the issue gratis, with your lunch, of a carafe of something that looked like flat lager. It had no name and no particular flavour. If anything it was like a faint fino sherry. I liked it.

The tradition is not entirely dead. There is sherry, of course; and its not-too-remote cousin Vin Jaune in the Jura, which is full of flavour. Not long ago I was in Arbois, the little Jura town where Louis Pasteur was born and did much of his thinking on fermentation, bacteria, inoculation and all the subjects in which he started the modern world. The wine-shop in the square was selling something labelled 'Vin Typé'. There is nothing officially so called, say the authorities. I bought a few bottles and served it at a dinner to country friends in France. 'Aaah,' they sighed, 'this is how I remember wine in the good old days.' Gently oxidized, in other words, with a faint smell of varnish; 'Pagan wine', my appreciative brother once called it. Recently I was sent what was clearly a fairly prestigious bottle from Argentina. A Sémillon (which sounds like 'Semijon' in those parts: they do something Welsh with a double-l). There it was, the soft, flat, over-exposed white wine. Oxygen had not turned it sour, on the contrary it had made it mellow.

Modern southern white wines don't even flirt with the idea. They are judged on how fresh their fruit, how high their acidity. And the new regime has turned up some excellent flavours from grapes whose names used to be hardly known.

Viognier is the first. We were driving to Provence, Judy and I (this was in the 1970s), and hesitated between the two hotels that then sparred across the Rhône at Condrieu. The Beau Rivage in Condrieu was the grander; the Belle Vue, across the bridge in Les Roches de Condrieu, appealed more to our budget, and its dining room had an alarming view of all the Rhône's brown waters swirling straight towards you. Condrieu was a legendary name to me: home of a celebrated wine I had never tasted and, I gathered, was almost extinct. There it was on the wine list. It came, with a curious black and gold label: Jurie des Camiers, viticulteur à Condrieu. The sommelier poured; I can taste it now. Its perfume was like a garden of unknown flowers. My first thought was the hawthorn in a May hedge, then freesias (or apricot; they are twins). Then I thought I must have smelled this in Germany, Rheinhessen, on the red soil of Oppenheim. Then I sipped, and felt it cool and plump in my mouth, a touch sweet, finishing dry. We ate quenelles de brochet. How do I remember that? Because the flavours are fused; I can see the pink and gold together. It was a moment of learning not to forget.

Next morning we set off to find M Jurie des Camiers across the river. Eventually we were directed to a tall bourgeois house in a garden; no sign of vines, or of people, until we heard the thwack of tennis. The young players told us our man lived in Lyon, there was no wine to sell but yes, please accept this bottle (fetched from the house) and card. It was the only Condrieu we did find. Georges Vernay was the principal producer, we gathered, but he was out, too. Where were the vineyards? Up there. Where precisely? Mixed in with the other vines, and the peach trees (and cabbages in some cases) up the extremely steep hill behind the village to the conspicuous and celebrated terraces of Côte Rôtie at the top. Further research revealed that the scented grape grew only here and was on its last legs: degenerate, decadent, no demand … and its name was Viognier. Furthermore it had its own Montrachet or Château Yquem: its holy of holies, Château Grillet. That was it, high on the ridge behind the wall. No luck calling here either, and when I finally tasted it I wished I hadn't bothered. It was brown and its fruit wasted. That morning, though, I called at the rival hotel to see what I could find. 'No Condrieu,' they said coyly, 'it's too soon. We have some *vin de table*, though.'

The glass the barman brought as *vin de table* was a shock. It was exotically perfumed – freesia and apricot – and extremely sweet. "We like it that way," said the barman, "but we can't call it Condrieu until it's finished." Perhaps this was why it was so rare: it was all guzzled half-fermented, as *paradis*.

Viognier has been rescued, and not only rescued but circulated round the wine-growing world as a jewel of price. It has not quite reached star status yet in any of its new homes, though in Australia it is getting there fast. Its perfume peeks out from many blends, the eye-liner for penny-plain Chardonnays from industrial vineyards. It is not an obvious menu-making choice; the reason, perhaps, why last year the sommelier suggested it at the restaurant that reinvented vegetables in France. The restaurant is Michel Bras, a lonely outpost of gastronomy on the heights of the Auvergne. You approach it from the cutlery town of Laguiole over wind-swept sheep-walks. On a fine morning, I have seen sun on the Pyrenees two hundred and fifty kilometres to the south.

Michel Bras paints pictures with vegetables high in the mountains of the Auvergne.

Bras is the poet-monk of restaura-teurs, an ascetic figure who expresses his passion for the austere Auvergne in dithyrambs as well as dishes. Lunch at his table starts with a perfect soft-boiled egg and a page of memoirs: eggs at his mother's knee, eggs as the expression of tenderness, the beginning of gastron-omy. You don't forget that egg, eaten with fingers of buttered toast before the immense landscape. What wine to drink with it? The sommelier (Serge is from Argentina) will be full of ideas.

Bras' signature-dish is the vegetables of the season composed as a painting, his *gargouillou*. A dry wine, a tannic wine, a sharp wine, an oaky wine would all stand between you and this garden-poem. The Condrieu was as fitting and natural as a bee visiting a flower.

There is nothing original about the trajectory Paris–Provence. It has been measured out in mealtimes since the Romans, and perhaps since the Greeks set up shop at the future Marseilles, made wine and traded it for slaves stolen from rival tribes by Astérix's ancestors. The rate at one time was one amphora to one slave.

Restaurants for the rich are spaced out along the way, at longer intervals now that we go faster down wider roads, but still forming an itinerary full of gastronomic nostalgia and romance. The two main roads from Paris to the south may even represent some kind of cultural distinc-tion: both head for Italy, but one over the Alps and one down to the Mediterranean and along the coast. Strangely, having left Paris by differ-ent gates, they meet twice en route, at Fontainebleau and Lyon. The Route Nationale Six passes the doors of celebrated kitchens at Avallon and Saulieu before crossing the Côte d'Or. This is the Burgundy road, past

Chagny and Châlons and Mâcon to Lyon, all names redolent of wine and the satisfaction of appetite. After Lyon its course becomes less certain. A good meal at Chambéry, no doubt, but then narrow valleys and mountain privations up to the Mont Cenis Pass and Italy.

The Nationale Sept leaves Paris by the Porte d'Italie, salutes the crown at Fontainebleau, then heads south to the Loire. En route to Lyon it threads the narrow streets of Moulins on the Allier, the capital of the Bourbons before they became kings of France, a crooked and difficult road to this day over high ground to Roanne, an ugly town of gastronomic pilgrimage to Les Frères Troisgros. After Lyon, though, the N7 is the greedy highway, straight down the Rhône via Vienne (la Pyramide), Valence (Restaurant Pic) to Orange and Avignon. There is a rudimentary poem in these names already. The whole route, all the way to Rome, is the ancient Roman Via Aurelia, by Aix-en-Provence, over the hills to Fréjus, threading the narrow coastal corridor, retitled the Moyenne Corniche, from Cannes to Menton and the Italian Border.

Before the Blue Train carried the *gratin* of the north to the Riviera everybody, one imagines, frequented the same hotels and discussed the same menus. There were leisurely travellers to the sun like Lawrence Johnston, moving between his gardens at Hidcote and Menton with his butler and ten dogs, and gamblers in a hurry like Wolf Barnato. He set off from London in his Bentley at the same time as the Blue Train, pausing only for a final bottle of champagne before scattering the chickens in his dust-cloud down the N7 – and arriving in Nice in time to meet the same train.

Not only famous restaurants serve good food. In the days when telephone numbers were single digits you ate well all over France. Pauchouse is a fish stew of the River Saône.

The red wines, you could reasonably argue, are more exciting on this southern route than the white. After Lyon they are Côte Rôtie, then St Joseph, then Hermitage and Cornas, then Châteauneuf-du-Pape and the Villages of the Rhône. But just as Côte Rôtie has its Condrieu, Hermitage and Châteauneuf-du-Pape have their white counterparts. Hermitage Blanc appeared on 19th century lists of the greatest white wines alongside Montrachet. More surprising, its special virtue was that it lasted a hundred years. Its secret? Two more grape varieties scarcely found elsewhere: Marsanne and Roussanne. Tweedledum and Tweedledee are perfectly complementary. Marsanne has a higher profile – an Australian fan club, indeed. Its characteristic of starting dull and over-heavy, then putting on nutty style after a few years, is well understood in such Victorian vineyards as Chateau Tahbilk. It is not a one-act turn, on the other hand; it is the main component of the region's oddest speciality, the succulent sparkling St Péray. Roussanne has more acidity, scent and nerve. It also ages well. None of which really answers the puzzle of the centenarian white Hermitage. What I find, and I have hidden away a few bottles for as long as thirty years, is that they say little young, and not much more old, unless you treat them more like red wines. Whoever said decanting makes no difference has not tried an old white Hermitage.

Turn left at Avignon for Italy and white wine grows strangely scarce. They will tell you about the coastal zone of Cassis near Marseilles, but don't hold your breath. Once in Provence, you must come to terms with rosé.

Many clichés have found their way into this book, but few will be as familiar as the one about the wine that doesn't travel. 'It was perfection,' it goes, 'as we sat under the pergola with the sea at our feet. They were wild, really savage, those anchovies in the salade Niçoise, the eggs had yolks by Van Gogh, the tomatoes were by Gauguin and the onions Cézanne. But the wine: I thought strawberries at first, fresh-picked in the woods. Then Vanessa said cherries and Sebastian said a touch of tar. That made Angelo come up with truffles. I can't remember who said mint. The bottles looked stunning with the beads of sweat running down. By this time we were too plastered to read the label. Anyway it was gorgeous, but when we tried to find it at Harrods they sold us this battery acid.'

I should love to know them all, these white wines from red grapes that hold sway from Aix to St Tropez and Nice to Draguignan. I can tell you that at Bandol, which has the best red wine of Provence, the rosés are deeper and rounder and

My daughter Kitty lives in the South of France and provides timely advice on which rosé to pick.

almost in earnest. The smart crowd at St Tropez on the beach at Club 55, the view of their bronze bodies obscured only by a gold chain or two, nibble their crudités and exclaim over the pale Rosé de Pampelonne, from vineyards by the sea. Consult a chic *caviste* and he will tell you that paler is better: what Californians call 'blush' is about right. But somehow I never pursue my studies beyond a second bottle. One can never keep frivolous thoughts at bay for long enough.

Turn right at Avignon, on the other hand, and (once you are over the hump of Tavel, the heavy orange rosé which every good Frenchman salutes like the Tricolor) the hills and even the plains of Languedoc present a more promising prospect. You are in New Wine World, with few fixed points of reference – of which most are red, and the potent muscats sweet. But the association of white grapes and limestone holds good here, too – as I discovered on the one-time island of la Clape.

This was the first Roman province of Gaul, its capital the little city of Narbonne and its monuments to Roman enterprise everywhere. Civil engineering does not get much more ambitious than at Ensérune, where hundreds of acres of farmland is sculpted into a single circular basin, draining mysteriously to a central plug-hole.

La Clape in Roman times was an island in the delta of the River Aude, a flat-topped chunk of limestone washed by the Mediterranean, unique I believe on the whole French coast. I went there prospecting for wines with my Wine Club partner Tony Laithwaite. Reds and rosés were the local norm (and Tony's system to follow the local Rugby heroes: the bigger the man, the better the wine). It was the time in the 1970s when things were just beginning to stir. Demolombe and Dubernet were the first oenologists to venture this far south. We had a barbecue by Demolombe's newly acquired ruin high on la Clape. Fish and herbs and a blunt herb-scented white wine I remember more clearly than all the potent reds that followed. It didn't have the spike of acidity that makes white wine refreshing, but somehow it didn't need it. It was dense, dry, smelling of the *garrigue* and the sea and tasting of honey-smeared rocks. I met it again later and was told I couldn't buy any, it had all gone to Air France First Class. Now all the wines on la Clape seem to be red. But it gave me a notion of what a white wine of the Midi can be. It stood out from the surrounding Chardonnays like a painting among prints.

There are almost no such wines in my cellar. The one Midi white my friends ask for, and I gladly supply, is the exotic invention of Aimé Guibert, who single-handedly launched the moribund Coteaux du Languedoc as a serious wine region in the 1980s with his Mas de Daumas Gassac. His white is, as an American friend put it, 'even more unique'; a blend of Chardonnay and Viognier and Petit Manseng a long way from its Basque-country home and, I imagine, a touch of Muscat for the scent. Like a Gewurztraminer, it is a wine no-one can fail to notice.

As I scour the Mediterranean coasts for white wines as memorable as its fishy feasts, I am ready for disappointment. The usual one is tastelessness. Wine-makers play safe, insulate their wine from the air, from temperatures above jolly cool, from natural yeast, from all reality, and sterilize it in the process. The curse of the Italian coast is Trebbiano, the bountiful blank of a grape grown to stretch Chianti, and in France (alias Ugni Blanc) to make Cognac. But recent years have produced far better things from Vermentino to Asprinio and Ansonica (or vice versa). Do they really need distinguishing, these coastal resources? My practice is to take the nearest, which means, from north to south, Vermentino (round La Spezia, on Elba, Corsica and Sardinia); Vernaccia (in Tuscany, and a different one in Sardinia), Grechetto (in Umbria), Malvasia (round Rome and on the islands of the Tyrrhenian Sea), Greco and Fiano (further south round Naples, Inzolia in Sicily). Texture and fruity succulence more than aroma is what these varieties offer.

Few things are as succulent as the Malvasias made on the volcanic islands of the Aeolian Sea, north of Sicily – Lipari, Stromboli and their neighbours. In the early years of the Wine Club we sailed (in a steamer; not all our voyages were wind-driven) from Greece to these islands in a replay of a regular run of the ancient Greeks. Very ancient Greeks: the Myceneans, many centuries before the rise of Athens. Perhaps the Phoenicians, too, even longer ago. Agamemnon's men went to Lipari for razor-blades. Blades, anyway: obsidian, the black shattered lava you find there, made the keenest edge then known. Quite possibly they took the vine that later became known as Malvasia, or Malmsey, both names apparently coming from the port of Monemvasia in the Peloponnese. Greece is certainly the source of vines, and wine-making technology, for most of Italy, most of Spain, most of North Africa, and even Portugal. On Lipari, sitting in the balmy evening air under a vine, looking out at the wine-dark sea, I had no trouble dreaming myself back to the creak and splash of galleys, triremes with three banks of oars slicing the grey rollers south of Italy. This wine seemed right for the fighters of the Trojan wars: amber, nut-flavoured, dense and strong.

Greece has turned its back on the sort of wine it gave to the rest of the world. I met perhaps the last traces of it on that other sea-girt volcano, Santorini, where scattered vines crouch from the scouring wind like birds' nests in the rocks. The cellars, equipped with ancient barrels, were caves in the cliff-face. Even under the Islamic Ottoman empire, Santorini

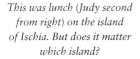

This was lunch (Judy second from right) on the island of Ischia. But does it matter which island?

produced its wine. It was the main supplier to the Russian Orthodox church, the sworn enemy of Turkey: a curious anomaly. Almost as strange is the recent revival of these vineyards to make white wine that seems to come from a different world; fresh, pale, crisp and totally 21st century. One of the best wines, indeed, of modern Greece.

The place where the Greek tradition of high-strength wine allowed or encouraged to turn brown took firmest root was not Italy but Spain. Andalucía perfected it. The fino of Jerez to my mind is the southern counterpart of champagne, a stylistic extreme turning disadvantages on their head. In champagne the grapes were unripe and too acid; in Jerez the opposite. What could be done about it? Painstaking processing is the answer.

There is hardly any sherry in my cellar. Perhaps its idiosyncrasy – that it is best almost as fresh as milk – is why it is so often overlooked. Sweet ones: a few. I'll come to them along with my other sticky treasures. But only one or two bottles of my favourite finos at a time. It doesn't positively go off with keeping (it does once the bottle is opened) but there is no virtue in storing it; no satisfaction in a wooden case or a pile of bottles biding their time. It is hard to persuade people to think of fino as a wine in the usual sense at all, its taste is so different: heady and dust-dry. No other wine tastes of olives (or goes with them so perfectly). But then no other wine so begs for food and is so often drunk without it.

Not the case in Spain. The browsing culture of Andalucía, tapas never far away, must explain the times its citizens choose to sit down to dinner – unless it is the other way round. Once during the September *feria* in Jerez we were invited to a formal dinner at 11.30pm. Determined not to do the predictable English thing and turn up on time we dallied (this was not easy) until midnight. We were the first to arrive. A long table was being laid in the garden. There was fino (we had drunk a little that day already) and tapas (not our first, either). At one o'clock we sat down with a most peculiar sensation: the tablecloth was drenched with dew and our legs and feet soaked. No-one commented.

Sushi and tapas, I realized when I first went to Japan, are first cousins. With sushi you sip saké. Saké and fino are not unalike in concentration and strength (though fino is not improved by being served hot). It would be fun, I thought, to have an investigating dinner tasting sushi with fino, and saké with tapas. The experts were a Japanese professor of culinary arts and the most urbane (and possibly even too diplomatic) Mauricio Gonzalez-Gordon, Marqués de Bonanza and the head of the house of Gonzales Byass.

We made it too complicated. We tried not only fino but manzanilla, not only manzanilla but amontillado, not only amontillado but palo cortado, not only palo cortado but old dry oloroso. The Jerezanos cannot resist it: they want you to see the whole range of what they make with their one rather plain little grape, the Palomino. (Japanese friends tell me you could do something similar with saké. I don't believe it.) Manzanilla is the purest and most appetizing of the set. It provokes saliva just to think of the little glass, beady with cold; a plate of prawns crisp and brown, and soft sand warm beneath my toes. I am swept away to where the manzanilla barns come down to the beach, to Sanlúcar de Barrameda. They put brine in the wine, do they? It could account for the tang.

They call palo cortado the indeterminate one: neither fine nor fragrant, in the jargon of the bodega. That leaves soft, rich and thought-provoking – thoughts like what to eat with it. Had we stuck to a fino or two, the same with saké, and concentrated more on the variety of miniature banquets that passed before us, I would be able to offer you some rare research findings. It was quite an evening, though.

IV   Red

The First Duty of Wine

HAVE YOU EVER confused burgundy and bordeaux? "Not since lunch." This honest answer is attributed to Harry Waugh; one of England's most gifted and popular wine merchants, whose palate kept going into his 95th year. Why would he have confused them? Or why would it matter? Wine-lovers love to quiz each other, to give each other a chance to look foolish. The two great classic French reds are the perfect starting point: theoretically totally different but, when they are good, both so appealing that in your enthusiasm you can (I can, anyway) plump for the wrong one.

So: in my left-hand glass, burgundy; in my right, bordeaux. One a Volnay, the other a Pauillac. How would I start to guess which one is which? I start by looking at the colour, holding each glass at an angle against something white. The tablecloth, for instance, or a piece of paper. The answer could lie here. If one glass is a light transparent red, either bright cherry, slightly purple or slightly brown, that's the burgundy. A self-respecting bordeaux can't be that colour. Why? The Cabernet and Merlot grapes have thick skin with a bluish cast; their wine may be darker or paler, but it can never be the translucent red of wine made in Burgundy from the thin-skinned Pinot Noir.

If the colour doesn't tell me, the smell should. Does one glass have a sweet, crisp, cherry- or plum-like smell; perhaps a bit earthy, like beet-root? That's burgundy. Does one smell of blackcurrants and/or green peppers, with a touch of iodine or iron and perhaps a whiff of pencil-shavings? That sounds like the Médoc to me; particularly Pauillac.

That all sounds simple enough. Unfortunately, though, it applies only to quite young wines. There may be other distractions, too; notably the greenish smell of raw oak or the coffee-like smell of oak that has been 'toasted' or singed. Either could have that. With two wines that are ten or fifteen years old and in any way atypical, confusion can start. If the colour and the smell together didn't make the answer apparent, the flavour might not either. But all this of course is a mere game beside the real point: do you like it? How much? And is it the sort of wine you want to drink?

There is a far wider choice of red wines than white. I am not, as you gather, one of those who think the first duty of wine is to be red. But there are many who do, and one can see their point. Red wines contain tannins. Tannins give wine texture, a 'grip' on the palate that can pinch like a shoe or scrape like sandpaper, but can also invigorate or caress, even invigorate and caress. A glass of red wine fills your mouth with warmth. It is more of a 'drink' – or so think my French friends. We sit in a café together. It's red for them and, usually, white for me. In a bad café it just shows they have more experience: bad white wine is even worse than bad red.

If the world offers us, say, ten really useful white grapes, it offers thirty red. And not only the grapes, but the traditions and cultures that go with them. Burgundy and bordeaux were the first to become luxuries and international icons. They have sown their seed round the world, but the red wine world still divides, neatly if not accurately, by the shape of its bottles into those with memories, or loyalties, or some kind of tendencies towards Bordeaux, and those in spiritual thrall to Burgundy. Straight-sided, high-shouldered, stiff-necked bottles for the first; a looser look, shoulders drooping, a well-tailored curve of the neck for the second.

In my cellar, as in the world at large, the Bordeaux Persuasion has the lion's share. It is partly my taste, partly because they tend to have the longest leases: when they come, they come to stay. I have never quite established why the standard lot of wine is a dozen bottles. It must enrage the metricators. Isn't it because 12 is divisible by two, three, four and six; and ten by only two and five? A ten-bottle case would be awkwardly long and thin. (Hard to believe, but champagne used to be sold in hampers of 50 bottles. Whoever lifted them?) Twelve bottles in a case allows you to observe and enjoy the early stages of a wine's life, track it coming to maturity, and still gives you half a dozen or so to drink when it really flowers. I find, though, that with far more good wines to choose from and their prices far higher, six bottles of one wine is the more practical number. I buy half-cases when I can. Besides, 12 weigh twenty kilos, and the cellar stairs get steeper every year.

Let me tell you about the prospect from the bottom of the stairs. On the right is the work-in-progress table, with wines to taste, recent arrivals, papers and the tools of the taster's trade. It has a shrine to history: an alcove with an amphora that Joseph Berkmann, an inspired and inspiring wine merchant and restaurateur, brought up, as a naval diver, from the seabed in Spain. In another alcove it has a dwindling stock, with mouldering labels or no labels at all, of vintage port I brought with me from London. One dozen was delivered in an old Haig Whisky case with a hinged lid like something from the First World War. For packing, they had straw jackets. For labels, just a streak of white paint to indicate which way up the bottle had been lying. The rest of the room is bordeaux in wooden boxes and German wine in cardboard ones. Most of the boxes are open. Work is in progress.

Claret. I am always using the word. Is it just an Anglicism, and an archaic one at that, meaning a red wine from Bordeaux; or does it signify a wine of a definite style? Is there, in other words, an archetype? A good place to look would be on the lists of those conservative British wine merchants who, like their forebears, select their own wine and bottle it under their private labels. Good Ordinary Claret is one of the best-selling wines at Berry Bros & Rudd in London. The English West Midlands and much of Wales thrives on Tanners' Claret from Tanners of Shrewsbury. Lay & Wheelers' Claret supplies much of East Anglia, Cockburn's Claret the conservative palate of Edinburgh, and the Wine Society's half the lawyers and doctors in Britain. Nor is the tradition dying out: you see supermarkets these days now labelling their own claret (subtitled 'Red Bordeaux').

They are light wines, usually a full but transparent red, no more than 12.5 per cent alcohol, and refreshing to drink. The main grape in most cases is Merlot (it is the main Bordeaux grape now) which gives it a rather leaf-green flavour. It is dry, lightly tannic, easy to swallow in liberal doses. It sounds rather like tea in this description. You could say it fulfils a similar purpose.

The Marqués Voyage

Shakespeare lifted whole plots from Froissart's Chronicles. I thought they were good stuff, too. But one episode made such an impact on my schoolboy mind that I can still quote it. In 1372 the English wine fleet sailing up the Gironde to Bordeaux numbered two hundred sail. Possibly not all on one tide, but what a picture: the estuary covered from side to side, the sea thronged with fat little wooden ships and their square sails. The tide turned at dawn and the armada crept along the marshy Médoc shore, blocks creaking, bow-waves rustling, conversations heard across the water. Men turned out to scrub the decks (did they in those days?) as they passed the fort at St Mambert which, a few years later, would be another Anglo-French battlefield – and, two centuries after that, be called Château Latour.

I always wanted to sail that passage, to see the same shoreline in the same pearly Gascon light from the shrouds of a square-rigged ship tight to the wind. I have done it now three times: once as crew and twice as a passenger, on ships ranging from a frankly dangerous old Balearic brigantine to the most luxurious clipper ever commissioned. All old sea-routes can stir romantic imaginings, but to me the Bordeaux run is fundamental to my very identity. Those tubby old cogs of Froissart's were the first claret-carriers, bringing wine down the Bordeaux river and over the heaving grey sea to the British Isles.

Claret was brand new wine, so fresh it had hardly had time to settle from fermentation. The wine fleet came to fetch it in October. If necessary the harvest was picked scarcely ripe to be ready for the rendezvous. A week of fair weather in early November meant it could be onshore all around Britain with a month to go before Christmas. The ships were like the Dunkirk fleet: anything that could be spared from any little harbour, most of them smelling of fish. Claret was the wine that was clear enough to travel. If you pierced a barrel two-thirds of the way down you could leave the rest, murky with unsettled sediment, for your competitors who missed the tide. For the wine it amounted to a rapid racking. Claret meant clear; it meant pale (there was no time for long maceration, nor a taste for tannin) and it implied first choice. In French there is no such word – nor even in America, either.

My first claret-run was in 1975. Tony Laithwaite was an independent, indeed a solo, wine merchant with a little business in Windsor, a rented arch under the railway his improvised cellar. He went to Bordeaux as an archaeology student from Durham and stayed at Castillon, the town on the Dordogne where England's army finally lost its Bordeaux dominion to the King of France. Thirty years later he has a château and a business empire based in the hamlet where he first drank claret. By 1975 he had so impressed the editor of *The Sunday Times* with the simplicity and probity of his little business, ferrying wine from Castillon to Windsor (hence its name: Bordeaux Direct), that the two cooked up the first newspaper wine club. They asked me, a long-time *Sunday Times* writer, to be its president.

Which is how the two of us took to the sea together.

Why? Salt water in our veins, no doubt. Why then? Bordeaux was in trouble. The price of its wine had suddenly halved. Israel's war with Syria had doubled the price of oil and the wine boom that started with the splendid 1970 vintage had gone into reverse. It would be a symbol of solidarity with our suppliers to sail the old route in the nearest thing we could find to a medieval ship. The *Marqués* was bigger, but the technology was not far different.

We invited the archbishop, the mayor and the burgers to see us off from the Bordeaux quay where, in our romantic minds, millions of barrels had been loaded for England. Never mind that up to the late 18th century they were loaded from the beach. If the mayor and archbishop were there I missed them, enthralled with the fall of topsails from the heavy yards, the mizzen boom slamming into place and the cracking of rigging taking the strain. The masts were dwarfed by the high span of the Pont d'Aquitaine carrying the Paris road (there was no bridge at all until after Napoleon). Then our little two-master was absorbed by the mist and tide as we headed for the sea.

Next morning we were still passing vineyards on the Médoc shore. We had a rendezvous with a lighter at Château Loudenne to load a deck-cargo of barrels to add to the six hundred cases of claret in the hold. Château Loudenne was where I had met my wife-to-be ten years before. Her family's business, Gilbeys, had shipped wine out of the little dock there for over half a century before it silted up and road transport took over. We went ashore to wait for the tide to turn and play a sort of cricket on the lawn with the pilots: one pilot for the river, one for the river-mouth. You never forget such golden days.

The Marqués *was our first sailing freighter from Bordeaux. Here she lies off the little harbour of Château Loudenne.*

The Bay of Biscay can be a millpond. So motionless that we dived off the bowsprit and swam round the ship. The *Hispaniola*: that's what she reminded me of. She was the very ship that carried Jim Hawkins, Squire Trelawney, Long John Silver and the rest to Treasure Island.

There would be nothing much more to report had the weather stayed that way. Just a long slow chug home, unavailable to our forebears. But late August is when sudden depressions arrive in northern Europe from the Atlantic. Forecasting equipment on the *Marqués* was rudimentary. You sucked your forefinger and held it up to the wind. We left the port of Brest (where we had put in, as far as I remember, to go to the cinema) with the promise or threat of a big wind from the west. Students of naval warfare will know that on-shore winds made possible Britain's blockade of the French fleet and the containment of Napoleon. We decided to come out and run for home before the wind blockaded us. It was a rash decision. We nearly drowned, and our wine was given a shaking. But the scene in the channel was worth the detour: we were a Dutch painting of a ship in distress, the foresails torn to shreds and flap-

*In the rigging.
An experience perhaps
better in retrospect.*

ping out ahead, red ribbons against the grey spray of the sea. White waves as high as the masts lifted the stern like a cork; the *Marqués* skied down them in a frenzy of foam.

At wind force ten, I learned, the surface of the sea blows off and races like a sandstorm. It is hard to see where you are going. If we had been on a lee shore it would have been shipwreck, but the English Channel gives you a long straight run in a westerly. We were trying to find Cornwall, but found the relative shelter of Torbay two hundred and forty kilo-metres to the east. As we passed the tall sheltering headland of Start Point it was like a door shutting against the gale. Anticlimax. Tony and I had finished our bottle of vintage cognac, we discovered, and were ready for more – cognac, wind: bring 'em both on.

It was many years, though, before we did another claret run. Mean-while the *Marqués* was lost in what sounded like the same sort of blow off Bermuda. But this time the sails did not split and she sailed straight on down. All hands perished.

When we went back to Bordeaux it was as trainees on a sail training brig, the *Astrid*, with a dozen members of The Sunday Times Wine Club. I was surprised by how many volunteered for the hair-shirt routine of keeping watches and handling the 16 sails on this approximate miniature of one of Nelson's ships. We left the same quay in Bordeaux with four hundred cases of claret. You opened a cupboard anywhere on board: boxes of wine. Again a reception for dignitaries on the quay, but this time a bad omen: the table, glasses, champagne, shrimp and mushroom *barquettes* were picked up by a gust and dropped in the river.

You don't need a second account of crossing the Channel in a summer gale. In mid-gale the first mate was standing on the deck-house roof surveying the efforts of his trainees to tame the writhing cordage and snatching sails. "You can't get the staff these days," was his remark. Next morning Weymouth Bay was a golden pond caressed by a zephyr. Just the thing for a sadistic skipper to give his exhausted crew some tacking practice. Three times about, three times 16 sails-worth of sheets and braces to free, haul and re-coil shipshape on their cleats under the morning sun. Our hands were raw when we slid smoothly alongside Weymouth quay, furling sails in succession, to a one-gun salute and a cheer from the shore. Absurdly, for a moment I knew how it felt to come home from a long voyage; to leave a cramped and dangerous wooden world for space, peace and the smell of green.

Upgraded accommodation. Our latest Bordeaux voyage was in pampered luxury on the old wine-trade sea route to the Bay of Biscay and south to Oporto and Lisbon.

SEA CLOUD II

The wines we carried home have long since been drunk. They were not grand wines, just the light dry reds that Bordeaux can still do better than anywhere else on earth. They are, come to that, faintly earthy, with a tang of the gravel about them and the sweet leafiness of the Cabernet cousins, Sauvignon, Franc and Merlot. When Bordeaux looks over its shoulder at all the world's Cabernets thundering up behind, it should remember one thing. Big and strong is easy. You can make Cabernet sweet, dark and alcoholic almost anywhere the sun is hot enough. So far, though, Bordeaux is the only place that makes great light red wines. Claret, in fact.

Bordeaux with Friends

I

F YOU WANT to give a wine enthusiast a treat, there is something even better than a bottle: introduce him to a fellow sufferer. To have a precious bottle of wine and no-one to discuss it with is a kind of torture. I frequently come across groups of friends who know each other's cellars, or cupboards, as well as they know their own. Sometimes they just pop round for an evening to see how a vintage is coming along; sometimes they formalize the affair, gang up to make a foursome or a sixsome, and call themselves a dining club.

If they have a recurring theme, these clubs, it is bordeaux. There is simply no other wine that comes in such quantity, in such variety, that lasts so long – and that above all is so eminently discussable. I have heard purists (strangely enough in Burgundy) object that bordeaux is a mongrel because it mixes two, three or four grape varieties. They are all being used, though, to make the same sort of wine. The differences arise because the local climate and soil favour one variety rather than another. And of course because each château has its tradition, not to mention each owner his or her taste. The interest (not that I am discounting the pleasure) is in recognizing the production of different properties and following them through different vintages as they mature. Train-spotting? More fun.

The Bordeaux Club (the pretentious part of its name is the definite article: for all we know there are scores of others) is a group of six friends who meet three times a year at each other's houses. It was founded by Harry Waugh, a wine merchant, and Sir John Plumb, a historian, biographer of England's first Prime Minister and Master of Christ's College,

*The Bordeaux Club
in pre-dinner champagne
session on our sunburnt
lawn. Jack Plumb is
the one in the straw hat;
Harry Waugh is on
the left.*

Cambridge. If its dinners and deliberations are better known than others it is mainly due to Michael Broadbent, who has recorded every wine and published his notes on many of them in his monumental tasting books.

It is seven o'clock on a January evening in Jack Plumb's rooms. He is sitting in a velvet smoking jacket below a glowing Renaissance portrait. "You're our champagne man, Hugh," he says (his way of saying you don't know much about claret, I fear). "I'm not sure about this Jacquesson 1976." I'm glad I'm not asked to identify it. I think it is a bit sweet and oddly raw for a famously hot vintage some twenty years old. When Jack doesn't like something he makes a point of saying so.

His dining room is downstairs, a panelled parlour hung with peri-wigged professors and lit by candles. It must have looked identical one, two or three centuries ago. I wonder, and we talk about, how different the food and wines would have been in the days of Jack's hero, Sir Robert Walpole. The food not very, I believe: college food without frills. We start with grilled fillets of Dover sole and drink Château Haut-Brion Blanc 1985. The château makes only a few barrels of its white wine, Bordeaux's most expensive by far. We decide, amicably, that in this vintage, rather almond-flavoured and not terribly lively, it is not worth it. There is no great choice among the white-wine châteaux of Bordeaux: we know all the notable successes by heart. We even resort to white burgundy.

With a bang of the heavy door the waiters arrive with the pheasants, roast, with big silver dishes of celeriac purée and Brussels sprouts and brown game chips and grey bread sauce. Walpole would have had no surprises. He would have loved the first claret, though. Château Canon 1982, St-Emilion, full of meat, velvety, rich and full of nuances (my notes tell me) but with what I called a minty fresh finish. Freshness is the touchstone of any great bordeaux. An eclectic lot, the wines were that evening; not a regimented comparison, all one vintage, or all one château, more a gossip with old friends. Château Pichon-Lalande 1978 was rather simple, I noted; its characteristic green-smoky smell of Merlot triggers memories of red Loire wines. This was the first vintage made by May-Eliane de Lencquesaing, one of Bordeaux's great hostesses and a friend of everyone at the table.

Château Latour comes up gratifyingly often at these dinners; the enigmatic 1975 not often. Enigmatic? There was no consensus. Everyone noticed now dark it was; tannic, too. To me it started full of fresh promise, then produced the hallmark Latour taste of earth and iron, then rather disappeared. Some said hold, some said drink – or even dump. A more interesting conversation than reaching for superlatives, in any case. And the next wine, a not very well-known château of a great vintage, made another good talking point. The Margaux Château Malescot-St-Exupéry 1961 could be called a sleeper; dark, sweet and spicy, very much a Cabernet Sauvignon, tasting more like Pauillac than Margaux, and finishing on a note of sweet decadence.

We were primed at this point for a First Growth of a delectable vintage, Château Haut-Brion 1953. Welsh, or more specifically Abergavenny, Rabbit had followed the pheasant. The Haut-Brion was poured. It was corked – and the only bottle. There is no hiding the disappointment when this happens. Of course Jack should have tasted it when he decanted it, as we told him. He would have been sarcastic with us. Corked bottles are an inescapable fact, though no-one agrees on exactly how frequent.

Then followed the inevitable stories of even more embarrassing disasters and corked wine policy in general. Figures as high as ten per cent of all bottles are sometimes claimed, especially by reformers who would like to see corks abolished and all wines sealed with screwcaps. Some blame bad hygiene, slapdash methods or over-production in the cork industry, which is largely Portuguese. Chemists have identified the elusive but catastrophic agent that lurks in corks and infects wine with its mouldy smell. If all wine-drinkers recognized it, and rejected every tainted bottle, the wine-trade would go bust. It is worrying to think that its profits depend on its customers' ignorance.

Michael Broadbent relates the latest of many tricky moments. He was having dinner with an important client of Christie's wine auctions. His host pours a precious wine, tastes it, pours it for all his guests. As soon as Michael lifts his glass he knows it is corked (or 'corky': further discussion on semantics). Dilemma: do you say 'What a pity, it's corked;' and embarrass your host and anyone else who has tasted it? Do you do nothing, and expect embarrassment yourself when someone else points it out? We are all in favour of course one (having just followed it ourselves with poor Jack's Haut-Brion). And if it's only slightly corked? "You mean like being slightly pregnant?" asks the rubicund farmer member of our little circle.

Happily no-one felt like pursuing the endless debate about screwcaps that dominated wine-talk at the time. Cork is demonised by some, sanctified by others. To the first it is insanitary; old technology, an unnecessary breeding ground for fungus that can wreck the wine. The only problem with screwcaps is the lack of mystique: they spoil the theatre. 'Wait,' say the others, 'you have no idea what may happen as wine matures. Corks allow wine to breathe; starve them of oxygen and how can you be sure they will age in the same way?'

And so to the Sauternes. More banging of the door and a cut-glass bowl of pears in red wine takes the place of the Abergavenny Rabbit. There is also a heavy silver jug Walpole would have recognized, brimming with yellow cream. Jack pours deep golden glasses of Château Rieussec 1976, fruit of a hot dry summer, a wine known for its colour and flavour like rococo caramel. How predictable we are: one member says he doesn't like Sauternes with pudding. He says it every time. Then comes the discussion that always reminds me of *Gulliver's Travels*, where two countries go to war about which end you should open a boiled

Sweet or cheese? The conservatory doubles as a workshop to explore this evergreen dilemma.

egg. The question of cheese first or sweet first divides England. Positions are so entrenched that I'm sure you could tell a Cavalier from a Roundhead, probably a Saxon from a Norman, and possibly a Roman from an Ancient Briton by his position on cheese. Rationalized today, cheese belongs after the main course, continuing the savoury theme and finishing the red wine. Unless you belong to the faction that sees the sweet as an intermezzo before a proper finale: cheese and a glass of port. We drink Cognac, a cup of coffee, get out our diaries, go to bed. There is much to be said for ritual.

Altogether on a grander scale is the Saintsbury Club. Wine in general rather than bordeaux in particular is the theme of this body of diners, but claret is inevitably preponderant in its cellar. Fifty members, the founders decreed, is the proper number. Fifty can each have a glass from the largest bottle used in Bordeaux: the barely liftable Impériale.

The 50 meet twice a year, in April and October, in the Vintners' Hall in the City of London. History oozes from the stones of a place where wine merchants have met for eight hundred years, on one occasion entertaining five kings at one dinner. London's ancient livery companies have something of the air of little kingdoms themselves, with a continuity of history and ceremony, of duties and privileges and responsibilities and robes and rituals a prince would be proud of. The Saintsbury Club is a mere guest here and only sixty years old, but it has a precious privilege negotiated by its founders: it has its own spacious vault in the Vintners' cellar.

Who was Saintsbury? The author of a book not unlike this one, but one which so caught the public's imagination that it has rarely been out of print in eighty years: *Notes on a Cellar-Book*. He wrote "There is no money … of the expenditure of which I am less ashamed, or which gave me better value in return, than the price of the liquids chronicled in this book-let." "Good wine," he went on, "has pleased my senses, cheered my spirits, improved my moral and intellectual powers, besides enabling me to confer these benefits on other people." After that the story scarcely hangs together. He was Professor of English Literature at Edinburgh University. He wrote a history of the French novel, was warned off wine for his health (half of his Cellar-Book is about gin, whisky, other spirits, beer and even liqueurs) and was not well enough to attend the club named in his honour, or even to receive its founders. They included André Simon, Hilaire Belloc (of the *Cautionary Tales*) and A J A Symons, author of *The Quest for Corvo*. Letters and wine were their two loves, and members of their club would be men (no women) whose love of wine is both 'catholic and articulate'. The custom is that its members stock the cellar with wine they like and look forward to discussing with friends, usually a dozen bottles at a time. There are some generous members.

The duties of the Vintners' Company include the annual 'upping', which means the catching, weighing and tagging, of a proportion of the swans on the River Thames. It is a duty the liverymen take very seriously.

Nobody pretends the food is notable at Saintsbury dinners, though it is far better than it was twenty years ago when a member innocently enquired whether there was a rule against bringing sandwiches. But the wines, and the way they are served, are classical. I pick a menu from my collection almost at random. A glass of champagne on arrival, and before taking places at a horseshoe table set with a great twinkling of glasses. A clear game soup (super classical, this) with a glass of the sort of old sherry or Madeira nobody serves any more: nutty velvet, oak perfumed and penetrating, poised between sweet and dry. Each wine is credited on the menu to the member who gave it. Then scallops in a cheese sauce or sole in a dill one with a glass of white burgundy. This was formerly the place assigned to hock, its function being, among others, to remove all traces of the sherry before the claret.

Two different clarets is the norm; less often two different red burgundies and very rarely Rhône wines, though everybody loves them when they come round. Convention says never claret and burgundy at the same dinner. Why? It is often done in Paris. I think there is a belief that however good they may be neither will gain by comparison. Lamb is the most frequent main course, with many vegetables. I scribble notes on my menu: Château l'Enclos 1982 "Very sweet, a little simple." Château Cheval Blanc 1985 "Starts mint-cool, then opens in autumn-leaf richness, but lively, racy, almost light on the tongue. Beautiful texture and dancing length." Too soon, I always think, the word goes round that one of the wines is the 'winner', as though it were a race, and a sprint at that. Better, I quietly philosophize, to give each its turn. But then I am a slow drinker (or perhaps talk too much) and the port generally comes round too quickly for me.

Is there no modern wine in the Saintsbury cellar? Are its members stuck in an era that has still not heard of the New World? You are bound to ask the question, so let me answer it. I believe I was the first member to present Australian, Californian and New Zealand wines. The first to be served was a Chardonnay. I should have sent it with a Caution, or rather a Best Before date. Unfortunately, the Cellarer flattered it by keeping it as long as he would a fine white burgundy. The one comment was that it was too old.

Port. All in good time, and in the Sweet section. The Saintsbury Club has its own convention, though. Whether or not we have cheese (sometimes yes, sometimes no) we always serve Digestive biscuits, those very British sweet and crunchy wholemeal affairs, with the most fragrant of apples, Cox's Orange Pippins. Whoever invented the combination it is excellent, and a fine foil for port.

Dinner ends with a comment, rarely controversial, from the Yeoman of the Cellar on the wines of the evening, and a hint about anticipated shortages in the cellar (there is never enough champagne). We step into the night primed for anything – in my case, on one October night in 1964, rather overprimed. I set out from Thames Street to St John's Wood, a distance of some five miles across London. I had made up my mind, even before the port, to ask Judy to marry me. We had, after all, known each other for several weeks. It started to rain. There were no buses after midnight. No taxis appeared either – and I had decided to walk. Judy, when I rang the bell and woke her, was not pleased to see me. In a curious way, though, I believe my sodden dinner jacket stood more in my favour than against me. Nonetheless weeks had to pass before I dared propose again.

It is fair to ask whether the opinions of well-dined judges, even on wine, are to be relied on. Even the much-respected Professor Peynaud, rather surprisingly, says in his standard work on tasting, "If you can remember what a wine is like the next day you didn't drink enough of it." (I take notes.) Things rarely, at least in my experience, go so far as they did at a dinner at one of France's great restaurants given by a generous host to celebrate all the famous vintages ending in five. The first he had in mind was 1865: we drank, I should estimate, most of the remaining stock. Fourteen wines and five rich courses into the dinner he proposed a joint. For a moment I was confused. Professor Peynaud, though, would have been amply satisfied.

In comparison with such extravagances our English efforts are small beer indeed. Texas was where I first discovered how far an American wine-collector was prepared to go. The year was 1979. Marvin Overton was a neurosurgeon from Fort Worth who evidently found fulfilment in Château Lafite. He had collected so many vintages, far back into the 19th century, that when he wrote to the Baron Elie de Rothschild, the presi-

The artist Louann Lipscomb was inspired by Manet to portray me with my host and hostess on a Texan picnic.

dent of Lafite in those days, to propose opening a bottle of each one evening, the baron agreed to contribute from the château's cellar. This took the array of wines back through 38 vintages considered either great or very good to the end of the 18th century. The dusty brick bin of bottles from revolutionary France at Lafite is the Médoc's most hallowed shrine. The baron duly delivered a bottle of the 1799, which with the 1864 and the 1825, remains among my most fragrant memories. Michael Broadbent was asked to comment on the wines. I've seen him perform on five continents at seances even longer and more extrava-

gant than this. Evidently the tasting was considered a landmark in Texas: by Resolution 601 of the Texas Senate the participants were officially welcomed to the Lone Star State.

Thirty-eight great wines in an evening, in any case, is beyond what I consider reasonable. The most regular and lavish thrower of such parties I have met is a Bavarian called Hardy Rodenstock. He invited me to his 16th annual rare wines tasting in 1995. All the figures, not only the wines, were impressive: 23 chefs, 30 waiters and ten sommeliers were involved. One hundred guests drank 29 wines at dinner, all served blind, and another 32 next morning.

This seance started with a 'flight' (the word for a group of related wines) of Château Rausan and Château Lafite between 1868 and 1832. Then four 1921s in magnums (Pétrus, the oldest I had ever seen: simply beautiful). Then the four First Growth 1921s in magnums. By now I was getting left behind: loving Château Margaux for freshness and Château Latour for ripeness, wanting to sip for ever – but no: three more 1921s to sniff and swirl (Gruaud-Larose near perfection) before a flight of Château Yquem. Yquem? The youngest was 148 years old: 1847. While this was sinking in, the 1825, 1814 and 1811 appeared. Abandoning my 1921 Gruaud-Larose (shall I ever taste that again?) I tried to think Sauternes. 'The 1847 has it,' said someone. 'Absolutely,' came the chorus. Maybe, but any one of those bottles alone would have been an evening of fascination and delight. If there was a winner, the rest were losers: three extraordinary survivors cast into the shadows. The table was still discussing the 1847 (and I was sipping the 1811) when a flight of eight more 19th century clarets landed in our midst. Panic. Somehow or other I scribbled notes on them. Three of Lafite's most famous vintages (1870, 1865, 1864) are not to be ignored. They can be wasted, though.

The First Growths

AWE IS PERHAPS the best word to describe the attitude of most wine-lovers to the Bordeaux First Growths. Awe goes beyond respect or admiration into the realms of the unknown. 'I once tasted Latour,' I have heard people say, as though they had once walked to Santiago de Compostela. I am tempted to answer 'Didn't you like it?' It does seem excessive self-restraint to deny yourself something highly desirable, even if it costs five times as much as you normally consider the boat pushed right out. There are ways: five clubbing together works well.

So why the awe? Three hundred years of marketing is the answer. It was the brainwave of the President of the Bordeaux Parlement in the 1650s to make a super-wine, on his own estate, and dangle it in front of London society. He did it with conviction – and one would love to know just why he thought of it and how he set about it. The timing is no mystery: Bordeaux was brimming with money, and London was well known to be recovering from a long fit of temperance under the Puritans. Bordeaux, moreover, was tired of dealing with the bargain-driving Dutch. A spot of conspicuous consumption was what M de Pontac had in mind.

Was Paris not the answer? Not in the 1660s. Louis XIV had a cold glitter about him. The age of perfume and champagne had yet to arrive. Pontac in any case went straight to the point. 'My boy,' said he to his son, 'go and open a restaurant. London could use one. One day it will be Paris's turn, no doubt, but now that they are rebuilding London after that colossal fire, I fancy a spot on Abchurch Lane, near the Monument.

You can call it Pontac's Head,' he said, 'and if they want to carry our line at the King's Head, or even the Boar's Head, you can offer them, at favourable rates, either our ultra-premium Haut-Brion or the Pontac branded line I propose to source from my other place, Château de Pez at St-Estèphe in the next hot area, the Médoc.'

One would like to know more about Pontac Junior, his crossing to London, his struggles with the English tongue, his girlfriends and where he found his chef. We catch a glimpse of the wine (not the man) in Samuel Pepys's diary. In no time at all it was attracting tourists to Bordeaux, the young philosopher John Locke among them, curious to see what land produced such different and distinctive wine, and surprised to find it mere sand and gravel.

There was similar land in the Médoc, and similar families forming estates with the same idea: the first of them the future Château Margaux, with Latour and Lafite close behind. The First Growths were first, in fact, in time as well as in quality. It was no mystery, apparently, which spots had the most potential. And there was more collaboration than rivalry between these similar, and soon intermarrying, investors.

What is mysterious is the method of shipping they adopted to reach their market. Peace between France and England rarely lasted long and the English excise men were active. There was no certain way of smuggling without being caught, so they chartered privateers, ostensibly on the English side, and captured their own shipments. Perhaps one day we will find the give-away papers; for the moment we can only imagine the nods, winks and kickbacks en route. In 1707 the entire crop of Haut-Brion was taken as prize of war on board one ship, to be offered for sale in London as New French Claret. When it happened again the next year, you would think the authorities would have smelled a rat.

When I followed in John Locke's footsteps three hundred years later, I found Château Haut-Brion much as he must have seen it, though sadly encroached on by the city; a pale stone country mansion with an air of quiet prosperity. Château Margaux looked out proudly from behind its giant portico, Château Lafite was anybody's idea of a quiet place in the country, low spreading under its centenarian cedar, its gardens dedicated to flowers and vegetables rather than statues and display. But what intrigued me was Château Latour, a château only in the courtesy sense that Bordeaux applies to almost any building with more than a few vines; frankly a pretty ordinary and disproportionately tall bourgeois villa rather down on its luck.

The pretext for my call was an article for *House & Garden*, not on wine but on the furnishings of such famous houses. The elderly manager of Latour, M Brugières, was good enough to take me inside, perhaps a little surprised himself that it held any interest. *House & Garden* did not print my photos of the faded flowery wallpaper, but allowed me to say I was "reminded of a grand, deserted, rather shabby boarding-house." I was glimpsing the last of a regime about to disappear.

Château Latour had just been bought, in that year, 1962, by what was described as 'Lord Cowdray's interests'. Lord Cowdray gave a party to celebrate at the Christie's rooms in London and, I remember, drank Scotch. His interests did not quite end the succession of ownership that had descended from the Ségur family in the 17th century. Their descendants, the de Beaumonts, had owned it in the complicated Napoleonic way ever since. They kept one (extremely valuable) share, and a thoroughly interested Beaumont continued to sit on the board. But Médoc landowners who actually live in the Médoc were, and are, rare. The Beaumonts had châteaux – immense, machicolated, rambling – in the more sociable and sporting Loire Valley. Hence the rather modest affair they built at Latour.

On my first visit I was aware that things were about to change. The wallpaper was peeling, but Latour had just made two of its greatest vintages ever, in 1959 and 1961 (the 1960 and 1962 were pretty good, too). Were 'the directors in dark suits everywhere', as I rather sniffily described them in my first book three years later, about to spoil an antique formula that clearly worked?

As it fell out, their first vintage, 1963, did not give them or anyone else a chance. It was a washout. In 1964 they were on their mettle, all set with new presses and new vats (stainless steel, in itself a revolution) to show what they could do. I have clear memories of that vintage in the Médoc, though not at Latour. The summer had been hot. I was invited to stay, as a journalist, up the road at Château Loudenne, in the more humdrum Bas-Médoc where there are no Classed Growths, let alone First Growths. My host, Jasper Grinling, had two beautiful half-sisters, Mandy and Judy. They just happened to be staying there, and I just happened to have met Judy at a party in London days before. It rained. It rained on our house-party, and it rained on everyone out picking grapes. Relentlessly. The only grapes it did not rain on were at Latour, where the new directors, itching to get cracking and remembering 1963, plumped for an early harvest. Latour made wonderful wine. A final bottle was still radiating its distant summer when Judy and I drank it on our ruby wedding anniversary forty years later.

In those days I had not the faintest inkling that twenty-five years later

I would be one of those directors (though rarely, if ever, dark-suited). What was clear was that Latour and the other First Growths, remote as they might be, were a driving force behind the whole culture of the Médoc. They were the pace-setters, uncatchable but always in view. Why uncatchable? It is an article of faith that the first investors, free to plant their vines wherever they chose, got the best ground. Others clustered round, planting as close to them as they could; the Rausans, the Léovilles and the Pichons must have hoped to catch up, even to overtake. Only one property ever has: Lafite's neighbour, Mouton. It took the patience and persuasion, as well as the wine-making genius, of a Rothschild to do it. And Philippe de Rothschild, unlike any of his forebears or almost any of his neighbours, lived on the job. He was promoting not only himself but the Médoc when in 1973, after fifty years of campaigning, Mouton-Rothschild was elevated from Second Growth (albeit explicitly the first of the seconds) to First.

Mouton could have been part of Lafite. If there is a mystery in the soil of the Médoc it is this. Lafite and Mouton both belonged to the Comte de Ségur, known at Versailles as the Prince des Vignes. Legend says he wore stones from his vineyard, cut and polished, as waistcoat buttons, a promotional notion that his successor Rothschild might have dreamt up. But Ségur drew a line between his estates and made two wines (or more accurately four: he owned Latour and Calon in St-Estèphe, as well). Can he have tasted different characters in the wines that came from the hill of Lafite and those from the adjacent plateau of Mouton? It is not difficult today, but that is after three hundred years of distinction, of developing a different culture on each property, propagating different vines, using their different indigenous yeasts, and indeed looking for a different result. Ségur seems to have seen it in the land or tasted it in the vats. It remains a mystery: the provoking mystery of terroir. Could other Second Growths, with different owners, have made better wine than the Firsts? Better, in Médoc terms, I doubt. Different, perhaps more in tune with the times; that might happen. But if the competition is to fetch the highest price, there is an easier way. Make yourself scarce; the formula of today's contenders to be the most valuable wine: the *garagistes*.

Why is it that hierarchies have an innate attraction? Democrats we may be, but we are still suckers for a pecking-order. We want something to be designated best, in everything from artistic merit to the line-up of a football league. What is certain is that it leads to a distorted market, in which perhaps half of the price is for the pleasure, the other half (it can be much more than that) for the reassurance and, of course, prestige.

The Marriott Hotel in Times Square was rather like a prison. Certainly there was no escape for the proprietors of châteaux and domaines and port lodges and bodegas and *cantinas* who had come to show their wares at the *Wine Spectator*'s annual show. Marvin Shanken, the proprietor of the magazine, was a sheep-dog crossed with a bull terrier. He believed in rounding people up and making them perform. When he first brought his publication to the summer wine exhibition in Bordeaux, Vinexpo, I asked some of the staff on his stand if they liked Bordeaux. 'We're not going to see it,' was the answer. It was none of my business, of course, but I asked Shanken if I could take one or two of them for a spin up the Médoc to see a château, or even a vine. 'No,' was the answer – but more fully expressed. I remembered this when I found myself at the Marriott drinking impossible coffee in a smoky bar with the proprietors of three of Bordeaux's First Growths. They were required to be on hand, in person, all day to pour little samples of their wine for a long queue of the magazine's readers. Lafite in America, I was learning, was 'Eric Rothschild's Château Lafite', and no substitute – for Eric – accepted. "Surely you can have more fun than this," I said. "You would in Japan [which I had just started discovering]. Why don't I organize a First Growth Show there?" This was in Japan's boom years of the 1980s, when wine-growers all over the world had Yen in their eyes. Some say China will be next.

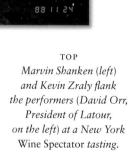

It was not I who organized it, but the firm I was working for as wine consultant, Jardine Wines & Spirits. When they heard that all the First Growths were game, including Château Yquem, they had the idea of a dinner of all the heroes: Japanese heroes, that is: sumo champion, poet, violinist, presidents of motor corporations. There was an extraordinary tasting, at which I introduced in turn the presidents and stewards (I can't think of a better translation for *régisseurs*) of Châteaux Haut-Brion, Lafite, Latour, Margaux, Mouton-Rothschild and Yquem. They each introduced two great vintages. It was the only such comparison of the First Growths I have ever witnessed. One little precaution, though: the same vintage never appeared twice; there were to be no direct comparisons – and they were right. In a direct clash one wine, however good, has to come second. We took a bullet train to do a second show in Osaka. Then came the

TOP
Marvin Shanken (left) and Kevin Zraly flank the performers (David Orr, President of Latour, on the left) at a New York Wine Spectator tasting.

ABOVE
Next stop: Japan. For some reason the Japanese market for wine was even more appealing.

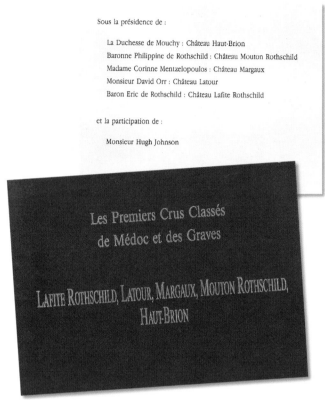

Sous la présidence de :

La Duchesse de Mouchy : Château Haut-Brion
Baronne Philippine de Rothschild : Château Mouton Rothschild
Madame Corinne Mentzelopoulos : Château Margaux
Monsieur David Orr : Château Latour
Baron Eric de Rothschild : Château Lafite Rothschild

et la participation de :

Monsieur Hugh Johnson

Les Premiers Crus Classés
de Médoc et des Graves

LAFITE ROTHSCHILD, LATOUR, MARGAUX, MOUTON ROTHSCHILD,
HAUT-BRION

TOP & ABOVE
*The First Growths rarely
go on tour together: one of
them is a sufficient draw.*

dinner. We were guests of Seiji Tsutsumi, the owner of much of Japan's railway system and described to me as four times as important as the prime minister. He lived in Tokyo (where space is measured out in teaspoons) in a modern house in an ancient garden, a century-old masterpiece of maples, cascades, bridges and lanterns.

Business-like analytical tasting-notes sound pretty flat at a dinner like this, however good the wines. I was required to sing for my supper: taste the wine, taste the food, think on my feet and say something to the point. There was a tricky moment when the first of the red wines was served with a gâteau de foie gras aux truffes. It was the legendary Latour 1961. Its bouquet was room-stopping; its flavours awe-inspiring – but it must be admitted that foie gras and such tannins are not made for each other. The effect was to emphasize the cut and denseness of the Latour; in fact, even at twenty-five years, its lack of maturity. I was reminded of drinking it in perfect harmony with dark cêpes at the château. My violinist neighbour was reminded of Smetana; I quoted him.

Lafite 1959 in magnums broke my reverie. Oddly, at first breath, the Lafite seemed just as massive and impenetrable as the Latour. But a few

RIGHT
*Japanese high society
(Asako Tsutsumi is haloed)
was duly impressed.*

moments revealed a depth of honeyed sweetness, a sort of feline charm matched with velvet. It filled your mouth at such length that it became almost monotonous. This was utter joy, perfectly set off by a dish of plain pale tender veal. The violinist said Handel. I didn't argue.

The next vintage, the 1953 of Château Margaux, was a huge step toward maturity from the full force of the first two wines. Its nose, I felt, was less a statement than a suggestion; its structure that of lace, delicately sweet with a touch of sharpness, in sly paradox with most persuasive harmony. I almost said Mozart before the violinist did.

Haut-Brion '49 was as great a contrast again. My notes on this go on and on. I could have mistaken the nose for Latour: a great male smoking-room smell. This was ripe but not sweet: earthy, rather. Deeper in colour than the Margaux, and explosively pungent. No wine that evening developed in the glass as much as this. However complete it seemed, each moment added another element of seduction: gathering sweetness, a limpid texture that made me think of cream poured over gravel. As the bouquet unfolded it became more smoky, autumnal, earthy, roast coffee-ish, and finally touched a note of caramel. I was too engrossed to hear what the violinist said, but I was hearing Haydn.

Mouton '45 in a Jeroboam was Napoleonic. My notes reveal that I was not as sober as when I tasted the Latour. "A roll of drums," I scribbled, "thunder on the horizon." The colour was almost threatening; the nose had such a depth of cutting Cabernet that one almost recoiled. In the second wave came the sweet creamy mushroom smell that I love in a great old champagne. Its bottom was unfathomable, yet the bite of Cabernet stayed young to the end – the smell of the empty glass growing only fresher and grapier. Beethoven, said the violinist and I with one voice.

It appears from my notes that by the time we were drinking the 1980 Yquem I was relying on the opinion of my neighbours, among them the wife of a painter. She told me all I needed. "Très sexuel," she said, and I repeated. As usual the tasting-note I borrowed was the best.

Is it because they can provoke such folly in descriptions that the First Growths hold their place in the world? They are extravagant, they switch on extravagant thoughts and extravagant language. They are (but it takes patience) as delicious in their different ways as any wine I can imagine. There is another reason, though, why they are such legends, so many people have heard of them and quite a few even drunk them: they are big. Château Latour makes as many as two hundred and twenty thousand bottles a year, Lafite two hundred and fifty, Margaux two hundred,

Mouton three hundred, Haut-Brion two hundred – and this is not count-
ing their second wines, which have (and indeed deserve) their own
following. In the luxury market quantities like these, at prices like these,
are significant brands – big enough to reach round the wine-drinking
world – and indeed beyond.

The way they are distributed is not what you would expect.
The Bordeaux market, for historical reasons that still apparently hold
good, is a game of pass-the-parcel. Château sells to *la place*, *la place* sells
to wholesaler, wholesaler to retailer and retailer to customer, sometimes
in a matter of days – and long before the wine is ready, or even bottled.
Each of these buyers has a clear idea of where his cases, often his meagre
allocation of cases, will end up. Their destiny depends not only on the
brand, but on the vintage. There are collectors' vintages, merchants'
vintages, great restaurant vintages, vintages for aspiring restaurants …
and so on down the line to vintages to be shipped as far away as possible
where the label is the only thing anyone knows. By diligent management
each vintage can be directed to the appropriate market and promoted
there. I have met the top management of a First Growth in parts of the
world not known for their wine appreciation. On holiday, no doubt.
It is essential to the system to help propel even wines no-one is proud of
through to where they will be swallowed. It does not always go according
to plan. The Château Margaux I was offered with Coca-Cola on ice in
the dark plush depths of Chateau Angel in downtown Kaohsiung had
fetched a record price at Christie's.

Château Latour

MY BUSINESS with Bordeaux had always been on the consuming end. I was well acquainted with some friends' châteaux, and had been a happy guest in many. But it came as a total surprise when in 1986 Alan Hare, the President of Château Latour (and Chairman of the *Financial Times*), invited me to lunch at his Club, the loftiest in the St James's Street firmament, and invited me to join the Latour board.

The Coffee Room at Whites was a cross between a ballroom and a school dining hall. The chandeliers, the portraits, plasterwork, the tall windows looking down on St James's, are 18th century London at its most elegant. The food, ordered by filling in a chit and brought by a wholesome matron, had a grown-up school air about it. Alan was always smiling, a slightly hesitant, most gentle man. I had a strong sense of *déjà vu* as he reached with the decanter over the shining mahogany to fill my glass. His brother, Lord Blakenham, had invited me ten years earlier, in that same room, to become involved with the Royal Horticultural Society's Journal. "Not technical stuff," said Alan, "but we'd like another point of view, and I think you'll find it interesting."

A day's work for a member of the board of Château Latour (this was in its years as an English outpost before a stricter French regime took over) started with

Alan Hare, left, President of Latour, and Pascal Ribereau-Gayon, consultant oenologist, confer in the presence of the Comte de Ségur, 'Le Prince des Vignes'.

a visit to the *chais*. The first-year *chai* first, where the wine of the latest vintage was still in active preparation, its barrels stopped only with a heavy glass bung to allow the *maître de chai* to make his regular inspections. Twelve hundred barrels lie perfectly aligned in six ranks, all the pale colour of new oak (the colour of Bordeaux stone, too) with their central panel, between dark protective bands of chestnut, stained claret red. It is the dress code of the Médoc; smarter than random red splashes. A cellar-hand in blue overalls is doing his rounds, using a can with a long spout to top up each barrel to the brim.

Ouillage (ullage in English) is a constant task as the wine evaporates and the oak absorbs it. The *maître de chai* leads the way, thief in hand (the thief is a short glass pipette; he plunges it into the heart of a barrel to draw a sample. One thief-full will put samples into three glasses). We follow, five of us, and concentrate fiercely on each dark red drop: too cold, too dumb, too tannic to taste like wine. The *maître* knows where each barrel comes from: which part of the vineyard, Cabernet or Merlot, the age of the vines, and its chances of becoming a Grand Vin or second wine, Les Forts de Latour, or even third, the wine sold simply as Pauillac.

It takes a sample or two, teeth-achingly cold, painfully masticated, to start distinguishing riper from less ripe, more fleshy from tighter-knit, short and abrupt in flavour from sweetly clinging. The wines from the Grand Vin barrels are a more imperious purple. The smell of cold coffee from the oak is overwhelmed by a sweet blackcurrant smell.

Being on the board of Château Latour was not always stressful, and my collection of menus is a reminder of the compensations.

Then down to the second-year *chai*, where the barrels go after nine months, sealed with white silicone bungs driven home and tilted to two o'clock. This is finished wine, selected and 'assembled' from its constituents of different plots and grapes around the vineyard. It is not yet homogenized into its final form. That happens in a big vat before bottling, a year and a half after the vintage. Taking a sample from a sealed barrel is a more complex operation. Across the end of the barrel goes a crossbar. The *maître* produces a tool like a little mattock, chops the blade down behind the crossbar and uses leverage to squeeze the barrel end. A thin squirt of wine comes from a tiny aperture bunged with a little point of oak. "*Le voilà. Le quatre-vingt-dix.*" Harry Waugh is the man we all look at. He was one of the first English directors and had tasted twenty-five new vintages. It was more the expression on his face than his few words ('very nice' was always among them) that pointed the way.

I feel more at home at the next inspection stop: the tasting-room, a small light-panelled oblong overlooking the yard, shaded by planes. The morning's exercise is to 'look at' (as wine people always say when they mean 'taste') the same vintage of the Grand Vin after six months in barrels from six different coopers. Is it really the same wine? The differences are frightening. A sample from a Nadalie barrel is vivid vanilla, one from Séguin-Moreau smells powdery and tastes beautifully fresh and cool, one from Radoux seems savoury, almost animal. What do I know about the long-term effects of these different containers? One could win a beauty contest today and years later be the weak link that prevents the vintage from being a great one. Somebody has to decide.

Then the previous two vintages are lined up for assessment, the younger still only samples from their barrels, the older now bottled and ready for shipping. At this stage in a wine's life a certain amount has to be imagined. They are much easier to taste than they were, but it is still a matter of analysis rather than enjoyment. The glasses are massive crystal. The wine stains them deep purple. The paper provided for notes is a rich cream vellum, befitting a First Growth.

I struggle for words for the familiar Latour flavour, the taste of the vineyard, and end up with my usual references to earth and iron. I am too verbal, I know; I should be analyzing tannins and acidity and extract. Thank goodness for the oenologists. The junior wine, the Pauillac, always tastes so good to start with that the two steps up, to Les Forts and the Grand Vin towering above both, still almost startle me. In wines this young it is almost as much about texture as taste: the sense of energy and grip on the palate, of something pent-up and hidden, is almost metaphysical. There is a column on the sheet for marks out of 20. I leave it blank. "Coffee and eau de Cologne," I write about Les Forts. Time for lunch.

It is a short walk back from the *chais* to the château through the vines, past the domed dovecote (everything is pale stone), the other emblem of Latour. The first, the lion, stands above the gateway, rather ambivalently I think. Doesn't he belong next door, at Château Léoville? There are two guests for lunch, but eight people is enough to fill the little hall. The architect of Latour had no idea about views: could he not have managed a room and a terrace worthy of this prime situation overlooking the river?

Champagne never tastes better than after tasting young claret, and lunch never smells half as good. Bruno cooks simple, savoury food; today the little menu card with its gold lion-crowned tower reads:

Pavé de lotte aux cèpes

Filet mignon de veau

Petits légumes glacés

Fromages

At least the decorator understood dining rooms. The round table almost fills it. The walls and curtains are red, the pictures big and the flowers small. The tradition is for the *maître de chai* to decant the wine, serve it, comment on it, and brief us mere amateurs on its past, present and likely future.

With the monkfish in its dark mushroom sauce we drink Les Forts de Latour 1966, fully mature, a little slender at this age but intensely fragrant. With the plump fillet of veal, pink and tender, and a pile of gleaming peas and beans and carrots from the garden, my favourite Latour vintage of all, 1959.

We all have our own ways of expressing the pleasure it gives us. Yes, it has the familiar challenging Latour flavour of gravel and iron. But the sun has come out on it. Or rather the sun of that distant great summer is lighting it now with summer evening light, shadows softening, clouds tinged red and tipped with gold. Where does wine find this consummate harmony, like a great orchestral chord where the ear loses the components, the woodwind and the strings and brass, the individual notes, and reacts to the thrilling whole? It reminds me of Daniel and that other lion: "Out of the strong came forth sweetness." And this is only lunch.

Times changed at Latour. The wonder of such châteaux is that while owners come and go the wine flows on like a river in its course. Rivers meander over time, undercut a bank here or silt up a foreshore there, but the Thames is still the Thames and the Seine, the Seine. Lord Cowdray's interests sold their shares to Allied Lyons. In a masterpiece of bad timing the Allied board then decided that wine was a poor investment. A small wine château in any case is an anomaly in the assets of a vast conglomerate; the more valuable it becomes the lower the percentage return on its capital. David Orr, the President succeeding Alan Hare, having been in charge of the vintages of 1989 (a great wine, almost roasted in September sunshine), 1990 (a triumph), 1991 (frosted, but one of the Médoc's successes) and 1992 (terrible weather, light but honourable) was told that Latour was on the market again. The Directors met at the château. A Paris bank, Lazard Frères, was asked to draw up a short-list of possible bidders in strictest secrecy in three weeks. First Growths come on the market in blue moons. The news was in *Le Figaro* next day. So much for banking secrets.

The owners of Chanel emerged as the one serious buyer. Negotiations began, and went on and on. They must have thought they were alone; the deal went back and forth. Payment for the land first, stock later ... I don't know the details. Then, on a Wednesday morning in July, François Pinault called. "If you will sign an understanding on Friday the cheque will be ready." Pinault, we rapidly learned, had made one of France's largest fortunes, in timber, in distribution, in shops and mail order and strategic deals in the USA and China. The cheque arrived.

I wondered, as weeks went by, where that left the board. Latour was now a Frenchman's private property. I wrote to him saying that I was passing through Paris and suggesting lunch. We met, with his *chef de cabinet* Patricia Barbizet, at his regular table *chez* Robuchon (weeks on

Under new ownership. The new team in the tasting room at Latour in 1994. François Pinault is at the head of the table, the current gérant, *Frédéric Engerer, behind his right shoulder.*

the waiting list for non-regulars). "Why did you buy Latour?" did not sound a very original question. "Because I could," was the answer. "When I heard a First Growth was available, and for the change in my wallet, I didn't need to think very deeply. Besides wine is my hobby, and Latour is my favourite bordeaux."

A hobby Latour may be, but a man like Pinault drives his hobbies hard. For me, board meetings became revelations of the difference between French and Anglo-Saxon attitudes. Sentiment gets short shrift. Staff numbers came steadily down.

There was no longer the pressing need for gardeners (we had spent productive hours discussing soils and drainage). The Pinaults were both distant and involved, rarely staying at the château but aware of every detail. They gave a generous lunch in my honour when I was voted *Decanter* Man of the Year and served my two favourite Latour vintages, 1959 and 1949. Madame Pinault arrived from Paris by train with a mountain of spring flowers for the tables. Three flagstaffs stand by the famous dovecote tower. One now always flies the flag of St-Malo, Pinault's home town; once the flag, he says, of fearsome pirate ships. That day one flew the Union Jack again.

I don't know, alas, what business schools teach you, but Rationalize before you Invest is a concept even I can grasp. Frédéric Engerer arrived as Pinault's lieutenant and new methods came with him. The routine work of the vineyards and *chais* is timeless (though not the decisions about personnel, machinery, how many hectares of old vines to pull up and replace). The stocks of old wine, though: how to make the most of them. The former owners seemed to see them as a sort of ballast to lend gravitas to the boat. The new director, a formidable taster as well as man of affairs, soon convinced the board that every vintage had its destiny, and most were ripe for theirs. Where his predecessors had seen tradition, he saw bottlenecks. The infinite advantage of a private owner is that he can rationalize to the bone and invest to the hilt without contradiction. When the moment came, in 1999, to start reorganizing or rebuilding almost all the working parts of the property, the wine (what else matters?) simply got better still. If I am right about the 2003, it will be one of the very great vintages.

As for me, I was fired for non-attendance. One meeting a year at Latour and two in Paris became the rule, naturally at the owner's convenience and not always with a great deal of notice. I was too far away to get back for several meetings. "Monsieur Pinault is concerned," said a letter, full of courtesy, "that all members of the board play a full part in the activities of the property." *Touché,* I had to admit.

Thank you, Latour, for many marvellous moments. Thank you for bottles past and bottles to come that evoke the Médoc more clearly than any others and yet heighten its mystery. Working at Latour gave me the chance to understand how the vines of one estate draw something unique out of the ground that becomes more and more characteristic with each year. When that character is a noble one the parallel with a human life is too obvious to ignore; Latour, in a great vintage, can even live for four-score years.

Bordeaux: Left Bank, Right Bank

Paris is traditionally divided, or was a generation ago, into the Right Bank and Left Bank of the River Seine. Right and Left had almost political resonance, at least in my mind. On the Right Bank are the Louvre, the Champs Elysées, monumental Paris, the financial district and fashion houses, the President's Palace, the apartments of the *haute bourgeoisie*. In a word, the Establishment. The Left Bank had been the aristocratic quarter before the Revolution; the remaining aristocracy shared it with students, with artists, with bookshops and jazz clubs. With politicians, too, admittedly, but Rive Gauche meant alternative, free-thinking.

Bordeaux uses the same terms, not for the city but for its main wine districts. The river, or rivers, are the Garonne, flowing through the city; the Dordogne, beyond it and converging with it, and the Gironde, which is the two united into a wide estuary. The Left Bank is the city side, the west, and in particular refers to the Médoc, the left bank of the estuary. The Right Bank refers to the Dordogne districts of St-Emilion, Fronsac, and Pomerol. You can almost reverse the political resonances here. St-Emilion has the ancient history, but if anything is the region of small properties

I thought I could make the geography of Bordeaux memorable for television viewers by drawing the estuary with a stick in estuarial mud. At least I remember it.

and revolution. Challenges to the old order are Right Bank stuff. The Médoc is the *haut bourgeois* area of châteaux in spacious domains, of ostentation and the Classification of 1855.

The Left Bank

Wine is the only possible destiny of the Médoc, the low-lying spit of gravel and clay and sand wedged between the Bay of Biscay and the broad estuary of the Gironde, where the waters of almost a quarter of France roll out to sea. The Atlantic has piled up some of the world's highest sand dunes on its western shore. Behind them stretch long wastes of maritime pines. An unemphatic spine of higher ground runs up the centre. Here starts a virtual monoculture of vines covering plateaux and gentle declivities down to the brown Gironde. There seems to be a single purpose in the existence of these buildings, whose pale stone picks them out among the green of vines in summer and brown of earth in winter. Pompous château and crouching farm, and the straggling villages that thread the roads between, are labelled as clearly as wine bottles with their destiny. Life is red wine here, and red wine is life.

The very office, the very desk where it was signed and the very document of the 1855 Classification are still in place in the Chambre de Commerce on the Bordeaux quayside.

Some days you can smell the sea. If you can't smell it you can detect its presence by the coastal parade of clouds and even a watery quality in the light. The sea buffets the land but also protects it. The winter is grey, damp but mild. Nothing stirs in the village; the château is shuttered. Development came late here: the Médoc was colonized at the same time as South America. It was still primitive a hundred and fifty years ago when Somerville and Ross, two Irish lady journalists, made their tour of what they called 'The Wine Country' and reported on the fleas and the lack of amenities. "It was those bare feet, crimsoned with juice, that took our whole attention …. At this juncture one of the bare-footed and blue-clad workmen approached with a small tumbler in his very dirty hand … we looked at each other in speechless horror."

That was when the Médoc acquired its most precious document, its Classification. At the time, Paris and London were competing with their grandiose Universal Exhibitions. London started with the Crystal Palace in 1851. Paris came back with its Exposition Universelle in 1855. How to put on a good show with the famous wines of Bordeaux? Answer: exhibit the best as winners in a competition.

The Bordeaux Chamber of Commerce consulted the wine brokers of the city. They pointed to a list that had been brewing for almost a century but had first been codified not long before by an English guide-writer, Charles Cocks. With a little fine-tuning this became the 1855 Classification of the 61 most prominent properties of the Médoc in five classes, determined by their prices. Why only the Médoc? That was their brief. Not to have included the more ancient vineyard of the Graves, south of the city, seems absurd. They could not leave out Château Haut-Brion, the first of the First Growths by historic right, but even Château Pape-Clément, founded by the archbishop of Bordeaux who became Clement V, the first Pope to reign in Avignon, was disregarded.

Did they have any inkling of what a landmark the list would be? Did they imagine that one hundred and fifty years later it would remain unchanged, except in one particular, however remote it might have become from actuality? In one sense it scarcely matters, now or then, because it succeeded so resoundingly in its main aim: to promote the Médoc. Why did it succeed? Because it looked like a rock of certainty in an ocean of variables. Like Robert Parker's 100-point system in 20th century America, it seemed to offer a short cut to an educated choice.

The variables, of course, went on – and go on – varying. Your place in the original order was based on form over many years, itself measured by price. It was not, unlike the pecking-order of Burgundy, soil-based, rigidly bound to the terroir. A Bordeaux château is not, or not necessarily, a particular parcel of land. Owners can buy and sell pieces of their property without losing their identity, or their place in the Classification. There are only two properties of all the 61 still under the same family ownership – and those, ironically, are not even French, but the Anglo-Irish Bartons of Château Léoville-Barton and the (then) English branch of the Rothschild family at Mouton. In this fluid situation all you can say is that a château is what it does. Many, thank goodness, do it beautifully. Others hardly do it at all.

The Graves

In terms of space in this cellar it is Médoc first, by a country mile, with Pomerol and Graves tying for second place, Graves out of proportion to its small number of châteaux. What is the special attraction of good red Graves? A flavour less rigorous, I would say, than that of the Médoc, mellower in tannin and milder in acidity. Half-way, you might say, to the St-Emilion effect of rich and meaty. Time and again my tasting-notes repeat the same things: "tastes of sun-warmed bricks," or sometimes "honeyed gravel." In a tasting of the First Growths Haut-Brion, the grand original from the Graves, is the mellow one. Faint, no; grainy though, rather than glossy: a savoury quality rather than bright fruit or a smack of the seaside, is the Graves ideal – and something our guests at dinner find hard to resist. This arid soil, mere sand and gravel, seemingly only fit for pines, has something like St-Emilion limestone below. Merlot plays a larger part in the mixture here than in the Médoc, too.

Château Haut-Brion is so pre-eminent that its little retinue of a dozen classed growths (too characteristically classi-fied under a different system from the Médoc, or any other part of Bordeaux) are often over-looked. Some make red wine, some white, some both, to the delight of encyclopaedists (or anor-aks, as we obsessive fact-collectors are unkindly called) but the bemusement of the majority. They are scattered through the suburbs south of the city in what was once the grandest real estate of all. The archbishop of Bordeaux made his wine at what is now Château Pape-Clément. Haut-Brion belonged to the Président of the Parlement. It is hard to find them now: housing estates penetrate far into the fringes of the pine forests. Try to drive through Pessac-Léognan, as they now call the northern, and best, part of the Graves, and the schools and supermarkets make you despair of find-ing a vineyard.

Château Haut-Brion, the first First Growth, was bought by Clarence Dillon, an American banker, in 1935. With his daughter Joan, Duchesse de Mouchy, in 1987.

Every second summer, when Bordeaux's world wine fair, Vinexpo, is playing in a stifling kilometre-long hall north of the city, I get lost in these suburbs looking for the Domaine de Chevalier. The pine forests shimmer in the heat of a June evening and the vines, when you find them, are deep cooling green. Between the vines on one night of celebration appeared fishing boats, a light-house, sea-serpents, a liner: a midsummer maritime mirage. They were painted cut-outs using the vine-rows as the waves. Under the pine trees round the winery (there is no château – hence the name Domaine – and the *chais* are spanking new) there were tables of oysters and every delight with the Domaine's wines and those of their friends in Burgundy, Champagne and Alsace. After dinner there was jazz. You couldn't believe the jiving crowd would be back tasting and doing business at the fair in the morning.

I have followed the Chevalier wines for decades, the white as one of sadly few dry white Graves to match up to my high expectations. The mystery is why they take so long, much longer even than white burgundy, to achieve harmony. They start raw, a not very seductive mixture of Sauvignon, Sémillon and oak flavours. Over the years the white champion has been Château Laville-Haut-Brion, sister wine to

La Mission-Haut-Brion, itself sister to Haut-Brion (they are a close family). Word gets around, though: it is not an easy wine to buy. Domaine de Chevalier can run it close, and Château de Fieuzal is one we often drink.

Red Domaine de Chevalier is also a clumsy starter but a good middle-distance runner. Château Smith-Haut-Lafitte is the one with the highest profile, as much for its vinotherapeutic spa, Les Sources de Caudalie (health through polyphenols, wine applied in unusual ways), as for its classic red and white wines. My favourite of the little group, stretched out like golf courses among the villas and pines, is Château Haut-Bailly. I once described its wine as being like 'long-simmered stock': benign, harmonious, satisfying. That, rather than pyrotechnics, is red Graves.

The Médoc

A tall grill of wrought iron guards the drive. Peering through, under a black-branched cedar, up cream stone steps flanked with vases of scarlet flowers, you see a cream stone house with a faintly seaside air, a jaunty turret here and there, primly grey-shuttered. Long barns of the same stone with red roofs enclose a grand yard. A century of siesta seems to be in progress.

The châteaux of the Médoc occupy a cultural niche of their own. They express the values of the *haute bourgeoisie* of the 19th century, between the Empire and the Belle Epoque. You could call it lavish austerity. It is *comme il faut*, seemly, orderly, often handsome – but dedicated to Apollo, you would say, rather than Dionysus; the god of authority (not to mention business), not the god of inspiration. In their long barn-like *chais* several hundred barrels stand in parade-ground order. In the salon the gilt chairs stand in groups, straight-backed and decorous, as the guests will sit for their conversation. There is nothing over-stimulating to the senses. The sideboard in the dining room is ready, the decanters in place. The sunlight creeps round the room; a warm smell permeates from the kitchen; there are voices outside and footsteps on the gravel.

This is where it all finds its expression and justification, the lonely landscape, the relentless vine-rows, the empty courtyard, the rows of identical barrels in the half-light. When the shining bottle is produced, its visiting-card label is inspected, and the ruby liquid cascades into the crystal glass.

Yes, it is emphatically the wine: redder than a ruby, deeper, more lustrous. Its scent combines the sea-locked land and its fruit, gritty earth and sweet currants, with pale staves of oak and even the nacreous Atlantic light, making a memory-trigger as strong as roses. And its power as it washes the tongue, this strangely ascetic draught: ripeness held in a precisely calculated grip of astringency, warm and cold at once, is as much a puzzle as a statement. Wine that satisfies soul and body together. Or intellect, perhaps, rather than soul. We claret-drinkers are not Rabelaisian roisterers. We may be when we go to Burgundy, but this wine we like so much is for sipping, not carousing. Sipping and asking yourself what it reminds you of, or whether you recognize it, or which vintage it comes from. To taste claret without this sort of self-examination is like looking at the answers to a crossword puzzle.

Claret-drinkers have a mental map (however inaccurate) of their favourite wine country to go with their recollection (however hazy) of the 1855 Classification. For the school of drinkers I am talking about, and in which I was reared, the Médoc holds pride of place.

I first saw the Médoc in 1961. Impressive it may have been, this landscape of apparently lordly domains, but no-one could call it welcoming. I don't remember seeing a single restaurant. There was scarcely a bar and certainly no sign saying *Dégustation, Vente* to indicate that there was anything for sale. Strictly speaking there wasn't. All the Médoc's wine was bought by merchants from *la place*, the market, in Bordeaux. A few long-established firms controlled the market from offices on the Quai des Chartrons. The trim cream stone and elegant ironwork facing the shipping on the river hid barrel-*chais* longer than polo-grounds.

An introduction to a château was unusual in those days and an invitation was rare, principally because the owners lived elsewhere. There were hospitable exceptions, but even they tended to occupy only the dining rooms and kitchens of their large houses. M Dupin of Château Grand-Puy-Lacoste was a legendary example. He would leave his chair at his richly furnished table to go into the echoing corridor and bawl to his cook, miles away in the kitchen: *'Antoinette. De la sauce!'* Where a château was warmly and permanently occupied it became a beacon to travellers. Château Ducru-Beaucaillou was famous for the smiles of the Bories, Château Langoa-Barton for the Englishness of Ronald Barton, Château d'Angludet for the shrewdness of Peter Sichel, Château Prieuré-Lichine for its unconventional dynamo of an owner, Alexis Lichine. I am sure other visitors would make

The computer revolution. These days the hosts of tastings for journalists have to provide tables for laptops, too.

different lists. Human geography is the most important kind; you navigate by the radiation from friends' houses. I was not a wine merchant whose business was in the warehouses of Bordeaux. My picture of the Médoc grew from visits, reading and drinking.

Sampling new bordeaux in the spring after the vintage is never an easy experience, nor one for the faint-hearted. Everybody says what a bad idea it is to be in such a hurry, but everybody goes. Two hundred journalists from around the world descend on Bordeaux at the end of March to taste. They arrive in groups in buses at a château in the vineyards where samples from a hundred properties in the neighbouring communes have been assembled. Long tables in a cold vat-room are thronged with the bottles. The visitors spend two hours worrying the cold hard wines for hints about their future. The critics peer, sniff, swirl and shake them, sniff again, take a note, swirl and sip. With a cold spoonful hurting their front teeth they suck and chew and calculate, close their eyes and meditate, scribble a note, or confide their conclusions to their laptops. Another wine and another; another decision, another sentence. Lips, tongue, teeth and fingers dyed blue, they plot the future of each raw unfinished wine. The art is to see through its distractions, its fierce tannins and apparent acidity, to what lies at the heart of it. How much sweet fruit is there to mellow and subsume the edgy elements? How much *charpente* (carpentry: as in the structure of a roof) to protect the fruit over the years?

Reputations hang on it, prices depend on it, this cold dissection of a year's hard work, a year's decisions and a year's luck. At noon, as the tasters file into the warmth of the château, their cold fingers closing round a glass of golden champagne, quiet remarks turn to murmurs and

Lunch after a long March morning tasting cold, half-finished wine is a moment of blessed respite. This was at Château Lynch-Moussas, a little Pauillac Fifth Growth very much of the family country house school.

murmurs to a clamour. Champagne doubles the decibels of any gathering. 'Did you see anything in the Giscours?' 'I loved the Palmer.' 'Can that be the final blend of the Lascombes?' A hundred opinions, definite or tentative, mingle and mutate, hesitate and congeal. The Merlots were ripe, the Cabernets green; the St-Juliens have it over the Pauillacs; the last to pick did best; you can tell the vines are very young or the barrels are very old at this château or that. Winners and losers emerge, stories are filed. The news has gone out, to be read and registered in wine-drinkers' minds round the world. A great vintage, Margaux the winner; or a difficult vintage, prices should come down. A decision, at any rate, and a hasty one, but a difficult one to alter.

The wines that have been judged are samples from a single barrel out of hundreds, of a vintage that is about one quarter of its way through the process of its *élevage*. Would its own cellar-master recognize it, in a whole morning's-worth of samples? Would he vouch for it as a fair sample? These are tough questions, but it is an unforgiving world.

So what is the difference between a good vintage and one its makers would qualify with explanations? A full mouth is one short way of expressing it. Really ripe grapes give the wine a sense of full veins pulsing, a texture gorged with matter, the sweetness of warm fruit and the flow of alcohol. Overripe means the taste of raisins, tannin that takes hold and a burn rather than a glow. Really underripe means scrawny, watery, weakly sweet and briefly sharp as it rapidly fades. 1968 was the last vintage with such a total collapse. In every vintage since some vintners have emerged with credit. The wine-maker (and the positive drinker: I am one of them) finds interest, if not satisfaction, in a good vineyard under difficult conditions. It will not be my choice on a restaurant wine list, but it will add to the categories of flavour I can bring up from my cellar. 'Why would anyone want less than the best?' is the question I am always being asked. For the sake of understanding would be the pretentious answer. The clearer to see the qualities of the best would be equally valid.

I was always drawn to the northern end of the peninsula, a long drive in those days from Bordeaux. You traversed long wet flats of poplars interspersed with the plateaux of vines. Margaux is the first significant village, but barely: two bends in the road, a cluster of high slate roofs, a *mairie* with the red, white and blue flag. The fields are pale gravel, flat and far-reaching. Are those country houses or factories dotting the horizon like ships anchored in a sheltered sea? Immense pale planes, geometrically aligned, lead your eye down to a palace, and beyond it to the grey Gironde.

Can I match a flavour to this landscape? How gratifying, and how simplifying, it would be. I tried in my Wine Atlas, but that was when the technology of wine-making here had barely changed since they gave up treading the grapes. The fashion today is for wines more shaped by fruit than soil, if that is a real distinction. More fruity, certainly, and much more oaky – and ready to drink at a younger age. Châteaux that follow fashion lose distinction. I am far from sure that I would know a Margaux from a St-Julien in the generic sense.

The convention is that Margaux does perfume and St-Julien does harmony, but with such abstractions the room for overlap is infinite. Margaux is certainly the best-known of the Médoc communes to what you might call the layman – probably, I think, because it shares the name of its one First Growth, and few châteaux attract so much adulation. It is the palace in the picture; its neo-classical portico, above steps like the approach to a throne, more intimidating than hospitable. Parties here are in keeping: one for the bicentenary of the Declaration of Independence will always stick in my mind. Three hundred or so guests had been regaled that evening on the north lawn with magnums of the Grand Vin in the vintage said to express every quality: 1953. Château Yquem 1937, its counterpart, according to the best authorities, had been generously poured. At this moment the sky lit up with fireworks. The guests rushed to watch – except for three or four with different priorities, who stayed in the tent and emptied glass after glass of a liquid considered divine.

Even First Growths can nod. Today Château Margaux is riding high, but it had a low period when its neighbour across the fields, Château Palmer, made some even more famous vintages. In 1961 Palmer made the most beautiful claret of an exalted year. Palmer's English name makes it, like Château Talbot in St-Julien, an easy choice for Anglo-Saxons. The story of General Palmer, of how he bought the château from a pretty widow on a long coach journey and introduced its wine to Regency London, is a cautionary tale. Society figures before and since have expected to prosper by their social connections, and Palmer had good wine to sell: fragrant, digestible; just the thing. The Prince Regent liked it; his port-drinking friends said it wasn't strong enough. Palmer tried adding various stiffeners: disaster. Poor man, he went bust. Perhaps the wheel of fashion is going round again today: certainly there are wines that taste stiffened.

To help our conjectures about what claret tasted like in those days there is a document full of surprises: the instructions to wine-makers of a Bordeaux broker called Paguierre. Among plenty of sound advice (pick your grapes later rather than sooner, for example) he sets out his surprising method of fermentation. He advises selecting the best grapes in the vineyard, to the extent of one-third of the crop, picking them over carefully for any duds and putting them, uncrushed and untrodden, into a large vat in which they are then covered with brandy. The rest of the crop is trodden in the usual way and the two lots fermented separately. The *mère-cuve*, or mother-vat, as he calls it, is rendered as airtight as possible. He was using, in other words, the technique now known as *maceration carbonique*, peculiar to Beaujolais rather than Bordeaux. Deprived of air, fermentation starts inside each grape individually. Preserved in brandy it would take a long time, but the result would be spectacularly fruity, and of course strong. Finally, he says, blend the two very different batches. I can think of plenty of people who would have paid four times as much for the *mère-cuve* wine unmixed.

Before you come to St-Julien, driving north, you pass a less prestigious patch, a plateau further from the river with not a single property listed in the Classification. I am drawn to it. It makes, or can make, a sort of rather raw-boned, saliva-inducing claret I like. You can taste, here, that there is no deep dune of gravel under the vines. Instead there is something more like Burgundian soil. 'The best vines,' everyone in the Médoc will tell you, 'have a view of the river.' None in the communes of Moulis and Listrac has one. Perhaps it is my instinct to back the underdog, but when I drink Château Chasse-Spleen, or Maucaillou or one of several châteaux with Poujeaux in its name I have a clear sense of where I am – and an excellent appetite.

Why should tastes change at commune boundaries? Appellation and geology are rarely synchronized. It is the size of the heaped-up stones that make up the Médoc, and the depth of the heaps that determines the drainage and the soil temperature – the fundamental factors in ripening grapes. There is no bump, no fault-line, when you arrive in St-Julien. It is Château Beychevelle that catches your eye, crowning a rise that could have been designed by the geography department to show you how the Médoc is constructed of stones swept down by the river from who knows where upstream. In

BELOW & BOTTOM Châteaux Beychevelle and Margaux must have looked even more palatially over-the-top in the wild and lonely Médoc of the times when they were built. The first is from the age of aristocrats, the second the age of bankers.

unnecessary splendour (who was there to impress in this backwater?) Beychevelle is the only rival to Château Margaux – royalist baroque rather than republican classical. I have been watching the broad black cedar of Lebanon in the courtyard facing the road gradually decline with age over the past forty years. It must be a contemporary of an even finer one that stood on the lawn of Château Lafite and was brought down by the great storm of 1999. There was devastation all round Bordeaux. Pine forests stretch down from the sea side of the Médoc (where the dunes are sand rather than gravel) down through the Landes almost to the Spanish border, two hundred and fifty kilometres south. They were so shattered that in places they remain as they fell, a tangle of trees uprooted and trees snapped. Nothing can be done.

The Médoc to me has always been tree, as well as wine, country. A *bouquet d'arbres exotiques* accompanies almost every château – amusing novelties in the garden for the builders; now landmarks visible for miles around. Grand ones like the Beychevelle cedar stick in the mind. There is one tree so prominent and so peculiar that I recognized it when I read the account by a hostage of his three-year captivity by terrorists in Beirut. Jean-Paul Kauffmann was a journalist from Bordeaux when he was captured. He writes of a tall tree, delicate in its pale foliage, standing alone by a stream, surrounded by vineyards. In his prison it says to him: 'to live is to be alone'. It is the swamp cypress that marks the boundary of St-Julien and Pauillac, where the vineyards of Château Latour, Château Léoville-Las-Cases and the two Châteaux Pichon-Longueville meet – to Kauffmann the *territoires royaux* of the Médoc. To me it has always been symbolic, too; an alien from the Caroline swamps declaring that this landscape is the work of man. Nature did not put vines here either. But can man determine what they produce? No, nor the commune boundary make any difference. It is what the vine-roots find deep in the soil that determines the wine and here, regardless of the boundary, are four of Bordeaux's most famous properties making four quite different styles of wine. Château Latour is stern and majestic, Léoville-Las-Cases ascetically fine, Pichon Comtesse fragrant and feminine, Pichon Baron a Pauillac of the cedar-scented, strongly structured school. The philosophy of each is to make the most of the terroir. How they do that, with what grapes, with oak vats or steel and with a hundred nuances, completes the definition of each château.

I have followed the vintage closely enough to see dozens of little differences that could add up to different qualities – or different styles – right through the harvest. The first difference to add to that of soils is the proportion of different grapes: Cabernet Sauvignon, Cabernet Franc and Merlot, with sometimes a few rows of the difficult but high-flavoured

Petit Verdot. Then there is the age of the vines, the way they are pruned and the regime of weeding and spraying the vineyards against diseases. There is the condition of the deep clay drains, necessary even in this stony soil. Out with the pickers you can see how carefully they work. There will be someone up on the trailer where the pickers dump their loads from the bins on their backs. Do they take out any mouldy bunches – and when the grapes arrive at the belt that takes them to be crushed, is there a sorting team? I have been given a pole with a prong on the end and told to flick out any remaining leaves, even while the grapes are tumbling in a blue cascade into the silvery screw that carries them off for crushing.

The atmosphere in the vat-room is tense. In the most modern, the product is given away only by the sweet smell. A battery of steely cylinders is all you see: the grapes are piped in overhead. In most vat-rooms the cylinders are massive tuns of burnished oak. Is one material better than the other? The steel tanks are easier to clean; the oak, some say, a kinder container.

'Typical Pauillac' is an oxymoron. Its three First Growths (no other commune has more than one, though Margaux is stiff with seconds) are so different that you might think they span the whole Médoc. I will borrow a description of the difference between Lafite and Latour I wrote in 1984 in my *Wine Companion*. "Lafite is a tenor; Latour a bass. Lafite is a lyric; Latour an epic. Lafite is a dance; Latour a parade." Musical cadence can give some idea, but it leaves out the taste. Lafite tastes of cedar, Latour of iron.

If I were looking for a typical Pauillac I would choose Château Grand-Puy-Lacoste – but then I love it and have followed its wine for decades. What does it do for me? It speaks the Pauillac language of Cabernet fruit and deep warm soil, and it seems to transmit energy. Vitality (I have said it before) is the most important quality in wine. I have fond memories of the château, too, once M Dupin's and now belonging to the Bories. It is not one of the river-front ones, but stands on the broad pebbly plateau behind the town. Behind it is an unexpected valley where swans swim on a hydrangea-bordered pond. In the days when no-one lived there, I trespassed in the deserted rose garden and took a cutting of a strange climbing rose the purple colour of young claret. I called it Grand-Puy-Lacoste. Now I can see it from my bedroom window. I said, didn't I, that sentiment can make a good wine even better?

A typical St-Julien? It should be easier. There is remarkable consistency, even of quality, in this scattered fleet of châteaux moored on the crests of the gravel waves from Beychevelle (and further inland, on the same roller, the most sturdily reliable of all clarets, Gruaud-Larose) to the three Léovilles on the Pauillac boundary. The one most faithfully followed in England, and a model in any company, is Léoville-Barton. There is an element of pride in the fact that this Anglo-Irish family has been installed here longer than the owners of any other Classed Growth. 1821 was the year when Hugh Barton bought the handsome chartreuse of Langoa (I can't remember why these single-storey, one-room-deep houses are called 'charterhouses') and a fifth of the huge Léoville vineyard. His five-times-great grandson, Anthony, is a Médoc landmark himself. When the pleasantries of tasting turn pretentious, a thing not unknown in the grander châteaux, the tall saturnine Anthony pricks the bubble. We have all been guilty of an excess of similes. "Wet dog," said Anthony one day, as a party of tasters sipped his wine and volunteered extravagant comparisons. "I certainly get wet dog." Raised eyebrows round the group, then nods of assent. "Sure, I get wet dog." Brenda the Irish Setter gave her master a wag from the corner of the room. Last time I was there we had the young 2002 in our glasses and I was struggling with an expression relating blackcurrants to tightly sheathed flower-buds. I didn't tell my host, though.

Another Pauillac château that could claim the title of most typical is Lynch-Bages, generous quintessence of the blackcurrant flavour of Cabernet Sauvignon, and home of the man who for many symbolizes Pauillac, indeed the Médoc, today: Jean-Michel Cazes. Cazes – burly, smiling, diplomatic, single-minded – inherited the local insurance broker-age from his father, who had set about restoring the dilapidated Fifth Growth. (Pauillac has 12 Fifth Growths, the whole of the rest of the Médoc only six. I'm not sure why). Presumably Cazes insured everything and every body in Pauillac. They all knew him and liked him (he was mayor too) and Lynch-Bages went from respected Fifth to the status of a Second. Tracking these trajectories is part of the fun of following claret. It had a head start in England: 'Lunch Bags' was easier to say than Pichon-Longueville Baron de Longueville. In due course Jean-Michel became czar of a new kind of wine empire, when the insurance company AXA decided that wine was here to stay and bought that very Pichon … Longueville, added the port house of Quinta do Noval and the Tokay house of Disznoko and put Jean-Michel in charge. The Médoc is forging more links like this one now, yet in essence it still feels as remote as it always did; what a 16th century writer described as *sauvage et solitaire*.

The man who first challenged the somnolence of the Médoc was Baron Philippe de Rothschild. This was in the 1920s when the somno-lence was profound. Phylloxera had ended the glory days of the 19th century, and the Russian Revolution and Prohibition had suddenly removed two important markets. Connoisseurs in England were enjoying a run of fine vintages made by loss-making châteaux. Philippe was a playboy scion of the branch of the Rothschild family who had settled in England. His forebear Nathaniel bought the Second Growth Branne-Mouton at a low point in the 1850s, just before the Classification. They had never built a château; it was simply a wine-farm. Michael Broadbent, whose notes are my only authority on such wines, gives a grim report of the 1858; by 1864 things seem to be looking up; the 1870 was terrific. In the early 20th century things drifted. In 1924 Philippe (then 22) produced the wine of the vintage. He bottled it all at the château (even the First Growths used to sell in barrels) and he commissioned an artist friend to design the label. In one stroke he had mapped out the future of the Médoc – no, of a new concept of wine de luxe.

Instead of building a château, Rothschild made a museum. He and his American wife Pauline (his first wife was killed in the war) rejected the bourgeois style of the Médoc and lived in airy modern rooms full of sculpture and books. They collected fine art of every kind and every age that related to wine or told its story, a collection that his daughter Philippine continues. Philippe was the aristocratic bohemian, spending the morning in bed (he received you in state, surrounded by pillows and papers and dogs) and writing, gardening, polishing his wine, his domain and his mind in the afternoon. You approached his door along a broad path of deep white gravel perfectly raked, conscious as you crunched along that you were leaving deep footprints. By the time you left, the gravel had been raked smooth again.

It took him fifty years of perfectionism to achieve his goal of changing the Classification of 1855 to have Mouton recognized as a First Growth, although that had been its unofficial status all along. No other changes have been made, and I suspect they never will; too many of the adjustments would be downwards. Of far greater cosmic significance, though, was his friendship with Robert Mondavi and their joint venture to produce a Napa Valley Mouton: Opus One.

—————————

There is little in the scenery to detain you in Pauillac. One day its riverside cafés and its little marina may blossom into fashion. It is the only possible resort between Bordeaux and the river-mouth. Indeed it has recently acquired the only fashionable hotel, another enterprise of Jean-Michel Cazes. Château Cordeillan-Bages is the place to eat (but only in spring and summer) the local lamb considered the perfect accompaniment to great mature Médocs. Agneau de Pauillac may be more of a generic term than an appellation d'origine, but its meaning is clear: lamb that has fed on nothing but its mother's milk, hence meat pale in colour and meltingly tender. The alternative is agneau de pré salé, lamb that has fed only on the meadows flooded by spring tides, whose grasses are tolerant of seawater and give the meat a distinct flavour. Agneau de Pauillac is sometimes steamed to accentuate its pale tenderness; with a vigorous young wine I would choose a gigot de pré salé, browned with shallots. And the cheese for great claret? Not one of the strong and salty cream cheeses, but something sweeter. My favourite is the hard round orange Mimolette from Lille (where they call it Vieux Hollande). Aged a year and a half it grows nutty, sweetens and seems to crystallize like Parmesan.

As you leave Pauillac, the gravel banks that produce the world's finest Cabernet (cue for an argument; another time) are brusquely interrupted. The last château is Lafite, screened by a yellow veil of weeping willows; then the road dips into a poplar valley. All the rain that doesn't become Lafite, I muse, drains out along this stream into the Gironde. Then abruptly the road climbs again towards a strange oriental building; there is a sense of arriving in the country. You are in St-Estèphe; the folly is Château Cos d'Estournel.

From here on the Médoc feels almost deserted. You are a long way from Bordeaux. The last big gravel dune rises to twenty metres above river level at this point, fringed with the northernmost estates that figured in the 1855 Classification. Its central domed plateau is dotted with châteaux, some just as architecturally ambitious, glorying in the ambiguous-sounding title of *crus bourgeois*. Is France a classless society when it makes such a distinction between the aristos and the traders? You hear rather less these days about the two humbler categories of estate: *crus artisans* and *crus paysans*.

Many times I have sailed this stretch of the river. From the water it is clear which vineyards have pole positions. Cos d'Estournel is only a poplar-plantation away from Lafite, Château Montrose is the precise counterpart to Latour in Pauillac, with a riverside hillock to itself. Its wine shares some of the characteristics of Latour: strong structure and the need for time to soften it. It is indissolubly linked in my mind with an incident I recounted in my first book, and which I have heard recalled so often that I shall keep the ball rolling by telling the story again. The owner, M Charmolue, out of pure kindness, I am sure, and not with any thought of my telling the story, put half a dozen bottles in the back of my hire car before I drove away. The next weekend I was staying alone up the Dordogne and ate my evening meal at a *routiers* café. I drank one of the bottles of Montrose with my dinner (ragoût, I remember, with lots of carrots). I loved it so much that I went out to my car, fetched the other five bottles and asked the *patron* to pour them for the lorry-drivers. They must have thought I was mad. They would not have known what a Second Growth was, but they raised their glasses politely, and were about to empty them when they stopped in mid-swallow. Broad smiles broke out; a rapt look came over their faces. The sweet autumnal vapours of the wine, and its clean sweet power in their throats, needed no explanation. No wonder I feel at home in St-Estèphe.

It was wine from the high *prairie* of St-Estèphe that was my first contact with the Médoc, too: the Château Les Ormes de Pez, which was bottled by that sterling and conservative British institution, The Wine Society. My father used to look no further; cases and vintages came and went. It was probably the 1953 I first encountered. It is more ambitious now, purchased and polished by Jean-Michel Cazes. Its neighbour Château de Pez has a far older reputation; constitutes, indeed, one of the mysteries of Bordeaux. This remote and unextraordinary farm was owned by the man who first seduced the London market with claret de luxe: Jean de Pontac, proprietor of Haut-Brion. De Pez was probably sold in London as 'Pontac'. Why here, right out in the sticks?

In his day, durability was not the issue. Nobody knew that these fields could make wine with a lifespan counted in decades. I came upon an old de Pez in a dark corner of my cellar not long ago. My notebook reads: "Pez 1966, bottled in London by Justerini & Brooks. Cork so loose that it moved when I put the screw in. It came out as though any connection was casual and temporary. Disagreeable resiny stink at first; decanted into my Suffolk jug it took an hour to come clean. Wonderful deep glowing garnet, white at the rim. Then sweet as raisins, like an old Napa Cabernet. It tasted sharp at first, then became the spirit of old Médoc, gently resinous, waxy, clinging; a *vin de médita-tion*, light and lacy, claret heaven." To taste wines as old as this and find them still alive, still individual and true to their natures, is like meeting some gifted and fortunate soul whose old age is expressed in a gentle sort of sweet vitality never found in youth.

Château Loudenne, playground of my youth. I have seen (or perhaps imagined) the ghosts of ancient Romans on its terrace overlooking the Gironde.

The best sites, the ones that really stand out as the natural places to build, that must even to primitive people have looked the likely places to settle, have a magnetism of their own. They line the riverside like natural balconies, their lands shelving down to the river-meadows. Château Montrose has such a situation; so does Château Latour, and so does Château Loudenne. There must have been a villa here since the Médoc was first settled. It seems self-evident, when you sit on the terrace and the night settles round you, that generations have had the same feelings, and seen and heard the same things. There is a yellow moon-track on the river, and an owl in the elms. The heat of the day is fading. The Roman I imagine next to me pulls his toga closer.

I think about Ausonius, the consul from Bordeaux whose name is given by tradition to another natural villa site, Château Ausone on the brow of the hill at St-Emilion. He retired from a glittering career in Rome to his Bordeaux home. In Germany he had written a poem about the vines reflected in the waters of the Moselle. "What colours paint the river," he wrote, "when Hesperus has brought the shades of evening." In old age (he was 84 when he died) Ausonius disappears into seclusion. Villa Ludenensis, let's call it, would have suited him very well: the elms, the owl, the ships waiting for the tide to take them upriver, and the light red wine.

The Right Bank

Jean-Pierre Moueix kept a legendary table at his country house on the Dordogne outside Libourne. Pomerol first became known to many through his hospitality.

Of all the dining tables in claret country, that of Jean-Pierre Moueix had, in its heyday, the highest reputation. Round it gathered those who had shown they understood, or were trying to understand, the dialect of the Right Bank. Claret is spoken with a different accent here, and rounder vowels. Young wines are less harsh, old wines more caressing. Great wines begin as ripe plums and mature into uninhibited excesses of honeyed cream.

In the 1970s and 1980s, Jean-Pierre Moueix was the high priest of the Right Bank and the emperor of Libourne, the market town on the Dordogne at the hub of the region's three vineyards: St-Emilion, Fronsac and Pomerol. Libourne is no Bordeaux. The Right Bank wines lived in the shadow of the huge prestige of the Médoc, its Classed Growths and business machine on the Quai des Chartrons. But Libourne also has a *quai*, a modest road beside the eddying waters of the Dordogne. Moueix set up shop here just before the Second World War as a négociant in the wines of the Libourne hinterland. I once asked him how, in the hard years after the war, he had prospered with such satisfying results. "It was easier for me," he said. He is a tall man, grave of manner, with the cello voice of an archbishop.

He stooped, and clasped his hands as he spoke: "When a salesman sets out from Bordeaux he has a big bag of samples: Graves, Médoc, Margaux, St-Julien, Pauillac, St-Estèphe ... it's a long story to tell. I turn up with two wines: St-Emilion and Pomerol. They are brothers, but different – and of course delicious. Even when they are young. Everybody chooses one or the other." This was in the north of France and Belgium, the traditional market for the Right Bank (while Britain was obsessed with the Left Bank, and Paris besotted with Burgundy).

As Moueix prospered he became a collector. First, of paintings. When he went to Paris he went to galleries. He had a natural eye. His house on the Dordogne became a shrine to the art of the early 20th century. At his table, over the glint of glasses, you were faced with the glowing colours of Dufy and the Cubist contortions of De Stael, de la Fresnaye and Picasso. It was unforgettable, the light angling through curtains into a world of fantastic form and colour while the wines went round, explained with what seemed excessive modesty: pure jewels from Trotanoy and Lafleur, Cheval Blanc and Pétrus – another world from the vigour of the Médoc, wines that flowed like conversation, dangerously easy, wickedly heady.

He sold a painting to buy a château. That was the mismatch in value in those days. In time he became proprietor of five and managed as many more, the business today continued by his younger son, Christian, while the elder, Jean-François, trades in the great names of all Bordeaux.

Half past ten on the Quai du Priourat. The brown Dordogne is sliding by in oily circles under the stone bridge and on through farmland to the estuary. Cars are parked under the trees for shade. There is a red door in a long stone façade and a brass plate: Ets J-P Moueix. Christian Moueix is tall, dark-haired and lean, with his father's gravity and courtesy. "We have just put out some of our own wines," he says. "Magdelaine, Le Grave Trigant de Boisset ... and Pétrus. May I join you in a quarter of an hour when you have had a chance to see them?" The tasting-room is austerity itself: a white corridor with a broad white bench on which ten black bottles are perfectly aligned. A typed list and a pencil are perfectly aligned, too.

It feels like desecration to pour the first wine; alarming when dense purple fills the glass; disaster when a purple drop falls on the white bench. I settle myself to concentrate, put all my senses into the first contact, the first raw, shocking impact of new-born wine. Try to be analytical, I tell myself. But I am distracted by the clean energy that hits me: fresh and somehow athletic. This is a Fronsac from a hilly area just outside

Libourne, the prettiest in all Bordeaux wine country but geologically less generously endowed than its neighbours. Fronsac is the perfect place for a country house (unlike Pomerol, a seemingly sterile landscape); its leafy combes are full of them, creamy stone cubes with grey shutters, spangled with the shadows of their tall planes, their vineyards tilting to and fro in a restless landscape. This is not the smell of Merlot, the plums-and-cream of Pomerol, but something more Médoc-like. Not far from the sort of virile claret I like in Moulis, I think. Move on: the first impression is the one to trust.

Château Fonroque: "This is sweet ripe Merlot, with an earthy, or maybe meaty, character; what I expect from St-Emilion. There is less tension: a sort of open weave effect." Château Magdelaine: "Far from open; the nose not expressive, but silky, polished, intricate in the mouth. The subtleties linger on. This is serious stuff." The Pomerols are a longer list. It is strange to think that until Jean-Pierre Moueix came along hardly anyone in the wider world had heard of Pomerol. Those who think that in France you are ancient or nothing should reflect on this. I knew the first English merchants to spread the word in England: Ronald Avery and Harry Waugh were teaching me while they were learning here. Did Moueix invent the style, too; the heavy emphasis on early-ripening Merlot, which on Pomerol soils as gravelly as the Médoc gives wine of a plummy, milky ripeness that appears evanescent at first, until you realize that it hides a steely spring? (The answer is no: I once tasted a 1921 Pétrus; that is what it was like.)

The mantle of the prince of Pomerol has fallen on Christian Moueix, responsible for Pétrus and a clutch of other seductive, harmonious wines.

Christian comes into the tasting-room. He knows the texture of every millimetre of Pomerol; the calibre of the gravel, the percentage of sand, and the depth before you hit clay. As everybody knows, gravel is warm. The more gravel, the riper the grapes. Château La Grave then should logically be the deepest, most potent, wine. No: it is fresh, sweet and clean with a light touch. Then Le Gay, more intense, restrained and impressive. Then Latour à Pomerol, sweetly dense, a bigger presence in your mouth but hinting more than giving; then lingering. La Fleur Pétrus: a sniff of oak and a bright minty attack, then scenting the palate with smoky black fruit, expanding as it goes. Trotanoy: almost hearty; forthright warm grapes to smell, but an enigma of tight tannin, even sharpness, under the warmth. Château Lafleur: astonishing aromas. Is that Cognac I smell splashed over the plums and cream? And Pétrus: strikingly darker purple than all the rest, the fresh-coffee smell of toasted oak, such sweet density at first that I can taste nothing through it; then a quintessence of fresh plum almost painful to hold in your mouth, were it not so creamy.

There is more to it than gravel. A layer of iron weaves through these fields. But by what perverse chemistry does the ripest, subtlest, most explosive flavour come from a patch of pure clay? Pétrus is a puzzle. Jean-Pierre Moueix did not write the tune, but he arranged the orchestration. Christian, too, loves understatement, and is prone to disclaimers. "It is nothing. We just take care of the vines" (a few years ago they stripped off all the topsoil and laid drains on the solid clay below); "we like a reasonable crop" (they remove half the grapes still green in July); "we pick on a nice day" (they rush in the whole crew, have even fanned the vines dry with a helicopter); "and we let the fermentation take its time." As for the château: there isn't one. Cocks and Féret's *Bordeaux et ses Vins*, the Bordeaux bible, contains a very bad engraving of a building with a rough stone tower. There is no evidence that such a thing ever existed: a simple farmhouse with the usual modest barn for a *chai* (and vats of cement, not oak or steel) is all there is. One never knows how much to trust this brick of a book, now in its 17th edition (the first was in 1850). It lists 7,400 'châteaux' in all Bordeaux (150 in Pomerol). I'm sure the acreages and the tonnages are right, but some of the descriptions read like partisan puffs, and the illustrations, judging by Pétrus, can be pure fantasy. I was asked to write the Preface to the 13th edition. "If a priest were asked to write a preface to the Bible," I said, "he would be wise to limit himself to recommending attentive reading … it is the nature of a classic to gain stature from its own idiosyncrasies. Here endeth the lesson."

When it comes to the Pétrus vintage, Lafleur-Pétrus just over the road serves as the homestead. The pickers, the cream of their trade, gather at the long table for the sort of meal that has disappeared, alas, from France's restaurants; business-like bounty: terrines and crudités, an entrecôte with creamy potatoes and haricots verts, cheeses and a glowing apricot tart. Bread by the metre and wine by the litre. Christian Moueix is there with his guests, so is Jean-Claude Berrouet, the scholarly *oenologue* who has made the Moueix wines for thirty years.

It seems there is still room for reinterpretation, or rescoring. Ten years ago the Moueix family bought another vineyard adjoining Pétrus, which in typical Pomerol fashion had a different layering of gravel, iron and clay. Also in typical Pomerol fashion it had a name borrowed from two neighbours. (They are unmemorable, these names, to the point of perversity; the result very often of old family parcels splitting up. It happens in St-Emilion, too.) Dump the old name, was their solution, and call it Hosanna. St Peter is at the gate; this is the chorus when they let you in. The first shout was in 1999, recorded in my tasting book as "Sleek, delicate …". It is almost Burgundian, this soil-driven variation on a theme.

For all the similarities of their wines, St-Emilion is quite different from Pomerol. Pomerol is very much a location, a gravel plateau delimited by its odd deposits of soil. St-Emilion is several places: a little capital city, its surroundings (on varying soils), and an idea that spreads out into the country round.

St-Emilion would be a honeypot, wine or no wine. The Right Bank (of the Dordogne and the Gironde) is a wall of limestone waiting to be cut. It gives the city of Bordeaux its seductive uniformity, all its buildings in creamy stone, and it does the same to St-Emilion, where the stone is simply sawn out from below ground and stacked in architectural symmetry above. The houses up the steep cobbled streets (the town lines a deep re-entrant in the hill) could have been built at any time in eight hundred years. Beaune is a place with much the same undatable allure, where the doorways may have been built in the days of doublets and the windows added for men in frockcoats. You pass from gate to cloister to arcade, to little squares crowded with tables, to rampart, to tower, among sacred buildings and bottleshops and many menus.

You will be tempted by the luxurious doorway of the Plaisance, the hotel that commands the view over the amphitheatre of roofs. Submit. It is a restaurant where the damask and crystal and vases of tall flowers do not deceive. Ask for lampreys. The lamprey (archaic animal; eel is the sleeker modern name) is the edible emblem of St-Emilion. He comes from the rivers, perfumed with river slime as mushrooms are redolent of the rotten leaves of the woods. He is chopped into little logs and simmered with leeks and red wine until he becomes the osso buco of the estuarial world, a brown stew with a riverine savour matched perfectly to rich red wine. Which could also be said of the cèpes, obese fungi sautéed in olive oil and breadcrumbs and garlic and parsley (how can a woodland fungus be richer than cheese?), or the entrecôte marchand de vin, a thick steak peppered and smokily caramelized, then dressed with bone marrow and shallots, fat and sharp. A nutritionist will prove to you that tannin combines with protein to everyone's benefit.

In St-Emilion you forget whether you are in a building or a cave. Wine-cellars are incidental in this subterranean maze. Mushroom-growing takes up more of the dank irregular chambers. In one episode of my television history of wine I tried to evoke the spirit of St Emilianus, a hermit

St-Emilion is hollow with caves, the limestone quarries of centuries. This was an episode in my history of wine series for television.

who lived, at least in legend, in a cave where Roman graves have been found. When the camera turned I grasped a flaming brand and set out into the claustrophobic dark. The flames sent fantastic figures leaping along the raw stone round me. More tunnels, an ossuary, a steep incline, and I emerged under a high rock vault into a scene of scarlet robes and candlelight. I had stumbled (with film-maker's licence) on a ceremony of the town's ancient parliamentary body, its Jurade, in its rock-cut monolithic church. Folklore is important to a wine region. Burgundy invented the genre with its Chevaliers de Tastevin. (It is not limited to France: even German Australians have their rituals in the Barossa Valley.) The Jurade's solemnity is so well rehearsed that one almost believes this is the city's real corporation. At vintage-time the elders in scarlet cry the *ban des vendanges*, the signal to start, from a tower accredited to England's (and Aquitaine's) unfortunate King John. The medieval, and Roman, resonance of the Right Bank makes the Left feel like a recent colony: Bordeaux's own New World.

The Jurade de St-Emilion, the town's medieval parliament, processes past the Café de la Poste, parasolled in chromatic harmony. Visitors who show sufficient devotion to the local produce are regularly enrolled.

The New World of bordeaux in the 20th century, on the contrary, started on this side of the river, and not in a château but in a garage. *Garagiste* is the self-deprecating term adopted by a band led by a son of the town called Jean-Luc Thunévin. They set out in the 1990s with no money to make great wine from vineyards with no pedigree. The techniques available to anyone wanting to make the sort of wines that score Parker points are mainly those of self-denial. First you accept a tiny crop: concentration is all. A garageful of wine reduced in volume and thick with 'extract', as chemists call all the elements that are left if you remove the water, can be fine-tuned more easily than traditional quantities. Massage the wine with tiny bubbles (a technique called *microbullage*) to settle its molecules in patterns agreeable to a discerning tongue. Give the wine strong aromas of new oak to absorb as part of its extreme flavour. Even give it new barrels twice to make sure no-one misses the smell.

In wines like these you have exactly what America, led by Robert Parker, seems to look for. They justify extreme language: words such as rich, sweet, jammy, dense and thick, and of course blockbuster. Smooth is not one of these buzz-words, but it should be. The alchemy of oak seems to clog the wine's pores, glaze it like the gesso on a picture frame. It has the same effect on my palate: the electrical impulses can reach the soft flesh at the back of my mouth but not penetrate the smooth coating that seems to flow in with the wine and cling like petals to a pavement – or Teflon to a pan, I sometimes think. I feel frustrated: why can't I taste the fruit – or the terroir? And smooth means dangerous: too easy to swallow for the drinker's good. These attributes point bordeaux firmly in the direction of California or Australia – certainly of a region with a warmer climate. Since the best vintages here are the warmest, it is a logical move. It would be difficult to sell large quantities, because by definition the concentration and care they need is expensive. Small, sometimes minute, quantities make them collectors' items, send their prices wild and attract other wine-makers to follow suit. Perhaps they foreshadow a revolution in the nature of claret. Wouldn't it be a disaster, though, for bordeaux to put itself in competition with vineyards where this style is dictated by nature?

Certainly it can't be done on a big enough scale to become the bordeaux norm. But more important, this is the only region in the world, or yet discovered, whose genius lies in making great light wine – light on the palate, light on the spirits, light on the constitution – great in its best moments, nonetheless, by any definition except that of blockbuster.

More to my taste is Château Figeac, on the gravelly plateau that extends from Pomerol into this northwest corner of St-Emilion, or indeed Vieux Château Certan, to take one Pomerol less seen in England. They are both determinedly non-varietal wines; that is the flavour of Merlot or the flavour of Cabernet is not the point. Nor is the flavour of oak. Vieux Château Certan belongs to the same Belgian family as the nearby micro-property le Pin, a mini-Pétrus with a correspondingly maxi price.

"Marvellous stuff," I see in my notebook. This is the VCC 1990. I am usually more conscientious than this, scribbling away about the colour, smell and taste in something like an orderly fashion. 'Marvellous stuff' means I was so pleased by the first sniff that scribbling seemed superfluous. I recovered myself enough by the end of the evening to add "light and full-bodied, if that's possible. The creamy texture has a firm frame. Perfect with the partridge." This was a dinner party at home. Finding a bottle of Le Pin to compare with it was not straightforward – nor, I must say, cheap. Its production, a quarter that of Pétrus (which in turn is a mere tenth the size of say, Château Lafite), makes it instantly collectable by, well, collectors. Exotic is the inevitable word for this opulent creature. It came on and on in waves of scented innuendo; one moment plums, the next Bourbon, the next salt. Racy currents of fruit came and went like meteors in a night sky. "A *grande horizontale*," I finally wrote – referring to its seductive powers, of course, not its morals.

Château Figeac is positively *Ancient Régime*: it stands in a park, a luxury not seen elsewhere on this intensely viticultural plateau. Through the park runs a stream, the one that drains Château Cheval Blanc next door. It was the prime spot when it was picked by its 18th century builder. Its land originally embraced what was to become Cheval Blanc in other hands, as well as the dozen small châteaux that include Figeac in their names. The Manoncourt family have owned it for a century; change of policy seems no more likely than a change of the flagstone floors. Policy is to minimize the gap with the Médoc, use Cabernet Sauvignon, tolerate toughness in the early years. Not everyone will pay attention to the quiet delivery of wines like these. Why should they? Shall I try to describe the 1995? This is a long attempt, but you can always turn the page.

"Sometimes we talk about grape varieties," I wrote as I tasted, "just for something to say, in the hope of some way into a taste that eludes us. The colour: we talk about that. More garnet than ruby, this, but a jewel cut in the round, the dome of a cabochon rather than a thing of facets. The smell: blackberry crumble poured onto forest earth, but flinty, with a seashell tang I associate with the Médoc. It flows in your mouth, then turns with something like a snarl. The mailed fist shows, and the bitterness of a minor key. Now the beef welcomes it; the appetite needs a spur. Figeac is discreet. It is grave. It has grace rather than charm. While I have been writing this the bottle has half-gone. Gamey; between Médoc and Nuits, iron and singed taffeta; caramelized beef."

This is a long description – but it's a long wine. It looks more and more like burgundy, too: it has the high-toned freshness, between mint and game. Then it is more gravelly; the grit is in the taste as well as the texture. Finally you discover that there is teeth-staining tannin still in this gentle wine. I ask Judy to find one word for it. "Balance," she says. I try to imagine how you would put a score on balance.

St-Emilion, as I said, is several places and an idea. The places are villages on its periphery which show at least some of its character and have the right to use its name. They are part of the same limestone escarpment. They enjoy at least glimpses of the same long view south over the valley of the Dordogne, and have the same spacious quarry-cellars. The idea goes on eastwards through country that has had few champions until now. The most distinguished, or at least most successful, is Tony Laithwaite, whose first Bordeaux Direct vanfuls in 1970 came from the cooperative of Puisseguin. It was by pure chance that he stayed for a summer vacation from university with the manager. Monsieur and Madame Cassin (he never called them anything else, even when he became almost a member of their family) were stalwarts of old provincial France, a breed of hair-shirt hedonists who knew, loved and had three recipes for every living thing in their countryside. It was enough to admire a leaf in Madame Cassin's garden to provoke an account of its interesting pharmacological properties and the best time of year to eat it. In the Cassins Tony discovered an openness to ideas and vigour in pursuing them that served him well. His own Cumbrian roots drove him in the same direction. He imported first the cooperative's wine, then the neighbours', and later on his own. The village of St Colombe where he found his student lodgings is now the headquarters of his company making wine all over southern France.

This fringe of the St-Emilion country is the Côtes de Castillon. Castillon la Bataille, in the Dordogne Valley below, was where the three-hundred-year English rule of Aquitaine ended. The English commander, John Talbot, Earl of Shrewsbury, is still remembered with respect. Having once been ransomed and sworn not to bear arms against France again, he led the charge unarmed. He and his son were both killed in the fight that gave Bordeaux back to France – a process that seems to have gone into reverse as you go on up the Dordogne and find *rosbifs*, or their descendants, all around you.

Tony Laithwaite started his life as a wine merchant on the fringes of St-Emilion, shipping direct to English customers in his van from the spot which is now HQ of his wine-making and -trading empire.

The spirit of claret (and its grapes) continues even after the appellation of Bordeaux (which is enormous: the whole département of the Gironde) comes to an end. The same wine-making techniques as the *garagistes* use in St-Emilion (old vines, small crops, new oak) can have even more radical results applied to grapes from what used to be a minor district.

We did a day-trip to Bergerac in the early years of The Sunday Times

Wine Club. The airfield, I seem to remember, doubled as the football pitch. Tony and Barbara Laithwaite were waiting to greet our plane from London with the mayor and the local firemen's brass band. They began to worry when our plane, instead of landing, made two or three un-scheduled circuits of the field. It was my fault: I had presidentially told the pilot to hang on until we had finished the champagne.

The last time I landed at Bergerac, now a grown-up airport, it was in a Global Express, a private jet that had brought us from London in a twinkling; scarcely time to eat breakfast. My host was Eugene Shvidler, a Russian who had bought a Bergerac château and wanted me to inspect it. In his Range Rover, threading the green lanes of this quiet, domestic, undramatic landscape, he kept saying "Look at these hills. Look at these trees. We don't have these in Russia." In the little room at the top of his old stone house (the word 'château' exaggerates – as usual) he has installed a big chair and telescope for watching the hills.

The next stop was St-Emilion, one of its more modest restaurants, where he had invited a dozen of his Bergerac neighbours to bring their wines for a tasting. Most vignerons in Bergerac make red wine, white wine and a not-quite replica of Sauternes. We tasted 36 very respectable wines, some with modern ideas, concentrated and oaky; others the simple light drinking that makes me relax and swallow. The new proprietor's wines acquitted themselves well – in the modern style. Then lunch: the Dor-dogne's favourite, confit de canard, and the *vin d'honneur*: Château Lafite 1964. My friend was amazed. How did they know he was 40 that day?

I left after the birthday cake, at signs that the party was taking a Russian turn, to taste the new wines at the Moueix establishment down the road. "Château Thénac?" said the scholarly oenologue, Jean-Claude Berrouet, when I told him where I had been. "That's where I made my first wine. In 1962."

The Bordeaux Persuasion

A CHECKLIST of all the world's wines of the Bordeaux Persuasion would be longer than it would be useful. Any number can play. Plant Cabernet. Plant Merlot. Plant Cabernet Franc, Petit Verdot, even Malbec, even Tannat – they are all the grapes of Gascony, of the basin of the Gironde, perhaps with common parentage, perhaps with mingling genes. One account traces the family back, via Roman Spain, to Albania on the Adriatic. Two thousand years of cultivation and selection have narrowed down the clones that suit the maritime climate of Bordeaux.

In the past two hundred they have been shown almost every wine-susceptible climate on earth, and put on at least a recognizable performance in most of them. For how long will Bordeaux be able to claim leadership over such talent, and such diversity?

The grapes are on the limits of viability in Bordeaux. Climate change for the warmer would be good for business, but at the first sniff of a new Ice Age Bordeaux would be in trouble. A good vintage in Bordeaux is by definition a warm, dry, sunny one. All the great vintages have been years of exceptional heat. The same, though, can be said of any part of France: wine-growing was introduced there from further south. Does this mean that more warmth means better wine? Not so fast.

California was the first place on earth to make wine comparable to some of the best bordeaux. It may have happened in the Napa Valley as far back as the 1850s. The oldest examples I have tasted were from the 1940s. Then came Australia. The first I became aware of were from the remote outpost of Coonawarra in the southerly panhandle of South Australia. Chile had already been making Cabernet for three generations by then, but whether any was comparable to bordeaux is very doubtful.

Chile

Chilean Cabernet first crossed my path in the 1960s as one of the cheapest red wines my friends could be prevailed upon to drink. I must have been convinced because I negotiated with the London importer for a whole barrel to be delivered to the spacious cellars of my new home in the country. Half a dozen friends bought shares. We grew excited as we heard of its progress: by lorry to Valparaíso (not far, it came from the Canepa winery, between Valparaíso and Santiago); by steamer up the long coast of Chile, past Peru and Ecuador and Colombia and across to the Panama Canal; a steamy tropical passage through the Caribbean; five days steaming on the rollers of the Atlantic and a gentle home run up the Channel to Southampton. It rested in a London warehouse while I paid as much as the wine was worth in duty. Then a brewer's lorry brought it up to Essex. Hurrah. But how to get it down into the cellar?

The driver was a drayman. He rolled beer barrels for a living. They have ways. A noose around the barrel, a turn around the axle of the lorry, aim it end on down the cellar stairs and lower away. Just in case, a lorry tyre at the bottom for a soft landing. What he had failed to notice, and I to remember, was that four steps from the bottom the stairs widen out. Unconfined, the barrel turned sideways and fell, bounced on the tyre and drove its end into the brick floor.

A weeping barrel is a sad sight. The iron hoops had slipped enough for the parched staves to open up. The smell was marvellous as the barrel turned red and the puddle grew. We grabbed hammers and ruined chisels bashing the hoops as tight as we could. We threw sacks in the pond and wrapped the barrel in them. Why hadn't they given it a good soaking to swell the staves before they loaded it? The story, though, has a more than happy ending.

I recommend a bottling party. Quality control is a serious business, and nobody shirks his duty. Nine or ten of us worked late into the night, taking turns to suck on the siphon and direct the tube into the next bottle. In preparation for the first day I had ordered 25 dozen brand-new bottles, or their equivalent in magnums.

Mystery: I came to the end of the bottles and I still had twenty centimetres of wine to go in the barrel. Alarm: I had to leave them there. No more bottles, and a trip booked to France. I rang round all my neighbours for empties, and stirred what seemed a shocking quantity of sulphur into the remaining wine as it lay exposed to the air in the barrel. I came back. It tasted fine. And we bottled the rest in a medley of old wine bottles, beer bottles, water bottles, even a rather fine blue half-gallon affair from a Victorian pharmacy.

It was the cheapest wine I ever bought: the barrel held 300 litres when I expected 225. But more important it was delicious. It had the ripe dark blackcurrant flavour of good-vintage claret with a dry, earthy tang. Had it been Bordeaux, it would have come from the far end of the Médoc beyond St-Estèphe, or possibly from the Graves. The 1968 (a very good Chilean vintage, as it happened) had none of the grace-notes of today's Super-Chilean; just densely ripe fruit with enough gritty tannin to keep you on your toes. We drank the last magnum twenty years later. By then it was time to say goodbye.

Chile close-up was fascinating and frustrating in equal parts. I went in 1975, but remember more about the scenery than the wines. I certainly reported in glowing terms on my return. "The scene," I wrote, "is a broad bungalow nine-tenths hidden by almost-tropical climbers and trees of great seniority. The sense of lush growth suggests the rainfall of Cork or Kerry: rivulets run and ferns fecundate in aromatic shade, cool despite a surprisingly high and direct sun. The verandah is on the grand colonial scale: a long gallery roofed but only one-walled, its peeling red-painted pillars supporting a broad barn roof of corrugated iron. Dazzling white in the background, high above but improbably close, hangs the ridge of snow that caps a mountain range so sudden that it seems to rise from the back garden to Himalayan heights.

"Glowing deep red on the table before you is a glass of wine that seems both familiar and exotic. It bears a strong family resemblance to bordeaux, and yet its flavour is sweet, ripe and open in a way that is rare in claret. It is very male wine, pungent and earthy, dense in texture, hinting of resin, yet with a strong tannic cut that leaves your mouth braced and ready for more.

"The voices around you are speaking Spanish, but it is more leisurely, less clipped and emphatic than the Castilian sound. You are in Chile. You are one of the elect who has gone beyond the mountains to a country of legendary fertility, which since the time of the Incas has been a cross between an allotment and the garden of Eden, a land that bestows its own romance on the traveller; that so stocks him with superlatives that he becomes a welcome story-teller on his return."

My stories included a visit to a ranch where sixty horses waited in one corral to carry visitors through the vines, the orange groves and orchards of walnuts – and the manpower was even greater than the horsepower. If a ditch needed cleaning, a whole village would be turned out to spend the day in and around it. I'm not sure whether it was any cleaner by sunset. This was the problem with the cellars, too: plenty of men with brushes but not much scrubbing. The barrels were massive ovals of the local timber, rauli or southern beech, painted, some of them, with linseed oil 'to protect the contents from oxidation.' If the Cabernet reminded you of cricket bats, I suppose no harm was done. Varietal names, in any case, were used with abandon. 'Chardonnay' was often Sémillon, and one 'Pinot Noir' I tasted ("not bad, slight Cabernet nose, oxidized") was, they told me, 35 per cent Sémillon and 65 per cent Cabernet Sauvignon.

I went back to Chile in 1984 with friends who had been my guides and interpreters many times in Spain, Jan and Maite Read, to help them with the first English book on Chilean wine. Things had changed less than I hoped. We were taken for a day at sea on a Chilean naval frigate from Valparaíso, mainly, I suspect, to impress us with the fact that the navy was a clone of our own. Even the orders on the bridge were given in English. Perhaps our impressions were coloured by the violent politics of the day – not to mention the frequent juddering of earthquakes. One beautiful estate we visited, Los Vascos (it now belongs to the Rothschilds of Château Lafite), had been badly tossed around. Night time in Santiago presented a quandary: stay in the hotel and be crushed or go out on the street after the curfew and be shot? My conclusion in the book was "it is impossible not to feel frustrated for knowledgeable and ambitious individuals and well run companies baulked by forces beyond their control." Twenty years later there is nowhere better for knowledgeable and ambitious wine-makers to try out new ideas.

Chile and Argentina were quite different. Chile made much of its wine, even then, for export to the rest of South America. It was trying to emulate, above all, bordeaux. Argentina had its own market, and its tastes were Italian. 'Your Plate River settler,' I was told, on my way to Buenos Aires, 'is an Italian who speaks Spanish, dresses like a Frenchman and thinks he's English.' I'm not sure I met that individual, but the settlers' tastes were certainly Italian. Picnics in Patagonia were accompanied by sweet and prickly red wine from two-litre *fiaschi*, Chianti-style (but wrapped in plastic instead of straw).

Chile, in any case, was temporarily displaced by California, by Australia, and before long by Italy and even Spain as a source of excellent Cabernet, not necessarily cheaper than bordeaux but offering different interpretations. The Napa Valley, to my mind, was ahead of the pack in quality. The other wine that no claret-drinker could ignore (though

Cabernet has nothing to do with it) was Rioja. Rioja is Spain's best shot at the bordeaux style. It was not the primary fruit flavours of all these wines that drew me to them so much as their glorious ability to move on. Five, ten, fifteen years in bottle gives them more than just a patina of age. It does what age does to individuals: makes them more themselves.

California

The Californian Cabernets I first tasted, when the pioneering Dr Loeb brought a box of bottles to a meeting of the Wine & Food Society at Cambridge in 1959, were very different from California's polished products of today. I would characterize them as sweet and lean; deliciously sweet, like blackcurrants become raisins, and sinewy in structure where the modern model has voluptuous curves. There were wines whose tannin overrode everything, but the good ones were balmy with balsam, balanced sweetness with delicious astringency, as uncomplicated as they were unsmoothed by any flavour of oak. With age they became leathery like skin long-exposed to the sun.

Dr Loeb had pupils in California as well as Cambridge. Gradually I came to know some of them – all doctors. The Rhodeses, Dickersons, Adamsons, and Dr Robert Knudsen (a bachelor with a zest for every sort of knowledge, and an impressively bald head) mysteriously knew the best chefs in London before we did and moved in a well planned frenzy of discovery. They debated the relative merits of the Moselles of the 1950s, the oysters of Colchester and Cancale, the tables at England's meagre supply of country house hotels. I was agog. Americans did not take pleasures lightly, or for granted. There was everything to be learned from their approach.

André and Dorothy Tchelistcheff visited Saling with Jancis Robinson, her husband Nick Lander and baby Julia.

The main subject of their study was the Napa Valley. I hope its winemakers were conscious of how much they owed to the medical fraternity of the Bay Area for its enlightened enthusiasm. Wine is made by its market; the best customers are sympathetic and critical; Napa and Sonoma were the beneficiaries. Napa had, besides its natural advantages, the gift of a resident genius, André Tchelistcheff, the winemaker of Beaulieu Vineyards (always referred to as BV). It was completely fitting in this frontier community (it still felt like that in the 1960s, even with a century of wine-growing behind it) that the lead was given by a Russian working for a Frenchman.

With hindsight we can see that there were many talents at work and that the spirit of the times would inevitably produce great wines. Many years later I wanted to compliment a French friend with a bottle of great Napa Cabernet. I chose my last bottle of BV Georges de Latour (Georges was the Frenchman employing Tchelistcheff) of 1968. My guest tasted it with a smile. "It's not the '68, Hugh, is it?"

"Christian," I said (it was Christian Moueix), "you are a genius."

"No," he said, "I was working at BV that vintage. I was bringing samples of Cabernet from the Rutherford vineyards to the winery, and hauling hoses around; you know, I was a cellar rat."

So the future *patron* of Pétrus was already getting his Napa legs. (Today he has his own winery there: Dominus.) Robert Mondavi had just opened the first new winery in the valley since Prohibition. The building is a calculated statement that California has its own wine history: it looks like one of the Franciscan Mission buildings whose adobe towers are scattered up the coast from Mexico. The next winery to be built, by Donn Chappellet on Pritchard Hill, took the opposite line: its three-sided pyramid in rust-red steel at the foot of a vast amphitheatre of vines is still, thirty-five years later, as modern in concept as any in the valley.

A Sonoma winery in the 1960s. The tanks were built of redwood – no hint of the glitz of California today.

It was by no means a gold rush in those days: not like the Médoc a hundred years before. A handful of old-timers, BV, Inglenook, Louis Martini, Charles Krug in particular, already knew the best dirt, as they called it, on the valley floor and the enclaves in the hills that had been assayed by such as Jacob Schram. There were old vines up there, and vineyard clearings gone back to forest. Exploring east and west of St Helena, up Pritchard Hill and Spring Mountain, and north up to Calistoga with

its mud springs and beyond by the little pass to Alexandra Valley, was a journey through paradise. You left the pastoral beauty of the valley, with its stiff battalions of vines, to climb among rocks and streams, madrone and buckeye and ponderosa pine. You glimpsed shy deer among the rocks and unflinching red-tail hawks in the pine-tops. You passed from burning sunshine to deep shade, then up to the rarer air of mountain meadows, where range answers purple range far up and down the coast. It is not for the faint-hearted, this landscape. Climb high enough and you can see the Golden Gate sixty miles to the south, white fog veiling its red towers.

My guide on my first exploration of the North Coast backwoods was Bob Thompson, a young writer working for the wine industry's corporate voice, the Wine Institute. I suspect he was as new as I was to some of the incipient wineries. He talked with modest authority about wine-makers and vintages and grapes and dirt, painting a picture of each actor in the Renaissance that was in progress. His own cellar had bottles going back to the beginning. So did my doctor friends'. It was time, I suggested to Bob, to write a book, a grammar of California wine to help people like me get started. (I always like writing about things I know nothing about.) We planned it, tasting and discussing together. Bob researched and wrote most of it, coining as he went a language to fit new tastes and attitudes. It was published in 1976 under our joint names as *The California Wine Book*. Then the sky clouded over. One of the wine-makers cited sued us for misrepresenting his business. What we said did not agree with what he told his customers. The easiest thing for a publisher to do at the sound of a lawyer is to dump the book in question. Not only did our book disappear immediately from the shelves but we were being sued for half a million dollars.

Bob Thompson (left) and I tasted our way round California. One visit was to the first home of Dominus, where Jean-Claude Berrouet explained he was not planning a western Pétrus.

Nathan Chroman saved our skins. He was the wine editor of the *Los Angeles Times*, and a lawyer. He wrote to the big names in the industry. Gallo, Mondavi, Brother Timothy of the Christian Brothers ... a score of them. They wrote to our persecutor. 'How can we expect writers to tell our story,' they said, 'if the moment our versions disagree we bankrupt them?' Peer-pressure had its effect and the suit was dropped.

Meanwhile in London a handful of us who had tasted the fruits of California's rebirth met for dinner. It was at Harry Waugh's house in Camden. Harry was already in his seventies, a veteran director of Château Latour, but bubbling with excitement about the new wines. The guests were Ronald Avery's son John, as enquiring as his father, Paul Henderson, the American owner of a Devon hotel, and myself. Frustrated that so few California wines were available in England (and perhaps elated with the success of The Sunday Times Wine Club), I had a club to propose. We would pool our knowledge and bring over the best California wines to share: not for profit, just for fun. The word Zinfandel occurs only in California, so that would be the club's name. We started straight away with a dinner at the Garrick Club. I still remember one of the 1968 Cabernets we drank, from Heitz's Martha's Vineyard. "It smells of eucalyptus," said Harry, and we all agreed.

We were not the only ones to be excited by California. In 1976 Steven Spurrier (he was the first English wine merchant in Paris; he and I were at school together) staged a historic tasting in Paris in which French judges found both Cabernets and Chardonnays from the Napa Valley, of which they knew nothing, better than some of the best clarets and white burgundies. Within a year British wine merchants were going to California and coming back with their own discoveries. The most influential was the elegant young Geoffrey Roberts, whose name for a while was almost synonymous with California wine – until he became equally enthusiastic about Australia. Looking back I can see that part of the reason for this stampede was disillusionment with France. Bordeaux prices spiked absurdly in the 1970s and then spectacularly flopped. It was a low period for burgundy, too. No wonder merchants were looking around.

In my Californian enthusiasm I took a party, members of The Sunday Times Wine Club, on a West Coast tour. I drove one of the overloaded station wagons all the way, one day, to Modesto, the farm town in the Central Valley which was being made famous by E & J Gallo. Ernest Gallo and his wife Amelia had invited us to lunch (a truly beefy pasta) by their swimming pool. I had never seen one with two palm-treed islands before. It was very early in Gallo's researches into the British market, but when we left he had heard everything we had to say about Gallo Hearty Burgundy and its prospects in our then-new supermarket wine departments. The next stage in the Gallo research programme was a weekend at Saling Hall. I had never met anyone who demanded answers to so many questions – including the names of the best local antique dealers.

The Gallos' was not the kind of wine country I was used to. It was the first winery I had seen that was too large to explore on foot. You were driven round to admire not only cubic miles of stainless steel but also a fleet of what Americans so romantically term 'big rigs', road-liners – trucks – with shining steel Parthenons for radiators and tall shining chimneys. Best of all, they had their own bottle factory. The Gallos not only grow grapes, I was told, they quarry sand for their glass. Every part of

What do you give Mr & Mrs Ernest Gallo for dinner? The best of British and French, judging by this menu. La Tâche 1962 was my all-time favourite burgundy.

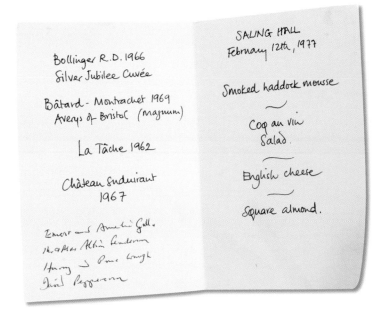

Bollinger R.D. 1966
Silver Jubilee Cuvée

Bâtard - Montrachet 1969
Averys of Bristol (magnum)

La Tâche 1962

Château Suduiraut
1967

Ernest and Amelia Gallo
Mr & Mrs Albin Henderson
Harry J Paul Gough
David Peppercorn

SALING HALL
February 12th, 1977

Smoked haddock mousse

Coq au vin
Salad.

English cheese

Square almond.

their business was unprecedented. Out of the wreck of Prohibition the country's two most single-minded brothers had chiselled an empire.

They may have started with such simple liquors as Thunderbird, which I had first met as a teenager late at night in Greyhound bus stations, but they progressed, diligently educating America as they went, to table wines they called Hearty Burgundy and Chablis Blanc. Whatever fabulous quantities they sold (and they told me they owned, among other plants, the two biggest wineries in America) they were anxious to learn and endlessly self-critical. Ernest interrogated anyone who got as far as his tasting-room. "Describe it to me, Hugh. Is it too sweet?" I frankly admired his Hearty Burgundy. It was far better than the red wine the Italians lived on, and indeed the French. I learned in the end, though, that converse with the Gallos was a one-way street. When I was researching my history of wine I wrote asking Ernest if I could come and use their famously comprehensive library in Modesto. The blunt answer was No, it was a company facility. But do come to lunch.

In the Gallos' tasting room at Modesto, Ernest on the right. Was that a 'Chablis Blanc' I was peering at so intently?

There was the Central Valley with its miles of vines flicking by, alternating with orange groves. There was the Napa Valley, still a pastoral idyll in the sixties but becoming more and more self-conscious as wine-culture visibly took over its life. There was sprawling Sonoma; not a county you could easily visualize as you can Napa. Napa is like the Médoc, long and narrow, with mountains in place of water. You can measure out Sonoma in historic landmarks, from the perfect toytown Mission and barracks and City Hall and Opera House around its original central square to the strange vision of Fort Ross (admittedly in the next county up the coast, Mendocino) where a Russian fur-trappers' Orthodox church survives. It stands, onion-domed, in a wooden stockade above the sea, from the time when nobody owned California.

South of San Francisco there was the increasingly phantom wine country of San José and the Santa Cruz mountains; phantom because its pioneer wineries, Paul Masson and Almaden among them, were giving up their vineyards and their identities to sprawling development and sprawling corporations. Across the Bay there was Livermore, a name I associated with two of San Francisco's greatest pleasures, the Crab Louie salads and Rex Sole browned in butter at a restaurant on Fisherman's Wharf. In the 1960s the choice of good white wines was not wide. I soon learned that Wente Bros Sauvignon Blanc was the best choice. Wente was a pioneer of the Livermore Valley. Its gravel soil produced California's equivalent to white Graves; after three or four years in bottle, completely succulent.

That was the recurring question: did these geographical areas, and the new ones emerging down south on the Central Coast, have tastable identities? Bob and I and our friends would have loved to find certainties. With such a moving target it was difficult. There was a rush of technical progress, there were more and more practitioners and there were surges of fashion, but local climate was apparently more of a factor than soil.

Whatever the question, Robert Mondavi was the man to ask. He not only made better wine than almost anybody in California, he loved to talk about it. 'In that regard,' always seemed to start the eloquent display of the latest bee in his bonnet; a useful phrase to latch onto whatever had just been said. The bees were high-velocity pollinators. Theories germinated everywhere. The terms that became Mondavi's theme-song were 'moulding' or 'crafting' or 'sculpting' or just growing more subtle wine. At Mondavi's you were likely to find yourself in the sun-filled tasting-room in the arcaded courtyard of the winery, through the Mission arch, lapped on the other side by a First Growth Cabernet vineyard, if only

Robert Mondavi can't help looking like a Roman Emperor – especially when he reclines by the pool in his Napa Valley villa.

California had such things. There would be a party with whoever had just turned up, Mondavi opening Châteaux Latour and Mouton-Rothschild to compare with his babies, his ear cocked for any hint that could bring him closer to his ideal. I hope someone has sculpted Mondavi himself. In white marble he would make a Roman Emperor to put most of them to shame. I never, alas, saw him and Philippe de Rothschild together. Their meeting was momentous. Both were great men, with plenty of prejudices (or at least entrenched ideas). But they knew they could learn

from each other. Their joint venture is Opus One. Is it a case of the mountain coming to Mahomet? (An unlikely trope, perhaps, for my subject matter.)

Mondavi's search is for sweet reason in wine. He preaches its benefits to health and society. He is indefatigable (a good gritty word much misused) in his pursuit of knowledge. He was well over ninety when Judy and I travelled with him in Spain. It is a joke of the business that no *bodeguero* (or any other winery owner) will let you go without seeing his bottling line. Bob placed himself next to this object of admiration wherever we went, Margrit his wife at his side to amplify what was said. "How many?" from Bob rang out loud and clear. "Is there any Merlot in that?" "Did you say 100 per cent Allier?" At lunch: "What's in this sauce?" In visiting a castle (where he is first up fifty stone steps) "Was that the crusading one, or his father?"

Knowing the man and knowing the wine could be leading me to wrong conclusions, but I think I see his openness in the subtlety of his finest Cabernets. Latterly this kind of wine has run counter to fashion in California; Napa especially. It is not big-ego wine. The points in the high nineties (and California is high on points) go to delicious fruit-creams made in such tiny quantities (though in premises very unlike a garage) that few ever taste them, or indeed relish paying their prices. The first time I was introduced to a group of them I said they were wines for cigar smokers – which I didn't intend as a compliment. I remembered this wryly when Marvin Shanken, who had changed the little *Wine Spectator* from a piccolo into a full orchestra, started a life-style magazine called *Cigar Aficionado*.

If a yacht is a hole in the sea into which you pour money, a Napa vineyard has become its terrestrial equivalent. There are 'consultants' who will construct you a vineyard in mid-air by blasting a hillside to fill in a gully, bulldozing new soil into place (and never mind the fauna, the flora or the downstream drainage). Their crews will prune, treat, weed and primp it like coiffeurs. Its exiguous crop will be massaged into wine of fabulous colour, depth, smoothness and juicy sweetness, redolent of … (follows a long list of fruits, smokes and stones). The word for such wines is 'cult'. You have been warned. As a writer once said to me in San Francisco, 'There is less here than meets the eye.'

Terroir, the signature of the soil, is something that has to be discovered over time. André Tchelistcheff coined the name 'Rutherford dust' for the one he knew best, an elusive scent that haunts the Cabernet of the bench-land between Oakville and Rutherford in the same way as cedar hovers over Pauillac. Stags' Leap was recognized in the 1970s as a hillside zone on the opposite side of the valley that basks in the evening sun but also catches a cool breeze from the Bay. Anyone can see how different soil and different temperatures will give different flavours. The question is, how much does it matter? You can plausibly divide the Napa Valley into a

dozen zones from Carneros to Calistoga: Mount Veeder, Spring Mountain
… they are not the same; they all sound good. To some extent the new
American Viticultural Areas (they were begun in 1983, in Missouri, of all
places) do that. Or, alternative plot, you can leave growers to establish
the identities of their vineyards as Joseph Heitz did with
Martha's, Joseph Phelps with Eisele or, way back, the
Finnish mariner founder of Inglenook when he gave his
patch of Oakville the unfortunate name of 'Napanook'.
Then it is up to the grower to make his wine consistently
distinctive. Step one is to match the grapes precisely to the
soil. The market decides whether what he is doing is interesting or not. There is no single model: Bordeaux does it one
way, Burgundy another; both are endorsed and protected by
law. But something tells me it will be a long time before any
sort of consensus turns to statute in California.

The truculent stance
becomes a man who didn't
tolerate fools. Joe Heitz
gave California confidence
with his exotic oak-aged
single-vineyard wines.
His Martha's Vineyard
was the first you could
describe as a cult.

I have not been able to follow as many California wines
as I should like. Some of the best are not easily available in
England, and the hurly-burly of a tasting allows you only to
keep up an acquaintance. So Bordeaux is by no means balanced by California in my cellars, nor do many of the
fashionable names appeal to me. Is self-parody a sin? Not in
California. More is more.

The truth is that, however good they are, I find they taste better in
America. Their big flavours work with the flavours of American food,
sweeter and often saltier than most in Europe, and certainly most at
home. When I was writing for *Cuisine* magazine in the early 1980s we
had a correspondent who compared some wines to rock music, to the
advantage of neither. She implied that they were beneath critical
attention – too popular, too common, too vulgar, in fact, to be any good.
"I can't admit this," I wrote. "To give pleasure to huge numbers is itself a
virtue. I don't like rock [that was then; I do now] but I do like jazz. From
the first creaky acoustic recordings to the smooth bounce of the big bands,
it goes, in the words of 'Careless Love', to my head like wine. Which wine
in particular is something I have long been trying to figure out."

I have tasted first-attempt Chardonnays that were like Dizzy Gillespie's
solos: all over the place. And the colour of his trumpet, too. On the other
hand a Stony Hill Chardonnay recently had the subtle harmonies and
lilting vitality of Bix Beiderbecke. Robert Mondavi's Reserve Cabernets
are Duke Ellington numbers: massed talent in full cry. Benny Goodman is
a Riesling from Joseph Phelps, Louis Martini's wines have the charm and
good manners of Glenn Miller. Joe Heitz, though, is surely Armstrong at
the Sunset Cafe; virtuoso, perverse and glorious.

Logically I suppose I should choose the California wines least like bordeaux and profit from the whole range of what Cabernet in different soils and climates can offer. Bob Thompson once teased me for being a cold-country Calvinist: liking wines I could drink without worrying too much about the sins of the flesh. If liking enough tannins and acidity to freshen your mouth is Calvinist, that's me. It is not so much sin as frailty that worries me, though, when I taste wines so concentrated, so full of extract, alcohol, glycerol and tannins burnished to a sheen that you are surprised they can pour. My instinct is that they are often bottled head-aches, and my experience has to agree.

If one Cabernet in California encapsulates this quality of freshness it is Montebello, from a vineyard remote on a hill above Silicon Valley (do they still call it that?) on one of the rollers of redwood-coated hill that seem like a green extension of the Pacific. The name of the winery, Ridge, is more apt than Montebello: from the edge you look straight down into the San Andreas Fault. It could be a canal down there, the straight line where the coast will one day break off from the rest of California. It is an odd place, you would think, to evoke the Médoc; but that is what Montebello does – and the Médoc at its best: firm, focused and slow to express itself. Paul Draper, the creator of Ridge, is a professorial figure, smart, smiling, trim-bearded, understated – and patient. He is unique among the elite of California's wine-makers in being as loyal to the state's own grape, the Zinfandel, as he is to its more prestigious Cabernet Sauvignon. He has proved to everyone's satisfaction that Zinfandel from old vineyards in cooler regions can make wine of the Bordeaux Per-suasion as good as almost any California Cabernet, and better than most. But then he chooses his grapes from the best growers, wherever they are, brings them up the long winding road to his eyrie, and makes his York Creek or Lytton Springs with as much care as, and similar methods to, his flagship Montebello.

What are the qualities of this Cabernet that travels so well and lives so long: the epitome of a great California claret? Intensity of flavour is the first, balance the second, and length the third. Imagine a line starting with the first taste of ripe, even cooked, blackcurrants. It proceeds, through hints of dust and hints of caramel, the same clear flavour precisely, at its climax as bitter-sweet as vermouth, uninterrupted to a close that seems indefinitely postponed. Cabernet to the power of Cabernet is what I wrote. Cabernet squared – it seemed to sum it up at the time. Wines like this are made only from old

Paul Draper brings out a barrel-sample of Ridge. Montebello Cabernet is his crowning achievement, but his Zinfandels show the same sense of balance and style.

vines, deep-rooted in challenging places, by someone who consults his palate every inch of the way. California has many formulaic, indeed bombastic Cabernets. But those that achieve harmony and age gracefully are among the loveliest on earth.

Australia

You would have to be pretty far gone in the claret habit to take Bordeaux as a role model for Australia. But then Australia was: this was John Bull's vineyard and, after port, claret was John Bull's wine. 'Claret' was the most popular table wine class in the Agricultural Shows that had, and remarkably still have, an important place in Australian life. 'Burgundy' was its rival, but since the same wine would be entered for both classes (and could conceivably win them) the stylistic difference was more in the heads of the judges than in anything more measurable. It was a funny way to go about making either to use the Rhône grape, but brilliantly pragmatic. Shiraz will make almost anything in Australia, from admirable fizz to 'port' and even, I believe, white wine of sorts.

The Bordeaux Persuasion is precisely the factor that led to Australia's greatest red wine, and hence to new ambitions for all Australia. Max Schubert was not a big wheel at Penfolds when he was sent to Spain in 1950 to study sherry-making (though sherry and port-making were what kept the wheels on Penfolds). It was not exactly part of the plan that he should visit Bordeaux on the way home. But he did, and he met Christian Cruse, a grandee of the ruling merchant class, who gave him great old claret to drink. He described his reaction to me forty years later: "I had no idea table wine could taste like that, let alone live that long." He had a magnificent nose: a sort of craggy trunk. Back home in Adelaide he tried to find a link between what he had tasted and South Australian grapes. The best were Shiraz, but he remembered the quite different tightness of bordeaux tannin and the way fresh acidity kept claret going in your mouth. Château Latour he particularly liked. There was no remotely equivalent vineyard in Australia. So he created a virtual vineyard, a completely Australian idea. It almost embarrasses me to say it, as a firm believer in terroir and the sense of place, but the vineyard for Penfolds Grange was wherever Schubert could find his ideal Shiraz at vintage time. It was what he did with it that would give it a sense of place.

His methods were without precedent. He fermented the wine in new American oak when he could get it. There is a strong green smell in American oak that could maybe, at a pinch, suggest the character, or at least the tannins, of Cabernet. When fermentations were boiling away in summer heat he used refrigeration to cool his new wine and slow it down.

Is it pure coincidence that at that moment in California André Tchelistcheff was also doing both these things? Schubert was anxious for acidity to freshen the richness of Barossa Shiraz: he allowed a measure of the volatile acidity which wine-makers normally shun. I am only guessing; there is certainly no recipe. In some years he would add a few per cent of South Australian Cabernet Sauvignon, not great in itself but bracing a just-too-soft blend. Whatever he did he was told by his employers to stop: it was undrinkable, they said – until they tasted it again five years later and saw what he had imagined from the start: Australia's own First Growth.

Australians tell this story with the fervour of an Englishman talking of Trafalgar. It poses all sorts of questions, the terroir one being the most obvious, but it set up a model of a great proprietary wine, a brand in fact, that now runs parallel in Australia with the concept of a single great vineyard. It also underscores the fact that Cabernet Sauvignon comes way behind Shiraz in (if there is such a thing) the typical Australian climate. The places famous for Cabernet are on the relatively cool southern edges, most notably Coonawarra, near the coast of southernmost South Australia, or the southwest coast where the Indian Ocean air-conditions the Margaret River.

The Margaret River is a long drive south of Perth through the bush. Nothing happened down here: no settlers, no harbours, no known resources, just trees. After the Second World War the government gave 100-acre grants, and not much else, to ex-soldiers. A man and an axe could get nowhere: it was misery. In the 1960s its emptiness, its climate and its great ocean surf attracted hippies. It has the rather sad beauty of temperate Australia; a wilderness of eucalyptus, trees with no apparent seasons whose leaves hang limp, whose bark peels, whose forest floor is sere. Where the axes never reached there are soaring stands of pale-barked Jarra, some of Australia's tallest trees.

Again and again Australian wine history has been propelled by doctors. Penfold was a doctor, and so was Lindeman. The medical men came to the Margaret River in the 1960s. By the 1970s three of them had the wine world talking. You might wonder what a small new vineyard area could add to Australia's

Gaia is the name of Jeffrey Grosset's Cabernet vineyard on a parched hillside above the Clare Valley. Despite conditions that look extreme, its wine is all harmony. The ruined building is called the Grog Shop – its original purpose.

palette. One answer, among others, was Cabernet with the promise of every quality. It was juicily and richly ripe, and it was vivid, with parallel flavours of blackcurrants and herbs. Perhaps Coonawarra came closer to Bordeaux, but this added an exotically vigorous note, as though the vines were in the peak of training.

Big showplace wineries are not the Margaret River style. Leeuwin Estate has established itself as the host of an annual open-air concert that has seen many of the world's great singers and orchestras, but there is nothing grandiose about its timber buildings, or the sort of sublimely simple food of its restaurant. Australian wine country is becoming one of the best places to eat on earth. The collection of modern art downstairs comes as a surprise out here in the bush. The way one estate's Chardonnay (like Puligny) can follow Riesling (like a warm Rheingau) and lead on to a refulgent Cabernet (like – ah, that's the question –) where none of these things has any obvious connection with the primitive landscape, comes as a shock. How can a remote region have come so far so fast?

Vanya Cullen pours a Chardonnay in her Margaret River restaurant.

Cullen's winery is in the densely planted centre of this new region, in the shallow Willyabrup Valley three kilometres from the endless beach and its crashing waves. Vanya Cullen succeeded her mother (it was another medical family) as wine-maker.

Are all Australian vignerons so endlessly experimental? This is the Médoc and Graves of Australia, or it could be. The Cabernet is acknowledged excellent. The Sauvignon/Semillon blend is a classic. So Vanya sits over a salad in her restaurant under a peppermint tree offering her Chardonnay ("intense, lovely, smoky and figgy with a citrus centre," I wrote in my notebook), her new Pinot Noir ("surprisingly mature, ripe cherries, quite light") and her blend of Malbec, Petit Verdot and Merlot. Everything from Bordeaux except Cabernet, in fact. I find it savoury with an exotic cherry brightness that reminds me of a favourite off-beat Alpine grape, Mondeuse. And the mainstream blend of Cabernet Sauvignon and Merlot? At eight years old as sweet as Lafite, on a broader base. Great claret, in fact.

It is definitely a feature of Australian wine country, the desire to try something else. Most of the world settles down to do one or two things well in a style it hopes people will recognize. Australians are encyclopaedic. 'You haven't tried Queensland Merlot?' (Or even) '... Korean Riesling?' 'I've just stirred up a spot of Sangiovese and Shiraz.' It is endlessly stimulating, but it makes it hard to keep track.

The puzzle I have with such creative, self-critical scholars of the vine is why their wines seem to get inexorably stronger. Not as much as in California, perhaps, where I find many wines hard to drink for their boozy burn. But even in such cool-climate areas as the Yarra Valley and Mornington, in the far south of Victoria, wines that used to be singingly ripe at 12 per cent alcohol are now made with 14 per cent. Is it the wine-maker's palate that is being corrupted, or his customers'?

"If only we knew," was James Halliday's answer when I asked him – about the alcohol that is, not about the corruption. "It's the last thing we wine-makers want. We suspect global warming, or specifically the thinning of the ozone layer and more ultra-violet light. Our vines are so healthy now that the fruit ripens too quickly. Perhaps there are too many leaves. Yeasts are becoming more resistant to alcohol; we use less sulphur. It is probably all these things."

Would it not solve the problem just to pick the grapes earlier, before they have had time to produce so much sugar? First, of course, you have to see it as a problem, which you don't if strength earns you high scores from important judges. Ripening, though, is not that simple: it involves all the constituents of the grape, not just its sugar content, maturing together. The acids have to reach ripeness and the skin has to mature. The pips change colour when they are ready to germinate. Birds jump the gun: they judge only by sweetness, but the wine-grower has to wait until the whole metabolism of the grapes has reached maturity – and the longer it takes, the better the flavour. It is the reason why the most marginal vineyards (north of the equator or south) make the best wine. Nearer the sun strength is easy, but flavour is hard.

Brian Croser and a clutch of coolers. He chills and stores the grapes and only gets around to crushing them after the distractions of the vintage.

There is certainly space to think in Australia, even if not everyone takes the time. You meet plenty of talkers, and sometimes people who have to have it teased out of them. Clams could learn from the taciturn Australian, but sometimes quiet revolutions are going on. Brian Croser is one of the philosophers. I talked to him once during vintage time, when the pickers were racing the red and green parrots to the fruit of the Piccadilly vines. I asked to see the crush, as they call the wine-making part of the operation. "We haven't got time for that now," he said. He didn't mean him and me, but the crush itself. He was putting the boxes of grapes fresh-picked into cold stores to be crushed when he had time to do it properly.

———————————

Croser country is the prettiest in South Australia: the Mount Lofty Ranges, as the hills above Adelaide are called. Adelaide is the trim little capital of an agricultural state, hemmed in with vineyards. Barossa lies to the north, McLaren Vale to the south, and to the east a hilly region that catches the breezes and the rain sweeping in from the Great Australian Bight, a position comparable to the Margaret River's, but almost six hundred metres up. My favourite Australian wine road leaves Adelaide to the southeast, climbs close to the top of Mount Lofty and drops down to Piccadilly, in the lee of the summit. The Adelaide Botanic Garden has its cooler-climate outpost there, a leafy retreat for plants that find the city stressful, too hot and dry, and Brian Croser has Petaluma vineyard. You are only an hour's drive from vines producing some of Australia's most potent red wines, but this is Chardonnay and Pinot Noir territory, burgundy, not bordeaux; Adelaide's answer to Melbourne's Yarra Valley. These extremes make nonsense of the perception of Australia as one warm industrial wine region. If the subtleties of soil and nuances of climate are to be explored anywhere in the New World it is here. This is Croser's contention, against a marketing machine that finds them inconvenient. He has a fight on his hands: big corporations like to keep it simple.

The Mount Lofty Ranges east of Adelaide have one of Australia's most temperate climates. These are Petaluma vineyards at Piccadilly.

"I honestly believe," he said, "that if all the Australian vineyards of today disappeared we could start again on fresh sites and do as good a job, or better." He is a solid, serious man who doesn't suffer fools – certainly no fantasist. It is hard to see how Piccadilly could be reborn elsewhere, but that is not the point. There would be different kinds of good wines from sites with different characteristics no less valid in their own ways.

The map of Victoria certainly seems to bear this out. Vineyards there spread with the gold fever of the mid-19th century. Gold fields don't necessarily have good dirt for grapes, it is customers they provide – and labour. The fact that Ballarat in the west turned out to be excellent red wine country, and Rutherglen in the northeast (to take just two examples) one of the world's most propitious sites for sweet muscats, was the sort of good fortune that could presumably easily happen almost everywhere. The age of the Australian continent, the oldest on earth, means that bedrock has been eroded over endless ages: deep soils are not hard to find. I opened a bottle of 25-year-old Ballarat wine to make sure I was not fantasizing: Balgownie Cabernet Sauvignon 1976. It was still deep ruby, with a dusty blackcurrant smell that could almost have come from a hot Médoc. It was poised between milk and leather, dried fungus and red velvet. Can you imagine swallowing a perfume that keeps going all the way to your stomach? That was how sweet-smelling and long-lasting it was.

Coonawarra was certainly no accident, and nothing to do with gold. It was more of a fruit farmer's lucky strike in the days when all Australia was up for grabs, and prospectors with narrowed eyes were calculating whether they were looking at sheep country, wheat country, somewhere to grow fruit or to stake a claim for the minerals below the ground.

This open flat country, eighty kilometres from the coast in the panhandle that extends South Australia into what might well have been Victoria, looked destined for sheep. Then a Scottish gardener looked at the soil on the sheep station and suggested growing fruit. The owner, John Riddoch, promoted it as the 'Penola Fruit Colony' and found 26 people to buy plots and plant vines. It turned out that the curious rectangle of land fourteen kilometres by one was red earth over limestone and a bountiful supply of sweet water. Rain clouds reached it from the west, even if scorching winds could arrive from the north. The whole region, and not just the Fruit Colony, looked right for vines. When the sheep-farmers put in deep drains to improve their pasture it looked even better. Drainage, coincidentally, was the making of the Médoc colony, too.

It takes a certain character to persevere with wine-making in the middle of nowhere. Where California had plenty of Mexican labour to hand, Australia had no workforce to call on, and out in the bush no amenities of any kind – not even anyone to buy what you made. But Coonawarra's red wines had something the rest of South Australia was not producing: a quality you could really call claret. Shiraz was the main grape here as elsewhere, but here its wine was bright and clear, lively rather than jammy, with moderate alcohol and tannin. Cabernet was in a minority, but even more clearly in the claret camp. For years only one family, the Redmans, pressed on, selling their wine in Adelaide. Then the big companies moved in, seeing Coonawarra as a place to use mass-production technology developed for bulk wines in the Riverland to the north. The labour-intensive work of pruning and picking was abolished: pruning was by hedge-trimmer and picking by mechanical harvester.

Today Coonawarra can be seen as a battleground. On the one hand are industrial wine-makers who aim to use vines to their fullest efficiency as converters of water and sunlight into sugar. There is no plant that does it better: the vine outdoes grass, grain or anything else in capturing energy. Australian wine, caught up in the conflict between conglomerates for supermarket space, has been going headlong in that direction.

On the other hand are prophets like Brian Croser who see the future as applying taste to terroir as the French have done, investing in the best matches of variety and land – of which Coonawarra and Cabernet is the perfect example. Then it becomes a matter of critical self-discipline – and hard work. "Of course a big leafy vine will give you lots of alcohol," he says. "Anyone can do that. But that is not why the names of French villages are world famous, and it is a total waste of a national asset like Coonawarra."

He has kindred spirits all over the world. The late Peter Sichel, a vintner and merchant who interpreted bordeaux and its often outrageous market to the Anglo-Saxon world for a generation, was one of them. "The ultimate achievement in wine," he said, "is to discover a terroir with a character potential." Only particular spots on earth, in other words, are capable of giving wine a recognizable and consistent character. It is no good looking in California's Central Valley, or the Murrumbidgee Irrigation Area, for a singular flavour. Mass-production in any field must research what its market wants and then find out the best way to make it. But if you are lucky enough to have a terroir that marks its wine with a memorable character, the last thing you should do is to adapt it to the market. You should educate the market to appreciate what it produces. And the public, you may ask; why should the public want what you make, rather than vice versa?

I have to quote Peter Sichel again. A good vintner with a singular terroir helps "the world's consumers to understand the extraordinary complexities of which only Nature is capable, and how these can be miraculously expressed from those little berries if man remains modestly satisfied with observing, understanding and assisting ...." As opposed, that is, to trying to "make wine to a style that conforms to a preconceived ideal."

I thought of these words as I listened to the heavyweights of Australian wine-making setting out their stall for the millennium and beyond to 2025 at a lecture session after the Australia Day tastings in London. These are the people Brian Croser is arguing with. However much Australians love wine, and however good they are at making it, modesty doesn't often come through. They make masterly wine by being masters of nature.

The word 'style' gives the game away. Have you noticed how Australians don't drink, or make, or sell wines? They drink, make and sell 'wine styles'. Nature doesn't do styles. Individuals, species, families, varieties are nature's units. And of course terroirs.

Italy

Florence, 1904. The Marchese Piero Antinori leaves his palace in the city centre, its vast blocks of rusticated stone blackened by time and soot, to drive to Santa Christina. The other side of the Arno, as he clatters up the road towards the monastery of the Certosa, the sun comes out from behind grey storm clouds, the bare poplars shine like bundles of bronze rods, mimosa sends wafts of honey across the road. Antinori is putting a plan into action. The Chianti he and his friends make on their estates is absurdly rough-and-ready. It was good in the past, even exported in bottles to England under the name of Florence. It was a puzzle why French theories for improvement did not work in Tuscany. At Brolio Castle Bettino Ricasoli certainly made improvements, after he was Prime Minister, using a blend of red and white grapes. But on this cold soil of the Chianti hills the main grape, the Sangiovese, is just too astringent. In most years you have to alleviate its bite as best you can, and the result is not exactly exquisite.

The Marchese has a case of Château Lafite with him. He has the means, he has the land, he has a warmer climate than Bordeaux. Why can't he make claret at Villa Antinori? The first thing is to try a blend: see what happens if he mixes his Villa Antinori with Lafite. He calls the cellar-master: they blend; they taste; the cellar-master makes a face, Antinori thinks it is a vast improvement. Bordeaux grapes are the way to go.

We know the outcome of this story. A hundred years later some of Tuscany's greatest wines are Cabernets and Merlots. Sangiovese has been taken in hand and subdivided. Now it is celebrated as several good but different varieties for different regions. One of Antinori's grandsons has created an international wine empire based at Santa Christina. Others have virtual Bordeaux châteaux on the coast where he bred horses. Chianti as Tuscany's most famous contribution to the table, symbolized by its pot-bellied *fiasco* in a straw jacket, has almost disappeared, and has

Two aristocrats on the castle walls at Brolio. The Ricasoli (centre, Count Bettino) and Antinori (right, Marchese Piero) families have written the history of Chianti for a hundred and fifty years.

few mourners. I am one, as I recall the simplicity of the thing, and the beauty of that bottle. It looked better in a field than on a table, propped at an angle against an olive tree in the light shade where the bread and ham and fruit were spread on a sun-speckled cloth. It elevated the peasant to possess such things; his muddy wine was made sacramental. At least that is the enduring myth of a country that still sees itself as an idyll from a perfect past, though its oxen are gone, its fields have been bulldozed, and its olive-presses and shrines are outnumbered by swimming pools.

As a new Bordeaux, Tuscany has done brilliantly. Antinori's idea was perfect: lace your Chianti with Cabernet and bottle it in a bordeaux bottle. His grandson Piero told me twenty years ago that Cabernet was the secret agent in his Villa Antinori Reserva. "One day," he said, "I hope we won't need it. We'll go back to Chianti made from only Tuscan grapes, but first we have to improve the grapes. Meanwhile it takes only ten per cent of Cabernet to boost the flavour." I have watched the various stages of conversion of Tuscany's vineyards, from haphazard old jumbles of red and white grapes using olive trees, even elm trees, as props and climbing frames, vegetables and all the colourful necessaries of a peasant life growing beneath, to today's trim monoculture. It is hard to deny that it mirrors a total change in the wine they produce. The difference is that the wine has changed for the better.

The roots of ravishing landscape and poor wine were the same: the *mezzadria*, the share-cropping system in which the peasants, the *contadini*, gained nothing by their efforts. The Tuscany I first knew was the paradox of a rich land whose main export was its population, to America. Wine was made indifferently from black grapes and white harvested in great swags, some from trees, some from trellises like washing-lines. They were thrown into a battered vat on wheels pulled by a pair of oxen and crushed with a club in the field. It was no wonder most preferred the wine in a state short of full fermentation, before it went both sour and bitter. A little sweetness and a gentle fizz made it drinkable. That was what was expected of Chianti, certainly in the trattorias of America that must have been its best customers.

I made it part of my research to investigate Italian transatlantic life at all levels on the steamship *Rafaello* sailing from New York to Naples. First Class dining was predictable international excess: foie gras, lobster, filet de boeuf en croûte … with French wines. Second Class was

This was the Chianti I first encountered, the contadini *using methods unchanged (at least for the better) since Virgil.*

business hotel food, rootless dishes with long names and second-rate wines with the best-known Italian labels. Steerage class was a fair: stout women in black ladling golden pasta; prosciutto, mortadella, the smell of dried tomatoes, and litre jugs of sweet young wine bubbling gently on each table. If humble Italians took such pleasure in the table, why should their wine be so haphazard?

My brother's long experience of life in what used to be a remote part of Tuscany, the Maremma, suggested one answer. "They don't trust a soul," he said. The word you hear most often in praise of anything is *genuino*. A pot of jam from its maker's hands, in her kitchen, is *il genuino*. If her sister made it she will assure you it is *il genuino* with a slight inflexion of doubt. From a friend in the market? Open doubt. Factory-made, with a label? Don't be ridiculous. This is not so much suspicion of trafficking as a habit of identifying things with their precise

Barrels being soaked by the public fountain before filling: a scene from old Italy.

origin. It doesn't necessarily mean the non-*genuino* is second-rate; it just lacks the pleasurable intimacy of knowing exactly where it has been. Is this a different sentiment from the one behind appellations of origin? One has reservations, of course, about anything run by civil servants – but wine, above all things, is the foodstuff whose exact origin matters.

Cabernet did turn Tuscany round. Gently, in its infusion into Chianti, but also dramatically, when an Antinori cousin, almost on a whim, planted it in a stony patch on his seaside estate at Bolgheri and made the first vintages of Sassicaia. This was in the 1940s. It is the Mediterranean coast at its most benign: gentle hills set back from the sea behind pine woods and pasture. Bolgheri is a fortified village approached by an alley of black cypresses suggesting a lordly domain – accurately enough: this is the fief of Florentine noblemen, their summer houses, their horse paddocks and orchards. Until the mid-19th century it was neither healthy nor safe; mosquitoes made it malarial and Arab pirates raided the coast for slaves. In 1770 they grabbed fishermen off the beach at Pisa.

Its fortunes changed definitively when Nicoló Incisa della Rocchetta planted Cabernet vines from Bordeaux to make his house wine. His cousin Piero Antinori tasted it; his oenologist Giacomo Tachis lent a hand, and Tuscany had its Archimedes moment: Eureka. Why had they been struggling to ripen red grapes in the cold hills of Chianti for all these centuries when they could have been making claret on the coast?

Answers as above: no inhabitants, no business. You made wine where the customers were – around Florence.

That was Sassicaia. By the 1980s it was Tuscany's most expensive wine. There was really no reason to be surprised. Why shouldn't Italian soil do what the Napa Valley had done? The Antinoris consulted France's greatest oenologist, Emile Peynaud, who was entirely encouraging. In succession they produced Tignanello and Solaia, blends respectively of Sangiovese with Cabernet and vice versa from Santa Christina. Tuscan wine was news as it had never been before. At a dinner in 1994 I served the 1975 Sassicaia with three Bordeaux First Growths of that good but tannic vintage. It was younger, darker and livelier than any of them, more distinctly Cabernet, more oaky, developing a slight gamey smell of maturity and ending with a hint of raisin; pitched midway, I thought, between Bordeaux and California. Its successors have clung to the Bordeaux model. Still less reason for surprise when in 1985 Piero Antinori's brother Lodovico set up in friendly rivalry next door at Ornellaia with a more opulent model in mind. Then he hit the American market square on the nose with the sort of sweet fat wine it loves, a Merlot called Masseto. Italy's answer to Pétrus? Possibly.

It is as radical as any New World development, this move down from the hills to the seaside. It has put the old estates of Chianti on their mettle. With or without the help of Cabernet (or Merlot, which ripens earlier and is more at home on clay) Chianti is having to assert its own personality to compete. You may ask what does the historical zone offer that is not more easily available on the coast? Even its noblest names, familiar from the Florence of the Renaissance and before, are hedging their bets. The price of land in the Maremma has soared, not just in Bolgheri, but much further south as well. My brother's view down from Scansano over rippling hills to the Argentario Peninsula has taken on new shades of green as vineyards spread over its pasture. Sangiovese, or the local variant called Morellino, not only ripens more reliably here, it gives wine with a juicy smack like, they say, Morello cherries. With stars in their eyes the local growers have bought French oak barrels, spanking new, to give their wine a touch of class. The price, of course, has to assert its new fashionable status. It is hard, even at the cooperative level, to find the old juicy wine we used to love, and its price has gone up in sympathy, too. The new oaky Morellino di Scansano is too often just another modern Tuscan.

What characterizes good Chianti can be expressed as restraint. It is not a naturally fruity open wine but something with texture and structure. Its tannin is deliberately abrasive and its acidity fresh and appetizing. In a good Riserva this is all filled out with flavour, warm and round, but still bracingly firm in your mouth – the character it shares with claret. It needs, if not the same length of years to mature, at least three or four. The parallels with Bordeaux go further: thirty or forty estates are on the scale of Médoc châteaux. Initiates can point to the sub-regions – the high village of Radda, for example, or the lower, warmer one of Castellina, or the Rufina hills east of Florence – which produce some of the best, with as much confidence and pleasure as a claret-lover tasting his way round the Médoc.

────────────

The way to explore any wine is to make comparisons. It may be the habit of a lifetime with me, but everyone finds it illuminating. I have done it as a last resort, sometimes, faced with a dire restaurant wine list. If you compare two similar wines it is most improbable you will not find one more agreeable than the other. Take pleasure, then, in the one you prefer. In Tuscany I often abandon the idea of a white wine (the Tuscans still have a long way to go to catch up in this department) and start a meal with the plain young Chianti they offer. When the first course is the everyday bruschetta, bits of dry bread with olive oil, with dried tomatoes or with rough pâté, light (or thin) astringent Chianti is a good appetizer. It opens the way perfectly to a Riserva, which will taste all the better by contrast. Better, of course, to open two wines from different zones, or a classic Chianti and one of the variants, garnished with exotic varietals, that are known collectively as Super-Tuscans.

Super-Tuscan was the name coined for non-conformist wines that charged, it sometimes seems, supernatural prices for venturing outside the rules. Strictly speaking that was what the Marchese was doing in 1904. The name appeared, though, in the 1970s when only a new port-manteau term could carry all the experiments that were going on. If Tignanello and Solaia led the way, they were soon followed by a crowd. No more was needed to claim it, I often thought, than a deep red colour, an overdose of oak and a black glass bottle weighing a kilo.

The Chianti we drink most is Fonterutoli, from the estate of the Mazzei family at Castellina. It appeals to my sense of history; this was apparently where the first wine to be called Chianti came from, recorded in a letter from Ser Lapo Mazzei to his friend, Datini, a merchant in Prato. The year was 1398, and the wine was white.

Fonterutoli is a hamlet on the Chiantigiana, the winding road through the hills from Florence to Siena. It is also a modest castle; the district known as Chianti was the Florentine front line in their frequent wars with Siena. From the battlements you could see the long line of Siena's walls as a rectangle on the horizon, with the silhouette of the immense watchtower breaking the line. I was delighted when I first went there to find that, six centuries later, the owner's name was still Lapo Mazzei. One big change: the wine was red.

The Mazzeis were typical in their reaction to the Cabernet revolution. They made wines with Cabernet, with Merlot and with Sangiovese in different combinations. Within ten years they had settled for Chianti as their flagship. The others are good wines, even distinctly Tuscan wines, but classic Chianti was simply more special.

We drank a bottle of Ser Lapo, Fonterutoli's 1990 Chianti Classico, when it was 14 years old. It was burgundy colour: brilliant light-holding garnet. The scent was as invigorating as damson; sharp, plummy but dusty and abrasive at the same time. It was somehow totally liquid, or limpid, or just lightly and happily flowing – and yet it made contact all the way down. Plums and crisp tannin sound more like burgundy than bordeaux. It is not like either, just that difficult thing to achieve, a wine as light as it is satisfying – and a perfect mouthful for lamb chops with rosemary singed on the grill.

The parallel development of Montalcino was also challenging Chianti. It is warmer down here, south of Siena, on the hills around the walled town of Montalcino, and warmer still in the great basin of the Val d'Orcia, where the little River Orcia skirts the foot of Monte Amiata. 'Monte Amiata keeps the clouds off,' is what you constantly hear. It certainly always seems to have its own cloudy halo.

It is a different Sangiovese they grow here, one with smaller grapes, thicker skin and, on this soil, giving darker, stronger, beefier wine: Brunello di Montalcino. I first saw this open landscape, very different from the complex contours of Chianti, from a helicopter, roaring up from Rome. I was invited by the Mariani brothers from New York, John and Harry, to see the vast tract of land in the Val d'Orcia they had bought and were transforming, with big yellow crawlers, into a vineyard for the 21st century. Already they had a futuristic winery, the most computerised I had seen, and were working, with a gantry as tall as Siena's tower, on the castle that surveyed the entirely restructured valley. Ezio Rivella was their oenologist, like Antinori's advisor Giacomo Tachis, a native of Piedmont. I was not sure whether this had anything to do with his surprising plan to

Burton Anderson is the American sports writer whose book Vino *was the first to explore Italy's modern potential. This was at Ristorante la Chiusa at Montefollonico, after 16 courses and as many wines as you see glasses.*

specialize in Moscadello – it was famous in the 18th century, the sweet Moscadello of Montalcino. Moscato is a tradition in Piedmont (think of Asti Spumate). More likely it was the Marianis' hunch that America would love it. They had been spectacularly right with the sweet Lambrusco from the Po Valley they sold, by millions of cases, as Reunite. But they were open to all ideas, including Brunello.

Twenty years later it is Brunello everybody wants. The brothers' New York showmanship was delicious. They gave a medieval banquet in their castle by the light of flaming torches and to the sound of trumpets, employing the *sbandieratori* of Siena to throw brilliant heraldic flags clear over the battlements. The food came in on litters, Brueghel-fashion. How accurate their medieval interpretations were I am not sure. A long cobbled ramp up from the base of the castle walls to the first floor they said was for launching a knight in armour. By the time his horse reached the bottom it would be clattering along so fast it would go straight through the ranks of the besiegers.

I have every reason to be grateful to the Marianis. When in the 1980s I was looking for a backer for my television history of wine, a costly project of 13 episodes, they didn't hesitate. "We owe something to wine," they said. Such were the laws surrounding sponsorships that I was allowed to mention the names of every wine producer I visited round the world in the series – except their Villa Banfi.

Brunello is the Tuscan wine, almost you could say the Chianti, for drinkers who might not catch an understatement. It could be called the maximum statement of the splendid Sangiovese. I will have to quote my own book on Tuscany to define its genius.

"While the Sangiovese remains king," I wrote, "its elusive flavour and highly strung texture will mark out Tuscan reds. The tension is between fruit, acidity and tannin with a distinctive patois. Some tannins can be felt as the spinal column of a wine; some as its *charpente*. The tannins of Sangiovese coat the whole mouth with a more or less marked astringency. They season food and create thirst at the same time. Too much becomes bitter; the right amount is as invigorating as a rough towel."

Cabernet has come to Tuscany to stay, but not to conquer.

Spain

Long before I could afford to drink good mature claret on a regular basis, I discovered Rioja. Rioja was mature almost by definition; certainly any that was imported into England (there were not many). I paid my first visit there in the early 1960s, and reported in my first book on the dismal state of Haro, its bodega-capital. I had no problem with its long lean wines, though: they had a juicy acidity and cleaning tannin around a core of red fruit that suited me fine. They also had the smell of strawberries and vanilla that I learned came from Tempranillo grapes and years in American oak.

Rioja set its sights on making claret from the beginning; extraordinarily early even in the history of bordeaux. Bilbão is its nearest port. Bilbão merchants were very aware of Bordeaux at the time of its commercial ascendance, when it was building its streets and squares and theatre as the first French port for the Indies, West and East. Copy bordeaux, they thought, and we can export Rioja. Copying bordeaux involved barrels and cellars. It was not to happen until Bordeaux itself was desperate for wine, when its vines were dying of phylloxera. At this point there were capitalists ready to invest in modern plant. The Marqués de Riscal built his version of a château, even planted Cabernets.

It was to Rioja's long-term benefit that the Cabernet didn't work. It is hard to see how a me-too Médoc in the highlands of the Basque country could have competed. The founders of Rioja turned instead to their native grapes and put more emphasis on the barrel. They learned to lighten and perfume the stout Tempranillo with Graciano and Mazuelo. In those days long-term cellaring in barrel was the standard way to stabilize and soften any edgy wine, from the Mediterranean to the Rhine. In Rioja it was used with added emphasis, and with strong-flavoured American oak at that. It gave the region its identity; it made it almost the monopoly supplier of distinctive fine wine to the whole of Spain (and its colonies); it also cunningly entrenched the capitalists who could afford large numbers of expensive barrels and cellar-crews to handle them. There were no little family domaines in Rioja.

Riotous behaviour in Rioja. The annual feast of San Pedro brings out the wine-squirting tendencies of the population. Everyone is armed with a bota, a leather wine-skin.

Rioja has not lost its powerfully original flavour. Nineteenth century technology is still an occasional feature of wine country elsewhere, but nowhere so totally as at my favourite Rioja bodega, López de Heredia. It was built in the last years of the 19th century on a railway siding at Haro. Like the merchants on the Quai des Chartrons in Bordeaux, the bodegas clustered as close as possible to the shipping. In the vat room below its jaunty brick tower, Moorish in parts, seaside gothic in others, you can see wine-making with no evident alteration from a hundred years ago; oak-age technology, fragrant grey-brown vats, pulleys with iron chains. In the rock-cut cellars below (the tunnels are the stone-quarries for the buildings above) lie fifteen thousand *bordelesas*, as they still call the Bordeaux-model barrels, used for aging red and white wines for up to fifteen years. In other wineries round the world they will proudly tell you that one or two men can manoeuvre all the cooperage, stacking it (the alleys here are five *bordelesas* high) or taking it for racking or cleaning. In this Rip van Winkle winery there are forty barrelmen, from the coopers who build them to the barrel monkeys who pile and unpile them, using only ropes, to the foremen who rack the wine. You will come across one in the dark in his blue overalls, stooped in candlelight over a ruby thread of wine, his glass gleaming as he moves to and fro checking for the first trace of sediment. A deep balsamic sweetness hangs in the air; black fungus covers the vaults around. One of them, a high dim room lined with brick bins of bottles, deeply cobwebbed, is the tasting-room. You have glimpsed caverns of stacked bottles glinting garnet or topaz as you pass. You stand around the broad table to taste vintages going back sixty years. It is not the place to take notes and analyze aromas. The bread and the thin scarlet ham are too tempting. Why has the wine been kept so long? Simply to become the perfect drink, refreshing and satisfying, not clamouring for comment.

You rack wine until it pours gem-clear into the glass – many times, in the cellars of López de Heredia.

I have a few bottles at home of Viña Tondonia 1964. The vintage has resonance as the year I met Judy. It was a great vintage for Rioja both red and white. Only Rioja does this: a polished jewel (years of racking really does polish the colour), pungent with sweet soft fruit and balsam. Balsam is related to resin but sweeter, and doesn't catch in your throat. There are two reds, from different vineyards, Tondonia (in a bordeaux bottle) and Bosconia (dressed like burgundy). The two concepts persist; the two French champions have long shadows.

Rioja is not the garden of Eden. The valley of the Ebro is open, austere, a great hammock slung between the snows of two Sierras. Stony towns, Tuscan-style, cap the scattered hills: Labastida, Laguardia, Haro, Briones. From somewhere in this country they conjure markets full of sumptuous produce. In the regional capital of Logroño, a whole street is given over to browsing. You go to the Calle del Laurel for the specialities of its bars with evocative names and permanent queues: Soriano for 'champi', white mushrooms grilled on bread with shrimps dipped in garlic and parsley oil; Perchas for fried pigs' ears; Diagonal for squid fritters; Sebas for stuffed peppers; Jubera for baked potatoes with mayonnaise; El Soldado de Tudelilla for sardines and green peppers; Pagano for kebabs. The wines of the day are chalked up on boards and keenly discussed. At a restaurant called Iruna, wave upon wave of tender vegetables appear. Your ham or chicken is incidental to the baked garlic, the white beans with clams, the celery in almond sauce, the grilled red peppers, the

borage fritters, the artichokes and peas and beans and huge white asparagus ferried with anxious looks by women in white who attend the old iron stove as if it were an altar.

The Riojanos seem to love building. Señor López de Heredia was conventional beside the builders of some of the latest bodegas. There is a long Spanish tradition, starting with the monumental white-arched warehouses of sherry country (buildings routinely likened to cathedrals) of giving wine a grand architectural frame. I have not noticed the Italians, for all their sense of theatre, clothing a factory in fantasy in quite the way the Spanish do. One new bodega near Briones stretches out across the landscape like a huge bird just landed on a lake and settling its silver feathers. At Labastida, where the Marqués de Riscal built the first *chais* in Spain modelled on Bordeaux, the architect of the Guggenheim Museum at Bilbão, Frank Gehry, has piled up weird slivers of shining metal like curled shavings from a plane. It could as well be a church as a winery. It will certainly bring visitors to Rioja.

"I know you like history," said my friend Miguel Merino, having just let me taste his new Reserva in his Briones cellar. "If you have half an hour before you go, a friend of mine has a collection you would enjoy."

Stained glass in Miguel Merino's bodega captures the luminous beauty of a glass of red wine.

Miguel is one of a new breed in Rioja; a small producer without the thousands of barrels that used to be obligatory before you could deal. The result already is more flexibility; experiments with grapes or barrels and individual vineyards that were not part of the old Rioja culture. Wider choice brings confusion, of course, but why should Rioja be immune? We went to see his friend's little collection. Dinastía Vivanco, the sign announced at the gates. The dynasty is Pedro Vivanco and his sons, and the collection, I was astonished to find, the most ambitious museum in the world of wine. Names like Vivanco's rarely surface: he is Rioja's biggest dealer in bulk wines. He is also, it seems, a magpie who has acquired everything from old tractors to Assyrian grave goods, from medieval manuscripts to Picassos, over a long life. Miguel's little half-hour turned into a day of absorption in ploughs and parchments, enzyme research and engravings, and I shall need more.

A hundred and sixty kilometres southwest of the River Ebro the Duero runs parallel, flowing the other way. Of all the places to set up a claret-plant these upper waters of what becomes the Douro, and gives us port, seem less plausible than most. Its city, Valladolid, was once the capital of Castile, and hence of Spain. Capital cities need wine, and the Duero Valley supplied it: the white wine of Rueda was apparently the best. The eccentricity of an imitation Rioja came about on a mixed-farming estate with the name of Vega Sicilia. The story is more Napa Valley than Castilian tableland. Money, connections and benign neglect started it in the days when it was radical even to equip your cellar with wooden fermenting vats (*lagars* and cattle-skins were the norm). Wine routinely stayed in barrel (for those who had barrels) until someone bought it. At Vega Sicilia in 1939 the 1916 vintage was still waiting to be bottled. Connections, though, meant that the farm had Cabernet vines among its stock of Tempranillo (or Tinto Fino by its local name). Chance gave it a well-drained north-facing slope down to the river. And its altitude (it is nearly twice as high as Rioja) gave it extremes of temperature: days hot, nights cold.

Owners who paid more attention to the accounts would probably have given up. (Brandy, sold in Mexico, was more interesting.) The district is notorious for spring frost, early autumn frost, and hail in between. But in making wine that was rare, intensely flavoured and long-matured they had stumbled on the formula for a cult. You could acquire Vega Sicilia only on a friend-of-a-friend basis. First it was given away (shoots and race-meetings were the milieu), then, and still, there were mailing-list sales. To start as a legend and build on it takes money. The tap was turned on in 1982 when David Alvarez – another Bilbão businessman – bought the estate, unseen. From the age of cobwebs and old wood (the age of López de Heredia in fact, but without that company's professionalism) he has changed what he called 'a fragile object' into the First Growth of a new region pulsing with competition.

Cult status demands certain things. High-profile wine is only the start. My kind of claret, made to be a light digestible drink, need not apply. Vega Sicilia is potent in every sense: high-intensity, high-tannin, high-acidity, high-alcohol, a blend of Tinto Fino with enough of the bordeaux grapes to take your mind (or mine, at least) off the varietal mix. Long-maturing in American oak removes the primary fruit flavours: you are left with a heady quintessence of what seems the taste of Spain.

The rest is style: relentless work on the detail. The place is spotless, and guarded like Fort Knox (cleaning and security is the Alvarez family business; the biggest in the field). I stopped my car one day to walk up to the pinewoods above the vineyard. Within five minutes a guard drove up to eject me. A Hispano-Japanese garden is the rather surprising frontis-piece to the austere old warehouses. Inside the tiles shine, the vats gleam and the barrels (made on the prem-ises) are as fresh as laundry. The bottles are embossed, engraved and numbered (fakes were not un-known). The corks are the longest, hand-selected. The tissue paper, I surmise, is from a special mill, and the wooden box, carrying an engagingly low-tech print of the bodega, is printed with each purchaser's name.

Vega Sicilia Unico is the Grand Vin, in Bordeaux terms, aged up to ten years in barrel, another three in bottle. The bodega releases it, or intends to, at the peak of its form and ready to drink, a Spanish

The Gran Orden de los Caballeros del Vino was founded in London in 1984 to encourage lovers of Spanish Wine. Its January investiture and banquet is a fixture on the London scene.

approach entirely at variance with Bordeaux, where the buyer undertakes the cellaring. Spain has very little tradition of laying down wine, nor does the modern world. "Keeping a bottle more than twenty-five years shows a lack of respect," says Alvarez. Or, one might add, a collector's instinct. The second wine is called Valbuena, only five years at release: some prefer the lighter, fresher version. Now there is a third, Alión, made in a separate bodega nearby; more modern and 'supple' (wine code for soft, as 'elegant' is for lean). And recently a fourth, from Toro, downstream on the Duero beyond Valladolid. Trying to "tame these unpolished and extremely potent wines" is Alvarez's stated aim. We were served a bottle of Toro in a restaurant with a party of America's most noted connoisseurs. They loved it; I'm afraid I asked the waiter for a glass of the house wine for my thirst.

ABOVE
Two nonagenarian vintners:
Alejandro Fernández (left)
started his Pesquera bodega
in 1972, six years after
the launch of Robert
Mondavi's Napa winery.

Emulation arrived on the Duero even before the Alvarez family. The legend was in place; the local cooperative cellars at Peñafiel found that horsepower comes easily to Duero wine; polish takes longer. Alejandro Fernández sold agricultural machinery before he started La Pesquera as a challenge to Vega Sicilia, just across the river. It is the Tinto Fino, and never mind bordeaux, that inspires him, and more recently 'Pingus' Sisseck, the nephew of my old Danish friend from Bordeaux, Peter Vinding. Where there was one winery in the whole region there are now a score; the world has expectations.

Claret? The Duero version has New World sinews with a Spanish twang, and its practitioners are fanning out all over Spain. Is there a Spanish national taste that these new wines have in common? It is a question you can ask about any country without finding a clear answer. How can there be? A national taste in food is something you take for granted. You can probably guess, blindfold, whether you are passing a Spanish kitchen or a Portuguese one, a French or Italian. The cooking oils and condiments are different. But there is no such thing as a national soil, or a national grape variety. Here are two glasses of Cabernet, one from Spain and one from Italy: which is which? Or one from Australia and one from California. There may be a stylistic clue, but few people could detect it. Logically, then, few people have a preference. Some see it as a mark of progress, even: if all wine is homogenized I shall never be troubled with a wine list again. Happily for those who love diversity and find discrimination one of the great pleasures of life, wine-makers who come near the brink usually back away when they realize their identity, too, will float away on the Cabernet sea.

In Spain, as in Italy, the most successful have done both: embraced the international taste without abandoning their own. Cabernet gives a breathing space while local grapes catch up. The Catalan house of Torres, in the Penedés hills west of Barcelona, set the example. It began as a trader in above-average regional wines in bulk. I still have one of their barrel-labels – a rare sight

today: a big bright red and yellow disc big enough for a barrel-head. The late Miguel Torres started bottling better and better wines without specifying the grape varieties. When his Gran Coronas Black Label started winning important medals he revealed that it was three-quarters Cabernet Sauvignon. It still is, but it stands as a splendid wine in its own right without mentioning its grapes. Meanwhile his son Miguel has experimented with almost-forgotten Catalan grapes and is gradually supplanting the Black Label as his finest wine of all with his truly indigenous wine, Gran Muralles, made entirely of traditional Catalan grapes, including some that were almost extinct until Torres revived them. Logically we can expect more and more native grapes, as well as the principal ones that produce such established Spanish classics as Rioja or Priorat, to step into the limelight and make their appearance on the international circuit.

Portugal

'Buy on an apple and sell on cheese,' is an old wine-trade axiom. An apple is a cold appraiser of a wine's constitution. No wine tastes its best with an apple, and bad wines taste miserable. Cheese is the opposite. It forms a forgiving fatty layer between you and the acidity; it plays off the tannins with protein. You miss the faults – or pardon them. Cheese is the salesman's friend.

When a vintner prepares a small feast at a wine tasting I always feel suspicious, cheese or no cheese. The ritual in the cellar at Bussaco might have set warning lights flashing. We went down to the crypt below the castle to see the *lagar* where the wine is still trodden in the ancient manner of the port country. Both the red and the white, Señhor dos Santos assured me. Treading white wine at the end of the 20th century argued a conservative bent, I thought.

Señhor dos Santos had brought a maid to do the cooking. He started opening bottles and she lit a funny little stove. It was no more than a pottery dish with pottery bars forming a sort of grill. She filled it with brandy (I hope it was brandy), set light to it and put the sausages on top. The smell ruled out any sensitive nosing but this was not, I gathered, a priority of the house. A pity because, as I had discovered upstairs in the restaurant, the Bussaco wines are an intimation of a lost age of Portuguese prosperity. The vintages on the list went back to the 1940s and though they were frail, these veterans, they were graceful, lean, sweet to smell and had a long pure line of flavour that spelt good claret in any language.

The castle is even more bizarre, built of stone quarried from maritime memories. The manueline style brings ropes and anchors into everything, marrying gothic shapes and spaces with a fleet's worth of rigging. It stands, what's more, in an enchanted forest on the pinnacle of a ridge wrapped year-round in sea mists. Exotic trees grow to unprecedented size in this perpetual bath. You can book the tennis-court any time before lunch: you will be playing an invisible opponent. The stream gurgling below the serpentine drive is deep in ferns and hydrangeas, and moss grows on your glass as you sit on the terrace.

Is this wine country? It is the eyrie above the vineyards. Nowhere so perfectly exemplifies the influence that rules Atlantic vineyards – or west coast weather – anywhere. West of Lisbon, Sintra is a similar fog-bound hill of deep mossy woods. Galicia grows lichen on its vine-stakes. The hills of Oregon and Puget Sound are endlessly irrigated by sea moisture born on the prevailing winds, and even on the west coast of Sicily, Trapani is a green knoll above the scorched vineyards of Marsala.

Bairrada is the name of the vineyards at the foot of the castle hill.

Evidently the local taste is for wine with a bite: the local red grape, the Baga, can carry black astringency to the limit. It is the Cabernet of northern Portugal, thick-skinned, late-ripening. Or rather perhaps the Tannat, the grape that gives its singularity to the knife-like Madiran of Gascony and the newly discovered reds of Uruguay. Whether it has the potential for greatness is doubtful, but few grapes push the principle of scouring, cleansing, saliva-provoking tannin further. (Its name incidentally also means elderberry.) Luis Pato makes Bairrada wines for today, still scouring but full of fresh fruit as well. I am always happy to find a grower going to the limits of quality of an unfashionable grape: Pato makes different *cuvées* from different vineyards as though he were in Burgundy. Strangely enough his favourite, Quinta do Ribeirinho, from his warmest, sandiest soil, has a smell of burgundy about it. They come into their own at ten years old or so with the Portuguese country food he serves: thick vegetable soup with a golden swirl of olive oil, roast swordfish and potatoes, duck (a signature dish, *pato* in Portuguese) with rice powerfully flavoured by duck liver, and runny-ripe ewes' milk cheese.

Who wants this sort of wine today? It is being overtaken by less overtly ethnic wines from the port vineyards of the Douro. Coastal fogs are a dream here; a good one or a bad one according to your inclination. Tradition used to be adamant that Douro wine was in the Injurious to Health category unless and until the port shippers had tamed it. A funny way to tame wine, you might think: to fill it up with raw brandy. Presumably all the good grapes went into the port, because they imported the table wines they needed in Oporto from another part of Portugal altogether; the Alentejo, south of Lisbon. One ancient *quinta*, Mouchão,

The Douro today is fast moving away from its traditional image. Water-skiing and velvety, even elegant, table wines are the new attractions.

The view from Noval:
only the Moselle compares
in dramatic beauty with
the high Douro. The village
of Vale de Mendiz
in the 1980s.

had apparently been supplying the port shippers' club, the Factory House, for a century with barrels to bottle, unattributed, as their house wine. It could be sumptuous, I remember, but the port always got all the attention.

Revolution up the Douro started with the realization that grapes rejected for port are still worse turned into table wines. Table wine grapes have to be in perfect condition, their crops modest, and the timing of the harvest is critical. Raisins must be rejected. Tolerances are finer than for wines that will be fortified.

Did the original inspiration come from upstream, the Ribera del Duero, where Vega Sicilia makes Spain's most expensive red wine? No, it was the long arm of Bordeaux again. In 1950, the senior wine-maker from the port house of Ferreira travelled to Bordeaux. He might almost have bumped into Max Schubert from Adelaide there; they were on similar errands. Fernando Nicolau de Almeida came back to the Douro, the highest and hottest part, to Ferreira's Quinta do Vale Meão, and made the first vintage of Barca Velha. Like Schubert, he aimed for claret in a different climate with different grapes. Like Vega Sicilia, his principal grape was the Tempranillo, known in Portugal as the Tinta Roriz. There were other grapes too; port has a fruit basket as big as that of Châteauneuf-du-Pape. Tinta Francesca was important in the blend, Touriga Nacional, the powerhouse grape of vintage port, less so. Barca Velha came into being in the 1950s, and reopened a question that had gone to sleep a century before: why did Douro wine have to be fortified? There had been fierce debate in the 1830s and 1840s: the British Baron Forrester accused the port shippers of ruining their wine with elderberries and brandy. Perhaps the answer is that it was easier to make, to keep fruity and to get to the market, pickled in alcohol. Certainly the British liked strong drink. Baron Forrester lost the argument.

When I first visited Vale Meão, conditions looked unpropitious for claret. It is a big *quinta* with a row of great granite *lagars* for treading – equipped, I clearly remember, with holes in the outside wall at fly-buttons height as a convenience. Barca Velha was then fermented in a wooden vat, Bordeaux-style, cooled by blocks of ice brought by train from Oporto. The wine was sumptuously full of port-like flavours, but more like a Rhône wine in strength and texture. It was rare, made only in ideal vintages, and for years seems to have had little influence. Only since the 1990s has the word gone round: Forrester was right, Portugal's best table wine may yet come from the Douro.

Certainly the time is ripe for it. They are wines in the modern manner, strong but soft, or at least with rounded edges. And they have reached the market at the same time as the new wines of the Spanish Duero. Douro/Duero is their mutual flag – a *rapprochement* in the spirit of a new Europe.

Burgundy

A WINE-GROWER from Burgundy has had a good year and takes his family to the Médoc seaside. On the way, with the sand dunes almost in sight, he finds himself surrounded by flat fields of vines. Odd, he thinks, they must make wine around here, too. Curiosity overcomes him. He stops, enquires at the *mairie*, and is directed to a daunting wrought iron gate. It looks a magnificent domaine, with an avenue, a turreted house and huge barns. He pulls into the gravelled yard, his children protesting. "Take them for an ice cream," he tells his wife; "I may be a little while."

The door opens and a man in a suit appears. "With pleasure," he answers, "follow me." Instead of leading to cellar stairs, though, he opens the door to a barn of astonishing length, full of immaculate files of identical new-looking barrels. He fetches two big crystal glasses and a pipette, thinks for a moment, then leads to a barrel in the middle of one of the rows. He takes out the bung, lowers the pipette into the wine, withdraws a sample and shares it between the two glasses. Monsieur Moutarde from Muligny takes the proffered glass and looks at the wine. What an extraordinary colour: darker than any wine he has ever seen. And the nose: powerful, sharp, like seashells and carpentry, but scarcely inviting. He tastes and just stops himself recoiling. The tannin stands his teeth on edge and puckers his tongue. He spits, contemplatively he hopes, into some intimidatingly clean gravel. "Very interesting," he says. His host evidently believes in starting with something rough to make his best barrels taste better. Then, as he looks around in hopes of a better barrel, the vintner says "Voilà" and hangs up his pipette. So this huge domaine makes only one wine? Or is he just stingy? They exchange pleasantries; M Moutarde confesses that he too makes a little wine. "Here is my card," he says, "do call if you are ever in Burgundy."

A year later our Bordeaux proprietor shuts up his château to go skiing in the Alps. As he drives through green rolling country a road sign reminds him of his visitor. The next pretty old village is Muligny. Here is the Moutarde establishment: a little stone house on the village street proclaiming *Dégustation, Vente*. A few minutes to go before noon; he knocks at the door. A woman appears in her apron, accompanied by a smell of roasting to make your heart beat faster. She glances at the clock and goes off to find her man. Our friend appears in blue overalls, with a bunch of keys, and recognizes his careful acquaintance. They shake hands, he opens a little door and leads down to a tiny cellar crammed to the ceiling with battered barrels. He unhooks his pipette, picks up two little round brandy glasses and unbungs a barrel.

What an extraordinary wine! It has practically no colour; just a pretty deep pink. But it jumps out of the glass, as sweet as spring, like the ripest cherries, with a background of damp ploughland and urgent growth. Our skier sips; his head is full of ravishing fumes. "Very interesting," he says, looking round at the other barrels with high expectations. M Moutarde hangs up his pipette. "Voilà," he says. "That was your Bordeaux idea of a tasting. Now," getting his pipette down again, "shall we have a Burgundy tasting?"

It may be a shaggy dog story, but there is truth in it. The distance between the two great poles of French wine, for example. The physical distance seems greater than it is because the country between is some of France's poorest and least travelled. A new autoroute is about to link Bordeaux and Lyon via Clermont-Ferrand, but the old route was a revelation of the rural life of ages past. I once drove it in winter; it felt like an endless alpine pass, narrow, snowy and winding, punctuated by small towns with deserted market squares. By train it was an overnight ordeal on a brown rexine bunk. Nothing to drink; not even water. When you arrived you had to adjust yourself to a different world. Bordeaux is a proto-Paris, boulevards of symmetrical smooth house-fronts, brasseries on the pavements, buses and bright shops and an accent like the south with a hint, is it, of English? Beaune is a little walled city of cobbled streets and steep roofs, houses that lean, a sense that this is true Europe, changing only in emphasis as you go east to exotic frontiers. Europe's five great rivers, a Burgundian once told me, are all within a day's journey (not walking. Riding? Flying?) of Beaune and the Côte d'Or. Hence Burgundy is the centre of Europe. He really meant the world. There was, in other

words, no great call for a Bordeaux-Burgundy link, either physically or culturally.

The bordeaux style has persuaded half the world; we have looked at a mere sampling of its applications. The Cabernets, as a family, are redoubtable travellers, and even without Cabernets bordeaux is a model to follow of strong-coloured, firmly structured red wine with fruit flavours and tannins in a certain relationship. And the burgundy style?

The Pinot Noir is not a great traveller. Up to a generation ago it was considered a total agoraphobe; the limits of its world were the Côte d'Or, Champagne (but for white wine) and the Rhineland, where its performance was so anaemic that only the locals would drink it. It is certainly a fussier plant than the Cabernet, even genetically unstable, so that clones with weird characteristics can appear at any time. But its other problem is the mysterious glamour of its origins. Even to taste a truly great burgundy (let alone to make one) was the wine-lover's Holy Grail. That moment of revelation, nose poised above the shining *ballon*, was not vouchsafed to everybody. The chosen, though, had sent back word that every sensual delight pales before the truffled violet silk of a Musigny, the oriental opulence of a Romanée-Conti or the martial splendour of a Chambertin. If you know the right man. If you know the right vintage. If you have chosen the perfect moment in the unpredictable alchemy of ethereal vapours. It is a lot to ask of a drink.

There was some truth in this picture, but two things have changed it. First, there are far more people who know the scientific principles of wine-making. Even in famous vineyards it used to be seat-of-the-pants stuff, even seat-of-grandfather's-pants. Luck played a major part. Now a great deal of burgundy is genuinely the best that can be done in the circumstances of each vintage. There is also a lot of more cynically made wine trading on its name, but are you likely to change human nature?

Second, the mantle of awe is lifting. Once you can see, however imperfectly, the reasons for the behaviour of a neurotic grape variety, you can calculate outcomes. You can even grow it in America or Australia without feeling that the instruction book has been left out of the box.

Pinot Noir, like Riesling, is a lens that brings the soil into focus. It captures soil, climate and vintage weather and reveals them without mercy. The Cabernet family blended together, as Bordeaux does it, cover for each other. Pinot Noir is transparent; it has thinner skin, hence less pigment and less tannin. There is less of a veil to see through, or hiding place for inadequacies. You can taste unripeness or overripeness, excess oak or excess alcohol with embarrassing clarity. Initiates can recognize the soil of each vineyard plot or *climat* (it also means atmosphere).

So (setting aside the glimpses of heaven) what are you looking for? How do you know it is burgundy in your mouth, and what justifies paying two, three, five, twenty times as much a bottle for the best? Parameters, please, starting with the basic.

It is quite alarmingly pale, this sample: a mere darkish rosé compared with a red from anywhere else, and I would say on the brick rather than the blue side of the red spectrum. It smells sharp, and if anything earthy rather than fruity. Beetroots bear some relation, with their shaggy tops on and specks of earth clinging to their dusky skin. But no, it is more sharply sweet than that. Cherries don't smell, but if they did this would be the scent. And in your mouth? It is very liquid; there is little palpable substance: more the feeling of a sharp white wine: thinner, in fact, than a good Chardonnay. There seems not to be much there, except a just aromatic sharpness, when things start to look up. A little soft round sweetness appears from nowhere. What was astringent becomes tender; a note of plum kernels or almonds fleetingly appears and you are left with a warm glow and an urge to try again. "A nice enough wine," as Dr Johnson once said (though not about burgundy), "but not a wine to invite a man to."

That was a starter-level burgundy, from the Hautes Côtes, the courtesy appellation for the cold vineyards at the top of the hills that have none of

Burgundy is translucent, unlike the dense colour of bordeaux. This is five-year-old Volnay, all purple gone and a warm brick tone taking over.

the privileges of soil and situation of the middle and upper slopes. What about a more hospitable wine, then, one we drink a good deal of at home, from a village rarely mentioned because it lies on the wrong side of the all-important main road, the N74? You orient yourself by this road, as you do by the road that snakes up the Médoc, the D2. It links the villages of Gevrey-Chambertin and Vougeot and Vosne-Romanée to Nuits-St-Georges, then further south to Beaune and on to Pommard and Meursault. You know for certain that every traveller from northern Europe to the Mediterranean since prehistory has been this way and seen the same cloud-shadows moving over the same hills. At Meursault there is a medieval chapel, its heavy grey door arch cut with savage zigzags, that appears to have sunk into the ground, so many times has the surface of the ancient road been raised.

All the good stuff lies to your right as you go south, on the slopes that swell and recede in a long frieze beside you. According to legend, Napoleon kept his marching troops at eyes-right as they passed to familiarize them with the heritage of France at its most glorious. There was a loud slap of muskets presenting as they passed the Clos de Vougeot. Or was that another general? (Napoleon drank Chambertin. Half-and-half with water.)

Chorey-lès-Beaune (*lès* means 'near') is the name of our house red burgundy – for the last two years; the grower, Tollot-Beaut. These wines are landscape made tastable, and not just at exalted levels. 'Minty' was the word I used for it when I first made a note of it. A ripe vintage brings a sense of fatness, too. You wonder if this is not a wine to lay down for the more advanced pleasures of maturity, but experience says no, the bloom of youth is the best part; two or three years is a good age for it. It is the sort of wine that tastes better cool, and not with anything too red-meaty. You have to go higher up the slope for the bone structure that makes flesh more shapely as it ages. Up to Savigny, for example, though you could take a slice through the hill at many points and come up with the same formulation: light wine at the bottom and a growing sense of fullness and energy as you go higher, with the climax about half-way up. Vitality is the sales point of Savigny. Its best wines are tight and punchy, not rich or deep. You feel a little pinch of tannin on the sides of your tongue. This is the kind of burgundy I find a domestic role for most easily: the most different, in a sense, from the big-boned mouthful of bordeaux and its kin.

In the days when nearly all burgundy was elaborated (perhaps assembled is a better word) by merchants there was a corresponding character allotted to each of the main appellations. How otherwise would the cellar-master have known how much of the different ingredients to add? The Côte d'Or divides in two, with Beaune not far from the middle. Wines from the Côte de Nuits to the north would be expected to be long keepers: darker and more tannic. Côte de Beaune wines would be lighter. It may well be tradition as much as geography that makes this so (and they were certainly owned and farmed in rather different ways), but why confuse your customers by departing from the stereotypes?

Gevrey-Chambertin? Stern and meaty. Morey St Denis? Rarely asked for: same recipe. Chambolle-Musigny? Lightish, scented. Clos de Vougeot? Middle-of-the-road. Vosne-Romanée? Hard to get: your best blend. Nuits-St-Georges? Tannic; you can use press-wine here to pucker their gums. Corton starts the Côte de Beaune; make this dark and solid, more like Côte de Nuits. Savigny? Light and sappy. Beaune itself? Sells well; should be smooth and easy-going. Pommard? They expect something more like Nuits; lots of colour. You can use a dollop of Algerian. Volnay? Paler; you can use a drop of white in this.

Where Burgundy meets its critics. A London trade tasting of the new burgundy vintage, just before kick-off.

Chassagne-Montrachet and Santenay, to finish off the Côte de Beaune going south? No great demand, but make sure they are a good dark red.

No-one in the wine trade has quite this cynical confidence any more, as far as I know. Besides, the balance of power has shifted from trader to grower. Even the biggest négociants now make more of their estates than of their brands. To blend is to generalize – even with the purest motives. How can you generalize about the competence, or indeed the tastes, of growers? That is Burgundy's problem, and at the same time its fascination. It is true of white wines too, but much more of red. The vigneron takes all the decisions. It is up to him how he prunes, how he treats his vines, when he picks and if he adds sugar. Then how far he takes the simple process of reddening, as you might call the steeping of the skins in the juice. It used to be the fashion to macerate them for twenty days or more; ten is now considered about right – depending on the vintage. If you heat the must it will pick up colour and tannin more quickly. If you don't keep the floating skins well mixed in with the liquid (fermentation pushes them to the top) it will hardly become red at all. The traditional way to do this is to jump in the vat, men only, no clothes; a risky business, never to be done solo after dinner. If you slip and there is no-one to haul you out, drowning is certain.

How easy is it to identify what part the vineyard plays and what part the vigneron? Not at all, is the answer, but what about a fresh try? It would be easiest, I thought, with a fairly small vineyard, one with a marked style and not too many different owners. I chose Chambolle-Musigny Les Amoureuses. Is there a vineyard with a more beautiful name? Even in translation 'Women in Love' is pretty good, but *Les Amoureuses* sounds like a languid swoon. I should be attracted to it wherever it turned up, but as the neighbour of le Musigny, Burgundy's finest vineyard, it draws me like a glimpse of stocking. There are only 13 acres of it, divided among ten owners – a fairly typical situation.

I mentioned my idea to Russell Hone, who with his American wife Becky Wassermann runs one of the best-loved (at least by Anglo-Saxons) brokerages in Burgundy. He volunteered to approach the ten growers and invite them to bring a bottle or two for a tasting at their old stone mansion in the village of Bouilland.

The drive up to Bouilland is one of the loveliest in Burgundy. You follow a hidden slash in the hills just behind Savigny. The vineyards disappear and you are deep in a Côte d'Or of a different nature. Deep woods of beech and oak cloak the steep sides of a narrow valley of meadows, where a stream dashes among the cattle, twisting and turning through alder clumps and shawls of wild flowers. Geology becomes dramatic here. Below in the vines you are not aware of the hard limestone crest that forms the backbone of the Côte, whose crumbled rock constitutes the magic of its soil. Up here it forms a canyon, crags for mountaineers who abseil down the sides. Bouilland lies in the bottom, a hamlet of stables and dairies that has never seen a wine barrel.

This is no test-bench analysis, this tasting, but an appreciation of a singular character by the people who know it almost too well to comment. When you compare closely related wines, slight differences seem more important. It is the argument for specializing, or at least limiting your choice. If it is the differences between things that appeal to you, if you are a collector by nature, they don't need to be wide. On the contrary, the obvious things that distinguish a rose from a marigold or an oak from a palm tree are hardly worth commenting on, while the barely perceptible difference between two roses, one with more petals or a more piercing scent, can make it worth the trouble of growing both.

Not all the growers came to our tasting, but all but one sent bottles. Russell lined them up on the long table in the galleried hall with the huge fireplace. He is an enormous man, built like Falstaff, this human gauge of

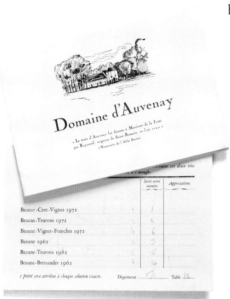

The toughest tasting test of all: the Domaine Leroy pits its vintages against the sharpest palates. Guests at a summer evening session at Auvenay were asked to match wines to a list of vineyards and vintages. This page was (by far) my best result.

the infinitesimal nuance. Monsieur Roumier's Amoureuses was creamy and delicate, with a satin character I described in my notes as 'luxury lingerie'. Mugnier's was tighter, with a sense of dissolved minerals. Drouhin's was minty and bright, Groffier's pure and sweet with a hint of almonds, Serveau's smoky, plummy and nutty. Moine-Hudelot's was softer, Amiot-Servelle's tight, crisp, lean and lovely, Bertheau's comparatively big and fruity; de Vogüé's (the benchmark of the village, the biggest domaine with the highest prices) notably potent and concentrated, sweet, oaky, plummy and fine.

They sound very different. My fellow-tasters saw something else: something that distinguished them from the vineyards all around. One said it was 'mobility', another a 'mathematical elegance' (which was beyond me). 'Ballerinas' was clear enough. Becky muttered, "The unbearable lightness of being." These may have been well rehearsed, of course, but they all pointed in the same direction: don't look for a macho wine in Les Amoureuses; all its energy seems to go into a tightrope walk. The name, the taste, the image and the reality add up to an identity; Burgundy calls it a *cru*. It is not a brand. Each grower interprets it his way. Both the identity and the variants on it are, believe me, worthwhile. And this is an exercise you could repeat fifty times up and down the Côte d'Or.

Chevaliers du Tastevin

A file of huge coaches, by no means camouflaged in their flashy liveries, snakes through the vineyard lanes. Five hundred guests are being manoeuvred into place. Every week from spring to autumn the feat is performed: the château in the Clos de Vougeot embraces, feasts and beatifies burgundy-dazzled pilgrims from all over the world.

The British do royal pageantry with inimitable style. Many countries do the military variety. Only France can stage a dinner with equally lavish proportions of ceremony and gastronomy, musical sauces and side dishes of slapstick. For five hundred people, moreover, and send them home wide-eyed with memories. One day, I tell myself, I will see the kitchen and interview the chef. Far better not, though; best just to sit pressed in on all sides with the spirit of festive greed and receive what the Chevaliers du Tastevin ordain. They evoke in their speeches and songs the spirit of Rabelais, of Gargantua and his unfettered appetite. They evoke Molière, too, and borrow his jokes without stint. The cultural part over, they concoct menus like five-act plays and bring on wines as players,

The fine figure of the chef, Hubert Hugot, at the Clos de Vougeot. Five courses for five hundred guests is small beer to him.

from fragile *ingénu* to supreme, mature, stage-dominating star.

Snails were the first dish, one spring night when I was there, by the dozen in ramekins in strong garlic-scented butter. The wine was Aligoté, one year old, the sharp palate-rinser white you rarely see outside the region, where its appetizer qualities are appreciated. In the stylized commentary of the menu (the style of Rabelais, that is) Aligoté is "alert, brisk." The South Seas snapper was the second dish, Suprêmes d'Empereur in the language of the menu, with green points of asparagus. They were "led on" by a "symphonic" white Chassagne-Montrachet. Third, and labelled Entremets, came a dish that must once have been the Burgundy wine-grower's comfort food, oeufs en meurette, eggs poached in red wine, matched with an 'upright' red Savigny-lès-Beaune, young and crisp and juicy.

The main dish, labelled Dorure, 'gilding' (of the lily?), was duck breasts with a mustard sauce. Were the servers tiring by this time? They don't tire here, but carry their vast dishes through the throng with grins and banter, offer them with grave courtesy, and even remember requests from guests capable of imagining any further desires. At a different dinner, not to be forgotten, the Dorure was a casserole of chickens' oysters, the plumpest-tasting morsel from the back of the bird. (Its name in Burgundy is *sot l'y laisse*: 'you have to be an idiot not to eat it' would be a fair translation.) There were ten on my plate; a chicken has only two. So five hundred guests spelt the end that day for five thousand chickens. The wine in this case, according to the menu, 'moistened' the dish. It did more than that

Hunting horns and musical banter, with outbreaks of 'all-together-now', punctuate a banquet of the Chevaliers du Tastevin.

for me. It was an appetizingly tannic, hard-hitting young Nuits-St-Georges, the home town of the Côte de Nuits, just down the road from the Clos de Vougeot.

Cheese in Burgundy is considered the climax of the feast. Burgundy's favourite cheese, indeed, pushes the decibels of flavour to the limit; after a ripe Epoisses, a custard-coloured drum sagging into deliquescence as it rots, there is no dish you could serve. Strange the custom, therefore, of keeping the best, most mature wine, the one with most nuances to offer, to fight this flavour-storm. Reason, and my nose, always tell me to go easy with the cheese to explore the complexities of the wine. Reason often loses.

This performance has taken nearly three hours, interspersed with fanfares from scarlet-coated huntsmen, speeches, the swearing-in of new Chevaliers and songs, some predictable, some sharply funny, from the Cadets de Bourgogne; 'Lads of Burgundy', you might say.

BELOW & BOTTOM
*The proceedings
at a Chevaliers feast
tend to involve giant
ice-cream snails
and at least one too
many speeches.*

By the end every guest knows the chorus and has lost all inhibitions about the hand-waving and hand-clapping it demands. All inhibitions of any kind, indeed. Last dish on the scene is a monster white snail, carried head-high on a litter round the hall, which proves to be a head-clearing ice cream. You have had the last wine; Burgundy has no equivalent to Bordeaux's Sauternes. Noble rot does not strike the Chardonnay or Pinot Noir, or not in these vineyards. With the boiling coffee (described by the menu as "apt to stimulate the subtle vapours of the brain") there is Marc de Bourgogne, the potent-smelling distillation of the dry grape-husks after pressing. You will hardly notice the coach ride home.

What is all this about? Burgundy's business is selling a legend. Its plant is its vineyards, of course, but almost as important is the perpetual theatre of medieval buildings and rituals. You are never allowed to forget that monks created the vineyards, that Dukes realized their value and made them famous, or that Beaune runs Europe's most famous hospital on their charitable proceeds. The Chevaliers du Tastevin was founded in the Depression of the 1930s as the hospitality arm of the region; its genius is to make a technicolour version of history seem like the mainspring of Burgundy even today. Dinner at the Clos de Vougeot reiterates the message from the vineyards. Burgundy makes two kinds of wine, but in endless variety. The character of each flows directly from the land, and so, demonstrably, does the quality.

Têtes de Cuvée

They can afford to be exclusive, the few domaines that own the crown jewels. The hottest ticket of all is a tasting at DRC, as its often-frustrated clients know the Domaine de la Romanée-Conti. Its ultimate wine, Romanée-Conti itself, sells for as almost as much per bottle as a full case of a First Growth claret. Needless to say, there is a waiting list.

Bashfulness is no guarantee of distinction, but Château Pétrus and the Domaine have this in common: nothing is done to attract attention – or even to admit to existence. No name plate. Buildings that blend into the background. It is the vines that are important, of course, but even here if you are looking for so much as a stone wall to demarcate Burgundy's most precious patch you will find only a little one, and on only one side. A stone cross is the silent clue.

The director of the DRC, Aubert de Villaine, follows the same pattern: passionate austerity is his style, and daily hands-on operation. No cellar-master in attendance, even, to plunge the pipette and draw the samples. The *patron* surveys each sip you take (and prefers you to tip back into the barrel the wine you have not spat or swallowed).

The Burgundy cellar routine is always the same, progressing from the least to the most. Only here all the wines are Grands Crus. The barrels, you notice, are pale and new. The cellar is severe, clean, brick-arched and business-like. De Villaine leads to a barrel on the left near the door. A brief dribble into a tasting glass: Echezeaux. There is nothing mysterious

Horse-ploughing is kind to the soil and welcome to the photographer. The ploughman here in Vosne-Romanée comes, he told me, all the way from Hamburg for his springtime session.

about this smell: sweet ripe cherry juice faintly seasoned with oak. Nothing to wait for – or so it seems; I could drink this as it is. I should wait for ten years. Another barrel, another dribble: Grands Echezeaux. Another degree of sweetness, with a sense of something more profound going on. It has a gentle bite, then goes on giving for twice as long. I use the word 'sappy', more because I like it than because I really know what I mean. Vital, juicy, perhaps. In French, *sève* means more: all the elements leading to a succulent finish. Fair enough. A third barrel, the other side of the aisle: Romanée St Vivant, closer to the village, only a hundred metres from the cellar where we are standing: seemingly lighter, less sweet cherries and more spice. Less *franchise*, says our guide; I translate this as 'candour'. A cagey character, St Vivant.

Aubert de Villaine, proprietor-president of the Domaine de la Romanée-Conti, takes a sample of the ultimate red burgundy from its barrel.

Richebourg (the next dribble) is higher on the hill, in what looks like the prime part; the 'kidney of the slope', they call it. This is sweet. It smells and tastes almost roasted with ripeness. Oak gives it a smell of coffee, but meat is the main impression. There are terms of art for all these things, words that have instant meaning for initiates. To me it only makes sense to bring my own. Is there any touchstone, any flavour that always signals success? The character I look for, the one that gives me a shudder of pleasure in any red burgundy, I describe to myself as cherry brandy – the sweet Cherry Heering made in Denmark rather than dry, spirity kirsch. When I first met a DRC wine, before they had become international superstars, there was a current myth that they rinsed out the barrels with brandy, cherry or otherwise.

Now La Tâche. It gives little away. It seems less potent than Richebourg, more precisely drawn but also more suggestive. Strange that I can read tastes into it. If I think port I can taste that; Cabernet and it is in there somewhere; Syrah the same. Then it is the length. Line is the word. It defines something at the outset (don't ask me what) and goes on like an arrow with this precise indefinable flavour to the very end and long after. It is a sense that only great wines give you, and it promises bliss hereafter.

One more: the culmination. Romanée-Conti (there are only twenty barrels) smells as straightforward as Grands Echezeaux to me: very sweetly fruity, stonily clean. But "deeply savoury" is what I called the taste: swirling, not linear like La Tâche. Almost baroque in fact. "*En déshabille*," says de Villaine, which means in its dressing gown, or at least with its hair mussed up. There will still be bottles of this, and people trying to describe them, in fifty years' time.

It takes one click and two whirrs of the machine to sell wine in such short supply, and wine this good, only one whirr. Allocation is a form of commercial diplomacy used to leverage the value of something coveted to sell what is less coveted. No-one can buy a bottle of Romanée-Conti alone – that is, without buying other wines. First you must be on the mailing list, which soon spawns a waiting list to get your name on the mailing list. Then comes an email warning: the offer is tomorrow: drop everything and stand by for the postman. The offer comes: a handsome folder. 'Few estates,' it says, 'were fully able to profit from the exceptional conditions last year' (or words in this vein). 'The winter was harsh; we feared drought; just escaped hail; risk of frost; desperate precautions at flowering time; rain in July, humidity in August, exceptional temperatures, essential to thin crop by a half, a perfect leaf canopy saved grapes from scorch, touch-and-go at harvest; we alone avoided the rain; miraculous result. Tiny crop; unprecedented demand.'

My tasting-notes are terse beside the ones that follow. The dictionary is ransacked, the thesaurus torn apart to find synonyms for ripe, strong and long. 'If you miss all the other wines of the vintage, or all the other vintages of the domaine, this is the one you must have. Only, sadly, there is a mere fraction of what we need.' Your chances depend on how much you have bought in the past. More crucially, they depend on how many other wines you buy, or try to buy, regularly from their list. Meanwhile, each year, the list of producers billed as utterly exceptional grows, their prices are promoted to reassuringly high levels, and the machine whirrs on.

There is a difference between the way bordeaux and burgundy come and go in my house. There is no wholesale, and very little whole-dozen, buying of burgundy, no stacking up of pale pine boxes for opening in ten years' time. Bordeaux remains an easily tradable commodity. I fear the majority of those who buy the blue-chip wines by the case see them as rather unwieldy ingots – if indeed they ever see them at all; less trouble to keep them in a bonded warehouse and shuffle pieces of paper.

Burgundy, for me at least, is a retail commodity: two bottles of this, three of that (if I'm lucky). It is even delivered in cardboard instead of wooden boxes (with very few exceptions). Cardboard disintegrates in a cellar, so you unpack the chubby bottles, enjoy them cool in your hands, hold them up to the light-bulb to see their almost-scarlet through the glass, read the label, those multiple family names like a litany in your head – Gagnard-Delagrange, Confuron-Cotetidot – and choose their places in the rack. How many times will you glance at their red capsules before you decide the time is ripe? Burgundy does not repulse you with a wall of tannin if you start too soon. The taste of Pinot Noir is clear, and can be delectable, from the start. Tannins shape the flavour, though, and can soon cut you off from the fulfilment you are hoping for with their pincer-movement on your tongue. The flowers, the truffles and the forest floor in autumn, the velvet and the inner fire take over only if you bide your time.

How long? It is harder to tell with Pinot Noir than with Cabernet. 'Drink it when it tastes good,' is reasonable advice, but how do you know you are not prematurely ending its glowing prospects? I have tried many times to prolong the pleasures of a wine I love for its fresh flavours, only to find that pedigree tells. My everyday Chorey is good for three years, four after a great vintage like '99; then it runs out of energy. A wine from a better vineyard, higher on the hill, will take a year longer to say what it has to say but keep adding new thoughts for another two or three years. And Burgundy has more than one living museum of ancient wines that seem to have no limit to their hold on life. Fittingly the Château de Beaune is where a large supply of them live, in the cellars of Bouchard Père & Fils, founded in the 18th century and now owned by Joseph Henriot, a champagne merchant famous for his hospitality. Cellar is hardly the word for the dark labyrinth of caves and crannies contained in the medieval ramparts. Vintages starting with the figures 18 seem routine; the wines are not. Most are from the Côte de Beaune, from communes such as Volnay and Beaune itself, less famous for their longevity than the Côte de Nuits.

When a 75-year-old wine is the youngster in a group I can become disorientated. "Still dark red; can this really be Pinot Noir?" I wrote on my menu recently about a 1929 Pommard Rugiens from the Bouchard domaine. "In your face seems the right term: confrontational, alcoholic, crisply tannic, cinnamon-spicy, then rolling on and on." It was almost a relief that an 1870 Volnay Santenots had calmed down. "Could almost be an old white wine," I wrote. "There is a caramel softness to the flavour, but tannin still tightens the palate and contains an extraordinary length of sweetness." Asked to guess its year I would have been half a century adrift. What were we to make, then, of a white wine, an 1858 Meursault Charmes (from the vineyard almost next door), that still smelled fresh, still cooled the palate with a breath of lemon, before its winey energy started to ebb? There are explanations: this was before phylloxera, crops were tiny by today's standards and flavours concentrated … but what must these wines have been like when they were young?

The curse of burgundy at all levels is a sense of thinness, transparency revealing no flesh beneath, especially in a cold and wet vintage.

I appreciate what I see as freshness and a light touch, but it can easily go too far to become meanness and acidity. The majority has always voted for a more robust drink – and merchants have been happy to oblige. They made a discovery not many years ago at the oldest merchant house in Beaune, the house of Champy, founded in 1720. One of the attics was full of mysterious milk-churns, to all appearances dating from the 19th century. What were they for? Eventually the archives revealed that they were used in an operation to concentrate the wine by freezing it and removing the ice. *Gelage* was the term used, and the price-list proves it. *Vin gelé* was one-and-a-half times the price of the natural article.

If greater concentration is one of the secrets of making better wine – and that is certainly the impression you get as you progress, at a tasting, from village wines to Premiers and Grands Crus – there are easy ways to achieve it. The simplest is to run off some of the juice to make rosé before the serious maceration begins, the process called bleeding or *saignée*. There are more high-tech methods: evaporation under a vacuum or reverse osmosis. It is interesting to hear the best growers turn down the idea. Why? Because they trust wine to make itself better than they can?

There is a philosopher in every good wine-grower. Better, he says, to accept that cooler vintages make lighter wines than to put them on steroids by concentrating them. It is the ignorant who think bigger is better. The best you can do is cultivate a moderate crop, not too much or too little, and pick the grapes at the right moment. 'Phenolic maturity' is the term today, but the exact moment has been recognized for centuries. Two hundred and fifty years ago the association for the improvement of Tuscan agriculture, the Academia dei Georgofili, appealed to a Burgundian monk for help in making wine more like burgundy. Dom Denise was a Cistercian, an oenologist from the monastery that had established the Côte de Nuits seven centuries before. Among his clear instructions on vines and vineyards and pressing and cellars (and distillation), he describes exactly when to pick.

There never was a vintage, he says, when all the grapes were ripe at the same moment. Nor should there be; the wine would be too strong. You need some grapes overripe for colour and strength, some underripe for freshness and balance. How to tell? Pick a single grape. Look at the little woody tuft from inside it that stays attached to the stalk. It should be a purply red. If there is any green round the hole in the grape, it is not quite ripe. Suck the juice through this hole. If the grape is ripe the pips will feel dry in your mouth. The pips of Pinot Noir should be dark brown (and those of Chardonnay, beige). Chew the pip: it should taste like a ripe almond. Then squeeze the skin between your forefinger and thumb: it should stain your finger dark violet, the colour remaining after you have rinsed it. A saccharometer will tell you how many degrees of potential alcohol you have, but ripeness is much more than a simple matter of sugar. A good grower still uses his forefinger and thumb like a monk.

Beaujolais

You could never mistake Beaujolais for the Côte d'Or. Not the country, nor the wine. The Côte d'Or is walkable, at least in width if not in length. It is tidily arranged and easily remembered. Beaujolais feels immense: a veil of vines drawn over the lower slopes, up the valleys, over the middle slopes, into the steep interstices of the forest that crowns a respectable range of mountains. On the upper slopes you almost expect to hear cow-bells. Look east over the river-plain and you can see the shining white flanks of Mont Blanc. What on earth are people doing, you ask yourself, growing vines, and with such precision, such weed-free tidiness, marching like soldiers up fields as steep as roofs, in sharp corners where a tractor would be a liability? Barely scraping a living, is the answer.

We all know what made us turn our backs on Beaujolais. For a year or two in the early nineties it was fun to follow the crazy race to be first home, by hovercraft or helicopter, with the raw new vintage. We forced ourselves to swallow the pale purple banana-flavoured acid as though it was a once-in-a-lifetime chance. The producers were all too pleased to take our money. One year I went down to film the juggernauts leaving Georges Duboeuf's great factory yard at midnight. They had a rag-time band with a Sousaphone whose oompah-phrrrt just about summed it all up.

It was a discovery, at the time, that any wine didn't have to be kept a year or two to be drinkable. For the wine trade to do anything in a hurry was pretty revolutionary. Strange to think that we now expect most white wines, at least, to carry last year's date. Beaujolais as sold almost anywhere beyond the bistros of Lyon used to be a dubious dark-coloured brew. Then suddenly it was party-time, a sort of worldwide vintage celebration when you dared to drink wine straight from the vine. In Japan the trick still seems to work. In the West we rapidly lost the taste for it – and sadly, it seems, for Beaujolais of any kind.

BELOW
The Gamay vines of Beaujolais lead independent lives, with no wires or trellising, sometimes to a great age.

BOTTOM
All the hoopla over Beaujolais Nouveau did the region no good in the long run.

There are other reasons, too. We became variety-obsessed at about the same time, latching on to Chardonnays and Cabernets from no matter where. But nobody outside Beaujolais plants the Gamay. If there were an Australian Gamay, the name would be on everyone's lips. If Beaujolais grew Pinot Noir, it would be in every line-up. But no. Funny grape, funny region. There are no comparisons to be made – so why complicate life? Let's have a Merlot.

Once in a while, though, there is a vintage that moves the goalposts. 2003 was one of these: all over Europe it gave the little wines their chance to shine, while such intense heat left many of the great vineyards, whose privileged positions make them the emperors of average years, floundering. In Beaujolais the whole population was rubbing its eyes.

It was not easy. There was hail to start with, so only half a crop. Nobody was ready for the heat-wave of the century. Nobody had ever seen ripe grapes in mid-August. Everyone was on holiday. I heard the story from Guy Marion, right-hand-man of Georges Duboeuf, the unchallenged king of the region. Marion has tasted with Duboeuf every day for thirty years, from 12.00 to 1.00pm and from 6.00 to 7.00pm, every vat made in the enormous Duboeuf winery and every vat brought in from many hundred small producers. You might say he has a considered view.

We had lunch at Le Cep, the cheerful shrine to appetite in the square at Fleurie, full of merry broad-beamed grey-heads in sports shirts and tans. There were twelve different vegetables with vinaigrette, all fresh, for a first course, then a casseroled pigeon, then endless cheese. We drank a Pouilly-Fuissé 2000, mature and nutty, then Moulin à Vent 2000. Nothing evanescent about these.

Marion told me how the alarm bells rang in August when the supermarkets suddenly had empty shelves. They stock up for the picking season and the influx of workers when the holidays are over. A great telephone call-up brought everyone back from the beaches to sweltering labour and emergency rations.

And of course things can go wrong when you harvest hot grapes and the cellar is a sauna. Not every vat was a happy story, and the technicians from the research centre were still away. I was cherry-picking, though; the privilege of a potential customer, and what I saw and tasted were curvaceous creamy wines carrying the different characters of the different *crus* to levels I scarcely imagined. Nobody had to add sugar for once – and natural alcohol is good alcohol.

It was warm again when I was there the following May, the sun burning among the fresh sprouting vines and the cool of a cellar a welcome retreat. Wine-growers are rarely at their most enlightening as they squeeze between their barrels, pipette in hand, fetching samples of what they hope are their best wines. They tend to speak in enthusiastic clichés. That year, though, the clichés did not go far enough. Not only were the wines richer, with wilder and more exotic perfumes, but the Gamay had an unaccustomed element: smooth silky tannins that could shape and structure its cherry-ripeness into something almost formidable.

Here is an example, a Brouilly tasted with a grower on the terrace of his house perched among steep vines at Lantignié, with a long view back to the Brouilly 'mountain' to the east. "Clear full red with violet lights," I wrote, "smells of black cherries with a suggestion of bananas, but cooked and creamy ones. Sweet and fresh on the palate, then rapidly tightening up like a silky corset around the fruit." The impression was repeated again and again. Brouilly is usually the easy-going one of the Beaujolais *crus*, the favourite of Paris cafés. In the more serious *crus* of Moulin à Vent and Morgon, and even in Chénas, the corset had bones hidden in its silk.

In a sense the *crus*, the ten villages in the north of the region that make the most stylish and longest-living wines, are the bane of Beaujolais. The French appellation laws, in their lofty wisdom, deny them the right to print 'Beaujolais' prominently on their labels. True, the word 'Bordeaux' is in very small print on the label of Château Latour, but no-one is in any doubt of the connection.

Brouilly, Chénas, Fleurie and the others are logically, geographically and gastronomically part of Beaujolais-Villages, the northern (and superior) half of Beaujolais, but the law fumbles the relationship. Fleurie is not sold as top Beaujolais but, more important, simple Beaujolais gains no kudos from its best wines. There is far too much of the basic produce (large amounts are routinely condemned to compulsory distillation) and no practical way of raising its game. Any that gets as far as a bottle must be considered in the upper echelons. I would never turn down a chance of trying one, but nor would I hesitate to dip deeper for the extra sous that would buy me a Beaujolais-Villages. Simple Beaujolais, even in a good year, always seems to me to disappear as soon as it hits the palate (and a good thing too, is a common remark). With Villages wines you stand a better chance of a flavour that lingers a little. I have never mastered, and probably never will, the territorial subtleties of the Villages. But light soil is its secret: free-draining granite and sand in contrast to the cold clay in most of

Guide, philosopher and friend, a good sommelier practises what he preaches. Michael Williams at the Plateau Restaurant in London's Canada Square.

Beaujolais. You usually taste the best in the cellars of growers who have land in the *crus*, whose wine-making is in any case more ambitious.

My notebook says of a Beaujolais-Villages of a little sales cooperative of go-ahead growers at Oingt, the village seemingly named by a goose, "This is light but limpid with a palpable texture, smells of ripe banana and peardrops, tastes of cherries. Nice sappy acidity, ending with a wild strawberry smack." Not bad, I thought, at five euros a bottle. My notes on some of the 2003 *crus* become lyrical, rising at times almost to hysterical. The awkward question remains: when and where do you drink them?

The traditional answer is in a bistro – in Lyon they call them *bouchons*, where the food is seriously home-made and the idea of a printed wine list, restaurant-style, would be absurd. The patron buys wine by the barrel, and the wine that flows fastest (important when you have a barrel) is Beaujolais. Bistros, though, are going out of fashion: will they return? That kind of cooking is hard work, and that kind of drinking doesn't go with driving. Restaurants, on the other hand, have a nose for what is fashionable, and prefer the profit margins on more exalted wines. Even to imagine asking for a bottle of Fleurie in a restaurant with a list of Argentine Malbecs and old-vine Barossas is to feel terminally naff.

At home, then? What could be more carefree? Beaujolais (by which I mean not just Beaujolais, or even Beaujolais at all, but Beaujolais-Villages and all the *crus* – see how the appellation tells against it) is excellent drinking on its own. Its low tannin makes it an easy swallow without food and a cool glass makes a good aperitif. It is perfect café wine, which translates as good in gardens, too. But I suspect it scarcely occurs to anyone with a cellar of maturing wines to include it. It needs fast-tracking, they feel, like most white wines. It almost gets in the way.

Will a great vintage change this perception? It will be up to the *crus* of Moulin à Vent and Morgon, perhaps Chénas and Côte de Brouilly, maybe Juliénas, maybe Fleurie, to show what they're made of.

The Burgundy Persuasion

I HAVE ARGUED that the influence of Bordeaux on wine-producers has percolated round the world, and that wines bottled in its high-shouldered bottle are all, even if subconsciously, acknowledging that influence. Can you say the same for Burgundy? Is the slope-shouldered bottle a sign of allegiance, of influence, or of some kind of spiritual bond? If you see a bond between Burgundy and the Rhône, the theory is not absurd. If you don't, it still divides the world into those with Bordeaux in their thoughts and those with a different set of values. At the very least, that is how I organize my cellar.

Pinot Noir has had many pioneers in venturesome places. David Lett was the first in Oregon: an excellent idea.

On the right, in what I see as the whatever-next department, are the burgundies and the growing number of other Pinot Noirs, the Rhône wines and the Syrahs (whether known by that or their Australian name of Shiraz). With them go the cluster of wines from Piedmont made from Nebbiolo, Barbera or Dolcetto – grapes peculiar to this subalpine enclave. They probably did have burgundy in mind when they first bottled Barolo. It was at the same time in the 19th century as Rioja was modelling itself on bordeaux.

If Tuscan landowners two hundred years ago set about imitating burgundy, it is fair to assume that it crossed the mind of every other aspiring wine-grower in the Old World and the New. They all tried; they all, at least in their own estimations, failed. Bordeaux they found (fairly) easy: you just plant Cabernet. The result might be approximate, but it was a cracking good drink. The bordeaux idiom, in any case, was wonderfully amenable to interpretation, Cabernet or not. Burgundy was altogether more elusive.

The easy approach was to bracket wines with less tannic structure, fuller, sweeter and generally friendlier wines, as 'burgundies'. This was the thinking of the Australian wine shows. The Gallo brothers with their Hearty Burgundy would not have disagreed. Great wines have come into being with this philosophy: in Australia, for example, the almost treacly versions of Shiraz from Barossa and Rutherglen and McLaren Vale, originally made as tonics to sustain generations of English maiden aunts – or so the story goes.

If Barolo and Barbaresco aspired to be like burgundy and found an equally valid quality of their own, others took a purist view and pressed on with the burgundy grape. They were looking for the taste of Beaune or Nuits or Chambertin; all they got, though, was Pinot Noir. It tasted either like a cold vintage in Burgundy or a hot one, but never (they thought) like a good one. Pinot Noir may be a delicious flavour, but it was not their dream. The places that came closest were ones with weather just as temperamental as Burgundy's. In the 1960s the dogged David Lett in the green hills of Oregon, south of Portland, found the right flavour, he thought, despite frustrating rain. In Australia, Andrew Pirie declared that green was the clue: to make French-tasting wine you had to go where the grass stayed green all year round. His solution was Tasmania.

"Plant Pinot Noir where the summer grass stays green," said Andrew Pirie. He was the first man to get a doctorate in viticulture in Australia – and went to Tasmania. His Piper's Brook Pinot Noir proved him right.

Californians adopted Carneros, in the relative cool of San Francisco Bay, as their best hope for Pinot Noir. In Australia the spotlight turned on the Yarra Valley. It was the 1980s by now. Hamilton Russell made good Pinot Noir at the Cape. Then it was New Zealand's turn.

In favour of growing Pinot Noir, even if your Beaune fell short of your dreams, was its talent for

making bubbly taste like champagne. Champagne indeed has nearly twice as many Pinot Noir vines as the Côte d'Or. In California it was worth growing anywhere you were aspiring to champagne-like bubbles. Then, if the grapes looked promising, you could make red wine with them, age it in French oak, and hope to fool your guests. That is exactly what James D Zellerbach did in his Hanzell Vineyards in the hills above Sonoma, and enough people thought the same way to start the ball rolling. It was not the Hanzell grapes that made the difference, though, it was the French oak. From that year, 1959, dates all the California wine, all the New World wine indeed, that smells French – or nearly.

Stirring the pot is essential with Pinot Noir. This is Bob Sessions at Hanzell.

Chardonnay was the first beneficiary. It was a minority interest in California until it met Zellerbach's oak. Cabernet Sauvignon benefited just as much when Joe Heitz in the Napa Valley charged twice the going rate for his first wines from French barrels in the early 1960s. Soon French barrel-makers were surprised by the orders from California. Pinot Noir, grown on soils very different from Burgundy's and under a much hotter sun, continued to taste bronzed but sulky, oak or no oak.

The first I tasted that moved me came from a place where green in summer was a dream. You remember the first time you drive to such extreme places. Chalone is a winery on a limestone outcrop in Monterey County, far south of San Francisco. The road winds up and up a bare mountain where it seems unlikely anything would grow. At the top, stripped to the waist, wiry and chestnut brown, was Dick Graff, too reasonable a man to be called a fanatic until you saw him at work. "This is California's Burgundy," he said. "It doesn't look like it [very true] but it has the soil." He gave soil primacy over everything (he even had to truck up water) at a time when nobody in California – and certainly not the theoreticians at the University – mentioned it at all. His Pinot couldn't taste as fresh and sappy as the original, not in that climate, but it was beautifully made – and so was his Chardonnay.

For Dick Graff, limestone soil was the key factor when he made Chalone Pinot Noir.

Another plan, of course, was to forget about Burgundy and make a different wine altogether from the same grape. Whenever I am in San Francisco I go to the Fairmont Hotel at the top of Nob Hill to hear one of the world's corniest Dixieland bands in surroundings of old-Hollywood vulgarity. Beer or wine? One night I noticed a Pinot Noir by the glass.

It came from a big winery far inland where the grass is rarely green. It was dark, thick, sweet, simple and delicious, with more Pinot Noir flavour than you can fit into a Riedel glass. What was the proper response? 'There you go!', perhaps.

Essential bird netting before the vintage at Coldstream Hills gives the vineyards a vaguely phantom appearance.

Once it was clear that Cistercian methods were not the only ones, possibilities multiplied. In 1985 James Halliday convinced me that he had found ideal grapes in the Yarra Valley, and in 1986 made Pinot Noir I thought a Volnay grower would approve. I became more and more convinced when year after year in the cellar it matured as good burgundies do, became less vividly fruity, silkier and even gamey, without losing its voltage of energy. It was time, I thought, to bring contestants from round the world to the table and see if they suggested any conclusions. We met one spring morning in James's house, its verandah looking north over the vineyards of Lilydale. (Australians use words such as dale, valley and mountain with poetic licence: not all have perceptible contours. But these are steep, the sort of plunging vinerows I associate with the Rhine, studded with green points of light as the new leaves catch the northern sun.)

That day a group of us tasted eight wines of the same year without knowing what they were, and described them to each other. I learned so much that I kept my notes. The first (later revealed as a Côte de Beaune Villages from Joseph Drouhin) was lovely to smell: fresh open minty fruit, then surprisingly dry. Its whole profile was lean, however pretty. The second was a New Zealander from Martinborough Vineyards. It smelled as sweet as a haymeadow but had much less shape. It started soft, then finished sharp. Already too old, I thought, at four years.

Number three was the regular Coldstream Hills bottling and the cheapest wine there. It was a strong clear red, it had an intense red fruit smell with a friendly suggestion of oak. It was silky already, but vital and penetrating with bright acidity. I loved it. Next came a Californian, Calera Jensen, from the same region as Chalone. It smelled of raisins and felt creamy in my mouth: a different aspect of Pinot Noir, but without enough flavour to cover the alcohol, and coming to an abrupt stop. Fifth was intensely attractive: fresh, sweet, minty and vigorous, adding one flavour to another in a crescendo that lasted and lasted. Just as well, it was much more expensive: Clos de Vougeot from a distinguished grower, Mongeard-Mugneret. Number six was Coldstream Hills Reserve: far darker than the burgundy, sweeter and seemingly simple but in a tight brace of tannin that made me write simply "Very young, intense, strong. Keep." Then seventh came a wine from Lombardy, Casotte Bellavista, a clear cherry red with a flavour of creamy toast from the barrel. There was something attractively cool about the palate, then a dry finish without much fruit in the middle. Finally a Mazy Chambertin from Armand Rousseau, the most illustrious Chambertin grower. "Full of colour for Pinot Noir," I wrote. "Deep sweet fragrance. Fleshy but svelte. No sign of oak but a powerful chassis of tannin. Not a flasher."

This was not nearly a broad enough sample, even for those early days. My notes are vague. I repeat them, though, because years later I remember the occasion so clearly, and they seem to represent the position of Pinot Noir round the world at the time – with a bias, naturally, to the Yarra Valley. The Côte d'Or was fairly, in fact generously, represented. California looked too hot, Italy too technical, New Zealand too callow. These were probably all wines from young vines. Oregon should certainly have been there.

Ten years on the early vines should be mature; it is fair to take stock. All eyes are on New Zealand. It took a long while for New Zealand to find its true vocation because for years it looked in the wrong direction. In the 1970s it came to believe that Germany was its best model and foolishly planted Germany's least interesting vines. New Zealand Muller-Thurgau was about as exciting as, let's say, German Merlot. Then came the sensation of Sauvignon Blanc so tasty that people queued for it. Then good Chardonnay – but that's not hard to find. Finally the grape with the longest list of frustrated suitors. Enthusiasts claim that, for Pinot Noir, New Zealand could be the Promised Land. The best examples already have sweet fresh smells of minty fruit and earth, depth of flavour, vigour of attack and more and more length. "Smells of Bonne Maman blueberry jam," I wrote about one that particularly impressed me, "but also rooty, suggesting thyme, and even ginger. Crisp and plummy, hiding its alcohol [it has 14 degrees] well. Perhaps a slight hot moment just before the long blueberry finish. Excellent with a salmon steak fried in oil, herbs and balsamic vinegar." Some are too alcoholic for me, but that is true everywhere.

What remains, in New Zealand and everywhere else, is to start defining the appellations, staking out the best soils and aspects, doing, in other words, what has kept Burgundy busy for a thousand years. It will happen much sooner than that. Give it, perhaps, fifty. Can you imagine the excitement of farmers who not long ago thought sheep were their destiny finding the world hanging on their pronouncements about Pinot Noir? How are you pruning it? How's the flowering coming? Are you sticking with Tronçais again this year? A New World indeed. Already in Martinborough and Marlborough and Christchurch and Central Otago a spectrum of vivid new Pinot flavours, some more luscious than any in Burgundy, some stressing the earthy note, are the start of a new chapter, and my excuse for a new wine-rack.

Gaja

Put me down in a vineyard anywhere you like and I will work out where I am. The hills or lack of them, the vegetation or lack of it, the design of the vineyard, spacing of the vines, their trellis and pruning, the soil, even the light (let alone any buildings) will provide the clues. But there are a handful where no clues are needed: a glimpse is enough. The Moselle, the Douro, the Médoc are *sui generis*. And so is the Langhe, the ridge-backed hills of tall-staked vines culminating in Barolo and Barbaresco.

A passionate man, a coiled spring, a fountain of energy: Angelo Gaja tells the past, present and future of Italian wine.

It is always autumn when I am there. Or winter. Or a drenching day of summer rain. Piedmont is an enclave trapped in the Alps: from any hilltop you can see the encircling ridge, half the year white with snow. Angelo Gaja has his own hilltop; his villa commands the vines of Barbaresco from their summit. He is a man who takes a commanding view of everything that touches wine. In Italian wine, they say, he makes the weather.

The Gaja *cantina* is a fortress behind an iron shutter. The bell buzzes far away. Inside is a working courtyard, a desultory little garden, a marble hall – and a short man in a frenzy. Angelo Gaja revs away in low gear like a mountain bike – always. One night I heard my name shouted across a square in San Francisco. "'Ugh!" Unmistakable: it was Angelo, with five people in tow. What was I doing this evening? Tomorrow? We must meet; had I tasted ...? And we did: next day, a hundred kilometres north in St Helena. I don't mind how far I go.

In Barbaresco again. "Look what we 'ave. Everything." The tasting table has forty bottles lined up behind ninety king-sized glasses. "What you want? Everything?" These are wines that I rarely drink, and nobody does often. "You say. Stefano will open." Hurry: he's always in a hurry. "First come 'ere. Come and sit down. I will tell you." And he does.

Sitting across his office table, the tasting postponed, he tells me the history of Italian wine, its problems, its possibilities, its background, middle ground and latest developments. How Chianti was ruined by the wrong vines, bastardized by rapacious newcomers, and is recovering. The formula for its future success. Piedmont: how neglected it was; how there were only two thousand when there should have been five thousand plants per hectare. How the wine was left in barrel far too long; often dirty barrels, too. The whole sad state of Italian wine a short generation ago (and these were the prestigious regions). The long work of recovery – starting with planting new vines. Now (Angelo swats a wasp. It dies) the renaissance is spreading from Piedmont and Tuscany (and Friuli, too: the Protestant northeast was always relatively clean and tidy) to all parts of the peninsula. Italy is surrounded by sea: just look how God made it for vines.

Thirty minutes later the dissertation was done – and worth a doctorate. This was a deep thinker's mind with the tap turned full on. Look at Italy's natural advantages: the Apennines down the middle offer every combination of altitude, latitude, shelter, exposure, inclination, drainage, soil, subsoil you could possibly desire. Eight hundred metres up on Mount Etna you can grow good Pinot Noir, that sensitive northern grape, within view of Africa. But why would you want Pinot Noir when Italy has three hundred and fifty grape varieties, not in a botanical garden but in regular cultivation?

Look at the Italians. Is anyone more creative? They are smart, pushy, individual, original, full of energy. They want to cut a dash with something new. And they are (lots of them) rich: it is no crime to have money and spend it, especially when you are taking the neighbourhood with you. The technology is terrific, consultants are brilliant – you just have to ask. There is a lot of changement (Angelo's favourite word) in the world. And it's not just the rich and famous recycling the profits from their sports cars and fashion houses and cosmetics and publishing. The humble growers at the cooperatives are in love with their land (some of them anyway). Merchants mass-producing famous names try harder than, for example, merchants in Beaune (also tendentious). Italy's trump card: restaurants. It comes back to the food. Everyone understands it. In comparison French food is too refined, too complicated. Italian restaurants are cheerful eateries, like Chinese ones. Japan is now in love with Italian food. It's the same style as theirs with different flavours. (Quite so, I think. I'd swap noodles for pasta any day.)

Angelo is the man who taught Italian wine self-respect. His father was a traditional Barbaresco farmer. Nobody much wanted the hard red wine that the Nebbiolo made in the Langhe, and even less the thin stuff they made from their second grape (out of five or six kinds), Barbera. And could they get their heads round Barbera being a grape and Barbaresco a place? Angelo made it better – he was not the only one – and he charged more. A great deal more. He made a better mouse-trap and the world beat a path down the autostrada from Milan, left at Asti, along the River Tanaro (poplars, lush vegetable plots), zigzag through Isola d'Asti, Costigliole d'Asti, Castagnole Lanze and their nut-orchards (this is Ferrero Rocher country), left again between the battalions of vine-stakes and up the hill to his iron door.

The tasting. We settled for 24: just the new releases of the last two years, starting with the Chardonnay Angelo planted (he was the only one) to show he had no Piedmontese prejudices, and named Gaja and Rey (his mother's family name). If fine white burgundy is violins and violas, this is a cello. It is golden, massive, smelling of ginger biscuits – always a good sign. I am seduced.

Now wines from young Nebbiolo vines, ruby red, smelling of plum stones and French oak. Well-designed wine tastings (and cellars) start the list with something quite open and obvious and progressively tighten the screw of intensity and bite. The vines get older and the vineyards steeper as you go. The best sites around here are known as 'Sorí' this and 'Costa' that. Sorí Tildín is full and round but far from soft. It tastes of tar and violets – and luxury. Sorí San Lorenzo starts with startling sweet intensity, then reminds me of burgundy in its fruity transparency, then flashes a touch of caramel, then clangs shut tasting of iron and iodine. It shuts but doesn't stop: the taste (which taste?) goes on and on. The most important question to ask an adolescent wine like this is 'How is your balance?' Is there too much of anything (alcohol, tannin, oak, acidity) to prevent harmonious continuity?

Costa Russi, another Barbaresco, next. This is darker – slightly. It smells of paper and fresh mint. I find it broader and deeper and more savoury, descending to deep notes of caramel and tar and cough mixture. Pow! I think we are disturbing a sleeping child. And this is just Gaja's local produce. Remember he has an all-Italian perspective. In the 1980s he set up shop in America's favourite Italian vineyard, Montalcino in Tuscany, and before long in the new Arcadia of the Maremma, the Tuscan coast south of Livorno. Will these new wines say more about Tuscany or about Gaja?

They smell very different. I've never found a one-word description for the smell of Tuscany's grape, the Sangiovese. I used to think roasted chestnuts, but decided that was an image for the whole wine rather than its smell. Texture is its real give-away: it feels like tweed in your mouth after the silk of Nebbiolo. It is the astringency of tannins that dry and pucker your tongue and palate – at this level a very pleasant feeling. Tannins can be bitter: this is ripe and benign, and in any case made sweet and creamy by a generous dose of French oak toasted to the point of caramel. No wonder America dotes on Montalcino; this has the fashionable density and sweetness with a beguiling rough edge. Sugarille is the name of Gaja's Brunello di Montalcino. "Extravagant elegance," I jotted down; "openly luxurious like a cavalier's neckcloth. Promiscuous."

Gaja's third winery is his latest passion. He gets up at four in the morning to drive the four hundred kilometres from Barbaresco to Bolgheri before the radar traps start blinking. Bolgheri is a different world from either the gothic alpine heights of Piedmont or the classic Tuscan hill-town of Montalcino.

Angelo Gaja saw a place for himself in this new Bordeaux. By 2000 he had acquired a property alongside Sassicaia and Ornellaia and bigger than either of them. He likes names that tell a story. His Cabernet vineyard in Barbaresco is called Darmagi ('What a pity'), his father's reaction when he replaced the old Nebbiolo. The new estate is called Ca'Marcanda, meaning 'I had to wrangle over the price', and its junior wine Magari, which is apparently a verbal shrug of the shoulders.

How was the Ca'Marcanda? Far from obvious. I thought I could taste the Piedmontese mentality behind the fashionable blast of coffee from toasted barrels. It was prune-ripe but tight and deep. Like a Barbaresco? Like Angelo Gaja.

Slow Food

The white truffle of Piedmont is a fungus of awesome power. I first met it in Genoa, at a wine fair with a hundred stands that filled a tall building around a central staircase. We were tasting on the second floor, our heads full of the fresh scents of Friuli from a dozen green-brown bottles, when a strange miasma crept through the fair, as unmistakable as a gas leak and as impossible to ignore. What on earth? No question of tasting wine any more. This strange aura, like the wildest of cheeses become gaseous, had to be tracked down. The crowd was in motion – down to the door. A rather grubby farmer was standing there, arguing, holding a newspaper bundle. Why couldn't he, he was saying, sell his truffles at the fair?

Alba, south of Turin, is Italy's truffle capital, and October high season for the hunt. Slow Food, the nearest thing on earth to a gastro-political movement, has its headquarters nearby in the city of Bra. Its founder, Carlo Petrini, is possessed by the quality of everything to do with food and drink. "Slow" (he says it low and deep, starting with a z) "began the day McDonald's opened a branch in Rome. Food should never be fast."

And slow became the cool of the table. "Come to Alba," he said, in heavily Italian French, "we will go 'unting the truffle together."

At dinner he said, "Bed early tonight. We must be up at three." For a slow breakfast, presumably, but even then .... Did we have to hunt the nocturnal truffle? Was it possible to go on a day shift? "You will see." That was not likely, I thought, at four on a winter's morning. We paraded at three, drank coffee in a hurry, and were off into a dark drizzling fog in a small smelly car with a small smelly dog in the back.

We spent the next two hours slithering through bramble and elder on steep slopes, trying to follow the dog by torchlight. Its master was in the same predicament. His instructions to the dog and his curses were indistinguishable, delivered in a patois more French than Italian. Our torches occasionally picked up the muddy hound scratching under a bush. By the time its master had reached it, it had moved on. Once an hour, it seemed, with great excitement he said, "Si, si;" and crouched over the animal as it scraped at the dirt. What did dog get, I wondered, as man took over the excavation and straightened up in triumph? We slid down to join him in the thorns. He was holding what looked like a pebble.

Dawn, the rain setting in, and a handful of pebbles. "Andiamo. Breakfast." We filled the car with mud and wet coats and drove steaming back to the village. The market was assembling: stalls going up. We filed into a café, the warmth, the smell of bread and coffee overwhelming. Breakfast was unforgettable: three fried eggs arrived gleaming on a white plate, to be buried in marbled brown slivers from a truffle the size of a bun. Not one of ours. And a bottle of Barbera, deep mulberry-coloured wine as subtle as an alarm clock. Finally I could ask, "Why so horribly early in the morning?"

"Because," our huntsman said slyly, "no-one must see where we were going."

"Or coming from?" I said.

The reason for secrecy, however approximate, became clear when we went shopping in Alba. On the stalls in the truffle market women were sitting behind piles of pebbles, pale, chestnut or nearly black. Some of the customers had jewellers' magnifying monocles to screw in as they said 'Permesso?' and picked up a tuber to examine. Ninety grams on the little brass scales: L30,000,000.

Bra is the capital of Slow Food. Its offices share a galleried courtyard with their own restaurant, kitchen, workshop and exemplar of all that is slow. In the dining room everything is simple, comely and to the purpose. The walls are yellow plaster, the table cloths rough white linen, the chairs rush-seated wood. They are not restaurant dishes on the menu but recipes from a Piedmont that Slow Food struggled to keep alive. Carpaccio?

A fashionable word for a thin slice. Calf's cheek? Jelly or gristle from the days when the squeal was the only thing that got away, but painted with a deep green pesto tasting of ground-up leaves. A glass of Arneis, a local white wine rescued from oblivion. Then fried rabbit, juicily anatomical, and a jug of young Nebbiolo, like a handful of berries to crunch. A cottage industry, apparently, this Slow business – until you see how it is conquering the world.

Italy's biggest wine tasting is the annual Vinitaly trade fair at Verona. Its biggest open to consumers is a Slow event that fills the former Fiat factory in Turin, a building so vast it has a race-track on the roof. In one of the halls where Topolinos were born is a bar with a thousand red wines in racks to the ceiling, in another a thousand whites. Your ticket entitles you to taste any of them. Across the hall is vast *salumeria*: every conceivable ham, sausage and salami, and a mountain of bread. Between the two families have settled down to lunch. A small boy runs over to fetch a Chianti for mother and a Barbera for father. Am I hallucinating? If only, says Carlo, the whole world would slow down like this.

Slow is the magazine of the Slow Food movement, published in four languages and circulated in 45 countries. It is no foodie journal: no recipes, but cultural commentary.

The Warm South

"**P**ROVENCE IS A COUNTRY to which I am always returning, next week, next year, any day now, as soon as I can get on a train ...." I read Elizabeth David's words in her *French Provincial Cooking* the year I became editor of *Wine & Food*. "Pale soups the colour of summer frocks," she writes, and the soups, and the mood, stick fast in your memory. No writer I know can be so feminine and so forthright at the same time. I was smitten. She was twice my age, and my confidante when I was wooing Judy in such a tearing hurry. She sent us to Provence on our honeymoon. As witness I have a red check-covered exercise book with "What We Ate on Honeymoon 1965" in my writing on the flyleaf.

"Lamastre. Tuesday is market day. Six in the morning the dealers start setting up their long stalls, the farmers start arriving with their sheep and calves, goats and geese. Under an intermittent drizzle the bales and boxes are dragged from trucks, hampers and umbrellas are opened and plastic awnings as long as cricket pitches are tied from tree to tree around the market place. The hammering and hooting, the animals' cries and the first bursts of bargaining are punctuated by the tinny strokes of the clock on the Hôtel de Ville. Half past six; seven, the sound of mallet on iron, of hammer on wood, of saw in a plank, of goats bundled in sacks to be weighed, of scooters skidding angrily among the artichokes and oranges."

Lamastre was the first place Elizabeth sent us en route for Provence. The Hôtel du Midi was her favourite memory of old provincial France, a *Relais Gastronomique* from the age when backfiring motor cars and stately bicycles carried people on unhurried tours. It is a long climb through brown beech woods west of the Rhône Valley, above the country of Hermitage and Cornas and St Joseph, the names on Mme Barratero's wine list and the inspiration of her cooking.

In those days, dinner started with soup. (It was a practice so established that in PG Wodehouse 'the soup and fish' meant a dinner jacket.) Sometimes it had a title; on our first evening at Barratero's it was potato soup, and one of the best things I had ever eaten. Sometimes it was just *potage*, and so skilfully concocted that there was no point in trying to spot the ingredients. The barbaric French habit then, as sadly still, was to start with a 'cocktail', often just white wine and blackcurrant syrup. The white wine was usually Hermitage Blanc, far from the legendary quality, alas; the red was the point. We drank Hermitage 1957 with a leg of lamb, Côte Rôtie 1959 with roast chicken, Cornas 1959 with pigeon casserole and Hermitage 1953 with a melting beef stew. None of the menus is a struggle to translate. There were five simple courses, dictated by the stalls in the market. We were learning French provincial cooking where it was born.

'Tendency of the French to entertain lavishly.' The artist Gort captured in a series of drawings the preoccupations of the French petit bourgeoisie. This is the true world of French provincial cooking.

Tendency of the French to entertain lavishly

If I had met these wines before, I did not recognize them. The only Rhône wine commonly drunk in England was Châteauneuf-du-Pape, one of the repertoire of dark reds of uncertain origin offered by the brewers who monopolized much of the nation's drinking. Hermitage and Côte Rôtie were offered by the most grown-up merchants as part of the historical repertoire of a gentleman's cellar. Today it is considered bizarre, short-sighted, even stupid, that wine regions outside Bordeaux and Burgundy were so little known. But even in French wine literature they were often lumped together under such titles as les Demoiselles d'Honneur, or just Vins de Pays. They belonged, that is, in the provinces. They also provided crutches for weak wine from Bordeaux and Burgundy in need of a boost. In the 19th century the English were known to prefer their claret stiffened with something stronger – and not in secret, either. Lafite 'Hermitage'd' even fetched a premium over Lafite *au naturel*.

At Lamastre then we were at the gateway to the south, about to descend the Rhône Valley and see winter turn to spring. The first vineyards we saw reminded me of the Moselle; ledges of vines teetering on cliffs as though sunshine were a rare commodity to be strained for and hoarded. Côte Rôtie was painted on its terrace walls. Over a hundred and sixty kilometres south of Burgundy, what was the need for this sun-obsession? The cold-blooded Pinot Noir and the Gamay have come to the end of their territory: this is where the Syrah starts.

Or rather where it ends. Whoever brought it to France (more likely Greeks than Romans, certainly from the eastern Mediterranean, possibly even from Persia) settled it in the south, in Provence. Then they prospected with it up the increasingly chilly corridor of the Rhône, beyond

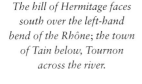

The hill of Hermitage faces south over the left-hand bend of the Rhône; the town of Tain below, Tournon across the river.

where olive trees will grow and where the oaks lose their leaves in winter. They found the perfect site for it on the granite hill of Hermitage, its back to the north wind where the Rhône makes a sweep to the left. Fifty kilometres farther north, on the bend above Condrieu, the north wind shelter was more crucial still. These are both tiny sites to plant, barely the size of a single Côte d'Or commune. It is surprising that their wines were so famous, not that they were so little known.

You would be more likely to take them for bordeaux than burgundy. Syrah is a tannic grape and makes a densely flavoured wine, unlike the transparent Pinot Noir. It is a chameleon, through, with no clear note of fruit or leaf comparable to the blackcurrant flavour of Cabernet Sauvignon. Figs are part of its character in age, but not in youth. In Côte Rôtie it can develop delicate raspberry-like sweetness; in Australia its alter ego Shiraz can taste of blackberries – a relationship that looks close but tastes distant. Only here, moreover, in the northern reaches of the Rhône, is the Syrah a solo performer. Down in Provence it is almost invariably blended with grapes that are easier or more productive to grow.

At home I follow the vintages of the few producers of the best Hermitage and Côte Rôtie as I do great growers of the Côte d'Or. Each time I open a bottle I resolve to make it a habit (it would be an expensive one), but relapse into my claret-drinking. Of the two, Côte Rôtie has the more fragrant memories, of bottles that grew so fine and delicate with age that they could have had Margaux in their veins, except that with age Syrah grows leathery. It was the custom to add a proportion of white Viognier to the Syrah to lighten, perfume and soften the wine. Some growers still do. The barrels were old, the wine at least a degree less alcoholic than today's prize-fighters. But if Côte Rôtie has been comprehensively reinterpreted it was happily by a master of his craft. Marcel Guigal brought modern concepts here, new barrels to the fore. He has succeeded at every level, from bottlings as rare as Romanée-Conti to generic Rhône wines as easy to drink as they are to buy. His Côte Rôties are not the wine I learned to love, but who am I to complain?

What is the best age for today's wines? Between ten and fifteen years is enough. With much more age than this the smell comes into the category of 'empyreumatic'. The Aroma Wheel came up with this, not me: it means related to fire – in this case singeing, perhaps. There is a flower that has this smell to some degree: the wallflower. At other moments I think of a fly-blown butcher's shop. Clearly the word 'complexity' is not out of place.

Not even a very good vintage of Hermitage lasts as long as good bordeaux. A great one, perhaps: Jaboulet's La Chapelle 1961 is in the league of Super-Wines, like Château Palmer of the same year; wines that strike awe in the taster and fetch fortunes at auction. The rule, though, is

for the tannins to leach away. Often they form, with the pigments, a dark crust stuck fast to the bottle. There remains a leathery astringency rather than the gentle grip of fine bordeaux. Strange to say it is the white wines of Hermitage that can go on for thirty or forty years.

If it sounds as though Syrah is a grape for collectors, isolated on granite crags, the true picture is not quite so restricted. Côte Rôtie and Hermitage have a burly brother in Cornas, an appellation that appeals to the sock-it-to-me school of wine-lovers, and a gaggle of cousins in the much less restricted districts of St Joseph and Crozes-Hermitage. Cornas is a bottle to keep for the end of a warm-day lunch, when the senses are not at their most alert and cheese sounds a good idea; the racier the better. A dark red glass, beefy and brisk at the same time, lubricates the proceedings perfectly. Cornas can be sweetly red-fruity and yet carry a rasp of concentration. It is the southernmost of the Syrah-solo wines, and tastes like it.

St Joseph can sometimes match Cornas, but there is no guarantee: the name applies to scattered vineyards over most of the sixty kilometres of riverbank between Condrieu and Valence. Local knowledge is essential. The student of terroir can have a field day comparing a patch of granite here with one of pebbles there. Crozes-Hermitage at least sounds a safer bet. It is a smaller district than St Joseph, but largely on the wrong side of the Hermitage hill. The same remarks apply. Nonetheless when we were looking for a wine everyone would enjoy and notice (but not too much) at my daughter Kitty's wedding, she and I both thought of the same thing, the Crozes made by the champion of Hermitage, Paul Jaboulet Aîné of Tain l'Hermitage. We drank magnums of Domaine de Thalabert 1999, three years old. It had precisely the combination of sweetness and grip that a wedding breakfast needs, but I know the few magnums I salvaged for anniversaries will grow more raspberry-like, more smoky and subtle, for ten years at least.

Is your heart in the Mediterranean, or in the green fields of the North? Are you gregarious, take life easy, put sunshine first on your list of desirables? Then your natural choice is wine from further down the Rhône. Northern wines are about intellectual rigour, purity, patience; in the warm fields of the south they produce the smoothest flowing wine they can and incorporate as much punch, spice and grip as they dare.

This is the recipe for Châteauneuf-du-Pape, and the formula for all the vineyards that cluster round the Rhône as it heads for the sea. It is based on the grapes that are easy to grow and big producers of alcohol; above all, Grenache. There are stony vineyards where old Grenache vines stand as sturdy as stunted trees and give formidable wine, not dark but rich, soft and very strong. Offered an easy life, on the other hand, Grenache can also make pale, empty-tasting wine, as so many southern reds and rosés witness. Vast vineyards of Carignan supply thinner reds and Cinsault fair-quality blending wines, but these are names you rarely hear. The vines vintners want to talk about are the ones that provide the spice and grip: Syrah and Mourvèdre.

The southern Rhône is a confusing region in many ways. I tend wrongly to think of it as, and even to call it, Provence. The centre of ancient civilization, the cities whose Roman facilities are still in working order, lies on both sides of the Rhône, from Nîmes in the west to Aix-en-Provence in the east. Strictly speaking, Provence lies further east, it is the Languedoc to the west, but they meet along the Rhône; Orange and Avignon lie at the heart of it, whichever label they wear. It is the same with the vines: their appellations demand local knowledge. Sifting the vintners, their estates, their choice of grapes and their appellations is no easy task.

Châteauneuf-du-Pape looks reassuring. There is an almost bordeaux structure, it appears, to its château-like estates under one unifying appellation. But you are forgetting the grape varieties: 13 of them, at the producer's discretion. Of the finest domaines, one (Château de Beaucastel) uses all 13; another (Château de Rayas) uniquely Grenache. Every estate has its own recipe. Perhaps you should be able to detect the pepper in a wine with a high proportion of Syrah, or the hard tannins if Mourvèdre is a main ingredient. If all the soils were the same, or all the cellars, or all the philosophies, you could establish some order. But some vineyards are covered with river-bed stones, begging to be photographed, and others with dull sand; some cellars are bright with new barrels, others dim with dusty casks – and as for philosophies, there are no two that match. My favourite story (I wish it were true) is that one sells his best wines at half price under its second label. The reason? Millionaires are less likely to appreciate it than clients who demand value for money and taste before they buy.

There are half a dozen domaines whose wines would appear at the head of a classification. Beaucastel has the highest profile and makes rich, even gamey, wines; Vieux Télégraphe; Châteaux Rayas, Fortia and La Nerthe and Clos des Papes are all estates deserving their fame, but there are smaller cellars, not remotely comparable with châteaux, making individual wines as good or better. There is also so much nondescript Châteauneuf that the label is no guarantee of anything, except possibly strength. It was the first appellation to be controlled, yet the official system has never satisfactorily pinned down its identity or set a threshold for its quality.

More and more today, as well, Rhône wines are made with a new American market in mind. Its requirements are made clear by Robert Parker's description of a Châteauneuf-du-Pape to which he gave a hefty score. "Pure sex in a bottle … with gobs of fruit, sweet tannin, loads of glycerine and no hard edges, this will make even the most puritanical American rethink his anti-drinking policy." It might not be so tempting for one who likes red wine, though.

Provence (or the southern Rhône) has never been made orderly, Bordeaux-style, for a far-flung moneyed market that likes its investment in wine to be tidied up in advance. Some of the most glorious Châteauneuf I ever possessed, in fact, came from (or via) Bordeaux. I found a dozen bottles mysteriously labelled Châteauneuf-du-Pape 1937, Jean Sanders, Barsac, at a price that indicated that no-one could vouch for it. Sanders, I suspected, was the Belgian owner of my favourite château in the Graves, Haut-Bailly. I bought the case, and learned how lovely fifty-year-old

Châteauneuf from a Bordeaux merchant can be. I could list strawberries and raisins, smoke and tar as its flavours, but to little purpose. What I remember best is just sweet warmth: sweet without sugar, warmth without heat; perfect equilibrium rather than classic structure or precise line.

This is why these wines of the southern Rhône are so good to drink quite young as well as old. They are burly rather than surly; they can be fiery, they are certainly heady, but there are no sharp edges to deter you. They are not wines I would want to sip alone; they need the strong tastes of lamb roasted with rosemary, and ewes' milk cheese, herb-scented from the *garrigue*.

Once, to get a sharper focus on the confusion of villages that make up the appellation Côtes-du-Rhône-Villages, we borrowed a house in the somnolent square of Sablet, where at night the only sound was the tinkle of the common fountain. Our host was André Roux, who for thirty years ran his family's Château du Trignon on the edge of the village. You are tucked in under the eastern hills of the Rhône Valley here: first the craggy limestone of the Dentelles de Montmirail, then the majestic symmetry of Mont Ventoux.

The debate goes on: Jean-Marc Sauboua (left) is wine-maker to Direct Wines, Tony Laithwaite (right) his boss. I am holding forth about the nuances of one Rhône commune against another.

Châteauneuf-du-Pape lies below you to the west. Each vigneron we visited had his own interpretation of what it meant for a wine to be a Sablet, a Séguret, a Gigondas, a Vacqueyras or a Beaumes-de-Venise (the last was easy: it is the universal aperitif of the district, a pale amber sweet Muscat Vin Doux Naturel. Two at lunchtime guarantee a siesta).

How much is geology, how much history and habit, is always the question. It can be physically obvious: in Sablet, for example, where the soil is sandy (it used to be known for asparagus, which grows best in sand) the wine is lighter than next door in Gigondas. But there are other villages with folk memories that affect their wine-making traditions. A group of them once belonged to the Avignon Popes, for example, an aspect of their terroir no sifting of soil could reveal. I convinced myself that Gigondas was generally a fatter wine than Vacqueyras; since the mix of grapes is rarely the same from one cellar to another (except that Grenache is always in the majority), it is hard to be sure. Using new barrels, as some do, complicates the equation to the point where you wonder how much it matters. André Roux made a Sablet and a Gigondas but only he, I suspect, knew exactly how much of the difference lay in the soil and how much in the proportions of Grenache, Syrah and Mourvèdre involved. He experimented, as many did in the 1970s in the south, with the Beaujolais technique of *macération carbonique*, which starts fermentation inside each individual grape before any are crushed. The result is almost exaggerated fruitiness. Done with discretion, it did wonders for sales.

For whose benefit, you sometimes wonder, do the French elaborate their layers of bureaucratic control and define more and more appellations contrôlées? Surely not only for the compilers of wine atlases? No; in the French psyche there is an urge, going back to the encyclopaedists of the 18th century and possibly long before, to construct a pigeon-hole for everything. There are *fonctionnaires* longing to complete the list of every wine-growing commune in France: what it grows, what its grapes are, what its wines taste like and how they should be made. It is, of course, of little use to the consumer: it is the market, not the rule book, that structures the way we buy.

Part Two of our honeymoon was in Provence proper at a little inn, Lou Paradou, another of Elizabeth David's favourites, just outside the now-fashionable village of Lourmarin. Mid-March is still earliest spring, even in this sheltered corner of Provence, under the lee of the Luberon Range. We were the only guests in a house raring to cook. Over the morning coffee and *pain grillé* our host, the chef, announced he was going to the market in Aix and asked us what we wanted to eat. 'Whatever you find,' was our answer. The red check notebook records his haul: pumpkins, thrushes, radishes, red mullet, lamb, black truffles, veal, fennel, salsify, kidneys, quail, apricots, endives, croustade de fruits de mer and countless cheeses. It is typically eccentric of the English (or so the chef thought) to eat outdoors even in March, but picnics are sacred. We would find a bright corner where the wind was tempered by a hedge or a wall, and bring out our feast. The Rosé de Provence was cold enough without any chilling.

At night they set the table for us by the fire. The wines we drank were Châteauneuf-du-Pape and something you never saw at home, Bandol Rouge. I did not know Bandol was made from a different grape from everything else we drank, only that it tasted just as I thought wine in Provence should taste: roasted, like lean meat and olives, with the clear cut of tannin you find in Barolo. At ten years or so it grew gamey

Days of innocence: honeymoon at Lou Paradou. Nobody had heard of the now fashionable Luberon in those days.

and herby. Why, I wondered, did Provence make so much rubbishy rosé (although the Château Simone at Lou Paradou was excellent) if its red was this good? The answer was that Bandol grows Mourvèdre, or grows more Mourvèdre and grows it better. Bandol is on the sea between Marseilles and Toulon, in two little valleys behind one of many south-coast harbours. Next question, then: why are there so few vineyards near the sea? One answer: there were more, when there were fewer villas.

The future lies in the opposite direction, west along the coast and in the hills of the Languedoc. It was France's New World in the 19th century, planted in big estates to make industrial wine and industrial brandy. It became notorious as the Midi, for routine violent *manifestations* when demand for ordinary wine failed to meet the ever-growing supply. Did it lack anything the New World could supply – in space, climate or conditions? Freedom of expression was the missing ingredient. It was locked into regulations Australia would not tolerate for a millisecond.

The official way out, to step off the treadmill, is to embrace a new set of rules and make Vins de Pays. Vins de Pays have been a great success; even a rung on the ladder to full official approval and an appellation. In the early years of the Wine Club the emerging red wines of the modern Midi were an important new resource. Our members immediately took to the reds of the Corbières and Minervois, hilly regions of quiet stony villages we explored with delight. It was hard to believe there had been a hiatus of half a century or more in the life of vineyards with such obvious potential. They were tainted, like the industrial vineyards of the seaside plain round Sète and Béziers, by decades of overproduction and under-investment, by planting with the worst grape varieties and making up the deficit of strength and flavour with imports from Algeria.

There was nothing inherently wrong with the vineyards of the plain, either. If they were in Australia, we realized, they would be world famous by now. Vins de Pays were all very well. They are not freedom, though. Freedom is the right to call your wine Cabernet Réserve with your own name, to ignore regional regulations and do whatever you can do best. In France?

Determination works, though, even here. Aimé Guibert is the living example. Since he identified and planted a singular plot of soil, at Aniane in the hills above Montpellier, his Mas de Daumas Gassac has rarely been out of the headlines. He had advice from Bordeaux, on the highest level, that Cabernet would enjoy his soil. He made a wine no-one would associate with the old Midi, as far removed as possible from the Grenache,

Carignan and Syrah of his neighbours. Even the colour of his wine was original. I carried an early vintage into the room in a decanter to serve it to Michael Broadbent at lunch one day. It is the sort of low trick friends play on each other. He took one look and said, "Not the Mas de Daumas is it, Hugh?" Neither of us had ever seen a wine with quite such a black-red sheen. The early vintages were more solid than charming. By 1985 I was writing enthusiastic notes: "Figgy-ripe, fleshy and enveloping, hints of thyme, turbocharged, tannins potent but padded, vibrant finish." None of my notes seems to have recognized the smell of Cabernet. The point was made, and doubly made when Guibert introduced a highly original white counterpart, that any limits on the potential of the Languedoc were self-imposed.

Paris does not seem to have been as impressed as foreign investors were. In 2000 I was intrigued to hear from two friends, Robert Mondavi and Aimé Guibert, both asking me (as a man interested in trees and forests) to look at a wood at Aniane which Mondavi planned to buy. Guibert and his local friends described it as a rare example of ancient woodland with an important flora; sacrosanct, not to be touched. The Mondavi side pointed out the old stone walls crumbling among the trees: former vineyard walls, they said. That is what they looked like to me, too. Their plan was to (re)develop the hillside to make premium wine. My opinion was that the woods were valuable, but to call them unique was stretching a point.

The matter was settled in a political shoot-out. Mondavi was refused permission. Guibert had saved the environment, or at least the part of it that might have fallen into Californian hands. There are still hard feelings.

Australia

Australia is by far the biggest grower of Syrah in the New World. California first had it in the late 1970s, from Joseph Phelps in the Napa Valley. Now the 'Rhône rangers', led by Randall Grahm, are well established, and not only with Syrah, but also with the white grapes of the northern Rhône, Viognier, Marsanne and Roussanne. South Africa offers Syrah at bargain prices, and the first Chilean examples (Montes Folly was the first I met) promise as well as anything from South America.

Australia's Shiraz, though, has had centuries (nearly two) to prove itself. There are ancient vines on soils of every stripe in climates as different as the cool south coast and the sweltering Hunter Valley. It has turned out to be Australia's greatest treasure – and confounds any generalization about styles.

'Hermitage' was what it was confidently called by most self-respecting

growers when they were getting their best wine out of it. You could take
your pick between the Hunter model: soft, pale and earthy but mysteriously apt for aging, and the dark, rich salty Shiraz of parts of South
Australia. 'Sweaty saddle' was shorthand for a decadent whiff that acted
like a truffle on food that had no other grace-notes. It was particularly
pungent, I remember, and rusty with iron, too, in wines from a spooky
part of the coast called Langhorne Creek where, in my ignorance, I fanta-
sized about Ned Kelly among the ancient trees. I was, of course, in the
wrong state, hundreds of kilometres out, but such was the impact of the
bush on an impressionable mind. There was a dish that made a deep
impression with these wines, too: the Carpetbag Steak. It was a fist-thick
fillet in which the cook cut a deep slot to fill with oysters. When the steak
was cooked, the oysters were nicely warm.

The Hermitage of Hermitage in those days was Penfolds Grange
(it dropped the borrowed name in 1990). Some called themselves
Hermitage, others clarets, others burgundies. But long before you
reached the peak there were memorable wines under the labels of the
Hardys and the Hill-Smiths, the vintner-barons of Adelaide, and their
equivalents in Victoria, and from such stalwart old family companies as
Best's Concongella, d'Arenberg, Wendouree and Bailey's Bundarra.
I always loved the combinations of European and aboriginal names, but it
was usually the strange native syllables that seemed best to fit the wines.

Bundarra, for example, was one of the boldest and most memorable
Shiraz wines of my early experience. Its label was black, with Hermitage
slashed across it in big red letters that spelled Danger. It came from
Glenrowan, in the part of North East Victoria famous for its treacly
muscats and 'tokay'. And indeed Ned Kelly. This is where in real life the
outlaw came to grief. I had never tasted any red wine so dense, bramble-
dark, bramble-scented, not sweet but profoundly fruity, yet with a sort of
cool focus to the flavour that made it fascinating. Many better wines have
been made since, but when I brought this home in 1977 people gathered
round in admiration. It was certainly nothing like a Rhône. When I last
opened a bottle I detected the density diminishing as the flavours
progressed. It still overwhelmed the food. It must have been this wine, or
one like it, that a visiting Frenchman described as 'food, drink and a good
cigar.'

The style seems caricatured in today's fashionable Barossa Shiraz.
Focus is what too many of them lack. Blackberry compôte and molasses
laced with bourbon (sometimes rum) sums them up too easily; the
bourbon smell coming from American oak barrels (unless, God forbid, it
comes out of a bottle). Nor is it hard to find examples with 16 degrees of
alcohol and a heady burn that their sweetness only partly hides.

'If it goes over 15, I'll show it the white snake,' one wine-maker told me. The white snake is the water hose. Practical chaps, these Ozzies.

———————

Old Barossa, for me, is personified in the figure of Peter Lehmann. It is still a region of grape farmers, most of them families of 19th century settlers from Silesia, rather than estates. The concept of the château, or indeed the Burgundian pattern of differentiated little patches of soil, is foreign to these broad, mostly flat, fields of vines. In the 1980s the farmer's life was a precarious one. Lehmann is a hard-headed philanthropist. He started a company to buy their grapes, process them and sell the wine on to wineries to finish – at his own risk, more or less. Masterson Wines, he called the business, after Sky Masterson, the gambler in *Guys and Dolls*.

I spent a day with him once in his little office by the weighbridge when the growers were driving their tractors up with their harvest. He was a burly man with an expression of amused surprise, blunt and affectionate in the approved Australian style. "Seven tons," he would say to a German-speaking farmer as tanned as a nut. "Have a schluck, Fritz. They look OK." Fritz would join his mates by the fridge, its door opening and shutting like a fledgling's beak as the cold bottles of Riesling disappeared.

This Australian Shiraz may have been sold as 'burgundy', but no-one, I suspect, ever thought that was its taste. It was not imitating anything; on the contrary it slowly established a new wine culture in which the wineries knew its qualities, whether it came from South Australia or New South Wales, and put them to use as they saw fit. It was shaped, they say, by the growers' 'broad backs and subtle minds.'

———————

Schoolchildren learn the essentials: a poster from the primary school at Tanunda in the Barossa Valley.

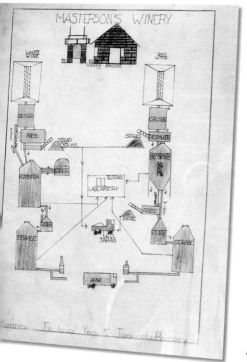

The not-so-secret weapon of the Barossa growers, or some of them, is their ancient vines. There are plants of Shiraz, and Grenache and Mourvèdre too, at least a century old, yielding little but concentrating, it seems, the flavour of quantities into their inky juice. Perhaps the frugal farmers kept their old vines out of inertia; in many cases it was the least ert of them who had the last laugh. A white wine boom in the 1970s saw fields of old red vines (particularly Mourvèdre or Mataro – they use its Spanish name) ripped up and replaced with white.

There are dozens of rigid little churches in the villages of Barossa. "They're dissident Lutherans," said Lehmann. "Whenever they have a row they build another bloody church." None has quite the aura of the little gothic church of Gnadenburg, a hundred metres above the valley floor on the hills known, in the true Australian spirit of topography, as the Eden Valley. Gnadenburg in English is Hill of Grace, the name of a vineyard of ancient Shiraz five generations in the Henschke family and capable, by common consent, of giving the wine that, with Penfolds Grange, clinches South Australia's case. Matched with the best Syrahs of the Rhône (in a spirit of comparison, of course, not competition) what seems to be the identical grape (Syrah and Shiraz are the same) turns out a plumper wine, richer in fruit if not so tight with minerals. The word chocolate is routine in describing ripe Shiraz flavours, and liquorice frequent. Blackberry, though, is almost universal – and of course oak.

The bearded Stephen Henschke and his wife Prue have always struck me as more Californian in spirit than Australian: reserved, earnest, amused, rather than challenging and dogmatic. They make an extraordinary range of wines for a smallish winery whose flagship is clearly Shiraz, starting with good Riesling and Semillon (both 'bonify', to mangle a French term, for ten years in the bottle) and embracing Sauvignon Blanc, Pinot Gris, Gewurztraminer, Pinot Noir, Grenache and Cabernet. Is it curiosity? Is it anxiety to please everyone? Four generations of Henschke's felt they were lucky to sell what they made, and without glory: it went in bulk to bigger wineries. The spirit of research seems to be the driving force. Prue is a scientist, and Stephen never stops probing. "What is the difference between these two reds?" he asked, giving me two glasses. They were young, quite light, nicely punchy; one I thought had a faint smell of oak. "They are the same," he said, "but that one had a cork, and this one had a screwcap." It had never occurred to me that a cork smelled of oak – which of course is what it is. Cork and screwcaps: the inconclusive debate rumbles on.

Australians are ambivalent about terroir – but when they discover it they let us know. Stephen Henschke among the old Shiraz vines of his Hill of Grace.

I was reminded of tasting with a different character, another German immigrant to Barossa, thirty years ago. His name was Wolf Blass, and he had just arrived via, at some point, the cellars of my friends Avery's of Bristol. His first English words all seemed to be four-letter ones; even in Australia they made an impression. Blass, working in Barossa at Tolley, Scott & Tolley (wine-makers, not solicitors) was as lavish with oak as he was with obscenities. If you missed the blast of oak in his wines you could not miss the Wolf Blass labels, as big as he could fit on the bottle. Blass was in complete contrast to the conservative Australian approach of the time (and Australians were generally more evolutionary than revolutionary). He won every Show medal, year after year. Wines that I thought undrinkably oak-stained when they were young have emerged in triumph. It takes a stockbroker to know who owns the Australian wine industry now, but Blass has a substantial share.

I am fifty-odd notebooks now from the red check-covered one. Rereading them has the effect of telescoping time: our first visit to the Rhône is as vivid in my mind as our last one to Australia. But is there anything substantial left of the world we learned about so avidly fifty notebooks ago? Beneath the surface, I believe, almost everything. Australia has pursued its destiny to make better and better wines with its unmistakable stamp. And in Provence the wines and the menus still have the predestined, ineluctable taste of their countryside.

Sicily

Two old pennies (we no longer have such small change) was what it cost to buy a white slab of ewes' milk cheese and a kilo of little peaches in a brown paper bag – and the wine to go with it. The peaches were so juicy that your chin was wet from the first bite. Effectively, wine in Sicily was free.

That was my first experience of this half-European, half-African island. It was the ruins of its ancient Greek civilization that I went to see, with half an eye on the seemingly out-of-place episode in which Admiral Nelson became Duke of a village on a volcano. I was lodging in what looked like the souks of Syracuse, in a bare little room with blue shutters up a white flight of steps off the market. My window had a view straight over the Ionian Sea in its dazzling purity. I paid less for the room because it was quiet; I was deprived of the amenities of the premium side of the house, the volleys of conversation and the scooters. Just up the road was the cathedral. The baroque veneer on an Athenian temple only made it feel more authentically pagan than the scrubbed-down ruined versions. The promontory of Ortygia protects the bay in which the Athenian fleet met disaster at the hands of the Syracusans and where, two thousand years later, the British fleet filled its water butts. The sweet water of the Arethusa fountain still flowed out into the salty bay, touching your body in a different way as you swam into it.

Byron's swim across the Hellespont feels no more remote now than that time of seeming innocence, when Sicily was unspoilt, unexplored, untamed, living in a historical limbo apparently equally attached to the ways of the Greeks, the Arabs, and Italy of the Risorgimento. Even crime seemed innocent, or at least routine: just the rules of the game. When I hired a baby Fiat to visit the temples of Selinunte and Agrigento, my landlady asked where I was going to park it. "In the street," I answered. "No no," she said. "Use my son's garage. You'll need the tyres when you leave."

The only wine with a name in Sicily was Marsala, the western province at the opposite end of the island to Syracuse, where an enterprising family from Liverpool set out to emulate Spanish Malaga. An order for fifteen thousand butts to victual Nelson's fleet in Malta had much the same effect as Sir Francis Drake's looting of sherry from Cadiz: it created a fashion among the impressionable English and a fortune for the producer.

Why go all the way to Australia when an island of equal promise for the vine lies off the south coast of Europe? The rebalancing of Europe by the European Community has been the making of Sicily, as it has of the Mezzogiorno, Spain and Portugal. The rules of the Sicilian game, though, have made it a story with many hidden sub-plots and many successful players, some known and some not.

Sicilians love to regale you with stories of what their rivals get away with. A Euro-grant for grubbing up a vineyard surplus to requirements. Another grant for planting a new vineyard (on the same land). A grant, sometimes, for planting olive trees on the same land, too. A grant for building a winery (a bargain, happily: the family were also the contractors). Finally (or more likely just for the interim) a grant to install a distillery next to the winery to distil the wine surplus to requirements. Da capo.

It came as a surprise when many of the wines with what we assumed to be a murky background turned out to be extremely drinkable. There were precedents. A wine called Corvo became an international restaurant standard as far back as the 1960s. No-one could argue with its genial easy-going ripeness.

Ducal titles fitted in with the other image of Sicily, *The Leopard* one of world-weary aristocracy playing its last cards with unfaltering style. It is still a valid image. Only a year ago we paced and repaced the baking streets of Palermo looking for a palazzo that merged with all the other immense baroque buildings lining the narrow cobbled streets. An air of exhaustion lay over everything; sleeping dogs the only life. The walls and monumental doorways were all equally shabby and forbidding. When we found the right door it opened into a galleried courtyard with stables below and a broad marble staircase. Dim, shuttered, stifling apartments led on and on. Were these paintings really the Caravaggios and Titians they seemed to be? Gathered in one of the drawing rooms behind tables covered with bottles were the aristocracy of the island, their coats of arms flashing proudly from new-minted wine labels. The wines were a revelation.

Sicily and the Mezzogiorno have an advantage over the conventional New World of Australia and the Americas: a quiverful of native grape varieties. Yes, they can grow Chardonnay and Shiraz, but who else is growing Fiano and Grillo and Falangina and Catarrato and Nero d'Avola and Negroamaro? Negroamaro means 'bitter black'. Perhaps that described its wine in previous generations; now it is the intense core of red wines from Puglia and the extreme south that show every promise of quality. Nero d'Avola? Avola turns out to be a little town remote in the southeast of Sicily as far south as Africa, and its Nero a potential southern Cabernet.

That afternoon, with the Celsius thermometer flirting with forty, we met Firriato's Harmonium (all Nero d'Avola); Planeta's Cometa (all Fiano, like honeyed melon); Vigna di Gabri from Donnafugata (all Ansonica, almondy, firm and appetizing); Grillo from Chiaramonte, Insola from Almerita and Catarratto from Rapitalà.

Confused? I was. Overwhelmed? A little. But I am confused and overwhelmed at tastings on home ground of two hundred versions of seven or eight familiar formulas from Australia. It is too soon to know how far Sicily, Puglia and the other regions of the south will develop their potential. In the field of mass-produced wine, Australia has something they will never have: enough river water to irrigate whole counties. It can keep refilling the supermarkets as long as people keep buying. Sicilian wine will never cost your smallest change again, but it will stimulate parts that other wines never reach.

The Wilder Shores of Wine

MY WINE ATLAS took me on some complicated travels, and my filming to some unlikely cellars, but nobody has ever followed the vine to the far corners of the earth with quite the energy and thoroughness of a sommelier from Paris called André Jullien. Anyone who thinks the French have never looked seriously beyond their own frontiers for anything to drink should read his *Topographie de Tous les Vignobles Connus*, first published in 1816. It was the result of apparently indefatigable journeys, followed by more journeys to add new territories to the editions of 1822, 1832 and 1848. By this time Greece, Turkey, Asia, Africa and America had come under his enquiring gaze – though exactly how many vineyards he visited himself is hard to say.

When he discourses, however, on the wines of the Caucasus, or even of Persia, he does it with such vivid conviction that you can easily picture the young Parisian, moustached and trim-trousered, no doubt, riding from cellar to cellar, tasting and annotating among the robes, the donkeys and the dust of the Levant.

"The mountain Tartars, who inhabit the highest part of the Caucasus," he writes, "bring to their city of Kislar stronger and better-flavoured wines than those of Terek; they keep better too, and form the normal drinking of people of means. These Tartars, though Mohammedans, make the wines themselves, and even augment their intoxicating properties by adding the seedheads of opium poppies to the fermenting juice. Then they drink the wines in public without reserve."

He traverses the Ottoman Empire with a fine palate for what little was then left of the once-famous wines of Anatolia, and especially Cyprus. In Trebizond he finds only raisins, but in Aleppo certain wines faintly reminiscent of bordeaux, and on Mount Lebanon sweet wines of noble quality, 'vins d'or', which fetch amazing prices in Beyrouth. On he goes through Damascus and Jerusalem ("strong white wines with an unpleasant sulphurous reek") crossing Arabia with its ambivalent attitudes to liquor but marked taste for palm-wine, until he arrives in Persia with its legendary "Schiras, the best wine of the whole Orient. [The wine is] red but not dark, with good flavour, body and plenty of vigour, sap and a very pronounced aroma, being neither sweet nor cloying but leaving the mouth fresh and the palate cleansed from whatever you are eating – a sensation of freshness almost like breathing in after a mint pastille .... The spirit of the wine is completely natural – no eau de vie is added. The warmth it produces in the stomach is gentler than most wines recommended for their tonic properties, and although very warm, not at all heady."

"People of rank in Persia," he adds, "drink Georgian and Schiras wines put up in bottles of Venetian glass, preferring them to wines imported from Spain, Germany or France. They conceal their drinking, whereas stricter Mohammedans inebriate themselves with opium and cannabis."

Modern wine writers rarely, if ever, pursue their researches with Jullien's vigour. True, there are different difficulties in the Muslim world today. One journey of recent times, following wine to its wildest shores, was made by Warren Winiarski of Stags' Leap in the Napa Valley. Winiarski's interest was in the varieties of fruit that are known to exist in the remote valleys of the Hindu Kush. Ancient strains of plants in great diversity: big juicy walnuts, roses of sumptuous perfume, peaches and apricots unknown in the world outside have survived who knows how long – and so, of course, have vines. Hunza, on the Silk Road, the one pass through from Pakistan to China, has a tradition of wine-making that suggests the possibility of ancient grape varieties, either indigenous or left behind by travellers during two thousand years and more of traffic. Winiarski's researches were inconclusive. He found less cultivation in Hunza than he had hoped, but nevertheless a variety of apparently wild vines growing wherever some rocky outcrop prevented the goats from browsing them. There were also sufficient apparently planted vines, on pergolas and the walls of houses or trained into trees Italian-style, to produce a substantial crop. But it was hard to find evidence of wine-making. Plenty of other visitors, though, have tracked down covert supplies of 'Hunza-water', as it is called. They give it mixed reports.

I am impatient to taste what Winiarski's cuttings produce in the New World. All he has said so far is "Don't hold your breath."

At about the same time as Winiarski's journey I made an atlas-writer's start on the vineyards, such as they are, of the border country between the North-West Frontier Province of Pakistan and Afghanistan. Lucy, our daughter, was teaching at the school that then educated the children of anyone of rank in the province, called after the Chitrali eagle, Sayurj. Major Langlands, the headmaster, a much-appreciated relic of the Raj, was said to be the most respected man in Chitral. Boys and girls all wore grey flannel and grey jumpers. Lucy had done a good deal of research to prepare for her parents' visit. If there was any wine in the neighbourhood she had sniffed it out. The best lead was to the Kalash. Tradition has it that this tribe, living in three fertile valleys deep in the Hindu Kush, are not indigenous at all, but the final rear-guard, as it were, of the army of Alexander the Great returning from his Indian campaign.

Certainly they bear no resemblance to their Chitrali neighbours. Many are blond with high-bridged noses, certainly Caucasian. There are no Muslim constraints; the women wear bright clothes and not only show but also paint their faces for hypnotic dances to the beat of haunting drums. Their religion is apparently animist: they worship a rock, a mountain or a tree. In the Elysian landscape of the Bumboret Valley, where the vast silver branches of ancient walnut trees shade rushing irrigation channels, there is much to worship.

Kalash wine, drunk from those sturdy little French tumblers that start life as mustard pots, was thick, pinky-red, fresh and reasonably clean to taste, with the charm of wild berries but no special character that I can recall. Salty goats' cheese may have hidden its subtleties. Nor did I see anything that could be described as a vineyard. The vines here are on walls and up trees – as indeed they must have been in the Greece of Alexander the Great.

We had Chitrali wine too, but this I remember less clearly. I came back from the valley of

At the mosque in Chitral with my daughter Lucy and a broken right arm. Chitrali wine, of course, is unofficial.

the Kalash in bad condition. Our jeep had crashed into the rock wall on the inside of a bend in the road – much preferable to an excursion over the outside of a bend with a sheer drop – and my arm had been in the way. The Bumboret medicine man was perfectly business-like. He strapped my broken limb to a short plank and gave me I can't imagine what to drink. It made me so happy that I insisted on a dance to the drums with the Kalash maidens before we were driven back to Chitral.

For a few days we were stuck in this wildly beautiful place while I arranged to get home to mend my elbow, so Lucy gave a dinner party at the Mountain Inn. She invited a dozen friends and we all drank our aperitif of Coca-Cola in a seemly manner with the proprietor. Half-way through dinner Lucy was looking agitated and whispering. "We can't have it till he goes," she was saying. "He'll recognize it." 'It' was wine the chef had appropriated from the proprietor's private little vineyard. I wonder if he had the fine palate she credited him with. It was reddish, when it came – but there ends my tasting-note on Chitrali wine, and no more wine was forthcoming in the days I was waiting for a plane home. I signed a statement that I was alcohol-dependent to get a daily bottle of beer, and as my arm got more and more painful, began to think it was no exaggeration.

Either alcohol-dependence, or some dark Dionysiac urge (it must be more than just curiosity) keeps wine and wine-making going in places you would hardly believe. If Jullien has any modern rival for sleuthing after obscure vineyards it is a battle-hardened journalist and his writer wife who set off on a quest for the wines of the dark continent. John and Erica Platter were the first chroniclers, in the 1970s, of the rebirth of South African wine. Then they directed their energies to a strenuous, not to say quixotic, tour of every African country even suspected of the slightest viticulture. Their account of it was published as *Africa Uncorked*.

Tracking wine in bush, desert and jungle is very rough shooting in a trade where the birds are usually driven tidily over the guns, corks drawn. The thread that ties together the characters and places you meet in their book is not really the continent. Africa is the difficult, extreme, violent and deeply human location. It provides endless colour, adventure, beauty, hardship and absurdity. The true defining thread is the challenge of producing one of earth's most precious and refined, even sacramental, products when everything is stacked against you. Yes, wine is booze. But so is whisky, arrack, beer … and beer is so much easier. Why persist when Cerberus in the form of a doubtful pong and worse headache stands between you and desired oblivion? The same loony logic will make a gardener try for the peachy petals of a perfect rose in tundra or steaming swamp, or a musician write a concerto for a full orchestra and comb and paper.

Hilarious as it is to read the Platters' careful-stepping notes on fiercely 'rustic' wines (in normal wine-talk the most imaginative language is kept for the best; here it evokes the most obnoxious brews), the real point of *Africa Uncorked* is the dogged persistence, passionate aspiration, desperate longing or crazy courage it takes to be a wine-maker when nature says don't bother. And in Islamic countries where it puts a price on your head.

Take Algeria, where the Platters' journeys begin. What was once the world's fourth biggest vineyard has been pulled up, shot up and on top of that foully slandered by the French who created it and were once its best customers. To the militant Islamic Front wine was the symbol of everything they loathed and feared. On one of John and Erica's first visits they needed an armed escort. They might prudently have tasted in flak jackets. But the oenologists included young women in designer jeans. Shades; no burkhas. There's progress for you.

Morocco is ambivalent, legalistic. The French are moving back in. Tunisia is settled and worldly. Egypt is a mad collision between Islam at its puritanical toughest and the latest stylistic wrinkles from Bordeaux. A fervent Islamist wants his share of wine alright, but has the faith and patience to wait for the promised supply served by dark-eyed maidens in the gardens of Paradise. Meanwhile he quotes the Pharaohs in evidence and keeps an eye on the refrigeration unit.

The tropics set other tests – for grape-vines as well as their long-suffering proprietors. The vine needs the winter to rest. Where there is no winter, or only a hiccup in the rainfall, a vine sickens, tries to flower and fruit non-stop, and soon dies. For all the heat – be it dry, damp or saturated – the grapes don't ripen. Hence the paradox of having to shovel in sugar to make up for grapes that can still be green though already rotten. Not that there weren't good tries. Intelligent not-quites are surprisingly frequent, and there are just enough Eurekas to keep the show on the road. It is startling what ampelographers you'll find in a clearing in the bananas, dreaming their dreams, with their reference books propped open at M for Merlot.

So in Kenya, Ethiopia, Tanzania, Zimbabwe (where armed thugs can be a special problem), but above all in the East African islands, Madagascar, Réunion and Mauritius, would-be wine-growers head for the higher, drier and maybe even cooler ground. In Réunion, whose Pinot Noir and Chenin Blanc have the distinction of being *produits de France*, the Platters followed demented mountain roads to twelve hundred metres to find vineyards on the lips of volcanoes. In Madagascar a thriving foie gras industry gives the wine an improbable partner. (In Zimbabwe one recommended accompaniment was five aspirins.) Mauritius still has an aristocracy in its plantation houses, but one that is not too proud to import grape concentrate to ring the changes with paw-paw juice.

Everywhere the Platters went they found hope triumphing over experience. Fag-ends of brief colonial histories (Ethiopians still eat 'spigittii', Namibia enjoys German food) colour the often knock-about efforts of fanatics of the vine. There is almost enough detail in the Platters' faithful records for a travel agent to base the Ultimate Wine Tour on their pioneering odyssey. Air travel (terrifying), road conditions (what road?), accommodation from luxurious to "sleep standing up", menus ("barbed wire and grilled goat") and of course wines are chronicled with frankly astonishing good humour.

It was the elder Pliny, I think, who advised travellers in the ancient Roman empire to carry with them a flask of *conditum*, usually a mixture of honey and pepper, to mask the taste of too-local wines. The Platters learned the same lesson; their recipe: a bottle of liqueur de cassis. Only for emergencies, though. John and Erica are the world's gamest guinea-pigs. How about this for positive thinking? "The finish hangs about awkwardly, but give it a spritz and away you go."

Is this the wildest shore so far? A shepherd tends his sheep in the vineyards of Tianjin, near the coast east of Beijing, in a haze of industrial pollution. The wine is drinkable, but what will happen when China really takes up wine?

Back to the Start

I had to start my television history of wine somewhere. Thank goodness our diligent researches led us to Georgia. You could evoke Egyptians, commemorate Mesopotamia, quote the Greeks as a perfectly satisfactory prelude, but you couldn't imagine Kakhetia. Kakhetia may or may not be where it began, but it is where it is all going on – just as it always did: vines up trees, grapes trodden in a tree trunk, juice, stalks, husks and all, fermented in a *kwevri* in a hole in the ground.

You would recognize the *kwevri* from any cellar scene of the ancient world. It is the tubby amphora, the one intended to stay put. Stay put it has in Georgia. We filmed a farmer taking off his socks to tread his harvest in a hollow log. He then scraped the earth from a big plug in the ground sheltered among the bushes of his garden cellar and took a gourdful of last year's wine from the *kwevri* that was buried there up to its rim. It was brimming with the pomace, the stalks and pips and pulp and skins we throw away in the modern world. Bracing stuff: an acquired taste, I thought at the time. This year I received a parcel from a Tbilisi professor with a history of Georgian wine and a bottle to try. Devis Siskhla Saperavi from Khashmi in Kakhetia, it said in script I struggled to read. It was sumptuous: deepest ruby, vivid and generous and smelling of berries and rousing your mouth with a diamond edge of tannin. I could imagine it maturing into something exceptional. It was, the professor explained, the archetypical Kakhetian, the historical exemplar for all the great wines of the world.

Saperavi is the grape. Look for it in Moscow; it is the grape the Russians adore. The poet Pushkin (his name and stature seem to have replaced Lenin's in public places as Russia's favourite son) considered the best Saperavi better than the finest burgundy. I make no such claims, I simply wonder. What can you tell from such a tiny sample, and from a country with a thousand troubles? What we know is that Georgia has the oldest relics. In Tbilisi there are *kwevris* six thousand years old. This tiny, remote and isolated outpost of Christianity defines itself as the country of the vine, has five hundred varieties indigenous within its borders and invented (it says) the very word for wine. Saperavi may be its Cabernet (or indeed its Pinot Noir), but what potential for pleasure is locked up in vine-stocks whose names we have yet to hear?

'What region, what country, what continent is next?' has been the cry for the past thirty years of turbulent progress in the world of wine. We are beginning to see what Chile can do with Cabernet, New Zealand with Pinot Noir, Argentina with Malbec and Australia with Riesling. Italy, Greece and Spain are parading their ancient varieties, unknown elsewhere, for the first time. Georgia, the country whose name begins, like geography, with land, may not be next, but the last word will not have been said before we taste what the modern world can make of the oldest wine of all.

V

Sweet

Port

YOU CAN STILL SEE the hacks of the adze in the oak, and the brick bins are not too well put together. Nobody much, I suppose, was ever going to see the little wine-cellar Jones Raymond tucked in under Saling Hall.

His father Hugh bought the house in 1717, newly modernized: its red and blue bricks positively gaudy with their white mortar, the window panes gleaming, the smoke from seven chimney stacks streaming down wind, the topiary trim and the fruit trees pruned. The old cellars were the last thing he thought of. But his father had left him expensive tastes. On his first voyage to China he had had armorial porcelain done for Saling, painted with his heraldic fantasies in blue and red and silver. I have two of his plates here. He was a pioneer in his Chinese tastes, but then not many people built their own merchantmen and sailed them to the Far East. He flourished as a sea captain, trader, then a director of the East India Company and finally of the South Sea Company, the greatest speculative flop of its age.

The South Sea Bubble, when it burst, had cut him down to size,

Miraculously, the 1769 inventory of Saling's little cellar still survives. It shows a preponderance of port over claret, the reverse of today's pattern.

but not his taste in wine. The new fashion was port. He bought a barrel, and had the satisfaction of seeing it bottled in chunky dark brown bottles (they cost as much as the wine) and the bottles stacked in his new wine bins. His sister, Amy Burrell, inherited what he didn't drink: he drank most of it. I have the inventory here.

Compared with all other wines port was wonderfully sweet and strong. Sack from the Canaries was strong, too, but not with this great rasping taste of fruit. It was hard to make elderberry wine so fruity, or so potent. And there was no record of elderberry wine separating, as it were, from all its gross impurities, leaving them like dirty clothes in the bottle when you decanted it, and pouring like a magic liquid ruby into your glass.

Hugh Raymond had bought a dozen of Ravenscroft's new lead crystal glasses, gleaming tulips on turned balusters like the staircase. In his enthusiasm he then had the staircase redone with balusters to match his wine glasses, and added corkscrews on top. Once the fire was going in the hall chimney and the candles lighted, the ruby in his glass was the finest sight in the world, and he talked about the China seas and the cargo he brought home until he nodded off.

Port was a makeshift that came off, a jury-rig that caught the wind. It came into fashion with full-bottomed wigs and saw them out, then periwigs, then little wigs with bows, then long hair, then hair worn short, Prince Albert-fashion. By this time old makeshift port was gone, port-making was a fine art, and bottles of Waterloo port were treasured rarities half a century old.

It was the 175th anniversary of the Battle of Waterloo when I helped to drink one of the last of them. Michael Broadbent saw to it that not every treasure from his Christie's auctions disappeared from view. He had invited the present Duke of Wellington and David Sandeman, whose ancestor had pursued a friendly correspondence with the first

Duke, to dinner in the Christie's boardroom. I decided to wear my only heirloom, the red soldier's coat of my own ancestor, also of Waterloo vintage (he was elsewhere on the day). It suits me, or so I'm told, and fits in all particulars but one: the sleeves prove that we are (or rather I am) descended from apes. They reach my knees. His Grace, in any event, was pleased to compliment me. The port, though, was a wine of extraordinary quality: pink-amber, smoky and tarry and still very sweet, with the final quality of great old wines, an after-taste that refuses to stop.

A broken arm lent artistic verisimilitude when I wore my ancestral red coat (Captain John Henry Johnson, North York Militia, circa 1815).

I don't drink enough port. The relatively few bottles in the Raymond bin today go back to the 1945 vintage, which was as splendid in Portugal as it was everywhere in Europe. The very rich and still sweet 1955 is represented; then 1960, 1963, 1966 and most of the vintages up to date – though I shall not be the one to finish them. Why do I not drink more? Squeamishness about alcohol I fear is the answer, and the same in our friends. They will take a little peck after dinner, or look round longing for less alcoholic Tokay. And port is not a wine I (unlike Jones Raymond) open when I am on my own. I find it a little too hearty for the late night television news.

It is magnificent, though. It combines the virtues, if that's the word, of wine and spirits in a flowing fire, tasting, progressively, from (comparative) youth to age, of crushed berries and treacle, of chocolate and liquorice, of violets and walnuts and possibly cigars. Wine and spirits combined is of course exactly what it is, or rather half-made wine, most of its sugar unfermented and therefore in the phase of *paradis* (as they say in Burgundy) and what they are pleased to call brandy – though firewater would be a truer description. Hence the imperative of age. Extreme age is a matter of taste. Today's fashion (the same fashion that commends sweet, thick and potent table wines) is to drink it much sooner than I would. Modern palates are not afraid of the bite and appreciate the stewed-fruit sweetness. Think of Napa Cabernets. If I were pressed for time, perhaps: why otherwise mix two pleasures when you can have them sequentially, and luxuriate in each?

It is hard to understand when friends say (and they often do) that they don't like sweet wine. The same people have no apparent aversion to strawberries, or chocolate pudding, or mangoes, or sticky toffee pudding, or Tiramisù or … precisely. I hear it argued that sophisticated people choose dry wines and unsophisticated people are afraid their cover will be blown if they admit to a sweet tooth. They are not self-conscious about the rest of their diets. The reason for this aversion? They have yet to try a good example. And yet the choice is overwhelming. Can you think of a wine region that doesn't have a sticky version? Burgundy is the only one that comes to mind. So that's almost one to try per wine region round the world. The Sticky Section of my cellar is not nearly big enough.

The paraphernalia of port drinking changes little. I took this photograph for my first book in 1965. The glasses are English lead crystal of the 1700s.

I met port at a tender age, and in a different age, too. Before our era, in a sense. The old era ended when the River Douro, the traffic artery of the port industry, was dammed for hydro-electricity and the boats that connected the vineyards to the cellars were laid up for good. Harvey's of Bristol, owners of Cockburn's Port (founded 1815), were inspired to invite a group of friends and journalists on a last descent of the Douro by *barco rabelo*, the galley descended from the Phoenician ship, without apparent modification, that plied the river. The Vikings used a sports model, you might say, but the Douro version is massive, carries twenty or thirty pipes (a pipe is an elephantine barrel) of port and eight oarsman on a platform forward. They guide rather than row: the current does the propulsion. And a steering oar over the starboard rear is copied directly from the ones on the Pharaohs' tombs.

What starts as a lazy day on the placid river gets more exciting. With the sardines and ribs and bacalhau and manchego a wooden flask is passed around, itself as round as a cheese, with a drinking spout. A suck on it is gloriously warming: this is, appropriately, 'wood' port, tawny in colour and by name, aged ten years or so in old dusty pipes in Cockburn's old dusty lodge near the river's mouth. You are about to need the courage. The river's rocky canyon narrows, the current flows on before the pointed prow – and disappears. You notice nimble footwork among the oarsmen, a Portuguese 'Ao!' goes up, and the floor removes itself from under your feet. Sheets of brown water fly out either side. That was rapid number one.

All port was delivered to Oporto this way: or rather to its left-bank

The ancient model of barco rabelo *no longer carries the crop down from the high Douro, but its descendants make excursions on the now-placid river.*

suburb, Vila Nova de Gaia, a hillside huddle of the long-roofed lodges of the shippers. The barcos tried to sail back upriver, but more often were towed laboriously by men and oxen. The Douro rejoices in its remoteness, and in a savage fertility that marks it out as a fiefdom of Dionysus.

I once met the god in person here. It was on a night of silver moonlight so bright that the leaves were visibly green on the steep terraces. We had been hot all day, and were tired, we had eaten flesh and drunk young wine, and we went out to breathe cool air and bathe in moonlight. Suddenly we were possessed. We found the invisible grapes and pressed them with our hands, sucking the sweet juice, rubbing it into our hair, over each other's bodies, dancing in the dark, laughing and chanting songs we didn't know. We were satyrs and maenads, and so much ourselves that the recollection makes me tingle with self-knowledge. I have never looked at the black figures cavorting on an Attic vase without thinking of that night. The next morning the palest blue sky was marbled with just perceptible clouds, silvery-buff with flecks of gold. Poussin would have painted the heavens this way above a stately Doric temple, arcades and gardens and shrines peopled with togaed figures, one burnt sienna, one lapis lazuli.

There is no need, nor room, for temples in this stupendous landscape. It is built like a titanic theatre of many stages whose wings rise a hundred metres and whose tiered auditorium, vast amphitheatres to hold tens of thousands, stretch to the horizon. The sun catches green points on their rhythmic surface, ribbed like the crawling sea. Every seat, every bench and ledge, every stage and every wing is green with vines.

Just after Judy and I were married we stayed at the Quinta da Roeda, the farmhouse of the Croft (established 1678) estate. It was the ancient world with cushions; white arches framing garden plots of sumptuous fertility, vegetables and orange trees, and the simple routine of cultivation unchanged. Robin Reid, the manager, set off to visit remote farms whose wine he hoped to buy. They were getting ready for the vintage, sweeping down the granite *lagars* ready for the treading; sluicing out the barrels. He went round each barrel, sniffing for vinegar that could taint the wine. He counted bunches, tasted them, calculated the crop and moved on. Virgil describes it. Port in those days came from the ancient world.

Folklore, especially in England, sees port as a British invention. Nobody has drunk more of it. It features largely in the politics of the early 18th century when it became a symbol of English animosity towards every-thing French. Many historians have puzzled over the capacity for port of 18th century Englishmen. William Pitt the Younger was instructed by his doctor, at the age of 14, to drink a bottle a day. (At 21 he was Prime Min-ister.) Three bottles a day was no means exceptional. However you make allowance for historical differences, it is not a healthy ration. Assume the bottles held fifty centilitres rather than today's seventy-five. Assume the port was considerably less fortified; say sixteen degrees rather than the twenty-plus which is standard today. At this rate many men drank the equivalent of two full bottles of modern full-strength table wine, on the scale of Châteauneauf-du-Pape or a Napa Cabernet, in addition to their regular beer, claret and white wine – every day. They started early and went on till bedtime. Pitt had a glass beside him in the House of Commons. The business of government, in other words, was carried on, and with prodigious energy, by people (Pitt was not the only one) who were seldom sober.

Reading between the lines of history it seems that sobriety as the norm is an invention of modern times. The British were probably no more given to drink than any other of the northern races. Even the French. I remember a case reported in the Paris press in the early 1960s. A building labourer was in court for habitual drunkenness. The court heard that he drank the extraordinary quantity of sixteen litres of red wine a day. How much, it enquired, did his colleagues usually drink? The average, it transpired, was six litres. Could it have been because the British were relatively sober that they prevailed, time and again, on the field of arms?

All wine is a cultural artefact; one that has been symbolic for as long as port has can be almost too heavy with meaning. Vintage port conjures up as much a mood as a flavour. Each category, in fact, has its own scraps of social history attached. Ruby (the trade now has various terms to make it sound more venerable) was the youngest, thinnest and cheapest. I picture it in the sort of wine-bars – they were called wine-lodges, like the warehouses on the Douro – now almost extinct. Yates's in Manchester had lofty rooms and hard furniture, with sawdust on the floor and a rack of barrels behind the bar. The customers were old, or seemed old to me, and drank their 'schooners' (how did a glass come to have the name of a ship?) methodically, as though it was their job. Port and lemonade was a long sweet drink to give you a longer respite.

Tawny was written on another of the barrels: a paler liquid. A drink for sophisticates? There are several ways of achieving a light brown wine: the most expensive is to start with a dark red one and wait for twenty years. Fine Tawny is barrel-aged: the purpose of a hundred dusty rooms full of clumsy grey butts overlooking the river at Vila Nova de Gaia. The flavour of old oak gradually takes over from the flavour of fresh grapes and strong spirit. Ten years is enough for some; others like the tangier taste of twenty, or even thirty. The texture changes, too, eventually; in the best wines, to a silky syrup.

Why do we not drink tawny port at home? Each time I come back to it (and it is a guaranteed fall-back, always smooth, somewhere off-caramel, old-oaky, walnut-scented) I think it will be habit-forming. If I haven't formed it, it is because it is a crowded area: sherry and Madeira occupy the same space, and I enjoy them all.

You can play Guess the Vintage with any wine of a single year. A great many of us do, even if only subconsciously, each time we try another bottle – if no-one tells us, that is, and the label is out of sight. It calls for a little inquisition of the wine, and a rummage through your memory to find a match. It doesn't work, of course, without local knowledge: I would be all at sea with most regions of the vine; only fairly competent with the most familiar. The inquisition, though, is always worthwhile. Port with a vintage is an obvious target. Vintage, after all, is its name.

Guess the Vintage is almost mandatory, especially in a wine so stiff with ritual. And there is a Wimbledon of the game, too: the Factory House in Oporto, the last survivor of a species of club once commonplace, if not universal, where expatriate traders gathered in numbers. Trading-floor, dance floor, officers' mess and drinking-den to generations of the British employed in the port business, it stands, conspicuous as a wig and frock-coat, in the quarter of Oporto long since abandoned by fashion; the heart of the old town.

The library is the most poignant part, big enough for a college and all the books worn with use, their backs ragged with fingering. They are the novels, the memoirs and biographies of the age before the Age of Communication. There were long hours between the cricket matches and games of croquet. Of recent books there are very few, and not many members left either. Wednesday lunch is assembly time. Members meet in the stone-vaulted hall open to the street, where in the 18th century they

The old town of Oporto. Michael Broadbent trained as an architect before becoming the auctioneer and chronicler of great and antique wines. He keeps his eye in with subtle and evocative drawings.

did business. Someone once said of a London club that it was like a duke's house where the duke was dead; much more so the Factory House in the 21st century. The rooms (ball, drawing, dining and drinking) are up the ducal stairs, lined with portraits of old members at their most

dashing in the uniforms of their regiments. Lunch is not a long affair, though substantial and far from solemn. Then members and their guests move into the room next door and take the same places at an identical table. The whole room, in fact, is the same. But you would not want the smell and clutter of a dining room when you were drinking port.

Did I say Wimbledon? There is no resemblance at all, except perhaps a blazer or two. The game does not take long. There is a decanter in front of the Treasurer. He passes it round. The glasses are small; fat rubies in crystal, alone on the polished board. 'I think I recognize this,' says a member; 'it's one of yours, isn't it, David?' It is not worth playing for high stakes: what are the odds when it must be a wine from one of 16 shippers, and there are perhaps forty vintages in the cellar? It is a matter of professional pride, though, to be able to match the richness of Fonseca's, the sweetness of Graham's, the vigour of Dow's or the authority of Taylor's with the characteristics, and the maturity, of a '77, a '70, a '66 or a '63.

ABOVE & BELOW RIGHT
The ballroom and the dessert room at the Factory House in Oporto, where British merchants have talked port for over two centuries. A film crew is not de rigueur.

The inquisition over, there is plenty to talk about. They are rivals and colleagues at the same time. There are technical developments, new regulations, tricky farmers, the traffic, new wrinkles in the business that can always be improved. Their great purpose is to extract the maximum

colour and flavour from the grapes, if possible without the patient crews who used to tread them, and in many cases still do. The port farmer works harder than any other wine-grower. The slopes are steep, the soil hard and the weather extreme. The men carry the grape-baskets on their shoulders, sixty kilos at a time: there is no other way. Then they form lines, women and children too, and tread the purple soup thigh-deep in the stone *lagar* until midnight, the foreman calling '*Um, dois, esquerdo, direita*,' 'One, two, left, right,' and an accordion going back over a lifetime of songs.

The test is the taste. If a grower can reach the same rich density of extraction with an Autofermenter or a robotic *lagar* he will – except at little farms up rocky tracks when there are not enough grapes to fill one. And the taste decides whether your best wines add up to a vintage worth declaring – a form of arithmetic only long-experienced palates can do. It is a rare year that finds the shippers unanimous. In every year one part of the valley does better than another, one grape than another, one *quinta*

Accordion and drum lead a file of harvesters, carrying the crop in baskets on their shoulders, along a steep Douro terrace.

than another. There is no absolute, and each blender has a goal in mind, which he must either reach or abandon. In Champagne, a vintage wine is a selection: you can select for it in most years if the market demands it, and your customers will know what to expect. On the Douro to declare a vintage is to make a commitment to an idea whose time is still a long way off. Nobody can be sure, when the fierce fluid is first assessed, what it will become after twenty years or so in confinement. Yet you can taste the flicker of clouds over the canyons fifty years later. That, at least, is the legend – and I love legends. This is where Hugh Raymond comes in.

The Noble Rot

HE GLOOM of a great brick vault was lit by iron chandeliers the size of cart-wheels. Along one wall ran a table with three vintages each of Châteaux Lafite, Latour, Margaux, Mouton and Haut-Brion. Opposite the First Growths was another table with the full range of wines from the Domaine de la Romanée-Conti. The rare champagnes were in one corner, vintage ports in another, and Château Yquem gleamed gold on a table in the middle. Then the fairway was encumbered by barrels, not of wine but of oysters and lobsters, the tables piled with sirloins and saddles, and the press of guests more organized, as we stood in line for a gargantuan buffet.

A lobster, I thought, would be the proper way to start. I was 23, and hungry. The old gentleman beside me in the queue, a tell-tale ribbon in the button-hole of his grey suit, smiled at me over his spectacles. When he saw me examining the lobsters he asked, in faintly French English, "What will you drink with that, my friend?"

"I'm not sure," I answered.

"I suggest you take a glass of Château d'Yquem."

I knew Château Yquem from decadent days in Cambridge as the grandest of all pudding wines and the ultimate show-off bottle. We had a silly student name for it: Wickham White. I had even drunk it, with the college's patent crème brûlée – about the only dish that could compete with, and spoil, its glorious creamy sweetness. With lobster? Who was this eccentric Frenchman?

He introduced himself as Bertrand de Lur Saluces. I knew that name: it is written in gold on the most sublimely simple of all wine labels: Château d'Yquem Lur Saluces, and a vintage date. I was queuing with the most illustrious name in all Bordeaux, inheritor of Château d'Yquem from centuries of noblemen with the same name and title, and President of the organization of Classed Growths for twenty-five years – and he was suggesting I drink his sacred wine with lobster. I did, and so did he, and it revealed a sweetness in lobster I did not know was there.

The scene could only have been at a Lebègue tasting. For a few of the sunlit years of youth I was on the list for what amounted to the Ascot, Henley and Chelsea Flower Show of the wine world. Guy Prince the chairman was an inspired showman. His firm's cellars were no different from a score of vaults under London's Victorian railway stations, but he made the dim spaces under London Bridge his fantasy Burgundy and Bordeaux. Anyone can put salesmen on the road, he used to say; far better spend the money on a party for high rollers. Invitations were not easy to come by; encounters like mine were the essence of the thing.

FAR LEFT
The Marquis Bertrand de Lur Saluces.
ABOVE
The Lebègue tasting under London Bridge where we met, and
BELOW LEFT
Château d'Yquem.

Further lessons followed when I called on the Marquis at Château d'Yquem and at his house in Bordeaux, an 18th century *orangerie* mysteriously isolated in a back street. I learned the first truth about the first of the golden wines of Sauternes: you don't argue with people who drink it. It made its name simply as the greatest of all white wines, Bordeaux's answer to Le Montrachet. In times before our modern anxiety about what goes with what (and the very notion of pairing wine

and food was unknown to our ancestors) the best foods simply called for the best wines. Turbot, being the biggest and best fish, was a natural choice (preferably with truffles and cocks' combs). Oysters and Yquem are frequently mentioned.

At one lunch at Yquem the first dish was a stupefying foie gras served warm with a sauce of Sauternes (presumably Yquem) and white grapes (peeled and pipped, of course). The second course was the big surprise: my old friend icy oysters and hot sausages, with the nearest Yquem gets to a second wine – or a dry one – Château Ygrec. The scheme was to jolt your appetite back into action for a little feathered game.

———————————

The green-ribbed apron of vines slopes down from the military walls of the château, east and north towards the Garonne and west towards the scattered village of Bommes and the River Ciron. It seems a fact of life that this is sweet-wine country. North they make dry white Graves, then further north red and more red, but here on this airy hill the wine is golden and concentrated and as sweet as wine can be. Does anyone know why?

They don't exactly know when, or rather when it was made sweet with serious intent, so to speak, rather than just tending that way. Sweeter wine fetched a better price with the 17th century Dutch. Here, as well as up on the Loire in Anjou and Touraine, across the river in Loupiac and Ste-Croix-du-Mont, up the Dordogne in Bergerac and Monbazillac, anywhere they could, they looked for sweetness, and propagated the sulphur match to sterilize it against fermenting on the way home. The sweetness of Yquem hit the headlines when the extraordinary vintage of 1847 was bought by the Czar's brother at an egregious price and bottled in gilded crystal. Could it be tastes that had changed? Champagne, after all, was routinely sweet until an eccentric first ordered it custom-made dry – and that was in the middle of the 19th century. Sweetness became a topic as its opposite became the norm. It's a theory. More likely, I think, that here in Sauternes it was a matter of vintage variation, some years much sweeter than others and considered better. There were more sweet vintages at Yquem than anywhere else. There is even an intriguing suggestion that the topic was avoided because the reason, or rather the agent, that caused sweetness was not a pretty sight. Its name, not particularly pretty either, is *Botrytis cinerea*.

———————————

What wonderful organisms they are, these fungi. From the succulent boletus to the bouncy little Paris mushroom, the sinister ink-cap to the fragrant *mousseron* or the savoury chanterelle, they have flavours that are neither vegetable nor related to flesh. Often, linking earthy and heady or yeasty elements of taste, they seem nearer to the essence of wine than any food. They take over cream and give it thrilling strength. As truffles they embrace some of the most elusive flavours and the most garlic-reeking. Yet in nature their role is merely to destroy, to seize on an organism full of the ripeness of the sun and draw it down into the grave.

Spores are their mode of attack, and a vineyard is subject to millions. Most of their attacks are malign. When they land on the wrong grapes they cause havoc. They destroy any that are thin-skinned and bloated, pecked by birds or pierced by wasps. Yeasts and bacteria join the attack and the result is vinegar. They destroy the pigment of black grapes – which is why there is no red wine in Sauternes. On the other hand on healthy, thick-skinned, ripe white grapes they show their benign side. They put down roots, or the fungal equivalent of roots, through the skin to the sweet juice inside and use it for food. The grape shrivels, its acids are consumed along with its content of water. Mouldy it may look, consumed by tiny grey-brown hairs, but its juice attains an incomparable sweetness.

Benevolent *Botrytis* comes with autumn mists. It is not precise in its demands, but its rendezvous with the right grapes demands precision. Regions with autumn mists learned that it was worth playing for, and comes in autumns when mists alternate with drying sunshine. Subsistence farmers could never take the risk. The noble rot was a gamble, and the way to shorten the odds was to grow fewer and better grapes.

Tokay is the probable progenitor of the whole business. In the 17th century its aszu wine, painstakingly made with laboriously selected grapes, was considered a wonder – and by the King of France, no less. The Lur Saluces were on the scene, not yet at Yquem and not yet united to the Yquem family of Sauvage, but nearby at the feudal château of Fargues. The desire for sweet wine was strong in Italy, too, but sun-drying the grapes to raisins was the way they set about it. Germany and Alsace took advantage of seasons when benign *Botrytis* struck. Methodically? Nobody really knows.

With dessert, with cheese, or just on its sumptuous own? The Sauternes-drinker's dilemma. Plums are one of the fruits I love to crunch with the golden wine.

The Yquem method is the model for all southwest France, insofar as anyone can afford it. The first cost is in pruning hard for small crops; a far higher one is picking only the *Botrytis*-smitten grapes. Patient pickers must go round the vineyard again and again in successive *tries*: a dozen turns is not unknown. A score or so of Yquem's neighbours, the classed growths of Sauternes and Barsac, make the commitment. They are wonderful wines, at least as distinct from each other as the red wine châteaux of the Médoc: all the more remarkable, it seems to me, because *Botrytis* seems an all-smothering force, reducing grapes into indistinguishable pellets of corruption. On the contrary, in fact: in concentrating juice they concentrate character; the essence of each different soil tells more strongly than ever. The châteaux adjacent to Yquem, Rieussec to the east, Suduiraut to the north, Guiraud to the south and the Peyragueys and La Tour Blanche to the west, come closest in richness. Châteaux Coutet and Climens and the Doisys, across the Ciron in Barsac, play variations of a more elegant theme: less cream and more lemon.

Few wines mature so consistently or for so long as fine Sauternes, their colour deepening from straw to glowing orange. From right to left: 1995, '83 and '67: three excellent vintages.

Very sweet grape juice ferments uneasily to start with. Given good yeasts and a not-too-cold cellar it will go on to produce very strong wine. Were concentrated sugar the only thing *Botrytis* provided, there would be little more to say. But it also infects the juice with an antibiotic of its own, known as botryticine. Yeasts coming from many generations in the same vineyards and cellars, antibiotics born of specific fungi ... I don't know the science, but the result is an unusual fermentation. The must, thick with sugar and thick with fragments of the perished skins, bubbles uncertainly for many weeks – at Yquem, in new oak barrels every year. Then it just stops. Fifteen degrees of alcohol is the maximum these yeasts can tolerate – and in the presence of botryticine they struggle to get that far. The must will have been sweet enough in theory to produce a wine of twenty degrees or so, but at least five degrees-worth of sugar, or a hundred grams per litre, remains as the sumptuous sweetness that preserves such wines not just for years but for decades, while a molecular gavotte at a pace as slow as time perfects their flavours.

Wine-lovers round the world were given pause when they heard, in 2003, that the Lur Saluces family, after so many centuries of perfecting Yquem, had sold it to a collector of trophy brands, the president of LVMH. They succumbed to the problem that bedevils all family inheritance in France. Napoleonic law prescribes how family properties must be divided among the heirs of each generation. Distant cousins can demand their share and force the sale of any property. Alexandre de Lur Saluces, who ran the château for thirty years with a perfectionism unequalled in the making of any wine, had to concede to jealous relations. To renounce the most admired of all such dynasties for mere money, and to a corporation famous for collecting brands, seemed perverse to say the least.

––––––––––––––––––

I drink far more Riesling Ausleses from Germany than I do Sauternes. My notebooks are full of little lyrics to their virtues. A fresh and punchy Kiedricher Gräfenberg of 1991 from Robert Weil, for example ("immense richness with a limes and minerals bite"), or a Schlossbockelheimer Kupfergrube from the state domain on the Nahe 15 years older. "Sublime dessert wine," I wrote. "Every dimension immaculate: silky texture, still richly sweet, lingers with touches of grapefruit and oil. Handled rhubarb and strawberry mush perfectly." It is a lot to ask of an old sweet wine to face up to rhubarb.

The difference lies both in the grapes and in the cellars. Riesling is aromatic with high acidity, Sémillon (the basis of Sauternes) tasty but low on aromas – and low in acidity too. The sugar content may start at the same point, but fermentation turns far more of the Sauternes sugar into alcohol. The Germans have learned how, essentially by keeping the cellar cold, they can play sugar against alcohol to achieve almost any balance they want.

In the past, conventional terms however complicated (how ripe the grapes, picked at what stage of *Botrytis* ...) helped you to understand each barrel and the prognostics for the bottled wine. The great sweet wines, though, were an art form riding on the back of the real industry. It helped even more to know the grower, if not personally, at least by reputation, and to study the coded messages of his labels and capsules. Modern times are not like this – as the German wine law of 1971 made all too clear.

In the idealistic world that still, despite all temptations, lingers in the cellars of the best German growers, the kinds of sweet wines they offer are clearly understood. Ignore the law that gives a table of sugar-contents (or 'must-weights') for each category from a lightweight Kabinett wine to a Trockenbeerenauslese. In the rare case that a grower picks grapes sweet enough to make the latter, or with a potential alcohol of over twenty per cent, he will certainly want to give you the statistics, but in truth style is more important than substance. It is the flavours brought on by *Botrytis* that make an Auslese a beautiful drink. *Botrytis* seems to explore and enhance the character of a good vineyard. Yes, in a warm autumn there are fine Ausleses made from grapes dried by sunshine without *Botrytis* – and there are merely sugary ones. There are more and more dry Ausleses, too, though realizing the alcoholic potential of very sweet Riesling usually gives a heavy graceless wine. The ideal Auslese is a seized opportunity, an inspired selection from a vineyard touched by the friendly fungus. Perfectly ripe grapes with no *Botrytis* make a different wine: a Spätlese, tasting of fresh green-golden fruit. Ausleses (in my fantasy, at least) have passed into overripeness: the juice is stiff with flavour; age will make it creamy and old age find in it the tell-tale citrus tang of nobly rotten Riesling.

So sensitive were the palates of those who loved Riesling, before our age of regulations spoilt the fun, that debates would take place around a barrel, a dark upright Füder shining in lamplight. Grey heads bent over little tasting-glasses. 'Feine Auslese, at least,' says one. 'That cask is a good Auslese, but this is better. It is rounder, but longer than a rat's tail.'

'Feinste Auslese, brother, I would say. The tone of the slate is remarkable; this is almost a great wine.' – And so they would deliberate form, like trainers round a ring, until every grade from Feine to Hochfeinste had been debated and the palm given to *Füder* No 27, except by those who loved the hint of peaches in *Füder* No 30.

No growers needed quite the persistence or the ingenuity of those on the Rhine, let alone the far-northern Moselle, to make their wines sweet. The ultimate German productions are Beerenauslese and Trockenbeerenauslese, originally meaning picked grape by grape and dry grape by dry grape respectively – dry of course meaning desiccated by *Botrytis*. There was no Sauternes-style industry to be made of these final-fling harvests, often long after the bulk was picked and cellared. Sometimes a single tiny cask of TBA, 'small enough to take to bed to keep it warm,' as a grower in Bernkastel once told me, was the apple of its maker's eye. It could be nearer to the Essence of Tokay than to Sauternes in sweetness – hence almost unfermentable, bed or no bed. In these wines, but also in many less extreme cases, there can be a sense of sublime fulfilment of the grape (the grape being Riesling) that happens nowhere else.

Vins de méditation (it sounds better in French) is the best description of these other-worldly wines. What is there to meditate on? In a young wine the eruption of a garden from your glass. The mysterious (and theoretically impossible) way Riesling seems to leach minerals from the ground. There is no new oak, no secondary fermentation to cloud the prism; slate, sandstone, quartz or loam brighten or intensify or round out the flavour. With age, the onset of exotic fruit and honey and oil, perhaps spice, and changes of texture. Red wines, I sometimes think, age like the skin of a man, eventually growing tight and leathery. Great sweet Rieslings age like a woman's skin, growing even more supple with time. Age certainly enters my meditations: a bottle of 1971 TBA has been with me more than half my life.

No *Botrytis*? No late-autumn apotheosis of mist and mellow

fruitfulness? The last throw of all is to leave the grapes (they must be miraculously well-preserved, to last until winter) hanging on the vine until they freeze, and pick them at dawn. Like truffle-hunting, it means an early start, but at least the quarry is visible: sad frozen bunches on leafless vines under plastic sheets to protect them from the weather. They must be frozen hard for the press to squeeze out the sugary pulp and leave the water-content behind as ice. Given the guarantee of icy weather, though, it can be done on an industrial scale difficult with haphazard *Botrytis*. Ice is not particular: it will freeze all the fruit in a vineyard.

When the fruit-growers of Niagara hit on the formula for their vineyards in the 1970s they created Canada's natural contribution to the world of wine. Ice-wine is a tingling hit of sweet and acid that takes over your mouth like a lemon sorbet.

Early rising: picking frozen grapes at seven o'clock on a December morning in Bernkastel. To make ice-wine the water in the grapes must be frozen solid so it will separate in the press from the sweet quintessence.

I am not usually given to half-measures, but Sauternes is a wine I do buy in half-bottles. It is not so much its strength (no more than a California Chardonnay these days) but its richness that makes one glass impressive and two as good as a feast. Its sugar shot is too intense to go on sipping for very long – in its early years it is almost as sweet as I can bear, without the counter-balancing acidity that makes me usually choose German wines in preference. The mouth-cleaning tang of Tokay is one of the qualities that drew me to it: acidity again. Baron Philippe de Rothschild lived and entertained as thoughtfully and elegantly as anyone in Bordeaux. No doubt he traded Mouton for Yquem (the champagne houses come by First Growths this way, too). Certainly he had a remarkable collection. His habit was to decant Yquem – often half a century old – and put the decanter in the coldest part of the fridge. I swear I saw ice-floes in a decanter of wine the colour of a Havana cigar. Each sip stung – and then spread in an aura of candied fruits and caramel and even, it seemed to me, tobacco as you swallowed.

Intense sweetness is the mark of Austria's dessert wines from its eastern province, the Burgenland, too. The Ausbruchs of Rust and the low-lying region around the reedy Neusiedler See may be as old in origin as their rivals in Hungary, the aszus of Tokaji. Alternating fog and warm sunshine can almost be taken for granted; perhaps in Tokaji more so than three hundred kilometres to the east. I remember enquiring, in the 1970s when they were almost unknown, for Ausbruch wines. It was at the town hall of Eisenstadt, the capital of the region, a small town dominated by the vast yellow mansion of the Esterhazys, where Haydn went to work every day on a new *divertissement*. Was there any way, I asked, that I could sample these historic wines? Did anyone still make them? I was taken into the cellar. Which vintage was I interested in? Around the walls on shelves were dusty bottles going back for decades. And did I prefer Welschriesling, Weissburgunder, Muskateller, Müller-Thurgau? Each grower, it seemed, must enter six bottles for the annual competition. Four or five stayed on the shelf. It was a gluttonous afternoon.

These days the sweet wines of the Burgenland are more often known by the modern names of Beerenauslese or Trockenbeerenauslese than Ausbruch. Since the 1980s they have become one of Austria's success stories. The country, surprisingly uninterested in its own wine up to that point, suddenly realized its potential. Now their growers vie for ever-sweeter and more exotic flavours. Alsace is at it with Sélections de Grains Nobles. Even California and Australia have found ways of making grapes rot in a good cause. The only question is who is going to drink all these sticky rivals for an inevitably limited moment in anyone's daily life? I will play my part, but my glass a day after dinner, and a second one with the late-night news, is not going to stem the tide.

Tokay

Hungary, 1985. A posse of hussars in incredibly grubby uniforms galloped up to greet us in the main square of the town of Mór. They were led by a horseman in that improbable Hungarian cowboy kit apparently looted from a Catholic seminary. In their outstretched hands they held brimming beakers of wine, half a litre at least, miraculously unspilled in the cavalry charge. As they reined to a skidding halt, down went the wine in one beatific swallow.

Forty years of more-or-less Communism had no more broken the Magyar spirit than centuries of harrying by Austrians and Turks. Budapest was the first city of central Europe back on its feet; but then it had never entirely lost its raffish energy, nor even its slightly wistful elegance. The Magyars (the Hungarians' name for their own high-spirited race) are some of Europe's great originals. Impetuosity, charm, impudence, theatricality distinguish them sharply from their neighbours and for long their oppressors on either side: the Austrians and the Turks.

A less familiar proposition is that Hungary is the only country in the world besides France and Germany to have an ancient, original, truly classical style of wine-making of its own. Georgia could perhaps give you an argument, and Portugal at a pinch (though neither – port apart – has ever really been in the fine-wine business). But the flavours now familiar to us from Italy and Spain were creations of the 19th century. Hungary has made precious wine for four centuries at least. The Anglo-Saxon view of wine has always been coloured by its accessibility. There is no easy shipping route from the Danube to the Thames.

It is not hard to describe the way Hungary's traditional wines differ from French and German. 'Fire' is the word the Hungarians traditionally use for the quality they are looking for. Don't be put off, though, by an image of alcohol and chilli peppers cauterizing your tongue and taste-buds. By 'fire' they mean vitality and high flavoured sweetness.

I fell in love with Tokay tasting around a barrelhead in a candle-lit cellar. Religious men, they say, can be sure of heaven hereafter; the rest of us have to catch glimpses of it here on earth.

Trips behind the Iron Curtain were always fascinating in what they revealed of how Europe used to look. There was a startling simplicity and innocence about the uncluttered streets, the cities standing (if they were standing) just as they had been built and, above all, the absence of words. There is nowhere you can look in a modern town without reading: advertising, instructions, warnings, labels everywhere. Every word alters your perception, distracts you, occupies some tiny part of your attention. Times Square is all words; St Mark's Square: no words. At one time, if there were not portraits of Lenin defacing the place, the whole of Eastern Europe was like St Mark's Square.

That is how I remember Hungary in those days: big, cold, shabby Budapest and remote, muddy, time-warp Tokaj. In my first Wine Atlas I used a photograph of the Tokaj market place: a peasant in boots, layers of waistcoats and a stocking cap by a cart jumbled with old barrels on ruts of frozen mud. It would have passed for a scene from Dostoyevsky, at least to me, knowing little of Russia, my head filled with images of chilly gloom. (The Hungarian authorities hated the picture and asked me to change it.) What I remember best about my first visit, in 1970, was the warmth and noise of the little inns, the beauty of hot red-brown goulash, and the colour of the wine. Even better than the taste I remember the amber gleams of bottles half-hidden in cellar-moss like white wool. This was in the state cellars of a town with the resounding name (but it took days of practice) of Sátoraljaújhely. The wines we tasted by candlelight, sitting round a black barrelhead, went back to the 19th century in stages of ever-greater loveliness. It simply seemed that the older they were, the more hues of chestnut and squirrel and dead beech leaves entered into their reflections of amber and gold, the fresher and more flowery they smelled. "Celestial butterscotch" was what I wrote about all of them, but some sent me on hunts among violets and roses, wallflowers and hyacinths for the smells that I couldn't pin down.

This was not the Tokay that was on offer in London. It was Edward Roche, a Polish wine merchant in Soho, who represented the Hungarian State Cellars and arranged my trip. He told me, I remember, that his father in Gdansk used to drink half a litre of 'plain spirit' at lunch every day. Plain spirit was 98 per cent pure alcohol. State Tokay had just enough of the butterscotch taste to be recognizable, but little of the amber light and none of the flowers.

Tokay was not, I was saying, one of London's wines. Everybody had heard its name, but as something remote, exotic, fabulously expensive, miraculously potent and impossible to obtain. It was by no means the only wine to have aphrodisiac claims made for it – and who had been failed by champagne?

I was an admirer but no expert, then, when Peter Vinding started talking about reviving a great old tradition that seemed to be spluttering. Peter was always a romantic. His dream of a great wine château in Graves had come to nothing except some beautiful bottles of wine. Reviving Tokay seemed much more far-fetched – but suddenly not impossible. I had seen the beginning of the end of the Soviet system in Moscow in 1987 when the first edition of *The Moscow Times* suddenly appeared on the streets. It was in English, not much more than a pamphlet, but it contained simple truths that had not been uttered in Russia for two generations. If such stuff appeared in print and nobody stopped it, we reasoned, the whole Soviet lie would be eroded in a flash. Gorbachev had written *Perestroika*: the writing was not only on the wall. By 1989 Communist rule was in chaos; it was Hungary that breached the dike by opening its borders. The Iron Curtain that isolated Tokay, the one great wine region trapped behind it, was disappearing.

Was there anything we could do? The dreamer in me was stirred, and so was the memory of that extraordinary flashing amber wine. If I could have tasted the wine that inspired Homer or Virgil I would have gone to any lengths. Why any less for the wine that Pushkin and Tolstoy drank, and that Peter and Catherine (both Great) considered one of the privileges of the Tsars of all the Russias? But was there any way of joining in?

In 1989, under the rump of the Communist regime, the only way was a joint venture. Peter's backers organized a meeting in Budapest, then in the little town of Mád (the name attracted plenty of ribaldry) open to all the wine-growers. They had borrowed the schoolhouse for the day; partly, I think, with the quaint notion that they would need a blackboard to show the growers what a Joint Venture looked like. They hired two interpreters from rival companies, as a precaution against collusion, and set out their proposal: the growers were to contribute their land, the foreigners all other capital. The company would then pay the growers for their grapes. Its name, after some discussion, would be Royal Tokaji (Tokay in English, and French, spelling).

Isztván Szepsy (left) has become an iconic figure in Hungary for his championship of Tokay. This was outside his cellar in 1990 with Peter Vinding.

We wandered round the bleak little town after the meeting. It had not seen a pot of paint for fifty years. There was one rudimentary shop-cum-café and nowhere to stay. But Peter had done his research; he led me to a cellar, announced by no more than a door in a low wall by the road. "This is Isztván Szepsy," he said. "His family invented Tokay. Just wait until you taste his." Szepsy was a slight man with a stammer. It was an exaggeration to say that his ancestors invented Tokay, but someone with the same name is credited with making the first sweet aszu wine for the ruling family of Rakoczi in 1650. Ancestry was not the point, in any case, when Szepsy took us down the narrow dark stairs into his little rock-cut warren of a cellar, scarcely tall enough to stand in. There was a row of old dark barrels, almost miniature by French standards, and behind the stairs a few more, of strikingly pale new oak. He drew samples from one of these. "Five puttonyos," he said, as he passed us the glasses.

Perfect wine needs no explanation, however exotic it may be. The rules are the same: it smells inviting, invigorates your mouth as it comes in, expands into new dimensions as you hold it on your tongue and lingers sweetly after you swallow. This smelled of apples and quinces and pears, honey and hay. It sent a charge of energy through your whole body as you sipped. It opened vistas of fruit and butterscotch and marmalade – too many impressions to record – on your tongue and clung to your throat like oil to silk, refusing to finish or go away. At the heart of it was a golden blade, glowing and cutting; the spine of acidity that is the hallmark of great Tokay.

There was a lot to explain. Szepsy had been the highly efficient vineyard manager of the Borkombinat, the nationalized State Cellars. When the instructions were to maximize production he thrashed the vines up to astonishing yields of, he admitted, tasteless grapes. The system was that they hoovered up all the growers' wines for a set price, regardless of quality, and put them through a pastiche of the traditional cellar practices, aging them as quickly as possible, pasteurizing the results and shipping them off to fill a quota. There were different quality levels:

apparently the Soviet Union got the worst, in exchange for tractors too wide for the vine-rows – so they were replanted twice as far apart and twice as high, with five wires. Vines that big don't ripen grapes enough for sweet wine – but there is always sugar.

That was Szepsy's day job. At the weekends he was cherishing his family's vineyards (each member of the family was allowed one-third of a hectare). He was growing the extravagantly small crop that makes great wine, picking the grapes one by one as they ripened, overripened and shrivelled, performing the rites that the earlier Szepsy had initiated, and aging his wine for the six or seven years that custom, and his palate, demanded.

Our question was, Would he help us with the new joint venture? He said Yes, for a year or two. There was no Royal Tokaji winery; just a space behind a building on the central square which had served at one time as a bishop's palace. On the slope behind was a typical entrance to a Tokaji cellar: a monumental doorway, unrelated to a building, leading straight to a flight of stone stairs. Below, the dark, narrow-bore tunnels wandered about, on several levels and with many bends, for nearly two kilometres. Cellars are more important than buildings: Isztván brought in wines from some of our shareholders in 1990 and 1991. I still have bottles, now deepening amber. Our own first vintage, 1993, was made in the open air.

More important than either is the quality of the grapes, and not all our grower-shareholders had got the right idea. The tumbrils from the vineyard arriving at our improvised cellar contained a fair proportion of rubbish, including what in California they call MOG: Matter Other than Grapes. Luckily for us, Peter had recruited a young Frenchman, Samuel Tinon, from Ste-Croix-du-Mont across the river from Sauternes. He was as tough as he was independent. He stayed in lodgings in the village right through the autumn and winter while Peter commuted between Mád and Bordeaux.

Samuel surprised the Mádites. When the police chief (one of our partners) turned up with mud and stones in his grapes our staunch lieutenant told him where to put them. For three days the village shop refused to sell him groceries and he had to go to neighbouring Tarcal to eat. But the penny dropped: what was the point of muddying the name of Mád? Who were they trying to cheat?

Nothing about Tokay matches other models. The grapes, soil, weather conditions, method of harvesting, system of fermentation, yeast, barrels, aging process and cellars are all *sui generis*. The key word, though is aszu. Aszu means dry, although the wine is as sweet as possible. It is the grapes that are, ideally, dried and wizened to the state of mouldy raisins by the same *Botrytis* as Sauternes. The quality of Tokaji Aszú (its full Hungarian name) is measured by the proportion of wizened grapes in a vat, and hence the sugar content. By tradition and convention it is measured in puttonyos, which are buckets, of the precious material that has to be picked grape by individual grape. Six puttonyos is the highest number normally used in a year when aszu is plentiful. Five makes wine as sweet as most Sauternes, or a German Beerenauslese. The balance in the vat can be either wine from the same vineyard, or unfermented juice made of the grapes the *Botrytis* has ignored.

Two grapes make up the blend: the sharp and tasty Furmint and the more fruity Harslevelu. In Sauternes, Sauvignon Blanc and Sémillon play similar roles, but here the acidity of the Furmint is decisive. Without it Tokay would not have its trade mark tang. In Tokaj, as in Sauternes, Muscadelle is a discretionary third partner, but here it is more highly prized. Perfectionists will delay the harvest until November if necessary for *Botrytis* to dry as many bunches as possible. It is a cold business, shuffling round the vines in the mud with two buckets: one for aszu, one for grapes juicy enough to make the liquid base.

Learning the ropes was not straightforward, or uncontroversial. It was a long time since so many perfectionists had been let loose in Hungary and there were several opinions as to whether, for example, the aszu should be fermented with fresh juice, with wine already fermented to dryness, or even (as everyone used to do) with the wine of the previous year. The good news was that 1990 was a good vintage for aszu, and so was 1991. Better still, we discovered that most of our vines were on land that had been classified, long long ago, as First Class. The classification of 1700 had fallen out of use over the years. It was something like the Burgundian system, based on the qualities and characters of different fields. In practice it tended to be overlaid by something more akin to Bordeaux, where the name of the property or its proprietor is given more weight.

The names of our fields, or rather the broad swathes of the hilly country where our partners had vines, started out unpronounceable, then became familiar, and over the course of five years and four vintages began to stand for quite distinct flavours. Mád lies in a trough in the foothills of the Zemplén mountains. The full name of the wine region, in fact, is Tokajhegyalja, the Tokay foothills. The vineyards occupy much the same space as in the Côte d'Or, both in total area and their situation on the lower and middle slopes of a range crowned with forest. Of our some-what random portfolio, Birsalmas turned out to be the light and lively one, Betsek the hearty one, Nyulaszo the steely one and St Tamas more bosomy. Tasting them together, in the damp darkness of the cellars, was just what a burgundy tasting would be like if Burgundy made sweet wines, a progression with variations. They are as sweet as honey when they are young, these aszu wines, yet sweetness so balanced and held in check by the sharp-tasting Furmint that they leave your mouth whistle-clean. Sometimes you can almost persuade yourself the wine is dry. As for the flavours, a great deal of muttering goes on as people compose imaginary fruit salads. Quince (which I always think of as a pear crossed with a truffle, so unearthly is its savour) is in most recipes. Apples and pears figure largely, sometimes apricots, also oranges and lemons. Orange is the touchstone smell for *Botrytis* wines, especially in old age. A great old Sauternes, a Tokay or a Trockenbeerenauslese hints of marmalade, whatever else is in its repertoire.

In the early 1990s the Hungarian government announced a privatiza-tion programme. It invited bids for many of the best vineyards and cellars in Tokaj. Investors arrived from France (principally) and Spain. The Alvarez family, owners of Vega Sicilia, bought a once-famous property with the name of Oremus ('let us pray', in Latin). The French insurance company AXA bought Disznóko with a beautiful site on the way to Mád. Another French company, Grands Millésimes de France, owners of Château Beychevelle in the Médoc, bought a hillside called Hetszolo between the towns of Tokaj and Tarcal (on the Burgundian analogy you might say between Vosne-Romanée and Chambolle-Musigny) and set about regrading and replanting it to make a model modern vineyard. Hungarian exiles and German aristocrats staked claims: it was a brief gold rush – except that nobody found gold. I also had my eye on a vineyard and a neighbouring cellar and, when I heard how low the expected price was, a grand old college building as well in a wooded park among some of the best vines of Tarcal.

Bids in the privatizing auction had to be at the Ministry in Budapest by a date in December. Not just cash offers but business plans, CVs of the bidders, details of the potential benefit to the economy – all in septupli-cate. By January I had had no response. Another week: still nothing. I rang the Ministry. "Oh, I'm sincerely sorry," said the minister, "we should have told you. We cancelled the auction of your lots."

"Why?" I asked.

"Because there was only one bid."

"I can send in as many as you like," I said. But the chance was gone.

Mézes Mály, the vineyard I was most interested in, was not in the auction and was far from easy to acquire. Its 18 hectares had been divided into plots of one-third of a hectare, owned or rented in different ways by thirty or forty families. Its wine had not had an identity of its own for many years; it was lost in blends, either at the Borkombinat or in little private cellars. Its name, though, is the most illustrious in the whole region. The first reference to it is in a deed of sale of 1571. It was cited in document after document as the source of Tokaji's most precious wine. In the classification of 1700 (all in Latin) it is described as *Pro mensa caesaris primus haberi*, or first choice for the royal table, a distinction it shared with one other vineyard, Szarvas, which remains state property.

I went into partnership with Royal Tokaji to try to reassemble this illustrious plot. We were helped by Deszo Pataki, the 'hill-judge' of Tarcal, an official with a role similar to that of a mayor but concerned only with vineyards. We spent many afternoons in his cellar ruminating on wines he had made from different plots within Mézes Mály. Sitting on a plank bench, the black-mossy walls lit only by a glow-worm of a light bulb, things seemed to grow clearer with one glass, only for the next to cast them back into obscurity. There were voluptuous flavours of honey, then musty ones, then a glass recognizable as a muscatel; then one that pierced like a needle.

Physically Mézes Mály is undramatic but distinct. It is the lowest slope of a series that rise from the plain, an unstrenuous mound facing south and west, backed by higher hills. Its soil is almost devoid of stones: loose, silty and deep. What character would this give the wine? Apparently that of honey. The name means 'honey corner'. "Do you want the house?" said Pataki. In the middle of the vines, on the crest of the mound, there stood a long narrow yellow building, evidently the workers' shelter. "Nobody uses it," he said; "Why don't you buy it?"

That evening Peter and I walked up to the shelter. It had half a roof, and traces of a former kitchen. We took a bottle of young aszu wine and sat on the steps watching the sun go down. There was nothing picturesque about the scene; more an elemental majesty. The hills and forests lie behind on the ancient volcanoes. This is an apron of fertile ground at their feet, a little curtsy before the flat monotony of the Great

'Johnson Var', *Johnson's Castle, is the ironic name the locals have given to the little yellow cabin in the vineyard of Mézes Mály, source of deeply honeyed wine.*

Hungarian Plain, the Alföld. The vine-leaves did not stir; they seemed submissive to the scorching sun. "Go on," said Peter; "why not?" It was a challenge.

Tokaj has turned out to be almost as hard to sell as it is to make. I fondly imagined that once they had tasted this nectar unlike any other wine everyone would feel as I did. The last thing I expected was fierce disagreements about the model: one school of instant experts said that our wine (and by extension most other growers' as well) was old-fashioned. It should be fresh like Sauternes, they said. We were allowing it to oxidize in the cellar instead of keeping it in strictly airtight conditions to conserve the flavour of the fruit.

When shall we start picking? Family and friends on the verandah of the yellow house. You can count on perhaps six good aszu vintages in a decade; 1993 and '99 were potentially great ones.

I am no theoretician. No technician either, with no scientific training. The pragmatist watches and listens. There is something going on in these cellars that happens nowhere else. In this soft volcanic rock, at low temperatures and high humidity, the microflora is unique. The cellar-mould growing on the walls, the barrels and bottles like white moss, then turning grey, then black, is not like this in Germany or France. No doubt the microbes, the yeasts and bacteria that inhabit it are different, too. Tokay by custom, and until recently by law, stays in the permeable environment of small barrels in these conditions for at least four years. How close the interaction between wine and cellar can be I have watched with amazement. At intervals they clean the thick accumulated cellar mould off the walls, moving the barrels into another tunnel. If an empty barrel is lodged next to a clean wall, the rock remains bare. Put a full one there and within a week mould will start to form on the wall nearest to the barrel – or rather nearest to the wine. The wine very slowly turns amber and takes on a taste and a unique tang distantly related to sherry.

Hungarian scientists have been poring over it for a century. Darabbantartas is the word, I'm told, for the process of exchange between the sugars and acids of the wine and the cellar environment. Amino acids, I'm told (but here I am right out of my depth) become or create or conjure up aldehydes in these conditions. Sherry is matured in dry *bodegas* at over twenty degrees centigrade. Could the process be related but different in damp cellars at ten degrees? The result, in any case, is umami, the mysterious fifth flavour to add to the known four: sweet, salt, sour and bitter. Umami is the tempting one: the taste of appetite. Tokay has, or should have umami. I am prepared to be very old-fashioned about this.

———————

What has been happening here since 1990 has been called the Tokaji Renaissance. The classical period for this national treasure came to an end almost a century ago. It began in what in England were Tudor times. It entered on the world stage as the creation of the Rakoczi Princes of Transylvania; the official starting date, 1650, is certainly long after its special qualities emerged. Ferenc Rakoczi, embattled against Turks on the one hand and Austrians on the other, used it to attract the attention of Louis XIV. In this he succeeded: it instantly became an honorary French wine, *le Vin des Rois et le Roi des Vins*. Practical help from Paris, though, was not forthcoming. The French, the Austrians, the Russians and the courts of Poland and Prussia were avid enthusiasts throughout the 18th century and most of the 19th. Tokay came to a precipice, therefore, when those courts, this entire system of European life, was exploded by the First World War. But Europe is rebuilding itself; its eastern countries are alive again. Was the 20th century simply the Intermission?

Isztván Szepsy has become a national figure, standing at the same time for traditional standards and liberal ideas. He set Royal Tokaji on the right lines, but he preferred independence to working for a foreign company. He dreams of returning his vineyards to the historic method of cultivation before wires and trellising: each vine standing alone, staked and tied up afresh each spring. He prunes for a tiny crop to maximize the chance of *Botrytis*, and then leaves his harvest until November. "Make your base wine from the grapes at the top of the hill," he told me. "*Botrytis* starts from the bottom and moves up. But pick late: the more strength and character, the better." He ferments all his wine in barrels of local Zemplén oak, many of them new. The results can be astonishing: a bewildering balance of intensity and delicacy; certainly great Tokay.

What to drink meanwhile? Aszu wines are for the long haul: traditionally a year in barrel for each puttonyos of richness – and then some more. Fermentation of so much sugar can take years to come to a natural stop. In the ultimate Tokay, the quintessence of all this, fermentation barely starts. Essencia is the name for the produce of the best aszu alone. The aszu is not added to base wine or must; it is not even pressed – except by its own weight. 1993 was a good aszu vintage, in beautiful weather. In the sunshine clouds of spores rose from the piles of raisins in a golden mist. In our rudimentary winery we stapled plastic sheeting to the walls and piled the fruit over a system of plastic drainpipes to catch the priceless drops. This viscous liquid, as much as eighty per cent sugar, will never ferment in earnest. It may reach three per cent alcohol, but your marmalade is as likely to become champagne as this is to become a normal wine. Historically it was often fortified with brandy to make more of a drink of it.

Meanwhile, turnover demands bottles to sell. Szepsy's answer, soon followed by most of his neighbours, is a Late Harvest wine made without selecting the aszu, with no puttonyos or refermentation, made as it would be in Alsace, where long ago they paid Tokay the compliment of adopting its name. They can be hard to resist, such smoothly, grapily sweet wines; they slip down scarcely making contact, it seems, as they go. Sadly they miss the point, though. The fame of Tokay was not made by a simple fermentation of sweet grapes – not even nobly rotten Furmint ones. It was made, like Yquem, by an almost perverse selectivity; like champagne by provoking a second fermentation; and like sherry by profiting from the microflora of the barrel and the cellar. Together they produce flavours that come about in no other way.

Madeira Party

THEY SOMEHOW FAILED to evoke the glory of Pharaohs, those thin red wines labelled Cru des Ptolomées and Reine Cléopâtre. It can't have been wine like this that was buried in Tutankhamun's tomb, bearing a label with the vineyard, vintage and vintner's name. If I had to choose one of the tombs in the desert near Luxor for my personal use, I'd take one of the ones decorated as arbours of vines; rather in the Sorrento-restaurant style, you might say. The royal tombs are scary with bird-headed gods in pompous processions. The tombs of common people (perhaps not very common, to have a burial chamber as big as a restaurant) are simple desirable places to live out eternity in the shade of a vine. What sort of wine, I have always wondered, did the ancients really drink?

When we spent Christmas on the Nile, a family party of nearly thirty of us, I had the commissariat job. How was I going to transport enough good wine for our thirsty party to ancient Thebes? What would be good at Christmas, appropriate to the ancient world, and transportable? I hit on Madeira. Far from being fragile in transport, Madeira thrives on it. It was a favourite of the Indies, East and West: sovereign in hot weather. A little goes a long way (gastronomically, that is, as well as geographically). And everybody likes it.

As it turned out, hot weather was not the problem. An icy north wind blew from the desert, swirling the dust in the grim temple courtyards with its bitter smell of cold smoke. We hurried back to the ship, to cluster round our short-wave radio and listen to the carols from King's College

Chapel three thousand kilometres away in Cambridge. We sipped the tawny comfort of Madeira, a honeyed glow perfectly in keeping with Egypt, I thought, ancient or modern. How complex are beliefs. The captain had only one navigational guide on his gleaming bridge to pilot him through the shifting shallows of the Nile: a copy of the Koran.

I have always thought of Madeira as the perfect sailing wine. But then sailing takes up a good deal of my thoughts. Chablis and ships, even champagne and ships, are somehow not such natural partners. Madeira uniquely combines tang and glow. Failing Madeira, old nutty sherry, or old nutty tawny port; they roll round the mouth in the proper fashion. But only Madeira has a core of acidity that keeps it bracing while it soothes – and keeps it alive for generations.

1830 is my favourite vintage. It would be a preposterous statement about any other wine. It was 160 years old when I bought it, and I was still able to buy two dozen for less than the price of a current First Growth claret. Others, sadly, have recently noticed that the price of such wine is too good to be true, but still antique Madeiras sell far below their intrinsic value – simply, I suspect, because most people don't know they are there, or anything else about them.

The label tells me everything about my 1830. It is Malmsey, the richest style and perhaps the original, the grape supposedly coming from the Peloponnese and arriving on the island in the 1500s. It was grown at the Quinta do Serrado in Cama de Lobos on the south coast just west of the capital, Funchal. It may have been fortified with rum, or at least cane

Madeira is unique among wines for tolerating exposure to the air, even in a bottle that has been opened. These are 19th century bottles, bearing the names of their original owners, kept on a dresser in one of the historic mansions of Savannah, Georgia.

spirit; some old Madeiras were. It was kept in cask in the warm ware-houses of the *quinta* for 105 years (topped up, I dare say, from time to time) and then transferred into glass demijohns. Fifty years later Mr Blandy found it fit to start drinking. It found its way to Christie's in 1988 and its journey ended at Saling.

I was never able to describe its taste to my satisfaction. I kept veering off into abstracts, 'concentration', 'balance'. To say it smelled of ancient timber and tasted of burnt caramel was nothing to the purpose, nor would 'vinegar' go down well in a Sales Point Document. Incense is certainly an ingredient, and oranges. If it makes you wince to hold something so piercing in your mouth, just give me your glass. I can handle it.

The wine we took to Egypt was nothing so precious. Let's say it had the true character of Madeira without the exciting quality. Madeira has been in slow-motion crisis for a hundred and fifty years; a crisis which is thankfully beginning to pass. At one point it almost died of discourage-ment. The worst form of mildew attacked the vines. Phylloxera followed and killed them. Old habits changed. Before Prohibition, East Coast USA was the main market for the best wines, nobody in Europe wanted any-thing except cooking wine, it seems; the French being the worst offen-ders. (Who eats anything with sauce Madère these days? Do you suppose it goes into Chef's hipflask?) For all these reasons they stopped planting the four grapes that make the four classic wines and fell back on one all-purpose grape, abetted I fear by nefarious hybrids. Companies as famous in their day as the great port shippers collapsed or had to pool their resources. Vintage Madeira almost died, and for years what appeared on the market led anyone who knew its great reputation to feel sadly let down.

What chance has any wine when its name is more familiar as a fault than as a virtue? To describe any other wine as 'maderized' is to say it is ruined: oxygen has destroyed, or is destroying, it; if it were iron it would be rusted. The effect on its colour is eventually the same.

Precisely why Madeira survives, indeed is created by, the very con-ditions that would be fatal to other wines, no-one really seems to know. It goes through a trial by ordeal that has the effect of stabilizing it once and for all. Today it is heated in massive saunas: six months at 50°C for a good wine. Originally it happened on ships, to wine picked up from the island, the last landfall on a long voyage west or south. The wine was not prepared in any way, the clumsy great butts were just put in the hold to take their chances. The fact that the longer the voyage the better the wine turned out was extremely convenient both for the ship-owner and for the distant customer – who would in many cases have been grateful for almost anything to drink. Stranger still it improved in a hot climate: a voyage through the tropics was worth two in the north Atlantic. The Indies, both west and east, became its natural market and its properties were soon discovered in the young cities up the eastern American seaboard: Savannah, Charleston, and on up north to New England.

Savannah in particular became its second home. I was hopeful, when I was making my television history of wine, that by some miracle the old American Madeira culture had survived. A remarkable amount of 18th and early 19th century Savannah is still standing. Would I learn anything about Madeira there? The miracle happened: I caught the last gasp of a tradition as old as the United States. The Madeira Club of Savannah, or a nostalgic remnant of it, convened in one of the dining rooms built for just this sort of ceremony. The polished mahogany, the silver and crystal, the soft-spoken Southerners with their formal manners, the silver-haired black butler adjusting the decanters, were briefly the America of Oliver Wendell Holmes and Andrew Carnegie – and indeed of Silas Weir Mitchell, America's most distinguished physician and author of *A Madeira Party*.

Now only a memory. The Madeira Club of Savannah reconvened in 1988, maybe for the last time. Dr Bernard Rhodes from Oakville, California contributed the oldest wine of the evening, a 1795 Bual.

Mitchell's short story is a lovingly mocking account of American manners of the middle 19th century, or rather those of the East Coast aristocracy of the time. Hamilton, the host, is entertaining three guests, all male, and inculcating Chestnut, who, poor man, has been away in Europe for thirty years, in the proper appreciation of wine – American wine, that is, which means Madeira. Dinner consists of terrapin and canvasback duck. (Our party ate the same.) Dinner eaten (we did not wait so long), the decanters of Madeira are put on the table and the stories begin. The wine is passed 'with the sun, gentlemen' – another gloss on the right-to-left circulation which is conventional for port, but which, for some reason, seems to upset liberal thinkers. Even my own children challenge me. Father, you are a square, they say (with some justice). Let's all agree, I answer, that we would hate to see two decanters collide. A one-way system seems only sensible – and 'with the sun' as good a rationale for it as any.

The last wine Hamilton serves starts a dispute. One of his guests swears it is not Madeira at all but sherry. The old man tells a story of the War of Independence, when British troops surrounded his country house and an officer arrived to arrest him. As a good host he offered the redcoat a glass of wine. "Wonderful sherry," said the Britisher. "I can assure you, Sir, it is my best Madeira," he replied. To cut the story short, he fetches another decanter, they finish them both, and the redcoat slides under the table.

Why America stopped drinking Madeira is unclear. Whisky seems to have taken over long before Prohibition. There were peculiarities, though, about Madeira that made it very much the drink of the rich. For one, it was never bottled, but transferred when ripe, like my 1830, from cask into demijohn, and kept in these rotund glass containers to be siphoned out for use. The most famous Savannah Madeira cellar, in fact, was anything but. The wine was stored in a sun-room at the top of the house to continue baking summer after summer. "The English know nothing about Madeira," said Hamilton. "They bottle all wine, and that is simply fatal. Madeira was never meant to be retailed." Which may well account for its disappearance from the market.

The best time for a glass of sweet sherry is the middle of the morning, or so old-timers have told me. In this case, in Jerez, it was more of a late-breakfast wine.

Sweet sherry does not carry such emotional baggage. It can be supremely luscious or ringingly nutty. It can be as brown and profound as liquid raisins. It can, indeed, be mistaken for excellent Madeira. There is a world of difference between the thrill of a fine old sweet oloroso and the utter banality of Bristol Cream. Bristol Cream was a name that once meant the very best of its kind. Sadly, no more. The wine trade on the whole has been shrewd at keeping its icons intact.

Every bodega in sherry country has its revered stocks of old wines, some sweet, some not. Using them it blends to any level of sweetness the market demands, or any quality. Sugar content is easy; the secret weapon for flavour is PX, or Pedro Ximénez, explosive on its own and highly persuasive as an additive. Sweet sherry remains, though, with rare exceptions, a construct. The true nature and destiny of sherry is to be dry, either fresh as fino, aged as amontillado, or fragrant and challenging (and crying out for aging) as oloroso. When I taste such wines as the treacly Methusalem of Gonzalez Byass, or Sandeman's Royal Ambrosante, I recant my heresy for the duration. But just as a dry port (or for me a white one) is difficult to justify, sweet sherry is little represented in my cellar.

The maps of Spain, Portugal and much of the Mediterranean are spotted with places where sweet wines are possible, have been plausible, and have largely disappeared. Some of the moments of highest demand were when the British came campaigning. The Napoleonic wars gave birth, or at least encouragement, to Marsala in Sicily, Malagá in Andalusía, Tarragona in Catalunya and several names in the battle-zone around Lisbon. True, the ancient Romans had probably enjoyed them before, but it takes a market to promote a name, and regimental messes and ships' gun decks were perfect for the purpose. I once spent a frustrating day combing the suburbs of Lisbon for vineyards to match silver decanter labels that passed for battle honours of the Peninsula campaign. Perhaps some of the names were just nostalgic fancies of war veterans.

The French, of course, did not have to look abroad but found their sugary encouragement in the vineyards of Provence, the Languedoc and the hills of Roussillon. It often mystifies foreigners that the French term for their equivalent of port is Vin Doux Naturel. What is natural, they ask, about a wine stopped in mid-ferment by a hefty shot of alcohol? The answer is the sugar. It is natural grape sugar in suspended animation, as it were, rather than – than what? Is the implication that the alternative would come from cane, or even, dear God, beet?

Compared with table wines these sweet specialities were never in big supply. They were the wines of welcome. Hospitality demanded more than just the daily drink for a visitor; still more did a wedding or a funeral. Sweet wine from an old cask is a different proposition entirely from the daily ration of red. Though the Midi industrialized its VDNs as the 'aperitifs' in every workman's bar in France, they still retained their local status. Now craftsmanship has returned, on a limited scale at least, it is surprising to find just how various they are.

Fashion favours first one, then another. The sweet golden Muscat of Frontignan near Sète was once the thing. Lunel had a turn, and Beaumes-de-Venise a real vogue. Then it was up to the hills to St Jean de Minervois for a more sprightly Muscat and, on an altogether bigger scale, south to Roussillon where the plain, unaromatic but businesslike Grenache makes the most popular VDN of all. Sommeliers in the top French restaurants navigate with more ease than I do among these potent wines and their appellations. When they propose a glass of Maury it will be red, and not necessarily up to port strength. Banyuls, from the coast and almost in Spain, is the touchstone: red Grenache (there is also white) cooked by the sun to fiery sweetness.

Once it was regular practice to maderize these wines, though not by sending them to sea. They were aged in casks or full-bellied glass jars in attics or in the sun, but in any case in contact with the air. The resulting flavour is described as *rancio* – for which there is no precise English translation. Rancid has the same root, and to an extent the same meaning, but is used of butter that has 'turned', not wine. In the right context the tang of *rancio* is strangely alluring, especially combined with the taste of oak. Madeira, Cognac, Banyuls are (or can be) all in this sense rancid. So can Australia's most treasured 'stickies', the liqueur muscats and tokays of north-east Victoria.

The tin-roofed sheds that shelter battered old barrels of Liqueur Muscat are the antithesis of a wine-cellar. A cellar is silent, cool, humid; a haven of unchanging temperature and dim religious light. The stickies of Rutherglen are out in the clamour of the bush, under the torturing sun, frozen on cold nights, protected only by their formidable constitutions. I swear that one of the sheds that Mick Morris showed me (the hero of *High Noon* would look neurotic beside this laconic Australian) was clad with corrugated iron that stopped a metre or so from the ground. Was it cooler for the lowest barrels, I wondered, to be in the direct sunshine than in the iron oven? Some of these wines had suffered these conditions for nearly a century, refreshed from time to time as they evaporated. There is no wine on earth so intensely, syrupy sweet, so viscous, nor so vividly – I could even say freshly – flavoured.

In a sense it scarcely matters how the sweetness is arrived at. The *Botrytis* route is one, the adding-alcohol route another, third is just plain dehydration. The European authorities like to prescribe exactly how every sort of wine is made, but the Italian farmer who pours you a little tumbler of brown vinsanto may not have burned the midnight oil reading the regulations. His wine may be anything from sweet to nutty dry with a smack of sherry. He will show you with pride the outhouse with racks to dry the grapes (sometimes on laths, sometimes on straw) and a small barrel or two. The creamiest and most aromatic vinsanto I ever had was aged under the roof tiles of a palazzo in a little Tuscan town in lozenge-shaped casks small enough for two men to carry. It combined, in fact, the qualities of vinsanto and a young Madeira. Never decline a glass of vinsanto, is my advice. It is a gesture of hospitality. It will lead you into the heart of a household faster than six bottles of red.

I believe in reading auction catalogues for the items that have no obvious origin, no scholarly apparatus, no obvious destination either – and consequently low estimates. A few years ago, Christie's sold some of the property of the Duke of Wellington, including the port I enjoyed in my ancestor's coat. The last items from the cellar were several lots of a dozen bottles of a wine simply called Molino del Rey. They were those beguiling hand-made brown pints made at the end of the 18th century with a big cavity, a 'kick-up' or 'punt' underneath. There were no labels; just a rather desultory wax seal. The bottles alone, I reasoned, were worth having. They had lain in the cellars of Apsley House, the ducal mansion at Hyde Park Corner known to generations simply as Number One, London since, apparently, the time of the victor of Waterloo, Prime Minister and national hero. I bid, and bought them.

I opened the first bottle (and years later, the last) with the finest judge of wine I know, Len Evans. It was greeted with a good Australian oath. What on earth? The wine, well into its third half-century, was extraordinarily sweet and creamy with a smoky softness but a clear tang of oranges. Was it wine at all? Could it be an orange liqueur that the Duke's butler did not know what to do with? But no, it reminded me of one of the last bottles of another legendary Muscat, Constantia from the Cape, I had drunk thirty years earlier: the same flavour of fresh oranges in a bath of warm cream.

Not long after, I chanced on a magazine article about the estates in Spain and Portugal that were presented to the Duke of Wellington after the Peninsula campaign by the two nations he had liberated from the French. Among them was one with the name Molino del Rey, in the mountains above Malagá. Mountain, in fact, was the name in use for Malagá in England. Hearing it had vineyards, the Duke dispatched a wine-grower from Bordeaux to advise on operations. For a few years in the 1830s barrels of the wine were sent to England. No more is known. Evidently some of the bottles were forgotten in the Apsley House cellars.

Len and I discussed the last bottle far into a summer night in 2003. We had drunk Krug 1971, Puligny-Montrachet les Pucelles 1992, Les Forts de Latour 1982, Château Margaux 1982, Quinta do Noval 1960 and my 1830 Malmsey Madeira. The others had gone to bed when I went to fetch the mysterious Molino. We were as dazzled as ever. Len pronounced orange rind; I said only freshly squeezed juice had the liveliness. "Honeyed heaven," I wrote, "for texture and softness. Touches of cloves and cinnamon and creamy smoke. It simply defies age: there is no sign of oxidation, no creeping volatility. Len and I agree: our life's top wine!" When I woke at four in the morning, I could still taste it.

The story has a happy ending. Telmo Rodriguez is a wine-maker from Rioja who carries his passion to other parts of Spain. He had heard my story of Molino del Rey, went searching and found a vineyard of ancient Moscatel vines in the hills above Malagá. He questioned the old people about their memories. Did they know how the wine was made in their grandparents' time? The grapes were picked when they were perfect, he was told, and laid out in the vineyard to dry in the sun. They were pressed in the olive-press, the only press they had, and left to ferment in small barrels until they stopped. Rodriguez set the wheels in motion again. He used new barrels. The fermentation (with a glorious smell of hothouse grapes) stopped at 12 degrees, he told me, leaving as much sugar in the wine as in Château d'Yquem.

When I first tasted what he calls Molino Real, it was like seeing a ghost. It was the ancient mountain reborn. The unique flavour of a wine I found perfect had been lying in the soil for nearly two hundred years, waiting for a curious vintner to give it life again.

Its life, in the last analysis, is what sets wine apart. There is nothing else we buy to eat or drink that brings us the identity of a place and time in the same way, that memorises and recalls (if we listen) all the circumstances that made it what it is. You can, of course, like a college examiner, submit every sample to the same critical appraisal and accept or reject it. Or you can embrace the identity, enjoy the circumstances, be transported to other places and times. Embrace even the mythology: it adds to the colour of life.

Index

PICTURE CREDITS

University of California Press
Berkeley and Los Angeles, California

Published in association with
Weidenfeld & Nicolson
The Orion Publishing Group Ltd.

Text copyright
© Hugh Johnson 2005
Design and layout
© Weidenfeld & Nicolson 2005

ISBN 0-520-24850-3

Cataloging-in-Publication Data is on file
with the Library of Congress

Manufactured in Italy

13 12 11 10 09 08 07 06 05
10 9 8 7 6 5 4 3 2 1

Design director DAVID ROWLEY
Designed by KEN WILSON
Edited by DIANE PENGELLY